Index to modern english

SAXON SERIES IN ENGLISH AS A SECOND LANGUAGE

GRANT TAYLOR, CONSULTING EDITOR

Index to modern english

THOMAS LEE CROWELL, Jr.
LATE PROFESSOR OF ENGLISH
COLUMBIA UNIVERSITY AND HUNTER COLLEGE

McGRAW-HILL BOOK COMPANY
NEW YORK
SAN FRANCISCO
TORONTO
LONDON

Library of Congress Catalog Card Number: 63-15019

7 8 9 10 VHVH 8 9 2 1 0 9 8 7 6

I S B N 0 7 - 0 1 4 7 3 4 - 5

preface

This book has grown out of fifteen years of answering questions of students and teachers about the English language. Those questions have concerned pronunciation, grammatical terminology, morphology, syntax, use of prepositions, spelling, punctuation, literary devices, style, and divided usage. The answers, I trust, will be clear to an intelligent though not necessarily expert user of English.

The book attempts to help educated persons whose knowledge of English is good but not flawless. It would be untruthful though pleasant to say that it answers every question about the language, but it does aim at aiding students and their teachers to eliminate those errors which repeatedly occur in the writing and speech of advanced students. A number of the illustrative examples are revisions of sentences taken from students' papers.

I have tried to view English as just another language in order to see the ways it says things differently from French, Spanish, German, Russian, Chinese, Japanese, and so on. A good deal of information has come from the efforts of linguists within the past twenty years; this book transmits their findings in nontechnical language. Nevertheless, it has not been my intention to state the similarities or differences between English and other languages. I believe that students can best learn English by using only English, not by paraphrasing it, translating it, or constantly comparing it with other languages.

Students and teachers, I hope, will find the book easy to use, for the sections are arranged alphabetically. In correcting a composition, a teacher can quickly direct a student to the discussion of a problem by writing on his paper the page number or the section number of the pertinent item—for example, p. 446 or W.18. Cross references are indicated by the symbol §. Phonetic symbols (see § Phonetic Symbol) are enclosed in brackets.

There are two exercise books which are keyed for use with this book: Crowell, *Modern English Workbook* and Fuller and Wasell, *Advanced English Exercises*. They have been built up and tested through use in numerous classes over a number of years.

Virtually every page of this book reveals my indebtedness to others who find satisfaction in studying or teaching language: grammarians, linguists, philologists, textbook writers, and, most important, teachers. I owe the greatest debt to my own teachers—Bernard

Bloch, Noam Chomsky, E. V. K. Dobbie, Cabell Greet, Albert H. Marckwardt, Andre Martinet, and Allen Walker Read—and to those cleared-sighted viewers in the field of English as a second language— Amy Shaw Abbot, Robert L. Allen, Virginia French Allen, William Cullen Bryant II, Mary K. Dobbie, Harry Freeman, Charles C. Fries, Helene R. Fuller, David P. Harris, A. S. Hornby, Frances Ingemann, Otto Jespersen, Aileen Traver Kitchin, E. Kruisinga, Robert Lado, William F. Marquardt, Lois McIntosh, Ainslie Minor, William J. Nemser, Eugene Nida, Harold E. Palmer, Jean Praninskas, Clifford H. Prator, Joseph Rankin, Earl W. Stevick, Jean D. Tafti, Grant Taylor, Florence F. Wasell, Harold C. Whitford, and R. W. Zandvoort. Among the countless others who have contributed directly or indirectly are Elaine H. Baruch, Karl E. Beckson, Leonard Bloomfield, Donald L. Clark, Louise G. Clarke, George O. Curme, Elizabeth S. Donno, Eugene Dorfman, Joseph I. Fradin, Louis M. Hacker, Zellig S. Harris, Archibald A. Hill, Mark R. Hillegas, Charles F. Hockett, Utako Inoue, Sanford C. Kahrmann, Joseph S. Kenyon, Thomas A. Knott, George P. Krapp, Louis H. Levi, George R. Levine, Howard P. Linton, H. L. Mencken, Lore Metzger, Annis Sandvos, Edward Sapir, James Sledd, Henry Lee Smith, Henry Sweet, Beatrice Tauss, George L. Trager, W. Freeman Twaddell, and H. C. Wyld as well as a great number of contributors to the publications *American Speech, College English, English Language Teaching, Language, Language Learning,* and *Word.*

THOMAS LEE CROWELL, Jr.

Professor Thomas L. Crowell, Jr., the author of *Index to Modern English*, dear friend and colleague, died in December, 1962. The patience, the great effort, and the wide range of knowledge this text required of him will be apparent at once to the reader. These qualities he had and gave freely, not only to writing, but also to the training of the many teachers with whom he worked and the multitude of both international and American students whom he taught at Columbia University and Hunter College for over thirteen years.

Tragically, Professor Crowell never had the chance to see the publisher's final editing or the galleys for *Index to Modern English*. If, then, there should be an error or misstatement in this final form of his work, the responsibility, as both editor and author's reader, must be mine.

GRANT TAYLOR

contents

A

B

C

D

E

F

G

H

I

L

M

N

O

P

Q

R

S

T

U

V

W

X

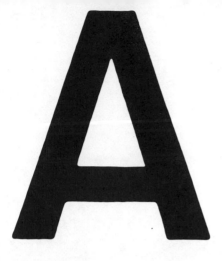

a

A VS. AN

1. The article *a* is used before words beginning with a consonant sound.

a baby	a history
A European	a hotel
a half	a one-armed man
a hand	a union
a hero	a unique course

2. The names of the following letters of the English alphabet begin with a consonant sound and, therefore, have *a*, not *an*, before them: *b, c, d, g, j, k, p, q, t, u, v, w, y,* and *z.*

The word *winter* begins with a *w*, and *union* begins with a *u.*

3. *An* is used before words beginning with a vowel sound.

an apple	an hour
an aunt	an instance
an effort	an odor
an example	an orange
an honor	an umbrella

4. The names of the following letters of the English alphabet begin with a vowel sound and, therefore, have *an*, not *a*, before them: *a, e, f, h, i, l, m, n, o, r, s,* and *x.*

The word *fall* begins with an *f*, and *half* begins with an *h.*

Also, see § Article (*A, An, The*), § Article—*A* vs. No *A*, § *H*- Initial, § Noun—Not Repeated, § Phonetic Symbol, and § Word Order—Adjective before Noun.

A VS. ONE

1. Although the words *a* and *one* have some similar meaning, they are almost never interchangeable.

2. In consecutive counting, *one* is customarily used instead of *a*—e.g., *one, two, three* or *ninety-nine, one hundred, one hundred one.*

3. Similarly, the use of *one* before a noun suggests contrast in quantity. For example, we would say, "I have three sisters but only one brother." Therefore, you should not use *one* as a modifier unless you mean "only one" or "one in contrast to another number."

See also § Article (*A, An, The*), § Article—*A* vs. No *A*, § Noun—Not Repeated, and § Preposition in Time Expression.

a

1. A few words, all beginning with *a-*, have a fixed position in word order: they follow the word they modify, either immediately or after the verbs listed under § Predicate Adjective. These words are the following: *afraid, alike, alive, alone, ashamed, asleep,* and *awake.*

> A man afraid is a man ashamed.
> Do you think it is alive?
> Please leave me alone.
> The girl seemed asleep.
> Their dresses are alike.
> He alone is responsible.
> I was ashamed of my action.
> I finally got him awake.

2. These words have equivalents which can be used before words they modify. Some of the equivalents are the following: *frightened* or *fearful* for *afraid; identical* or *similar* for *alike; live* for *alive; lone* or *solitary* or *only* for *alone; shamefaced* for *ashamed; sleeping* for *asleep; sleepless* or *alert* for *awake.*

> The frightened boy was pale.
> They sell live animals in that store.
> We saw a solitary hunter.
> The sleeping girl looked beautiful.
> They have similar dresses.
> Only he is responsible.
> The shamefaced man could not talk.
> The sleepless soldier stood guard.

ABBREVIATION   A.4

1. Following is a list of frequently used abbreviations. Most of them have a period, but a few do not. Some have no space after the first period; others do. A few are underlined or italicized in some literary and legal writing. For a list of contractions with apostrophes, see § Apostrophe.

A.B. (Latin, *Artium Baccalaureus*), Bachelor of Arts
ABC, American Broadcasting Company
A.C., alternating current
A.D. (Latin, *Anno Domini*), after the birth of Christ
adj., adjective
adv., adverb; advertisement
advt., advertisement
AFL, AF of L, American Federation of Labor
AFL-CIO, American Federation of Labor and Congress of Industrial Organizations
AM, amplitude modulation
A.M. (Latin, *Artium Magister*), Master of Arts
A.M., a.m. (Latin, *ante meridiem*), before noon
A.M.A., American Medical Association
anon., anonymous
AP, Associated Press
apt., apartment
Ariz., Arizona
Ark., Arkansas
asst., assistant
Aug., August
b., born
B.A., Bachelor of Arts

a

B.C., before Christ

B.S., B.Sc., Bachelor of Science

C., c., Celsius; centigrade; copyright

c., ca., about

Cal., Calif., California

Capt., Captain

CBS, Columbia Broadcasting System

C.E., Civil Engineer; civil engineering

cf., compare

ch., chap., Chap., chapter

Chas., Charles

chem., chemistry; chemical

CIO, Congress of Industrial
    Organizations

cm., centimeter

Co., Company

C.O.D., collect on delivery

col., column

Col., Colonel

Colo., Colorado

conj., conjunction

Conn., Connecticut

cont., continued

Corp., Corporation; Corporal

C.P.A., Certified Public Accountant

cu., cubic

C.Z., Panama Canal Zone

d., died

D.C., District of Columbia; direct
    current

D.D., Doctor of Divinity

D.D.S., Doctor of Dental Surgery

Dec., December

deg., degree (s)

Del., Delaware

Dem., Democrat

dept., department

dist., district

doz., dozen, twelve

Dr., Doctor

D.S., D.Sc., Doctor of Science

E., East

ed., editor; edition; edited

Ed.D., Doctor of Education

e.g., for example

Eng., English; England

esp., especially

Esq., Esquire

et al. (Latin, *et alibi*; *et alii*), and else-

where; and others

etc., et cetera, and others, and so
    on, and so forth

ex., example

f., following; and the following page

F., Fahrenheit

FBI, Federal Bureau of Investigation

FCC, Federal Communications
    Commission

Feb., February

ff., and the following pages

fig., figure

fl., flourished; reached the greatest
    development or influence

Fla., Florida

FM, frequency modulation

fn., footnote

f.o.b., free on board; not including
    transportation cost

Fri., Friday

ft., foot; feet

Ga., Georgia

Gen., General

GI, enlisted man in the Army

gm., gram

G.O.P., Republican Party

Gov., Governor

govt., government

gram., grammar; grammatical

Hon., Honorable

h.p., horsepower

hr., hour

hrs., hours

H.R., House of Representatives

I., Island

ibid. (Latin, *ibidem*), in the same
    reference as the preceding note

id. (Latin, *idem*), the same

i.e. (Latin *id est*), that is

Ill., Illinois

Inc., Incorporated

Ind., Indiana

I.O.U., I owe you

IQ, intelligence quotient

Jan., January

Jr., Junior

k., carat

Kan., Kansas

kg., kilogram

km., kilometer
Ky., Kentucky
l., line
La., Louisiana
lang., language
lat., latitude
lb., pound
lbs., pounds
lg., language
ll., lines
LL.D. (Latin, *Legum Doctor*), Doctor of Laws
loc. cit. (Latin, *loco citato*), in the place cited
log., logarithm
long., longitude
Lt., Lieutenant
ltd., limited
m., meter; married
M., Monsieur
M. (Latin, *meridies*), noon
M.A., Master of Arts
maj., major; majority
Mar., March
Mass., Massachusetts
math, mathematics
Md., Maryland
M.D. (Latin, *Medicinae Doctor*), Doctor of Medicine
mdse., merchandise
Me., Maine
M.E., Mechanical Engineer
med., medical; medicine
Messrs., plural of *Mr.*
mg., milligram
mgr., manager
Mich., Michigan
Minn., Minnesota
Miss., Mississippi
Mlle., Mademoiselle
Mme., Madame
Mo., Missouri
Mon., Monday
Mont., Montana
M.P., Military Police; Member of Parliament
m.p.h., miles per hour
Mr., a man's title, used before his name

Mrs., a married woman's title, used before her name
ms., MS, manuscript
M.S., Master of Science
mss., MSS, manuscripts
mt., mount; mountain
n., noun; note
N., North
NAM, National Association of Manufacturers
N.B. (Latin, *nota bene*), notice; New Brunswick
NBC, National Broadcasting Company; National Biscuit Company
N.C., North Carolina
n.d., no date given
N.D., North Dakota
NE., Northeast
Neb., Nebraska
Nev., Nevada
N.H., New Hampshire
N.J., New Jersey
N.M., New Mexico
No., number
Nov., November
n.p., no place of publication given
N.S., Nova Scotia; new style; new series
NW., Northwest
N.Y., New York
Oct., October
O.K., all right; yes; correct
Okla., Oklahoma
op. cit. (Latin, *opere citato*), work cited
Ore., Oregon
oz., ounce
p., page
Pa., Pennsylvania
par., paragraph
pd., paid
Penna., Pennsylvania
Ph.D., Doctor of Philosophy
pkg., package
pl., plural
P.M., p.m. (Latin, *post meridiem*), after noon
P.M., Prime Minister
pp., pages

a

P.R., Puerto Rico
pref., preface
prep., preposition
pron., pronoun
P.S., postscript
pseud., pseudonym
pt., part; past; past tense; pint(s);
  point
pub., published; publication;
  publisher
pvt., private
q.v. (Latin, *quod vide*), which see;
  see under that heading
R.C., Roman Catholic
reg., registered; regular; regulation
Rep., Republican; Representative
resp., respectively
rev., review(ed); revise(d); revision
Rev., Reverend
R.F.D., rural free delivery
R.I., Rhode Island
R.N., Registered Nurse
R.S.V.P., please reply
S., South
Sat., Saturday
S.B. (Latin, *Scientiae Baccalaureus*),
  Bachelor of Science
sc. (Latin, *scilicet*), namely
sc., scene
S.C., South Carolina
Sc.D. (Latin, *Scientiae Doctor*), Doc-
  tor of Science
scil. (Latin, *scilicet*), namely
S.D., South Dakota; Doctor of Science
SE., Southeast
sec., section; secretary
Sept., September
ser., series
Sgt., Sergeant
sig., signature
sing., singular
S.M. (Latin, *Scientiae Magister*), Mas-
  ter of Science
sp., spelling
sq., square
sq. mi., square miles
Sr., Senior
st., stanza
St., Street; Saint (masculine)

Ste., Saint (feminine)
Sun., Sunday
sup. (Latin, *supra*), above; super-
  intendent
s.v. (Latin, *sub verbo*), under the
  word or heading
SW., Southwest
syn., synonym
tech., technical; technical school
Tenn., Tennessee
Tex., Texas
Thurs., Thursday
tr., trans., translation: translated(by)
Tues., Tuesday
TV, television
TVA, Tennessee Valley Authority
ult. (Latin, *ultimo*), last; of last month
UN, U.N., United Nations
UNESCO, United Nations Economic
  and Social Council
U.S., U.S.A., United States of
  America
U.S.S.R., USSR, the Union of Soviet
  Socialist Republics
v., verb; verse
Va., Virginia
VA, V.A., Veterans Administration
V.I., Virgin Islands
viz. (Latin, *videlicet*), namely
vol., volume
vs., verse; versus, opposed to, con-
  trasted with
Vt., Vermont
W., West
Wash., Washington
Wed., Wednesday
Wis., Wisconsin
Wm., William
W.Va., West Virginia
Wyo., Wyoming
yd., yard
YMCA, Young Men's Christian
  Association
YMHA, Young Men's Hebrew
  Association
YWCA, Young Women's Christian
  Association
YWHA, Young Women's Hebrew
  Association

2. Use *U.S.* for United States only in informal writing or in the titles of certain governmental agencies such as *U.S. Department of Agriculture* and *U.S. Children's Bureau.*

3. Use the symbol & for *and* only in the most informal writing.

4. Spell out the names of states, days, and months when they stand alone.

> I will be in Georgia on the first Thursday in February.

Also, see § Capitalization, § Period, and § Underlining.

-ACE, -ESS, -ICE, AND -IS

A.5

1. A number of English words have an unstressed final syllable which contains the letters *-ace,* or *-ess* or *-ice* or *-is.* Those groups of letters are all pronounced alike: [ɪs]. Here are some examples of two-syllable words; the stress is on the first syllable.

furnace	actress	careless	business	justice	basis
Horace	empress	endless	darkness	malice	crisis
menace	goddess	harmless	illness	notice	Harris
necklace	hostess	hopeless	kindness	office	Lois
palace	mattress	reckless	sickness	practice	Louis
surface	princess	useless	weakness	service	Paris
terrace	waitress	worthless	witness	Venice	tennis

2. The following three-syllable words have the stress on the first syllable; they also end in unstressed [ɪs].

bitterness	artifice
coziness	avarice
holiness	cowardice
liveliness	precipice
loneliness	prejudice
loveliness	
sinfulness	

ADJECTIVE VS. ADVERB

A.6

1. Both adjectives and adverbs are used as modifiers, but both their forms and their positions are usually different.

2. The differences between an adjective and a corresponding adverb can be illustrated by the modification of a gerund (the *-ing* form of a verb). Let's take *thinking* as the gerund and then modify it with the idea of "rapidity." If we put the modifier before *thinking,* we will use the adverb form *rapidly.*

> Rapid thinking is an asset.
> Thinking rapidly is an asset.

In this section I will concentrate on the differences in form between adjectives and adverbs. The positions of adjectives are discussed in detail in § Predicate Adjective, § Word Order—Adjective after Noun and Pronoun, and § Word Order—Adjective before Noun. The positions of adverbs are discussed in detail in § Word Order—Adverb Modifying Adjective and Adverb, § Word Order—Adverb Modifying Verb, and § Word Order—Emphatic Adverb.

3. The suffix *-ly* has two uses. The more frequent one is as the *sign of the adverb*. It is added to most adjectives and to many participles.

ADJECTIVE OR PARTICIPLE	ADVERB
Ellen gave a *soft* sigh.	Ellen sighed *softly*.
Ralph was *safe*.	Ralph returned home *safely*.
The choir sang *beautiful* songs.	The choir sang songs *beautifully*.
The Franks have a *happy* home.	The Franks live together *happily*.
Ethel made a *surprising* reply.	Ethel replied *surprisingly*.
Carl danced with a *tired* air.	Carl danced *tiredly*.

4. The spelling of adverbs that end in *-ly* is usually quite regular: the *-ly* is added directly to the adjective or participle form. The place of stress does not change with the addition. Some examples are these: *complete – completely* and *sudden – suddenly*. In a few cases the spelling is altered:

a. If an adjective ends in *y*, change that *y* to *i* before adding the *-ly*.

> easy – easily   necessary – necessarily

The word *coyly* is an exception.
  A few short adverbs can be spelled with either *i* or *y*.

> gaily or gayly   drily or dryly

The word *daily* has only one spelling.

b. If an adjective ends in *-le*, change the final *e* to *y* for the adverb form.

> feeble – feebly   simple – simply
> possible – possibly   subtle – subtly

However, the adjective *sole* has a regular adverb form: *solely*.

c. Two adjectives that end in *-ll* add only *y*: *full – fully* and *dull – dully*. Remember to add *-ly* to words that end in a single *l*.

> real – really   usual – usually

d. In three adverb forms other changes are made: *true – truly; due – duly;* and *whole – wholly*.

e. If the adjective ends in *-ic*, the adverb ending is *-ally*. The only exception is *publicly*.

> Mrs. Porter called her child frantically.
> The conferees discussed the matter democratically.
> Mr. Sullivan expressed his opinion publicly.

5. The less frequent use of the suffix *-ly* is as the *sign of an adjective.* It is found on only a handful of words derived from nouns or other adjectives. The most common of them are the following:

brotherly	earthly	kingly	lovely	princely	sisterly
courtly	fatherly	knightly	manly	queenly	wifely
cowardly	friendly	leisurely	masterly	saintly	womanly
deadly	heavenly	lively	motherly	scholarly	worldly
		lonely	neighborly		

Mr. Clark is a friendly man.
Maria has a queenly appearance.
We heard a lovely voice last night.
Isabel is used to a leisurely life.

6. Sometimes but not often, *friendly* and some of the others of the preceding group are used without change as adverbs. Sometimes but even more rarely, they take an additional *-ly* as an adverb. ("He spoke very friendlily"). My advice is to use them as adjectives in phrases to show manner.

Joe spoke in a friendly voice.
Peterson walks with a manly stride.
Mr. Simmons treats his secretary in a fatherly fashion.

7. The words *early, hourly, daily, nightly, weekly, monthly, quarterly,* and *yearly* are used either as adjectives or adverbs.

An early riser gets up early in the morning.
That is a daily occurrence. It happens daily.

Certain adjectives and adverbs have specialized forms. They are discussed below.

8. *Fast, half, hard, late,* and *straight* are used either as adjectives or adverbs.

ADJECTIVE	ADVERB
The plane made a fast trip	because it went fast.
You get only half credit	for a half-finished test.
A hard worker	works hard.
A late student	arrives late.
A straight path	goes straight to its end.

9. The words *hardly* ("scarcely") and *lately* ("recently") look as though they should be used as the adverb form of *hard* and *late,* but, of course, they should not.

If you study hard, you will learn.
If you hardly study, you will not learn.

Lately, Juana has been coming to class late.

10. A few words can be used adverbially with or without the *-ly* and have the same meaning. They are *slow, quick, loud,* and *clear.* However, they can do so only in one position: after the verb they modify. Even then sometimes only the

-ly form is used. When they are used adverbially in other positions, they have the -ly. My advice is always to use the -ly form for the adverb.

> Duncan slowly walked down the aisle.
> Quickly everybody stood up.
> He clearly knew what he was doing.
> He turned slowly and faced the crowd.
> He spoke loudly and clearly.

11. Three words are used adverbially without -ly under special conditions. They are *sharp, sound,* and *wide.* After expressions of clock time, *sharp* is used to mean "punctually." *Sound* is used with *asleep* to mean "completely." *Wide* is used with *open* and *awake* to mean "completely."

> Ben arrived at nine o'clock sharp. *but* Lois spoke to the boy sharply.
> The baby was sound asleep. *but* Our team was soundly defeated.
> Open the window wide. *but* The window is wide open.
> The baby is wide awake now. *but* Mark is widely known as a speaker.

Also, notice that *widespread* is spelled as one word.

> The effects of the earthquake were widespread.

12. A few words are used adverbially without -ly with special meanings. They occur primarily in conversation or in casual writing. Generally speaking, use of these forms is not recommended by educators. Some of them are the following:

> *awful,* "very." I'm awful sorry. (Also: I'm awfully sorry.)
> *clean,* "completely." I clean forgot to mail your letter.
> *clear,* "completely." The boy ran clear through the house without stopping.
> *dead,* "completely." You are dead right. We were dead tired.
> *easy,* "in a moderate manner." Take it easy. [Relax.] Go easy on the boy.
>   [Be moderate with the boy.]
> *flat,* "completely." I am flat broke [completely without money].
> *good and,* "very." I am good and tired. Mary was good and angry.
> *mighty,* "very." The weather is mighty fine today.
> *pretty,* "moderately; rather." My course is pretty difficult. It's pretty hot today.
> *real,* "very." The novel was real good.
> *sure,* "very." I'm sure tired. Clarence is sure lazy.
> *sure,* customary in the interjection *sure enough.* "Will you do it?" "Sure enough."

Also, see § Intensifier.

13. The adverb of the adjective *deep* has two forms. We usually use *deep* when we refer to physical measurement or to future time but *deeply* when we mean "profoundly" or "intensely."

> The men buried the box deep.
> The body sank deep into the sea.
> Sam worked deep into the night.
> Would you like to see deep in the future?
> The student was deeply interested in the experiment.
> Mr. Lawrence deeply resented the woman's implication.

14. The adverb of *high* also has two forms. The more frequent one is *high.* *Highly* usually means "greatly," "extremely," or "with approval."

> The plane flew high in the sky.
> The pitcher threw the ball so high that no one could catch it.
> The story was highly amusing.
> Conceited people think highly of themselves.
> Hallie's supervisor recommended her highly for her work.

15. For the meaning "with justice," *justly* is used as an adverb. For other meanings, *just* is used.

> The criminal was treated justly.
> You will be justly rewarded for your efforts.
> Mary has just left.
> Mary left just now.
> Will you wait just a minute?
> You have just one more chance.
> We will do just as you say.

16. The adjective *kind* has the adverbial form *kindly. Kindly,* however, is also used as an adjective but not very frequently.

> The kind man spoke kindly.
> The kindly man spoke kindly.

17. The adjective *long* does not have an *-ly* adverb. The word *long* is used adverbially with the meaning "(for) a long time."

> A long speaker speaks long.
> I was long under the impression that Stuart was unreliable.
> Long after Mr. Fuller left, I realized what he had meant.

18. *Low* is used both as an adjective and an adverb. *Lowly* is usually an adjective meaning "humble."

> The room has a low ceiling.
> The plane flew low over the field.
> Please speak low in a hospital.
> Be a man. Don't act so lowly.

19. The word *near* is used both as an adjective and an adverb as well as a preposition. *Nearly* has a different meaning, that of "almost."

> Bob is a near neighbor of mine.
> Bob lives near.
> Bob lives near me.
> Mr. Crawford nearly died of pneumonia.

20. For the meaning "correctly," *rightly* is used before verbs. In other positions and for other meanings, *right* is customarily used.

> If I rightly remember, Randolph arrived in 1950.
> Maxwell rightly supposed that Sally was leaving.

> You did not guess right.
> Your guess was not right.
> You did not do it right.
> Right or wrong, I will be your friend.
> I am leaving right away.
> Nothing goes right with me these days.

21. Before verbs, particularly past participles, *wrongly* is used. In other positions *wrong* is customary.

> Stan wrongly accused Pete of the theft.
> You were wrongly informed.
> You guessed wrong.
> You have done it wrong again.

22. In speech *badly* frequently occurs in the construction *feel badly* meaning "regret" or "feel sick." In formal writing, however, the adjective form *bad* is customary in that and other expressions of attitude or health such as *look bad*.

INFORMAL	**FORMAL**
I feel bad about his loss.	I feel bad about his loss.
I feel badly about his loss.	

23. Similarly, *well* is used in expressions of health; *good*, in expressions of attitude.

> You look sick. Don't you feel well?
> You look happy. What makes you feel good?

Also, see § Comparison, § Spelling—Word with Suffix, § Part of Speech—Adjective, and § Part of Speech—Adverb.

AFTER **VS.** *AFTERWARDS*   A.7

1. The word *after* is used principally as a preposition or a conjunction.

> We can wash the dishes after dinner.
> We can wash the dishes after we have eaten.

2. Do not use *after* as an adverb. Although in certain constructions *after* is found as an adverb, in most constructions it is unidiomatic.

3. *Afterwards* is used as an adverb. Like many other adverbs, it can shift its position in a sentence.

> We can eat dinner. Afterwards, we can wash the dishes.
> We can eat dinner and afterwards wash the dishes.
> We can eat dinner and wash the dishes afterwards.

4. The words *afterward* and *afterwards* are interchangeable, but the latter seems to be used more frequently.

a

1. A number of English words have an unstressed final syllable which contains the letters *-age*. The *-age* is pronounced [ɪdʒ]. Here are some examples of two-syllable words; the stress is on the first syllable.

adage	breakage	garbage	manage	postage	usage
average	cabbage	image	message	salvage	village
baggage	courage	language	package	savage	voyage
bandage	damage	luggage	passage	storage	wreckage

2. The words *carriage* and *marriage* are also two-syllable words with the stress on the first syllable; in these words, too, the *-age* is pronounced [ɪdʒ]. The word *mileage* is similar: ['maɪlɪdʒ].

3. The following three-syllable words have the stress on the first syllable: *heritage, orphanage, parentage,* and *pilgrimage.*

4. The following three-syllable words have the stress on the second syllable: *advantage, discourage, disparage, encourage, mismanage,* and *percentage.*

AGO VS. BEFORE   A.9

1. The word *ago* follows an expression of time. It indicates a time prior to the present. It is used with the simple past tense.

> I saw Alice two days ago.
> John left a few minutes ago.
> We arrived here a week ago.
> That happened a long time ago.

2. The word *before* is used instead of *ago* to indicate a time earlier than another time in the past. It takes the same position as *ago.*

> Texas became a part of the Union in 1845. It had been an independent republic a long time before.
> When I went to visit Mrs. Sheaffer last week, I was told she had left two days before.

Also, see § Preposition in Time Expression.

AGREEMENT   A.10

1. The term *agreement* refers to the rules governing the selection from alternative forms of words on the basis of syntactical relationship. The selection is made on the basis of these features:

> *Number.* Some words are grammatically singular or plural.
> *Person.* The speaker or writer is grammatically *first person,* the listener or reader is *second person,* and any other person or thing is *third person.*

a

Gender. A noun or pronoun is grammatically masculine, feminine, or neuter.

Case. A few pronouns have a *subject form,* an *object form,* and a *possessive form.*

The following sections will survey certain aspects of agreement which may cause you trouble. Grammatical number is discussed in detail under § Singular vs. Plural. For the selection between adjectival and adverbial forms, see § Predicate Adjective and § Adjective vs. Adverb.

AGREEMENT—ADJECTIVE   A.11

1. The only adjectives in English that show agreement in number with the nouns they modify are *this – these* and *that – those.* In other words, we do not add *-s* to an adjective which modifies a plural noun.

> I like this blue car.
> I like these blue cars.
> That dress is pretty.
> Those dresses are pretty.

2. The adjectives *each, every, either, neither, much,* and *one* are followed by singular nouns.

> Each boy has his own book.
> Every girl comes on time.
> Either answer is correct.
> Neither man is qualified for the job.
> Much effort is wasted.
> One page is missing.

3. The words *either* and *neither* are sometimes used as correlative conjunctions. Then, they may be followed by plural nouns.

> You can have your change in either nickels or dimes.
> Neither tomatoes nor beans are good this season.

4. The adjectives *both, few, many, numerous, several,* and *various* and the cardinal numbers *two, three,* etc., are followed by plural nouns.

> Both boys have their own books.
> Few students are really lazy.
> Many people want to go.
> Two girls were standing on the corner.

5. As a correlative conjunction, the word *both* may be followed by a singular noun.

> Both rice and wheat are grown in that country.

For the difference between *much* and *many,* see § *Many* vs. *Much* and § *Many a.* For the use of *all, any, most,* and *some,* see § Singular vs. Plural.

a

1. A pronoun or pronominal adjective agrees in number, person, and gender with its antecedent—that is, the word or words the pronoun refers to.

2. Use *he, his, him,* or *himself* to refer to:

a. A masculine singular antecedent.

> That boy is very nice. Everybody likes him.
> My baby has got his first tooth. [My baby is a boy.]

b. A singular antecedent which represents a generalized member of a group which contains members of both sexes.

> A student in my class has to do his own work. [There are both men and women in my class.]
> Every citizen should exercise his right to vote.
> A teacher is usually very interested in his students.

3. Use *she, her, hers,* or *herself* to refer to a singular feminine antecedent.

> That girl has her own book.
> Elizabeth looked at herself in the mirror carefully.
> I can see that the baby has got her first tooth. [The baby is a girl.]
> A student at Barnard College has to do her own work. [All the students at Barnard are women.]

4. Use *it, its,* or *itself* to refer to a neuter singular antecedent or to a singular antecedent whose sex you do not know.

> That book has lost its cover. I will put a new one on it tomorrow.
> I can see that the baby has got its first tooth. [You do not know whether the baby is a boy or a girl.]

5. An inanimate object or an abstraction is sometimes personified and referred to as masculine or feminine. Such personification frequently occurs in conversation and in poetry.

> Love begins playing his old tricks every spring.
> My car is losing her youthful appearance.

6. Remember that the words *ours, yours, his, hers, its,* and *theirs,* do not have an apostrophe. *It's* is a contraction of *it is* or *it has.*

7. Be consistent in your reference. For example, do not begin with the first or third person and then shift to *you,* and do not begin with a singular and then shift to a plural. ,

> If *I* were very rich, *I* would go to Florida, where *I* could lie in the sun and sleep.
> *We* all have problems that *we* have to solve for *ourselves.*
> A *visitor* should see this country not through the eyes of others but through *his* own.

> *A group* aiming at special legislation is known as a lobby. *It* differs from a political party.

8. Do not be reluctant to use the first-person words. If you are talking about yourself, use *I, me, my*, etc. Do not use circumlocutions like *the writer*, and do not generalize with words like *everybody, people, they*, and *you* when you mean yourself.

9. Be clear in your reference. Sometimes you should repeat an antecedent to avoid ambiguity.

> Robert was a relief after my long visit with the family doctor. Robert [not *He*, which might be taken to refer to *doctor*] was young and gay.
> Some writers achieve fame in their lifetime or posthumously, but others always remain obscure. I do not believe that the latter [not *they*, which could refer to either set of writers] are necessarily inferior.

10. Do not use a pronoun to refer to something that you have not already clearly stated for your reader. Instead of *it, them, this*, etc., put down the words for the thought you have in mind.

> When I was ready for undergraduate studies, I did not have any choice about it. [What does the word *it* refer to?]
> We may disapprove of a political theory, but we do not have to fight them. [What does the word *them* refer to?]

11. The following words are grammatically singular:

anybody	each one	everyone	nobody	person	sort
anyone	either	everything	no one	somebody	type
anything	every	kind	nothing	someone	
each	everybody	neither	one	something	

Refer to all those words with a singular pronoun or pronominal adjective when you write. (In conversation those words are frequently referred to with a plural.) It does not matter if *anybody, each*, etc., are followed by phrases with plural words.

> Each boy has to make his bed.
> Everybody should do his own work.
> Each student in my class is working as hard as he can.
> Each of my students is working as hard as he can.
> Every person in this world has a right to his own opinion.
> That type of student is usually successful in his work.
> Everyone has his faults.
> Everything they do has its defects.
> Each student at Barnard is working as hard as she can.
> Every girl in all our classes has invited her father.
> Neither of those girls has told her mother the truth.
> The sort of girl that is respected by men is the kind who does her own thinking.

12. Three similar expressions which are used in the sense of "everybody in general" are grammatically singular but are different in gender: *man* is masculine, and *mankind* and *the human race* are neuter. In this sense neither *man* nor *mankind* has an article, but *the human race* has *the*.

> Man is attempting to subordinate nature to his will.
> If mankind is not careful, it will not have a place to call its own.
> The human race has certainly made its mark on the earth.

13. The words *you* and *they* are often used in conversation in a generalized sense.

> You have to look out for yourself in this world.
> They are very courteous to you in that store.

14. In writing, use words like *one, everybody, a person,* or *people* for the meaning of "everybody in general." Use specific words for particular persons or groups.

> Everybody has to look out for himself in this world.
> The clerks are very courteous to customers in that store.
> One should be aware of his own potentialities.

15. The pronouns *who, whose, whom, which,* and *that* have the number and gender of their antecedents. Be sure to make their simple predicates agree with them. Also, see § Subject and Simple Predicate.

> Any man who spends his day at his office expects to have rest at his home.
> Mrs. White, who has bragged about her children all her life, is quiet for a change.
> All of you who are leaving for your homes are excused from your last class.

16. Use the *-self* pronouns (*myself, yourself, himself, herself, itself, ourselves, yourselves,* and *themselves*) when there is an expressed antecedent in the sentence.

> I have cut myself. [*I* is the antecedent of *myself.*]
> John said he would do it himself. [*John* is the antecedent of *himself.*]
> You ought to be ashamed of yourself. [*You* is the antecedent of *yourself.*]
> I want the children to do it themselves. [*The children* is the antecedent of
>   *themselves.*]

17. In an imperative sentence *yourself* is used if only one person is addressed; *yourselves* is used if two or more persons are addressed.

> Do it yourself, John.   Do it yourselves, boys.
> Watch yourself, Mary.   Watch yourselves, girls.

18. Use the subject forms *I, he, she, we, they, who,* and *whoever* as subjects or predicate nominatives. Use the object forms *me, him, her, us, them, whom,* and *whomever* as objects.

> I do not know who is coming. [*Who* is the subject of *is coming.*]
> I do not know whom you mean. [*Whom* is the object of *mean.*]

a. When one of the pronouns is part of a compound, use the same form that you would use without the rest of the compound.

My father gave the book to my sister and me. [My father gave the book to . . . me.]
My sister and I read it at once. [. . . I read it at once.]

b. When you have a predicate nominative construction with the verb *be,* use the subject form. Remember, however, that the verb agrees with its subject, not the predicate nominative.

It is they who are at fault. [*They* is the predicate nominative; *it* is the subject of *is.*]
Tell me who it was. [*Who* is the predicate nominative; *it* is the subject of *was.*]

c. When the pronoun is linked to another object by *to be,* use the object form.

Imagine yourself to be me. [*Me* is linked to *yourself.*]
Whom did you expect him to be? [*Whom* is linked to *him.*]

d. When an "opinion formula" such as *do you think* comes inside a sentence, do not let it affect the choice between *who* and *whom.* As a test, mentally remove the opinion formula.

Who do you think did it? [*Who* is the subject of *did.*]
John is the boy who I think did it. [*Who* is the subject of *did.*]
Whom do you guess I saw? [*Whom* is the object of *saw.*]
The man whom I believe you mean is my teacher. [*Whom* is the object of *mean.*]

e. When a preposition precedes a dependent clause, use *who* or *whoever* for the subject or predicate nominative of that dependent clause.

Leave the package with whoever comes to the door. [*Whoever* is the subject of *comes.*]
Tell me about who examined you and what the questions were. [*Who* is the subject of *examined.*]
Sarah could not think of who he was. [*Who* is the predicate nominative of *was.*]

f. When the pronoun comes after *than* or *as* in a comparison, use the same form that you would use if you exchanged the position of the members of the comparison.

John is older than she. [If you exchanged the positions of the two members of the comparison, you would have "She is older than John."]
Mother likes John better than I. [The comparison is between Mother and me.]
John works as hard as I. [The comparison is between John and me.]
Mother gives money to John as well as me. [The comparison is between John and me.]

g. In conversation frequently only the object forms are used in comparisons like the above examples. Nevertheless, in writing, follow the rule in *f,* above. Also, see § Verb—Not Repeated.

h. After *before* and *after,* use the subject form if the pronoun is the subject of an expressed simple predicate. Otherwise, use the object form.

> I left after *he* did.
> I left after *him.*
> John left before *I* did.
> John left before *me.*

AGREEMENT—VERB   A.13

1. A verb agrees in number and person with its subject. For further discussion, see § Subject and Simple Predicate. Here are some suggestions to help you in the places that most often cause trouble.

2. If the complete subject can be referred to by *he, she,* or *it,* use the third-person singular form for the simple predicate. Do not be misled by a plural word in a modifier in the complete subject.

> Writing compositions is a good way to get practice. [The subject "writing compositions" can be referred to by *it.*]
> The destructive power of atomic weapons worries me. [*It* worries me.]
> The productiveness of their natural resources has been maintained. [*It* has been maintained.]
> The Board of Directors is responsible. [*It* is responsible.]
> The fabric of men's suits is important. [*It* is important.]
> Jim's way of dressing, speaking, and using his hands makes him odd. [*It* makes him odd.]

3. If the complete subject can be referred to by *they, you,* or *we,* use the plural form for the simple predicate. Do not be misled by a singular word in a modifier in the complete subject, and be very careful about two subjects that are joined by *and.*

> The implications in Prof. Leary's dramatic speech were astounding. [*They* were astounding.]
> The resources of nature have provided man with his livelihood. [*They* have provided. . . .]
> Dancing and every other kind of entertainment follow the dinner. [*They* follow. . . .]
> Dignity of concept and delicacy of line are expressed in the statue. [*They* are expressed. . . .]
> John and you have been selected. [*You* have been selected.] All the other students and I are going to the conference. [*We* are going. . . .]

4. If a clause begins with *there* and a verb form, make the verb form agree with the subject which follows.

> There is one thing that keeps worrying me.
> There are many tall buildings in New York City.
> There has been tremendous progress within this century.

There have been a few changes in recent years.
There were his wife and child to consider.
There was also his grandmother to remember.

5. If the complete subject can be referred to by pronouns joined by *or, nor,* or *but (also),* make the simple predicate agree with the nearest pronoun.

Mr. Bacon or his wife has to stay home with their baby. [*He* or *she* has to stay. . . .]
The living room, the bedrooms, or the kitchen has to be painted tomorrow. [*It, they,* or *it* has to be painted. . . .]
The president or the vice-president or both are going to welcome the guests. [*He* or *he* or *they* are going to welcome. . . .]
Neither Mary nor Billy has been invited. [Neither *she* nor *he* has been invited.]
Not only Norman but also his parents are coming. [Not only *he* but also *they* are coming.]
There is Florida or the Carolinas to choose from. [There is *it* or *they*. . . .]
There were not only his children but also his wife to consider. [There were not only *they* but also *she*. . . .]
Not the students but I was wrong. [Not *they* but *I* was wrong.]

6. If the subject is *who, which,* or *that,* select the verb form that would go with the antecedent of the pronoun. Be very careful when the pronoun is preceded by the words *one of those.*

It is I who am wrong. [The antecedent of *who* is *I.*]
I am the one who is wrong. [The antecedent of *who* is *the one.*]
It is you who are wrong. [The antecedent of *who* is *you.*]
You are the one who is wrong. [The antecedent of *who* is *the one.*]
It was they who were wrong. [The antecedent of *who* is *they.*]
The main trouble is probably the short range of our own lives, which makes it difficult for us to imagine eternity. [The antecedent of *which* is "the short range of our own lives."]
Shish kebab is one of those dishes which have to be cooked outdoors. [The antecedent of *which* is *those dishes.*]
The article is one of the best sketches that have ever been written. [The antecedent of *that* is "the best sketches."]
Mrs. Castro is the only one of those women who has a car. [The antecedent of *who* is "the only one of these women."]

ALL VS. WHOLE
A.14

1. A good general rule for the difference in use between *all* and *whole* is this:

a. Use *whole* with a singular countable noun.

He ate the whole pie.
The whole city is interesting.

b. Use *all* with an uncountable noun or a plural countable noun.

> He ate all the food.
> He ate all the vegetables.
> All New York is interesting.
> All the parts are interesting.

2. *All of* may be used instead of *all* or *whole* with a noun or pronoun.

> He ate all of the pie.
> He ate all of the food.
> He ate all of the vegetables.
> He ate all of it.
> He ate all of them.
> All of the city is interesting.
> All of New York is interesting.
> All of the parts are interesting.
> All of it is interesting.
> All of them are interesting.

3. The word order of *all* and *whole* differs.

a. *Whole* comes after an article (*a, an,* or *the*), a singular demonstrative (*this* or *that*), or a genitive word (*my, his, John's,* etc.).

> Effie spent a whole day in the museum.
> The whole class went to the lecture.
> This whole week has passed quickly.
> My whole day was ruined.

b. *All* comes before the definite articles (*the*), a singular or plural demonstrative (*this, these, that,* or *those*), and genitives (*my, his, John's* etc.).

> My counselor gave me all the advice I needed.
> All that information turned out to be correct.
> All those examples were quite interesting.
> All John's brothers are very tall.

c. When *all* modifies a subject, it may precede the subject or take the position of an adverb of frequency—that is, it precedes the main verb or comes after the first auxiliary, but it always comes after *am, is, are, was,* and *were* unless those words are final.

> All the boys go to school.   The boys all go to school.
> All the boys will go to school.   The boys will all go to school.
> All the boys were at school.   The boys were all at school.
> All those boys are students.   Those boys are all students.
> Some of those children are not students, but the boys all are.

d. When the pronoun *we, you, it,* or *they* is the subject, *all* takes the position of an adverb of frequency; it never precedes the pronoun.

> We all go to school.
> They have all gone to school.
> You will all go to school.
> It was all incorrect.
> Are they all students?
> Yes, they all are.
> After John's baggage arrived, it was all misplaced.

e. When *all* modifies *us, them,* or *it* or *you* not used as subjects, it immediately follows.

> John ate it all.
> I am grateful to you all.
> The woman thanked us all.
> A guide led them all out of the room.

4. *All* is used in a large number of set expressions. Some of them are the following:

> *at all costs,* "regardless of difficulties." You must see that movie at all costs.
> *all at once,* "suddenly." The building collapsed all at once.
> *all day* (or *night, morning, week,* etc.) (*long*), "the whole day." Paul has worked all day. I have been studying all week long.
> *all in,* "tired." After the examination Jim felt all in.
> *all in all,* "considering everything." All in all, Philip is a good student.
> *all of a sudden,* "suddenly." Grandfather jumped out of his chair all of a sudden.
> *all told,* "including all." All told, eighty persons attended the conference.
> *by all means,* "certainly" (a polite intensifier). By all means, go if you want to.
> *first of all,* "the first of a series" (used in place of *first* but not in place of *at first*). First of all, I will explain the symbols. Then, you will practice.
> *once and for all,* "now but never again." I will explain the problem once and for all.

Also, see § *Each* vs. *Every* vs. *All,* § Intensifier, § Preposition—Expression with, § Singular vs. Plural, § Word Order—Adjective before Noun, and § Word Order—Adverb Modifying Verb.

ALREADY VS. YET   A.15

1. Both *already* and *yet* have the meaning "by this (or that) time," but they are not interchangeable.

2. With that meaning, *already* is used in affirmative statements, and *yet* is used in negative statements. *Already* usually comes before the main verb or after the first auxiliary (and after *am, is, are, was,* and *were*), but it may also come after the verb and its complement, if any. *Yet* customarily comes after the verb and its complement, if any. Both words usually accompany the present tense, the present perfect, or the past perfect tense.

> The guests are already here.
> The guests are here already.

The guests are not here yet.
No one has done it yet.
I have already seen that movie.
I have seen that movie already.
I have not seen that movie yet.
When we got there, they had already left.

3. In both affirmative and negative questions *yet* is customarily used. In questions *already* conveys a sense of surprise.

Have you finished your composition yet? You have only a few more minutes.
Have you finished your composition already? You are very speedy.
Haven't you met Mr. Warner yet? Well, I will introduce you to him.
Haven't you already met Mr. Warner? I thought you did last week.

4. *Yet* also has another meaning, that of "however." See § Opposition Expression.

AMOUNT VS. NUMBER   A.16

1. The word *amount* is used with uncountable words.

Your grades depend on the amount of work you put into your studies.

2. The word *number* is used with countable words.

Frank and I were surprised at the number of birds in the zoo.

Also, see § *Many* vs. *Much* and § Singular vs. Plural.

ANOTHER VS. OTHER   A.17

1. The word *another* is always singular. It is always written as one word. It refers to an indefinite, different member of a series. It is not used to refer to the second of a known pair. *Another* occurs either alone or before a singular noun or the word *one.*

If you do not like that tie, put on another. You have a lot.
This shirt is soiled. I am going to put on another one.
It is very cold. You had better put on another sweater.
Wouldn't you like to have another piece of pie?

2. There are a number of expressions with the words *one . . . another.*

My friend Bruce is always busy with one thing or another.
A hobo is a person who wanders from one place to another.

The words *one another* are sometimes used instead of *each other* in referring to more than two people.

They all loved one another dearly.

3. The word *other* may be used before either a singular or a plural noun. If no noun follows, *other* is used to refer to a singular noun, and *others* is used to refer to a plural noun. *The other* is used for the second of a known pair, and *the others* is used for all the remaining members of a known group.

> The secretary told the applicant to come back some other time.
> Elizabeth was glad to go with the other girls.
> That movie was more interesting than any other I have seen recently.
> It is true that some books are duller than others.
> The little girl slowly closed one eye and then the other.
> Mr. Brown carried the heavy bag, and the children took all the others.

Also, see § Noun—Not Repeated, and § *Each* vs. *Every* vs. *All.*

ANTECEDENT   A.18

1. *Antecedent* is the term used for the word or words that a pronoun refers to.

> Mary needs a hat, but she can't afford one. [*Mary* is the antecedent of *she,* and *a hat* is the antecedent of *one.*]

Also, see § Agreement—Pronoun, § Subject and Simple Predicate, § *What* vs. *That* and *Which,* and other related entries in the Index.

ANY VS. *SOME*   A.19

1. The words *any* and *some* customarily indicate an intermediate stage between complete definiteness and complete indefiniteness. (Complete definiteness is usually indicated by the article *the.* Complete indefiniteness is usually indicated by the articles *a* or *an* before singular countable nouns and by no article before plural nouns and singular uncountable nouns.) Compounds such as *anybody,* *anything,* and *someone* function similarly to *any* or *some.* Before nouns, the *some* and *any* are customarily not stressed. However, the uses of *any* and *some* are different.

2. *Some* is used mostly in affirmative sentences, and *any* is used mostly in negative sentences, including those with words of negative force such as *hardly.* In negative sentences *any* occurs after the word of negation.

I received some mail today.	I did not receive any mail today.
There is somebody in that room.	There isn't anybody in that room.
Sam knows something about that.	Sam does not know anything about that.
Mae did the work with some help.	Mae did the work without any help.
Did you receive some mail today?	Didn't you receive any mail today?

3. *Some* and *any* before nouns are sometimes stressed. Then, they have special meanings. They may occur in either affirmative or negative sentences. Stressed *some* suggests contrast; it often means "special" or "certain in contrast with another or others." Stressed *any* often means "without exception" or "it does not matter which one (or ones or amount, etc.) of this kind." Sometimes stressed *any* suggests irritation or sarcasm.

> Somebody did not hand in his homework. [All the students except one handed in their homework.]
> Didn't you receive some mail today? [I think you received some although it may have been only a little.]
> Any girls who want to leave now may do so.
> Professor Moore will try to answer any question a student asks.
> Anything Mrs. Tolson says can be relied on.
> If I have any money left after today, I will be surprised.
> Anyone may find himself in an embarrassing position at any time.
> Did you receive any mail today?
> May I get you anything?

4. *Any* is used before a comparative to express emphasis.

> Do you feel any better today?
> I can not work any faster.

5. *Some* is often used before a numeral to express the meaning "approximately."

> Some forty persons bought tickets.

Also, see § Negative.

APOSTROPHE   A.20

1. The apostrophe has three major uses: (*a*) to indicate a genitive construction; (*b*) to indicate plurality for particular kinds of words; (*c*) to indicate an omission.

2. Be sure to place the apostrophe in its correct position. Study all the examples in this section. I will first discuss the meanings of a genitive construction and then give you the rules for the placing of the apostrophe.

3. A genitive construction is composed of a *genitor* and the genitive inflection. The genitor is the form before the apostrophe, and the genitive inflection is the following *'s* or *'*. In the construction the inflection indicates that the genitor is (*a*) a performer or (*b*) an affectee or (*c*) a characterizer. Those three categories can be subdivided into smaller classes:

Performer. The genitor has the meaning of "doer," "maker," "author," or "agent." A clear instance of that meaning is in a sentence like "Shakespeare's plays are often produced," in which *Shakespeare's* indicates that Shakespeare wrote or was the author of the plays. Another instance is in "John's gift to Mary was a watch," in which John is the performer of the act of giving. Other examples are in "We heard the ocean's roar," "The soldier's deeds earned him a medal," and "Women's tears are effective weapons."

Affectee. The genitor has the meaning of "that which is affected or acted upon" —a "receiver" or "undergoer" or "victim." In "The play ends with Hamlet's murder,'' Hamlet is the victim of the murder. A common instance of ''receiver'' is in ''Mary's gift from John was a watch,'' in which Mary is the receiver of the gift. Other instances of affectee are in ''The president's supporters were enthusiastic,'' ''Actors' admirers frequently wait at stage doors,'' ''Women's fashions are created in Paris,'' ''The student's grade was a *B*,'' and ''Washington's portrait hangs in every school building.''

Characterizer. The genitor has the general meaning of ''describer'' or ''limiter.'' A construction of this category can be one of at least three subclasses:

a. The subclass *possession* of the characterizing category is the one that usually comes to mind at the mention of the genitive; the genitor is the ''possessor'' or ''owner.'' In the sentence ''Bill's dog is very friendly,'' the *'s* indicates that Bill owns or possesses the dog.

b. Closely allied to possession is the subclass *connection,* in which the genitor is the ''referent.'' The genitive construction may have meanings such as ''related to the referent by birth, marriage, employment, or association'' or ''dedicated to the referent'' or ''forming a part of the referent.'' Examples are in ''The king's son was killed in battle,'' ''The club's members voted for an increase in dues,'' ''Harry went to see St. John's Cathedral,'' and ''Mrs. Thomkins dwells on life's tragedies.'' Quite often the referent is an expression of definite time like *today, yesterday,* or *last week,* as in ''Nothing is duller than yesterday's news.'' The referent may also be the determiner of a comparison; for example, in ''That young boy has a man's voice,'' the boy's voice is described as being similar to or characteristic of that belonging to a man. Another example is in ''That dentist keeps bankers' hours.''

c. A third subclass is *measurement,* in which the genitor is the ''unit of measurement.'' The measurement may be one of duration, extent, or value. Examples are in ''Mr. Green takes an hour's walk every night,'' ''We have two weeks' vacation for Christmas,'' ''That building is a stone's throw from here,'' and ''I bought a dollar's worth of stamps.''

4. Since the genitive construction may denote many different meanings, a careful writer stays on the alert to prevent ambiguity. For instance, without sufficient context, an expression like ''Paul's picture'' is ambiguous: it may be a picture painted by Paul, a picture painted of Paul, or a picture owned by Paul. Such an instance should be recast into an unambiguous construction.

5. The rules for the placing of the apostrophe in a genitive construction are the following:

a. With the letter *s,* at the end of words that do not end in an *s.*

the boy's teacher	the fox's tail	Hemingway's novels
a child's toys	the man's wife	John's brothers
children's toys	the men's wives	Mr. Smith's house

b. Without the letter *s* for plural words that end in an *s.*

both the boys' little dog	the Smiths' house
the two young princes' palace	the two young princesses' palace

c. With or without the letter *s* for singular words that end in an *s*. The alternative written forms may be pronounced the same way or differently—that is, both *actress's* and *actress'* may be pronounced either ['æktrɪs] or ['æktrɪsɪs].

the actress's role	my boss's office	a waitress's job
the actress' role	my boss' office	a waitress' job

Singular personal names follow this rule. Some first or given names with *s* are the following: Agnes, Augustus, Carlos, Charles, Dolores, Frances (feminine), Francis (masculine), James, Jules, Julius, Lewis, Lois, Moses, Thomas, and Ulysses.

Charles's mother	Dolores's cat	James's books
Charles' mother	Dolores' cat	James' books

Some singular family names or surnames that end in *s* are the following: Adams, Andrews, Barnes, Brooks, Burns, Collins, Davis, Edwards, Ellis, Evans, Harris, Hawkins, Hayes, Hicks, Holmes, Hopkins, Hughes, James, Jenkins, Jones, Keats, Lewis, Lucas, Meyers, Mills, Morris, Myers, Nichols, Owens, Perkins, Peters, Phillips, Reynolds, Richards, Roberts, Rogers, Ross, Sanders, Sears, Simmons, Stephens, Stevens, Thomas, Watkins, Wells, Williams, Willis, and Woods.

Have you seen Mr. Adams's hat?
Have you seen Mr. Adams' hat?
We are studying Robert Burns's poems.
We are studying Robert Burns' poems.

6. The foregoing rules apply not only to single words but also to groups of words which compose a construction in themselves.

the commander-in-chief's order	the commanders-in-chief's order
my father-in-law's house	my parents-in-law's house
somebody else's hat	

7. A genitive inflection is used after each of two or more performers, affectees, or characterizers of different things.

John's and Mary's grades are usually quite different.
My father's and my brother's raincoats are alike.

8. In writing, it is usually clearer and, therefore, better not to use a genitive-inflection construction in two instances:

a. If the last word is not the only performer, affectee, or characterizer

the house of my father and mother	*not*	my father and mother's house
the teacher of John, Bill, and Mary	*not*	John, Bill, and Mary's teacher.

b. If the last word is a part of a construction which is less than the construction which expresses the performer, affectee, or characterizer

the palace of the king of England	*not*	the king of England's palace
the beer for the boys in the back room	*not*	the boys in the back room's beer

Notice that "commander-in-chief's order" is clear because of the hyphens.

9. The genitive words *hers, his, its, mine, ours, theirs, whose,* and *yours* do not have an apostrophe.

> John has his book. Where is yours? You had better borrow hers.

10. Be particularly careful about the genitive words *its* and *whose*. Distinguish between them and the contractions *it's* and *who's*, which represent *it is* or *it has* and *who is* or *who has.*

> That dog has lost its owner.
> It's a fine-looking dog.
> Whose dog is it?
> Who's been feeding it?

11. Many stores, shops, offices, churches, hospitals, and magazines are frequently referred to by a shortened form of their name. That short form is usually a proper name with *'s*—for example, *Altman's* for *B. Altman & Co.* and *St. Luke's* for *St. Luke's Hospital.* Other similar ones are *Woolworth's, St. Patrick's* (Cathedral), and *Harper's* (*Magazine*).

a. Sometimes the short form has two proper names, but only the second name has the genitive inflection.

> I will meet you at Lord & Taylor's after I go to Franklin Simon's.
> You can probably get that article from Sears Roebuck's.

b. Rather frequently, particularly in conversation, a person's home or place of business is referred to by just the genitive construction.

> I went over to Paul's, but he was at his sister's.
> Florence was at her dentist's for two hours yesterday.

12. The apostrophe is used in a *double-genitive* construction like "a friend of John's," which has a different meaning from "John's friend." The difference is similar to that between the indefinite article *a* and the definite article *the.* When I use *a friend of John's,* I usually mean "a friend of his which I have not mentioned or specified previously." When I use *John's friend,* I usually mean "that friend of his whom I have been talking about or whom I will identify immediately by his name."

> Last night a group of students worked for quite some time on a puzzle. Suddenly a friend of Mary's exclaimed, "I've got it!"
> Last night Mary and a friend of hers, Paul Thompson, worked for quite a time on a puzzle. Suddenly Mary's friend exclaimed, "I've got it!"

The double-genitive construction is used when a possessor, affectee, or characterizer occurs with either a *count* word—*a* or *one, two, some, any, many,* etc.—or a demonstrative—*this, that, these,* or *those.* Contrary to some grammarians' statements, the double-genitive construction is not a matter of emphasis; it is due to a fact of English word order. Three kinds of words—genitives, count words, and demonstratives—customarily occupy the same position in a construction.

> *John's* old college friends
> *some* old college friends
> *those* old college friends

Since two words can not occupy the same position at the same time, the problem has been resolved by use of *of.* Either the demonstrative or the genitive may follow the count word with *of:*

> some *of those* old college friends
> some *of John's* old college friends

The genitive with *of* may go to the end of the construction with a count word:

> *some* old college friends *of John's*

It must go there after a demonstrative:

> *those* old college friends *of John's*

Notice the arrangement when all three kinds of words occur together:

> *some* of *those* old college friends of *John's*

13. In writing, the genitive inflection is often omitted from the performer, affectee, or characterizer when it is final in the double-genitive construction, but the "person" words always have their genitive forms (*mine, theirs,* etc.). Notice the different ways of expressing the same idea in the following groups of sentences:

> I always abide by a rule of my parents'.
> I always abide by a rule of my parents.
> I always abide by one of my parents' rules.
> That is a rule of theirs.
> That is one of their rules.
> Several characters of Shakespeare's are world-famous.
> Several characters of Shakespeare   are world-famous.
> Several of Shakespeare's characters are world-famous.
> Do you recall that poem of Wordsworth's?
> Do you recall that poem of Wordsworth ?
> I want you to meet a friend of mine.
> I want you to meet one of my friends.

14. In its second use, the apostrophe with *s* indicates plurality for *citation forms* —that is, figures, symbols, letters, and words which are being referred to as items in themselves. Notice that citation forms are underlined in manuscript and italicized in print. The *'s* is also usually underlined and italicized. Citation forms are further illustrated in § Underlining.

> Some Americans write *7's* that look like *1's,* but some Europeans make *7's* that look like *4's.*
> Your *z's* look like *s's,* and your *p's* look like *f's.*
> The teacher had only two *A's* in his class.
> You use too many *this's* in your themes.

15. Do not use an apostrophe with the plural of proper names with the meaning "people or things with the name of. . . ." Indicate that kind of plural by the addition of only *s* (*es* after the letters *s, z, sh, x,* and *ch* not pronounced like *k*). The names are not underlined or italicized.

> There are two Marys and three Roberts in our class.
> Are the Smiths coming to your party tomorrow night?
> The Foxes have already left for the Great Lakes.
> That house belongs to the Robert Joneses; the William Joneses live in the next one.

16. The third use of the apostrophe is to indicate the omission of certain letters or figures. Such omission occurs in three kinds of writing: general, informal, and special. The contractions used in general writing are appropriate for every occasion. Informal writing is used in letters to close friends and in representation of customary educated speech as in direct quotation and dialog of plays; its contractions are sometimes used by writers who wish to convey a personal relationship with their readers. Special writing can be divided into two categories: *poetic*, in which the poet wishes to reduce the number of syllables of a word for purposes of meter, and *nonstandard*, in which the writer wishes to indicate that the speaker is not using customary educated speech even though some of the shortened forms represent the usual pronunciations of educated speakers. Examples of the three kinds of contractions are given below:

a. General writing: Part of *of the* is omitted in the word *o'clock* and names like *O'Brien, O'Leary,* and *O'Toole.*

> Tom O'Toole came by to see you at eight o'clock this morning.

b. Informal writing:

1. Omission of the first two figures in years: *'55* for *1755; '05* for *1905.*

> The American Revolution began in '75.

2. Omission of various parts of auxiliaries and forms of the verb *be* and the word *not* when they are unstressed as they usually are in conversation: *'m, 're, 'd, 'll, aren't, can't,* etc. However, the auxiliaries are not contracted when they come at the beginning or end of a clause.

> I'm leaving. Are you leaving? Yes, I am.

3. Omission of the *u* in *let's* (from *let us*) and the *d* in *madam.*

> Yes, ma'am, let's see if we can't straighten out the difficulty.

c. Special writing:

1. Poetry: Omission of the letter *v* in *e'en, e'er, ne'er, o'er.*
2. Nonstandard: Contractions such as *an'* for *and, one o' them* for *one of them, 'im* for *him, 'er* for *her, 'em* for *them,* and *-in'* for the ending *-ing.*

> An' one o' 'em told 'er I warn't goin' that mornin'.

17. The following list includes contractions that you will encounter in your reading. In the brackets is the general writing of the contraction or an explanation of its derivation. The letter in the parentheses before a contraction indicates its

a

classification: **(g)** means "general"; **(i)** means "informal"; **(p)** means "poetic," and **(n)** means "nonstandard." I recommend that in most of your writing you restrict yourself to the general class; use the informal class only for letters to close friends or for direct quotations. Be sure to put the apostrophe in the right place.

(n) ain't [am not; are not; is not; have not; has not]	**(i)** mightn't [might not]
(n) an' [and]	**(n)** mornin' [morning]
(i) aren't [are not]	**(i)** mustn't [must not]
(i) can't [can not]	**(n)** 'n [and]
(i) couldn't [could not]	**(i)** needn't [need not]
(i) 'd [had; would]	**(p)** ne'er [never]
(i) daren't [dare not]	**(i)** n't [not]
(n) dassn't [dare not]	**(n)** o' [of]
(i) didn't [did not]	**(g)** O' [in proper names like *O'Brien* and *O'Riley*]
(i) doesn't [does not]	**(g)** o'clock [historically "of the clock"]
(i) don't [do not]	**(p)** o'er [over]
(p) e'en [even]	**(i)** oughtn't [ought not]
(p) e'er [ever]	**(i)** 're [are]
(n) 'em [them]	**(i)** 's [has; is]
(n) 'er [her]	**(i)** shan't [shall not]
(n) goin' [going]	**(i)** shouldn't [should not]
(n) g'wan [go on]	**(n)** sump'n [something]
(i) hadn't [had not]	**(n)** t' [to; the]
(i) hasn't [has not]	**(n)** -t' [-*th* as in *fourt'* and *tent'*]
(i) haven't [have not]	**(n)** t'ing [thing]
(n) 'im [him]	**(i)** 've [have]
(n) -in' [for -*ing* as in *comin'* and *mornin'*]	**(n)** warn't [was not; were not]
(g) let's [let us]	**(i)** wasn't [was not]
(i) 'll [will; shall]	**(i)** weren't [were not]
(i) 'm [am; madam]	**(i)** won't [will not]
(i) ma'am [madam]	**(i)** wouldn't [would not]
(i) mayn't [may not]	**(n)** y' [you]

18. Be careful about the pronunciation of the word *apostrophe.* The second syllable is stressed, and the final *e* is pronounced.

·Also, see § Suffix -*s.*

APPOSITIVE

A.21

1. An appositive is a statement of the content of a word or group of words. The appositive usually comes next to the word or group of words that it is in apposition to.

> My eldest brother, Timothy, left yesterday. [*Timothy* is the appositive to *my eldest brother.*]

32

Jim went to see his mother-in-law, Mrs. Curtis. [*Mrs. Curtis* is the appositive to *his mother-in-law*.]

Alice died April 22, on her birthday. [*On her birthday* is the appositive to *April 22.*]

2. Since an appositive is a restatement, you can test it by mentally substituting the same kind of personal pronoun (*he, him, it,* etc.) or *th* word (*there, then, therefore,* or *thus*) for both it and the word or group that it is in apposition to. Be sure that the substitution is for the entire appositive and for the word or entire group that it is in apposition to.

My eldest brother [substitute: *he*], Timothy [substitute: *he*], left yesterday.

Jim went to see his mother-in-law [substitute: *her*], Mrs. Curtis [substitute: *her*].

Alice died April 22 [substitute: *then*], on her birthday [substitute: *then*].

3. Be careful about the form of personal pronouns used in an appositive.

Only two students, John and *I*, got high grades.

The teacher gave high grades to only two students, John and *me*.

In the first example *John and I* is the appositive to *only two students;* therefore, the subject form *I* is used. In the second example *John and me* is the appositive to *only two students;* therefore, the object form *me* is used because of the preposition *to.*

4. There are two kinds of appositive: *restrictive* and *nonrestrictive.* Both kinds give additional information about the word or group they are in apposition to. However, a restrictive appositive tells the reader that the word or group is limited in meaning by its appositive. A nonrestrictive appositive intentionally does not restrict or limit the meaning of its word or group.

Let's take an example. Two writers, John and Bill, are going to use the words *my sister* in a sentence. John has only one sister. Bill has more than one sister. The two writers will use exactly the same words in their sentence, but, by using commas around the appositive *Mary,* John intentionally tells his reader that he has only one sister; by not using commas around *Mary,* Bill intentionally tells his readers that he has more than one sister.

John:	My sister	,	Mary	,	is older than I.
Bill:	My sister		Mary		is older than I.

In speech, there is usually a slight pause before and after a nonrestrictive appositive, but there are no such pauses around a restrictive appositive. In writing, the punctuation serves the same purpose as the speech pauses. It is the responsibility of the writer to use punctuation or no punctuation correctly to indicate to his reader whether the word or group is limited or not.

5. Certain words are often used with or as restrictive appositives.

a. The personal pronouns *you, we,* and *us* are frequently immediately followed by a restrictive appositive. Use no commas.

You men should be ashamed of yourselves.

We Americans have a reputation for being extravagant.

The Swiss family was very hospitable to us foreigners.

b. The words *all, both,* and *each* frequently serve as restrictive appositives. Do not mark them off. They usually immediately follow their word or group.

> My boys all go to school.
> Have my boys all gone to school?
> Jack Horner looked at the two pies and then ate them both.
> Should we each ask for tickets?

When *all, both,* and *each* are appositives to a subject, they precede main verbs but follow the first auxiliary or *is, are, was,* or *were.* However, they precede an auxiliary or *is, are, was,* or *were* used finally in a clause.

> My boys have all gone to school.
> My boys will all have gone to school.
> My boys were all at school.
> My boys are all students.
> Some of my children are not students, but the boys all are.

c. The *-self* words—*myself, ourselves, yourself, yourselves, himself, herself, itself, themselves,* and *oneself*—are *emphatic reflexive* restrictive appositives when they do not function as objects. They occur immediately after the subject or, if they are appositives to a subject, come at the end of the predicate. They are not marked off by punctuation.

> I myself will do it.
> I will do it myself.
> He himself is in doubt.
> He is in doubt himself.

The *-self* words may be in apposition to words other than subjects. When they are, they immediately follow.

> I will tell it to John himself. [*Himself* is in apposition to *John,* the object of the preposition *to.*]
> I will tell John himself what you told me. [*Himself* is in apposition to *John,* the indirect object of *tell.*]

Just for fun, here is an unusual though possible sentence that has two *-self* appositives:

> I will tell John himself myself.

Remember that the *-self* words are not always appositives.

> I have cut myself. [*Myself* is the direct object of *cut.*]
> I gave myself a lecture. [*Myself* is the indirect object of *gave.*]

d. The word *it* is frequently followed, but usually not immediately, by a restrictive appositive. The appositive customarily comes at the end of the clause. The appositive is or contains a verb form; the verb form may be an infinitive with *to,* an *-ing* form, or a simple predicate; the verb form may have a subject of complements or modifiers. In the following examples the appositive to the *it* is in parentheses, and the verb form is italicized.

It is nice (to *relax*).
It was John (who *told* me).
It was clear (that he *was* angry).
It was hard (to *break* the news to Mr Wheeler).
I thought it strange (that the men *had left* without their companion).
Rachel saw to it (that I *understood* what she meant).

The *it* in the first four examples above is the subject of the following simple predicate *is* or *was;* in the fifth example the *it* is the direct object of *thought;* in the last example the *it* is the object of the preposition *to.* Since the appositive expresses the content that the *it* stands for, such an *it* is sometimes called a "filler *it*" or "anticipatory *it*" or "preparatory *it,*" and the appositive is sometimes called a "deferred" subject, complement, or prepositional object. It is interesting to know that the antecedent of the *it* follows it in such sentences, but syntactically the *it* is the subject, complement, or prepositional object, and the clause-final verb construction is an appositive.

e. A restrictive appositive frequently comes after constructions beginning with the word *the* and containing words which have not been previously mentioned or limited.

The poet Chaucer is the most famous writer of Middle English.
Capitalize the word *Catholic* when it refers to a religion.
The clause "when it refers to a religion" is used as an adverbial complement in the preceding example.

Remember that citation forms like *Catholic* are underlined or italicized and that citation groups and definitions have quotation marks. Definitions are enclosed in parentheses if they are not part of the main structure of the sentence.

The word *lead* meaning "a kind of metal" is pronounced differently from the word *lead* meaning "guide."
The Latin term *deus* ("god") is the source of the English words *deity* and *deify.*

f. Another kind of restrictive appositive is the *epithet* appositive. It follows a name and begins with *the.* The *the* is followed by either a noun or adjectival form.

William the Conqueror lived after Alfred the Great but before Richard the Lionhearted.
Harry the grocer is a great admirer of Billy the Kid.

The numerals following names of kings are examples of epithet appositives. In writing, the word *the* is customarily not used with the Roman numeral, but in speech the *the* occurs with the ordinal number.

Written: George VI was the father of Elizabeth II.
Spoken: George the Sixth was the father of Elizabeth the Second.

6. Now I will discuss nonrestrictive appositives in more detail:

a. A nonrestrictive appositive is customarily set off from its word or group by a comma or a pair of commas. A nonrestrictive appositive frequently begins with the words *one, the one,* and *the kind.*

> My mathematics teacher, a very stern man, never smiles.
> Dr. Schultz was talking to Miss Frost, a nurse at the hospital.
> I want a potato peeler, one that will cut out "eyes" easily.
> Ellen took the black kitten, the one that nobody else seemed to want.
> Paul speaks Provençal, the kind of French spoken in southern France.

b. If a nonrestrictive appositive comes within a sentence and is fairly long or has internal punctuation, use a pair of dashes to set it off.

> The black kitten—the one that nobody else seemed to want—immediately appealed to Ellen.
> All the colors of autumn—red, brown, yellow, orange, green—mingled on the hillside.
> John and I—the hardest-working students, according to our teacher—got high grades.

c. A very long appositive in the middle of a sentence is likely to cause your reader to lose your train of thought. If possible, it is better to rewrite the sentence so that the appositive comes elsewhere.

d. A nonrestrictive appositive often begins with introductory words such as *namely, specifically, that is, that is to say, i.e.,* and *viz.* Put commas after the introductory words, and set off the entire appositive by parentheses or dashes (one dash if the appositive ends the sentence).

> Four students—namely, John, Paul, Bob, and Arthur—got *A's.*
> My most constant critic (that is to say, my wife) finds few virtues in me.
> We have only one thing to fear—that is, fear itself.

e. In writing, a nonrestrictive appositive often precedes a subject it is in apposition to. For that position, use a comma after the appositive if it has no internal punctuation; otherwise, use a dash. Quite frequently the summarizing word *all* is the word or part of the construction that the preposed appositive is in apposition to.

> A nurse, Miss Ross is quite accustomed to concealing her emotions.
> A poor man himself a long time, Dickens was well aware of the horrors of poverty.
> Red, brown, yellow, orange, green—all the bright colors of autumn mingled on the hillside.

f. A nonrestrictive appositive to a subject sometimes comes at the end of the clause, but it should not if there is any possibility of ambiguity. Use either a dash or a colon. The colon is preferable. (Remember that an appositive to a preceding *it* is restrictive and is not set off by punctuation.)

> All of the Blakes' belongings were lost in the fire: furniture, clothing, and keepsakes.
> All of the Blakes' belongings were lost in the fire—furniture, clothing, and keepsakes.

7. Use a colon before any clause-final appositive if the appositive is a series or could be a grammatically complete sentence by itself. However, use a dash, not a colon, if the appositive has introductory words like *namely.*

> The countries which participated in the conference were the following: Peru, Yugoslavia, Jordan, and Greece.
> Give your secretary what she needs: pencils, paper, and a good typewriter.
> When a friend buys a puppy, you are sure to hear all the news about it: when it is vaccinated, how much damage it does, and what intelligent tricks it performs.
> I find only one thing wrong with Henry: he is not very generous.

> Sometimes the first word of a complete-sentence appositive is capitalized.

> I find only one thing wrong with Henry: He is not very generous.

8. Do not use a colon for a series if before it there is no word or group for it to be in apposition to. For example, a colon would be wrong after *were* in the following example, in which "Peru, Yugoslavia, Jordan, and Greece" is the predicate nominative, not an appositive.

> The countries which participated in the conference were Peru, Yugoslavia, Jordan, and Greece.

9. Notice that the ordinary use of the colon is exemplified after the word *directions* or *instructions* as in the following sentence.

> Directions: Copy the following sentences, adding necessary punctuation.

10. It is pertinent here to point out that three uses of the colon are not related to its use before an appositive: (*a*) after a business-letter salutation such as *Dear Sir:* ; (*b*) in clock time such as *10:35 p.m.;* and (*c*) as the equivalent of *because* in a sentence such as "The boy did not attend the party: he was ashamed of his clothes." All the uses of the colon are discussed under § Colon.

ARISE **VS.** *AROUSE*   A.22

1. The words *arise* and *arouse* are not synonyms, nor is the second the past form of the first. For *arise,* the past tense is *arose,* and the past participle is *arisen.* For *arouse,* the past tense and the past participle are *aroused. Arise* is intransitive— that is, it never has a direct object. *Arouse* is transitive—that is, it may have a direct object.

> Whenever a political discussion arises in a group, it will doubtless arouse everybody.

2. With reference to people, both *arise* and its synonym *rise* are formal. *Get up* is conversational and informal.

> I arose at seven this morning.
> I got up at seven this morning.

Every student of English has my sympathy in his struggles with the articles *a*, *an*, and *the*. Here I am not going to attempt to review all the rules which some of you have undoubtedly labored over. Instead, in the following paragraphs I will try to group together those uses of the articles—or the omission of them—which may still cause some of you trouble.

1. First of all, I urge you to do this: listen to educated speakers. When you listen, listen carefully. Since the articles *the* and *a* are almost never emphasized, they do not stand out very prominently in speech, but they are pronounced. You will have to train your ears so that you will recognize that the little sound before certain words is an article and not a meaningless noise.

2. Also, get into the habit of pronouncing the articles in the way that educated speakers do: as little sounds that are virtually part of the word they precede. For instance, think of and say *the boy* as one word.

3. Do not be misled by newspaper headlines, advertisements, and titles of books, poems, and so forth. They frequently omit articles which are necessary in connected speech and writing.

4. All English nouns can be divided into two classes: those that are *countable* and those that are *uncountable.* A countable noun is, by definition, one that can be preceded by *one* (or *a* or *an*), *two, three,* etc. An uncountable noun is one that can not be preceded by a cardinal number. The *meaning* of a noun as it is used in a sentence determines whether it is countable or uncountable. The *form* of a noun—that is, its pronunciation or spelling—does not determine whether it is countable or uncountable. For instance, the word *hair* in the sentence "She has long hair" is an uncountable, but in the sentence "There is a hair on your coat" *hair* is a countable. In the sentence "Life is beautiful" *life* is an uncountable, but in "He had an interesting life" *life* is a countable. The matter of countables and uncountables is discussed in a little more detail under § Singular vs. Plural and § Article—*The* vs. No *The.* Also, see § *Amount* vs. *Number,* § *Few* vs. *A Few,* § *Many* vs. *Much,* and § *Such* vs. *Such a.*

Here I will make some very general observations and work from them.

5. Most frequently, both *the* and *a* (from now on I will include *an* with *a*) are restrictive: both refer to a group (a "species") which has more than one member ("specimen").

6. When I say *the,* I usually mean "that specimen which I have been talking about *and* which you know."

7. When I say *a,* I usually mean "a specimen which you do not know"— perhaps I know which one I am talking about, and perhaps you will know which one in a second, but at this moment you do not know.

a

8. Therefore, if *the* and *a* are restrictive (or limiting), the lack of an article must indicate the idea of "unlimited."

9. The difference between *the* and *a* usually causes little trouble. The difference between *the* and no *the* and the difference between *a* and no *a* do cause trouble. In the following sections I will base the discussion on the distinctions involved in using or not using an article.

ARTICLE—*A* VS. NO *A*   A.24

1. If you have trouble with *a,* you may find this test helpful: use *a* before a singular noun if that noun would be used in the plural without an article in a similar sense. That test, of course, is just a rephrasing of the fact that *a* has no plural form.

July is a month.	July and August are months.
John is a handsome boy.	John and Robert are handsome boys.
A nice girl doesn't swear.	Nice girls don't swear.

2. Before a singular noun denoting a member of a profession or a holder of an occupation, English uses the indefinite article. Also, see the discussion of fields of study under "Abstract words" in ¶ 4, *b,* of § Article—*The* vs. No *The.*

My brother William is planning to be a lawyer.
Herman Orton was an engineer before he died.
Mr. Thornton has been a clerk at Macy's for many years.

For no *a* with a predicate objective, see § Predicate Objective.

3. *A* occurs in the pattern "*a* + *very* + adjective + noun."

The ability to write is a very useful thing.
Morale plays a very important role in any organization.

A occurs in the same pattern before *most* meaning "very."

We spent a most pleasant evening with our old friends.

4. After expressions such as *kind of* and *type of,* an *a* is usually not used.

What kind of suit was Dean Brown wearing?
Juan is the sort of student that teachers are proud of.
That is the sort of thing I had in mind.
Mr. Greet is the type of man we need for the job.
What brand of cigaret do you prefer?
That variety of bird is extremely rare around here.
What make of car are you planning to buy next year?

5. *A* or *an* is used in expressions of time and measurement.

Our class meets four times a week.
Daniel makes ninety cents an hour. [He earns ninety cents an hour.]

> Ana Graniero visits her native country twice a year.
> Paul told me those shoes cost four dollars a pair.
> Butter was eighty cents a pound not long ago.
> Gasoline used to sell for fifteen cents a gallon.

Less frequently, **per** is used instead of *a* or *an* for such expressions.

> The car's speed was sixty miles per hour.

6. No *a* is used before *part of* meaning "a portion of." However, *a* is used in "a large (small, minor, etc.) part," and *the* is used in "the greater (or larger) part" and "the largest (best, etc.) part."

> Part of the letter was missing.
> Patrick forgot a small part of his talk.
> Students should study the greater part of their time.
> Alice's father gave her the largest part of his wealth.
> You did not see the best part of the movie.

7. *A* is used in expressions such as the following:

> *a couple of.* I saw Allen a couple of weeks ago.
> *after a fashion.* Len did the job, but I would not call it well done. He did it after a fashion.
> *all of a sudden.* The door slammed shut all of a sudden.
> *a long time.* It has been a long time since I heard anyone use that term.
> *as a matter of fact.* Albert did not take your book. As a matter of fact, he was not in the room.
> *be a pity.* It is a pity you can not go with us to the theater.
> *be a question of.* It was simply a question of choosing between the two applicants.
> *be a shame.* It's a shame that Mr. Adams spoke unkindly to you.
> *be in a good (bad, happy, etc.) mood.* A cheerful person is always in a good mood.
> *have a good (bad, busy, etc.) time.* Did you have a good time at the party last night?
> *in a hurry.* Pardon me. I am in a hurry to get to my class.
> *in a rush.* My boss asked me to finish the job in a rush.

Some other differences between *a* and no *a* are discussed under § *Few* vs. *A Few* (including *little* and *a little*), § *Many a* (including *a good many* and *a great many*), § Singular vs. Plural (particularly in the paragraphs on uncountables), and § *Such* vs. *Such a.* Instances of the omission of *a* are given under § *By*—Preposition, § *For*—Preposition, § *From*—Preposition, and § *In*—Preposition. Also, see § *A* vs. *One,* § *Hundred* vs. *Hundreds of,* and § Preposition—Expression with. For the difference between *a* and *an,* see § *A* vs. *An.*

ARTICLE—*THE* VS. NO *THE*   A.25

Historically, *the* is a demonstrative word. It is still used in a manner which can be interpreted as "this (or that)—and not any other." See § Article (*A, An, The*). The following sections list some of the major categories of the use of *the.*

1. Replacement for indefinite article. In its most common occurrence, *the* is used to refer to a previously mentioned specimen.

We own a dog and a cat. The dog is brown, and the cat is white.

The is used with certain words which refer to previously mentioned specimens: *former, latter, remainder, rest,* and *same.*

We own a dog and a cat. The former is brown, and the latter is white. They are the same ones we had last year.
Irma took only part of the cake. She left the rest (the remainder) for you.

2. Understood specimen. A speaker will often use *the* to designate a specimen that his listener or reader is familiar with. For example, a man and his wife may have a conversation like the following:

Mr. Allen: I'm going to leave the car at the garage on my way to the office.
Mrs. Allen: Be sure to tell the mechanic that the radio isn't working and the wiper needs to be adjusted.

Although the specimens in the above conversation have not been mentioned immediately before, the husband knows that his wife will understand *the car* to mean "the car we own," *the garage* to mean "the garage we regularly use," and *the office* to mean "the office where I work." Likewise, his wife knows that he will understand *the mechanic* to mean "the mechanic who works in that garage," and *the radio* to mean "the radio in our car," and *the wiper* to mean "the windshield wiper on our car."

a. Very often there is a specimen which is so frequently referred to that speakers automatically use the specifying *the* even though there are other specimens of the same species. For instance, there are many *suns*—that is, self-luminous heavenly bodies—but our solar system's sun is the one that we most often talk about. Therefore, a speaker will begin a conversation with "The sun's very bright today," and his listeners will understand that he means "this—our earth's—sun." Similarly, other items may have the specifying *the* with the meaning of "the present specimen." For instance, we say, "The weather isn't very pleasant," meaning that specimen of weather which we are having today. A number of words which are commonly used with *the* denoting the understood specimen are the following:

the air	the earth	the ocean	the sky	the universe	the wind
the Bible	the moon	the rain	the sun	the weather	the world

b. The process of "understanding" may be the explanation for our saying *the past, the present,* and *the future* as "understood specimens" of time.

History is the study of the past.
The present is the only time to do it.
You will have another test in the very near future.

3. Plural nouns. Do not use *the* with a plural noun if the singular of that noun in that sense would have *a* or *an.* This rule is merely a restatement of the fact that the indefinite article has no plural form. Note particularly that this rule must often be applied in the general statements occurring at the beginning of a conversation or a composition.

> When we talk about actors, we generally talk about their roles.
> Politicians have been called corrupted men.
> Great men can be scientists, musicians, or military leaders.
> I think that women prepare meals faster than men do.

The word *people* is so frequently used as an indefinite plural word meaning "everybody in general" that in many instances the use of *the* in front of it has an unidiomatic ring. The same is true for the words *humans* and *human beings.* (Those words are used in conversation much more frequently than the similar word *one*—"One has one's duty to perform.")

> People are pretty much the same all over the world.
> People in audiences should not cause disturbances.
> Variety is what humans seem to crave more than anything else.
> Long ago, human beings lived in caves and wore animal skins.

Also, see § Singular vs. Plural for instances like "the British" and "the dead."

4. Singular unlimited words. These include the uncountables, and they are the words which cause the most trouble, principally, I suppose, because their equivalents often demand an article. See § Singular vs. Plural and § Article (*A, An, The*) for additional discussion of uncountables.

a. Countable. A speaker may sometimes designate a species by one of its specimens. In other words, he may use *the* before a singular countable noun to mean "all the specimens of the species of" or "any specimen of the species." When "any specimen" is the meaning, *a* or *the* can be used. The specimen, I believe, is always concrete and tangible. However, do not use *man* or *woman* in this way.

> The horse has been replaced by the railroad, the windship by the steamship.
> Do you prefer the city to the country?
> Didn't you hear that news over the radio this morning?
> The hand is quicker than the eye.

b. Uncountable. When a speaker uses certain words in the singular with an article, he seems to be thinking of "a or the specimen of. . . ." When he uses the same words without an article, he seems to be thinking either of "every instance or aspect of . . ." or of "the idea of . . . without a specific example." Those words fall into four groups: *everybody* words, *mass* words, *abstract* words, and *object-activity* words.

EVERYBODY WORDS.
a. When *man* and *mankind* are used without an article, they convey a meaning similar to that of people in ¶ 3, *a*, "everybody in general."

> Man stopped wandering when farming bound him to a certain place.
> Pasteur was one of the servants of mankind.

In the "everybody" sense, *man* and *mankind* can be modified, but they will still have no *the.* Also, *man* is referred to as masculine singular, but *mankind* is referred to as neuter singular.

Civilized man can not live without cooks.
Man has his problems.
Mankind has its problems.

b. Similarly, other neuter words such as *civilization, humanity,* and *society* are used in the same collective sense. (Some of those same words are also used without *the* but with another meaning; see "Abstract words" below.)

Society frowns upon bad manners.
Is civilization losing its place in the world?

c. However, a similar expression, *the human race,* has *the.* It is referred to as neuter singular like *mankind.*

How long is the human race going to keep its place in the world?

MASS WORDS. These represent concrete items: things which can be seen, heard, touched, or felt physically. When a mass word is used without *the,* the meaning conveyed is that explained above, "every instance of . . . without a specific example." Some words used in this way are the following:

air	dust	ink	money	rice	tea
coffee	electricity	iron	oil	soap	water
copper	food	meat	opium	steel	wheat
cotton	gas	milk	oxygen	sugar	wool

Cheese is made from milk.
We need iron to produce steel.

a. A mass word can be modified without becoming specific.

We need fresh air and sunshine.
Do you like chocolate milk?
You had better get some bread.
Brazilian coffee is usually strong.
Atomic energy has great potentialities.
Kansas grows a lot of wheat.

b. If *the* is used with a mass word, the meaning seems to be "this (or that) particular quantity or specimen of . . .," and there is often an expressed contrast with another quantity or specimen.

Milk sours quickly in the summer.
The milk in the bottle was sour.

There is meat on the shelves.
The meat on the second shelf is fresh.

ABSTRACT WORDS. These represent ideas, attitudes, emotions, qualities, or actions. When an abstract word is used without *the,* it expresses such an idea, etc., as belonging to or potentially belonging to everybody or everything. When an abstract word is used with *the,* it becomes the possession of a particular person, object, group, etc. That particular person, etc., is expressed either immediately or in the context. The most frequent way of expressing such possession is the use of a phrase beginning with *of*, *to*, or *for* or with an adjectival clause beginning with *that* or *which*. Some words used as "abstracts" are the following:

advice	existence	information	murder	success
art	fear	knowledge	nature	time
beauty	freedom	life	peace	transportation
Christianity	happiness	literature	pleasure	truth
death	harmony	love	religion	war
desire	history	marriage	science	work
equality	hunger	migration	slavery	worry
evolution				

Death is inevitable.
The parents were sad about the death of their son.

You should study history for instances of evolution.
Andrew studied the history of Europe.

In some groups marriage is taken very lightly.
The women were talking about the marriage that had taken place that noon.

Sociologists concern themselves with migration.
Sociologists concern themselves with the migration of people within the borders of a country.

The beggar died from hunger.
Reading can satisfy the hunger that comes from the desire for knowledge.

a. A gerund (the *-ing* form of a verb used as a noun) is very often used in the unlimited sense without *the*. Notice that it can be modified. Also, see § Infinitive vs. Gerund.

Swimming is a good way to reduce.
Swimming in the ocean is more strenuous than swimming in a pool.
Mr. Brown does not enjoy talking.
Reading gives me great pleasure.
Careful reading is a requirement for a good student.
Reading carefully is a requirement for a good student.

b. A field of study is usually referred to by an abstract word without *the*. Some words of that type are *chemistry, economics, engineering, geography, law, linguistics, mathematics, philosophy,* and *psychology*. Such a word should not be capitalized.

Dennis is studying law because he wants to become a lawyer.
Is Tracy taking economics this semester?

c. Frequently an abstract word is modified so that its meaning is narrowed, but the specifying *the* is not needed.

Grammar is easy for me.
I think English grammar is easy.

Mr. Beck enjoys history.
Mr. Beck studies European history.

Literature appeals to Grace.
Grace likes romantic literature.

Mr. Doe teaches engineering.
Mr. Bailey teaches civil engineering.

Poets write about nature.
That is just human nature, you know.

Sociologists investigate migration, not only cross-boundary migration but also internal migration.

Human existence does not depend on war or science; science does not depend on war, but modern war depends on modern science.

OBJECT-ACTIVITY WORDS. When one of the following words is used without *the*, it denotes the activity or use associated with the object the word represents when it is a countable:

bed	church	court	lunch	sea	town
breakfast	class	dinner	prison	supper	vacation
chapel	college	jail	school	tea	work

I go to bed at eleven o'clock.
Please don't sit on the bed.

Emmy saw George after church last Sunday.
The grocery store is next to the church.

James is in class right now.
The class is on the second floor.

You have to go to college for four years.
Harvard is the college he wants to go to.

In most places in the United States, school starts in September.
The boys broke a window of the school.

I learned that fact in high school.
The high school in our town has recently been renovated.

Morgan was sentenced to ten years in prison for the crime.
Sing Sing is the prison that New Yorkers usually think of.

Mr. Joyce is not at work today; he is on vacation.
The vacation I enjoyed most was two weeks in Jamaica.

We were at sea for seven days on our trip.
The sea was calm all the way.

Mr. Bennett always shaves before breakfast.
Mr. Cox did not like the breakfast that his wife had prepared.

Hurry up. Dinner is almost ready.
The dinner was good, but I did not enjoy the speeches that came after it.

University is not used as an object-activity word: it is not used without an article. It is different from *college.*

> Did Patrick go to college?
> Did Patrick go to a university?

PERSONAL NAMES. The general rule is that a personal name is not preceded by *the.*

> William Bronson came to see me at my office yesterday.

a. At times *the* is used before a personal name to indicate that the person named is contrasted with somebody else of the same name.

> The Samuel Johnson who was a president of Columbia University was not the Samuel Johnson who was a famous English writer.

b. If the members of a family are referred to collectively, *the* is used with the plural form of the family name.

> All the Bronsons have gone to visit Mrs. Bronson's mother.

c. A distinction is made between a personal name and a *title.* A personal name is a permanent possession of the bearer, but a title is a designation by the special use of certain common nouns such as *president, king, doctor, lieutenant, private, professor, father, mother,* and *aunt.* A title may be applied to many specimens, but it is not the possession of only one of them; it may be preceded by *a* or *the* when it is used simply as a common noun.

> We have just elected a president for our society.
> You ought to talk with one of the professors about your problem.

When those common nouns immediately precede personal names, they become titles, but the general rule that personal names do not use *the* is not violated.

> George VI was a king of England.
> King George died in 1952.
> King George VI was the father of Queen Elizabeth II.

Such titles are capitalized when they precede the personal name.
The following titles are abbreviated when they precede the name: *Dr., Prof., Mr.,* and *Mrs.* (*Miss* has no period).

> I saw President Truman in Washington in 1950.
> Mrs. Collins called Dr. Berthel when her child got sick.
> When did Uncle Joe come home last night?
> We hope that Mr. Harper is going to marry Aunt Caroline.

Such titles may be used alone in direct address. They are then usually capitalized. However, *sir,* which is used instead of *Mr.* alone, and *madam* or *ma'am,* which is used instead of *Mrs.* alone, are not capitalized.

46

> When are you leaving, Doctor?
> I went there yesterday, Mother.
> May I help you, madam?
> Yes, sir, this is the right place.

For the omission of *the* with a title used as a predicate objective, see § Predicate Objective.

PLACE NAMES. The general rule that personal names do not use *the* also applies to names given to places. Similarly, the rule that *the* is used to refer to the members of a family collectively also applies to a geographic family or group: *the Philippines* and *the Rocky Mountains* are like *the Bronsons*. However, those two rules have some outstanding exceptions. Below are listed the chief divisions of geographic items and some related items and the exceptions.

a. Continent, country, or state: no *the.*

> Africa and Asia are larger than South America.
> We visited France, Italy, and Spain on our vacation.
> The state next to Connecticut is Massachusetts.

Exceptions:

1. The Ukraine; the Congo; the Sudan

2. A name with a plural form: the Netherlands; the Philippines

3. A name containing *Union* or *United:* the Union of South Africa; the Soviet Union; the Union of Soviet Socialist Republics; the U.S.S.R.; the United Kingdom; the United States

4. Official names such as "the Republic of Cuba" and "the Kingdom of Sweden"

b. Mountain: no *the.*

> Mount Everest is much higher than Pike's Peak or Fujiyama.
> Bear Mountain is a favorite recreation spot for New Yorkers.

Exception:

A mountain range, always plural, has *the.*

> The Rocky Mountains are west of the Appalachians.
> The Andes are in South America, and the Alps are in Europe.

c. Peninsula: *the.*

> Greece occupies the southernmost part of the Balkan Peninsula.

d. Island: no *the.*

> Greenland is the largest island in the world.
> Aruba and Curacao are off the northwest coast of Venezuela.
> Mr. Cox is going to Cuba and Jamaica on his vacation.

Exception:

A group of islands, always plural, has *the.*

> The Philippines are in the Pacific Ocean, and the Azores are in the Atlantic. Puerto Rico is a large island near the Antilles.

e. Desert: *the.*

> The Mojave Desert is by no means as large as the Sahara.

f. Ocean, sea, and gulf: *the.*

> The Gulf of Mexico and the Caribbean Sea are really part of the Atlantic Ocean.

g. River and canal: *the.*

> The Amazon is longer than the Yellow River.
> The Erie Canal does not carry as much traffic as the Suez Canal.

h. Lake: no *the.*

> Bear Lake is east of Lake Erie. Our cottage is on Smith Lake.

Exception:

A group of lakes, always plural, has *the.*

> The Great Lakes contain much more water than the Finger Lakes.

i. Falls: no *the. Falls* is always plural in form, and it is plural in number except when it is part of the name of a city.

> Niagara Falls are not as high as Victoria Falls.   *but*   Niagara Falls, N.Y., is famous as a honeymoon resort.

j. Beach: no *the.*

> Jones Beach is one of the playgrounds of New York.

k. City: no *the.*

> New York is larger than either Paris or Rome.
> Like Marseilles, New Orleans is a seaport.
> Have you seen the skating rink in Radio City yet?

Exceptions:

1. The Hague

2. Names such as "the City of . . ."

> Philadelphia is called the City of Brotherly Love.
> Charlotte, N.C., is often referred to as the Queen City.

l. Four of the boroughs which comprise New York City do not have *the,* but the fifth does: Brooklyn, Manhattan, Queens, Richmond (or Staten Island), but the Bronx.

> Many people who work in Manhattan commute from their homes in Brooklyn or in the Bronx.

m. Street and avenue: no *the.*

> Macy's is on 34th Street between Broadway and Seventh Avenue.

Exception:

If *Street* or *Avenue* is specified by a following *of* phrase, use *the.*

> The official name for Sixth Avenue is the Avenue of the Americas.
> There used to be a song about the Street of Broken Dreams.

n. Tunnel: *the.*

> The Holland Tunnel connects New York and New Jersey.

o. Park and square: no *the.*

> Have you been to Central Park?
> Times Square is a very busy place.
> We visited Alley Pond Park last month.
> New York University is near Washington Square.

p. Garden and zoo: *the.*

> The Magnolia Gardens are in Charleston, S.C., and the Bronx Zoo is in New York City.

q. Religious place names such as *heaven, hell, hades, paradise,* and *valhalla:* no *the.* These are sometimes capitalized when they are considered to be places, but they are not capitalized when they represent a condition of bliss or torment.

> Little Eva went to Heaven when she died.
> The accused man went through hell to defend his reputation.
> General Sherman said war was hell.

When such a place name is used with the meaning of "a place similar to . . .," then the indefinite article is used.

> That park is a paradise for bird lovers.

r. College and university: no *the* if *College* or *University* is preceded by a name.

> Bard College   Western State Teachers College
> Kalamazoo College Yale University
> Michigan State University

Use *the* if *College* or *University* is specified by a following *of* phrase.

> The University of North Carolina
> The College of the Pacific

49

s. Building: *the.*

> The Museum of Modern Art is in New York City, and the Albright Art Gallery is in Buffalo.
> Mr. Clark is staying at the Astor Hotel, and Mr. Perry is at the Waldorf-Astoria.
> From the Washington Monument you can see the Capitol and the Lincoln Memorial.

Exception:

Those with the word **Hall** do not have *the.* Some with the word **House** or **Library** have *the*, and some do not.

> Johnson Hall is two blocks from University Hall.
> The White House is much smaller than the House of Representatives.
> International House is in New York, and Blair House is in Washington.
> Butler Library is a branch of the New York Public Library.

NAMES OTHER THAN PERSONAL OR PLACE NAMES.

a. Businesses:

1. Those with a genitive: usually no *the.*

Lord & Taylor's	Macy's	Sears Roebuck's	Walgreen's

2. Those with *Company* as part of the title: *the.*

> The Edison Co.
> The New York Telephone Company

If *Company* is omitted: no *the.*

Du Pont	Eastman Kodak	General Motors	U.S. Steel

b. Ships: *the.*

the *America*	the *Andrea Doria*	the *Queen Mary*	the *Stockholm*

c. Periodicals:

1. Magazines: usually no *the.*

Collier's	*Life*
Esquire	*McCall's*
Harper's	*Natural History*
Harper's Bazaar	*Newsweek*
Holiday	*Vogue*

2. Newspapers: *the.*

the *Chicago Tribune*	the *Daily News*	*The New York Times*
the *Washington Post*		

d. Days of the week and months of the year: no *the.*

> I wrote to Carl on Monday and received his reply on Saturday morning.
> January is the first month of the year, and December is the last.

e. Holidays: no *the.*

| Christmas | Columbus Day | Easter | Halloween | New Year's Day |

Exceptions

The Fourth of July; the Russian Easter

f. Periods of history: *the.* Those with descriptive names are usually capitalized, but those without descriptive names are usually not capitalized.

> During the Middle Ages no scientist dared to talk about evolution.
> The archeologists discovered some implements of the Stone Age recently.
> Europe experienced profound changes during the Renaissance.
> Chaucer lived in the fourteenth century, and Shakespeare in the sixteenth and seventeenth.

DIRECTION WORDS. When the words *north, south, east,* and *west* are used as single-word adverbs, they do not have *the.*

> Austin looked both north and east before deciding which way to go.
> The Larsons live south of Mr. Croxton but north of us.

However, when those words are used in a similar sense in prepositional phrases, they are preceded by *the.*

> Austin looked both to the north and to the east.
> The Larsons live to the south of Mr. Croxton but to the north of us.
> Helen walked toward the east for three blocks and then turned to the north.

When the words *north,* etc., are used to refer to a section of the United States or of the world, they are preceded by *the.* They are usually capitalized in this sense. They may be modified—for example, the Midwest, the Deep South, and the Far East.

> The South produces most of the cotton grown in the United States, and the West produces most of the wheat.
> Mr. Bell thought of the East as having philosophy and the West as having technology.

COUNT WORDS. These include cardinal and ordinal numbers, Roman numerals, *next,* and *last.*

a. The is used before an ordinal number.

> I have read the tenth chapter but not the twelfth.
> William Phillips was a pilot in the Second World War.
> Don't forget that your income tax is due on the fifteenth of April.

Certain set expressions omit *the.* Also, see § *By*—Preposition, § *For*—Preposition, § *From*—Preposition, § *In*—Preposition, and § Preposition—Expression with.

> The problem is not as easy as it seemed at first sight (or first glance).
> On second thought, your suggestion appears quite practical.

b. No *the* is used when the count word follows a noun.

> Have you read Chapter X (or Chapter 10 or Chapter Ten)?
> Phillips was a pilot in World War II (or World War Two).
> Your income tax is due on April 15.

c. A special difference exists with count words and kings and queens. In writing, the Roman numeral follows without *the,* but in speech *the* and the ordinal number are used.

> Written: Elizabeth II succeeded George VI.
> Spoken: Elizabeth the Second succeeded George the Sixth.

d. Like other count words, *next* and *last* are usually preceded by *the.*

> The next thing Oscar said surprised everybody.
> Jane and Herman got married the next time they met.
> Mr. Baker bought the last box the storekeeper had.
> The last year that Texas was an independent nation was 1845.
> We arrived on the Fourth of July. The next day we had to return.

However, with words of time when the present is used as a point of reference, *next* and *last* are not preceded by *the.*

> Last week we studied Keats; this week we are studying Shelley.
> I was tired last night, but I feel fine today.
> What are you going to take next semester?
> Come to see me next Thursday.
> I am going home next Christmas.

DIFFICULT GROUPS OF WORDS. Following are certain groups of words with which some of you may have special difficulties.

a. Superlatives: These are usually introduced by *the.*

> Tea and coffee are the most popular beverages in the United States.
> Helen is the prettiest girl I have ever seen.

Sometimes you will see a superlative without *the,* but you will be correct if you always use *the.* The word *most* is tricky: without *the* it may be interpreted to mean "almost all." The following two sentences are different in meaning.

> The most beautiful girls are intelligent.
> Most beautiful girls are intelligent.

In the pattern "*a* + *most* + adjective + noun" *most* has the meaning of very.

> I had a most difficult time at the office today.

b. Parts of the body and clothes: *The* is often used in the unlimited sense of "everybody's." Sometimes, particularly in conversation, we use *your* in the same unlimited sense.

> The head is attached to the trunk by the neck.
> Your head is attached to your trunk by your neck.

In reference to a specific person, we customarily use the personal adjectives *my, your,* etc., instead of *the.* Notice that we frequently do not specify which hand, finger, toe, etc.

My head aches.
You have a spot on your cheek.
Sue has cut her hand.
Straighten your collar.
Peter hit his thumb with a hammer.
Put your tongue tip on your tooth ridge.

However, *the* is used after *myself, yourself,* etc., and before phrases beginning with "of your (his, etc.) . . ."

Sue has cut herself on the hand.
Straighten the collar of your shirt.
Peter hit himself on the thumb.
Put the tip of your tongue on the ridge of your teeth.

c. Disease: Use no *the.* Although some can be used with *the,* many can not.

Roy had pneumonia last winter.
Lew had a bad case of athlete's foot.
Influenza took many lives after World War I.

However, *a* is used with certain ailments, particularly those with *ache.*

I have got a cold.
Bill had a bad toothache.
Do you often have a headache?

d. Games and sports: Use no *the.*

Mr. Ames likes to play chess, but his wife prefers bridge.
Hilda beat me at checkers last night.
Football is one of the most popular sports in this country.
I like skiing better than skating.

e. Musical instruments: The phrase "play the (musical instrument)" means "have the ability to play the."

Do you play the piano?
Henry used to play the violin expertly.

f. Communication words: Use *the* with *radio* and *telephone* or *phone.* Use no *the* with *television* or *TV* unless you are referring to a specific machine.

We listened to the radio last night.
I frequently talk with Charles over the telephone.
We watched television a while.
We can't see the program because the television is broken.

Use no *the* with *by* meaning "by means of."

We got the news by radio (by telephone).

g. Languages: *The* is used if the word *language* is used. No *the* is used if the word *language* is not used. The latter is the more frequent way.

> Carlos is studying the English language.
> Carlos is studying English.
> Do you speak Spanish?
> Can you read Chinese?

AS VS. *LIKE* A.26

Four general rules can help you remember whether to use *as* or *like*.

1. Use *as* in a comparison beginning with *as, so,* or *such.*

> Ivan studies as much as Jane.
> Do it as quickly as you can.
> Constantine is not so lazy as you might think.
> Peter is interested in such things as astronomy.
> Emily prefers dark colors such as brown and purple.

2. Use *as* to mean "in the role or capacity of" or "with the function of."

> The actress was outstanding as Desdemona.
> Popin was finally hired as the janitor of the building.
> That word is used as a preposition in that sentence.

3. Use *as* if a subject and a simple predicate come next.

> Mr. Donner votes in every election as a good citizen should.
> Just as Esther expected, her father would not give his consent.

4. Use *like* in other kinds of comparison.

> Martha looks like her mother.
> Sam works like a beaver.
> Our dreams are like shadows in the dusk.
> Like every other student, Sara had difficulty with tenses.
> Mrs. Lloyd crept like a mouse into the nursery.
> Peter is interested in things like astronomy.
> Emily prefers dark colors like brown and purple.

Also, see § *Such* vs. *Such a.*

AS IF AND *AS THOUGH* A.27

1. The words *as if* and *as though* introduce clauses which contain expressions of opinion. If the speaker or writer feels that his opinion is true or is likely to become true, he uses the customary tense to show reality in that clause.

> It looks as if it will rain before morning.
> It seems as though the sailors do not have a chance.

2. Be sure to observe sequence of tense in such a clause.

> It looked as if it would rain before morning.
> It seemed as though the sailors did not have a chance

3. More frequently, the words introduce expressions that are neither true nor likely to become true. The verb in the clause then takes a past form to indicate unreality.

> Mr. Coleman always talks as if he knew everything.
> Act as though you were not afraid.
> Betty looks as though her last friend had deserted her.

4. However, if the main verb expresses past time, no shift in tense form is made in the opinion clause. For a similar patterning, see § *Wish* vs. *Hope* vs. *Want* vs. *Would Like,* ¶ 2.

> Mr. Coleman always talked as if he knew everything.
> Betty looked as though her last friend had deserted her.

5. Use *were* instead of *was* for the first and third person singular in clauses expressing unreality.

> I feel as if I were floating on a cloud.
> Henry acted as though he were sitting on a pin.

AS USUAL   A.28

1. Notice the form and the punctuation of the set expression *as usual.*

> As usual, Raymond was late for class this morning.
> This Sunday, as usual, Mrs. Martin will go to church.
> Oh, Millicent is talking about herself, as usual.

-ATE   A.29

1. More than four hundred words of more than one syllable end in the letters *-ate.* Some are used as verbs; some are used as adjectives; some are used as nouns; and some are used as two parts of speech. Both the pronunciation of the *-ate* and the place of stress in the word depend upon the part of speech the word is used as. The few exceptions are discussed separately below.

2. The ending *-ate* is pronounced [et] if the word is used as a verb. It is pronounced [ɪt] if the word is used as an adjective or as a noun.

3. The [ɪt] is not stressed. In two-syllable words the stress is on the first syllable; the stressed vowel is underlined:

agate	frigate	private
climate	pirate	senate

In words with more than two syllables, the stress is on the second syllable before [ɪt]:

accurate	chocolate	fortunate
affectionate	delicate	immediate

4. The [et] usually has primary stress in words of two syllables:

create	dilate	relate
debate	locate	translate

In words with more than two syllables the [et] has a secondary stress, and the primary stress is on the second syllable before the [et]:

appreciate	decorate	exaggerate
congratulate	demonstrate	originate

5. Most of the exceptions to the above rules are nouns in which the *-ate* is pronounced [et]. Only one of those, *debate*, has primary stress on the *-ate*. All the other two-syllable nouns with [et] have the primary stress on the first syllable: *cognate, inmate, nitrate, phosphate, playmate, roommate,* and *schoolmate.* Two three-syllable nouns have the primary stress on the first syllable: *concentrate* and *potentate.* Three adjectives—*innate, irate,* and *sedate*—are also exceptions: they have a stressed [et].

AUXILIARY

1. Words which can be auxiliaries are the following:

can	did	got	have	might	ought	used
could	do	had	having	must	shall	will
dare	does	has	may	need	should	would

2. Auxiliaries precede verbs in verb phrases. The last word in a verb phrase is called the *main verb.*

> You can stay. [*Stay* is the main verb; *can* is the auxiliary.]
> Robert has gone. [*Gone* is the main verb; *has* is the auxiliary.]
> You must study harder. [*Study* is the main verb; *must* is the auxiliary.]
> I do hope you will come. [*Hope* and *come* are the main verbs; *do* and *will* are the auxiliaries.]
> The boys should have told us the news. [*Told* is the main verb; *should* and *have* are the auxiliaries.]
> I ought to leave now. [*Leave* is the main verb; *ought* is the auxiliary; *to* is the sign of the infinitive form of the main verb. See § Infinitive vs. Gerund.]
> Martha used to help me. [*Help* is the main verb; *used* is the auxiliary; *to* is the sign of the infinitive.]

3. A main verb may be used with or without an auxiliary, but an auxiliary is not used without a main verb except in a *shortened clause.* A shortened clause is a construction with a subject and an auxiliary which is related contextually to a main verb which has been expressed but is not repeated.

"Who will sing?" "Jane will." [In the first sentence *sing* is the main verb. In both sentences *will* is an auxiliary.]

"Who said that?" "Bob did." [In the second sentence *did* is an auxiliary related contextually to the main verb *said* expressed in the first sentence.]

4. Some of the words listed in ¶ 1 above may occur as either auxiliaries or main verbs. Below, I will note their characteristics as auxiliaries.

5. Except in shortened clauses, as auxiliaries *did, do,* and *does* are followed by the uninflected form of a main verb. A subject or some other words may intervene.

I do my lessons at home. [*Do* is a main verb.]

Do you study very hard? [*Do* is an auxiliary; *study* is a main verb.]

Lorraine forgot the boy's name, but she did remember his face. [*Did* is an auxiliary; *remember* is a main verb.]

Mr. Paulson works, and his wife does, too. [*Does* is an auxiliary in a shortened clause related contextually to the expressed main verb *works.*]

6. As auxiliaries, the words *can, could, dare, may, might, must, need, shall, should, will,* and *would* have only those forms: they are not inflected with *-s* or *-ed*. Except in shortened clauses, they are followed by the auxiliary *have* or by the uninflected form of a main verb.

Alice must leave. [*Must* is an auxiliary; *leave* is a main verb.]

George must have taken it by mistake. [*Must* and *have* are auxiliaries; *taken* is a main verb.]

The movie should have lasted longer. [*Should* and *have* are auxiliaries; *lasted* is a main verb.]

Mother cans tomatoes. [*Cans* is a main verb.]

Mother can can tomatoes. [The first *can* is an auxiliary; the second *can* is a main verb.]

My father willed me his house. [*Willed* is a main verb.]

I have not seen that movie, but I will. [*Will* is an auxiliary in a shortened clause related contextually to the expressed main verb *seen.*]

7. As auxiliaries, *got, ought,* and *used* are followed by the *to* used as the sign of the infinitive. Except in shortened clauses, *got to* and *used to* in this use are followed by the uninflected form of a verb, and *ought to* is followed by the auxiliary *have* or the uninflected form of a verb. In rare instances, in shortened clauses *to* is omitted after *ought.* Also, see § Infinitive vs. Gerund.

"She ought to see a doctor." "Yes, she ought to. She really ought. She ought to have done so a week ago." [In all the sentences *ought* is an auxiliary.]

Sam got help on his assignment. [*Got* is a main verb.]

You have got to help Sam on his assignment. [*Have* and *got,* are auxiliaries; *to* is the sign of the infinitive; *help* is a main verb.]

We all used to help Sam. [*Used* is an auxiliary; *to* is the sign of the infinitive; *help* is a main verb.]

Here are a few other characteristics of the auxiliary *used:* If the words *in order* can be inserted between *used* and *to,* then the *used* is a main verb, not an auxiliary. Also, if any word other than a subject or a negative word like *not, never,* or *rarely* comes between *used* and *to,* then the *used* is a main verb. In speech, the auxiliary *used* is customarily pronounced [just], and the main verb *used* is pronounced [juzd].

> What was used to open the can? [The sentence can read "What was used *in order* to open the can?" Therefore, the *used* is a main verb, not an auxiliary.]
> Bill used to visit me. [*In order* can not be inserted between the *used* and the *to;* therefore, *used* is an auxiliary, not a main verb.]
> I used the key to open the door. [The words *the key* come between *used* and *to;* therefore, *used* is a main verb, not an auxiliary.]

8. The adverb *better* is followed by the uninflected form of a verb, and the adverb *rather* and the infinitive sign *to* are followed by the uninflected form of a verb or by the auxiliary *have* and a past participle. In addition *better* and *rather* are customarily preceded by *had, would,* or *'d.* In shortened clauses, the main verb is customarily not expressed.

> "I had better go to my office." "Yes, you'd better." [Both *had* and *'d* are auxiliaries. In the first sentence the *to* is a "true preposition" since it has the object *my office.*]
> Jack does not want to go. He would rather sleep. [In the first sentence *to* is the sign of the infinitive.]
> Jack did not want to go. He would rather have slept.
> The boy has to leave now, and I have to, too.
> You ought to have studied your lesson.
> Marion used to ski very well.

Also, see § *Had Better* and § Infinitive vs. Gerund.

9. As auxiliaries, *have, has, had,* and *having* are followed either by a past participle or by the infinitive sign *to* or the adverb *better* and an uninflected form. In shortened clauses the past participle and the uninflected form are usually not expressed.

> "Paul has seen the movie. Have you?" "No, I haven't. Do you think I have to?" "Yes, you'd better." [In all the instances the *have, has, had,* or *'d* is an auxiliary.]
> I do not have enough money to see it. [*Have* is a main verb.]

10. Certain auxiliaries and forms of the verbs *be* and *have* used either as auxiliaries or main verbs are sometimes called the *anomalous finites* because they have three characteristics which distinguish them from other verbs. These words are the following:

am	could	do	has	may	need	should	will
are	dare	does	have	might	ought	was	would
can	did	had	is	must	shall	were	

a. The anomalous finites can show negation by the addition of the adverb *not* or its contraction *-n't*.

Bruce must not stay here,	Bruce mustn't stay here.
I was not there yesterday.	I wasn't there yesterday.
The boys could not go.	The boys couldn't go.

Am is not contracted with *-n't*. *May* and *might* rarely have *-n't*: they usually occur in the negative as *may not* and *might not*. These finites have special negative forms: *can – can't; shall – shan't;* and *will – won't*.

b. The anomalous finites can occur before a subject in questions.

Are you going now? [*You* is the subject.]
Must I tell him today? [*I* is the subject.]
Doesn't Jim like school? [*Jim* is the subject.]
What did Gloria tell you? [*Gloria* is the subject.]

For a further discussion of that arrangement, see § Word Order—Split and § Word Order—Inverted.

c. The anomalous finites are used in shortened clauses.

"Who said that?" "Bob did." [*Did* is used instead of the repetition of *said that*.]
"I like him?" "I do, too." [*Do* is used instead of the repetition of *like him*.]

A *tag question* is an instance of a shortened clause.

John told you, didn't he? [*Didn't he* is a tag question.]
Mary isn't going, is she? [*Is she* is a tag question.]

11. The anomalous finites are customarily not stressed in ordinary speech. In informal writing and in dialog certain anomalous finites are contracted:

am, 'm	*have*, 've	*shall*, 'll
is, 's	*has*, 's	*will*, 'll
are, 're	*had*, 'd	*would*, 'd

I'm studying my lessons.
They've already done the work.
We'll go to school tomorrow.
He'd lost his way in the forest.

Those finites are not contracted if they begin or end a clause.

Is she leaving?
He won't go, but his sister will.

You will sometimes see the contraction *'ve* as the second auxiliary in a verb phrase ("I should've gone"), but you had better use the full form ("I should have gone").

The various auxiliaries and anomalous finites are discussed in more detail in other sections of this book.

BE—VERB   B.1

1. The various forms of the verb *be* are *am, are, be, been, being, is, was,* and *were.* Three archaic forms that you encounter in literature are *art* ("are"), *wast* ("was"), and *wert* ("were").

2. *Am, is, are, was,* and *were* have the characteristics of *anomalous finites* (see § Auxiliary).

a. In inverted word order, they go before the subject. See § Word Order—Inverted.

Was he here? [*He* is the subject.]

b. In negative sentences, they precede *not.* See § Word Order—Adverb Modifying Verb.

He was not here.
He did not stay here.

c. They precede adverbs of frequency.

He was seldom here.
He seldom stayed here.
He has seldom stayed here.

BECAUSE VS. BECAUSE OF   B.2

1. Use *because* when a subject and a verb follow. Use *because of* when only a noun, pronoun, or noun phrase follows.

Because he was ill, Mr. Rodriguez had to stay home.
Because of his illness, Mr. Rodriguez had to stay home.

BESIDE VS. BESIDES   B.3

1. *Beside* means "next to"; *besides* means "in addition (to), other than." They are not interchangeable.

A boy from Brazil sits beside me in class.
Besides food, we need air and rest.
It is too late to go for a walk; besides, I am tired.
Let's talk about something besides politics.

BIG VS. GREAT VS. LARGE   B.4

1. The three words *big, great,* and *large* have similar definitions, but they are not often interchangeable. Most large dictionaries have a discussion of the differences among the words. Below are examples when one of the words but not the others is used.

> *big business.* Labor unions say they must be strong to bargain with big business. The president of that oil company is a big businessman.
>
> *big man.* Mr. Simpson is over six feet tall and weighs more than two hundred pounds. He is a big man.
>
> *a great deal of.* Miss Tompkins spends a great deal of time helping her neighbors.
>
> *great enthusiasm (amusement, zeal).* Milton played the game with great enthusiasm.
>
> *great man.* Most Americans think that George Washington was a great man because he was the first president.
>
> *large eggs.* I want to buy a dozen large eggs.

BRACKET

B.5

1. Use brackets ([ ]) if you insert something into somebody else's piece of writing.

> Writing of Florence Nightingale, Lytton Strachey said, ". . . at that precise moment [1853] the desperate need of a great nation came, and she was there to satisfy it."

2. The word *sic* (Latin, "so" or "thus") is frequently used in brackets to indicate that quoted material has been copied exactly from the original.

> The wording of an eighteenth-century law has a certain inconsistency in spelling: "A certain Publick [*sic*] Office . . . known by the name of The Public [*sic*] Office. . . ."

3. Use brackets around phonetic symbols. See § Phonetic Symbol.

BY—PREPOSITION

B.6

1. The preposition *by* indicates position "near," "beside," or "next to" another position.

> The most comfortable chair is the one by the window.
> The big oak tree by the river was blown down last spring.

2. *By* indicates position "along a line near or beside" or "past" another position. With this meaning the preposition *by* is often used adverbially—that is, without an object.

> The river flows by the little village.
> Our friends drove by us without even waving.
> Our friends drove by   without even waving.
> We were standing on the corner when they went by us.
> We were standing on the corner when they went by   .
> Busses go by this corner every ten or fifteen minutes.
> Busses go by   every ten or fifteen minutes.

3. *By* indicates time "before" or "no later than" a specified time.

We will have the work completed by noon tomorrow.
Mrs. Adams thought the movie would be finished by 10:30 p.m.
All the guests had arrived by ten minutes after six.
By the time we got there, our friends had left.

4. *By* indicates a unit of measurement.

The workers get paid by the week, not by the month.
The patient was getting weaker by the minute.
The truck missed hitting us by a foot and a half.
The insects swarmed over the men by the millions.
That agency receives applications by the thousands.

5. *By* indicates agency—the person, animal, group, or human agency responsible for an expressed or implied action. See § Passive.

All the pictures were taken by a professional photographer.
Mr. Payne is highly respected by his associates.
The books used by the officers were very much out of date.
Have you ever been stung by a bee?
The explorers were attacked by savage beasts several times.
The actors were interrupted by loud laughter.
Several people were killed along the highway by trucks.
Our tension was relieved by a voice on the loudspeaker.
The book I am reading was written by a famous historian.
Some time ago I read a fascinating book by William Faulkner.

6. *By* indicates instrumentality—the device, tool, or technique employed to achieve an objective.

Can you see by the light of that lamp?
When I got to that country, I was shocked by the high cost of living.

7. For nonspecific instrumentality or agent, no *the* or *a* is used in the following expressions:

by air. Mr. Carlson went to Boston from Chicago by air.
by bus. My son goes to school by bus.
by car. Jim commutes between his home and his office by car.
by chance. I saw the President in Washington purely by chance.
by error. Paul's mail is often delivered to me by error.
by express. It will be cheaper to send that package by express.
by fire. The Ryans' home was destroyed by fire.
by flood. The crops on that land have been swept away three times by flood.
by foot (or *on foot*). Franklin traveled from Boston to Philadelphia by foot.
by force. The police entered the apartment by force.
by guess. Philip got the right answer simply by guess.
by hand. Those Indian blankets are all made by hand.
by heart. Have you learned that poem by heart?
by letter. Why don't you send Pete the news by letter?
by lightning. The old mansion was struck by lightning during the storm.

by mail. A catalog will be sent to you by mail.
by messenger. The note was delivered by messenger.
by mistake. Henry often receives his brother's laundry by mistake.
by parcel post. That store will send your order by parcel post.
by phone. I tried to reach Mr. Miller by phone, but he did not answer.
by plane. Did you go to Jamaica by plane on your vacation?
by radio. The Coast Guard got in touch with the ship by radio.
by ship. The troops will be transported by ship.
by subway. Mr. Coleman goes to his office by subway.
by surprise. The enemy captured the fort by surprise.
by telephone. The secretary gave us the information by telephone.
by train. We can go to Hartford by train.
by water. Much of the merchandise was damaged by water.

Instrumentality may be expressed by the following words without *by: airmail, express, parcel post, special delivery.*

Mr. Cunningham's secretary sent the letters airmail.
Paul's baggage was sent express.

8. Note the following distinctions: *by* without an article and *in* or *on* with an article.

We traveled from Italy to New York by boat.
We traveled from Italy to New York on the *Carpathia.*
My son goes to school by bus.
My son goes to school on a bus.
Jim commutes between his home and his office by car.
Jim commutes between his home and his office in a car.

9. *By* indicates the action involved in achieving an objective. *By* is followed here by the *-ing* form of a verb.

My secretary saved time by calling the company directly.
The stranger attracted our attention by shouting at us.
Pierre often makes himself understood by gesturing with his hands.
Our teacher ended his talk by saying he was satisfied with our progress.
The problem was eventually solved by putting up a large sign.
By acting as you did, you offended the young woman.

10. With a *-self* pronoun *by* indicates the meaning "without help" or "alone."

We helped Leon with part of his work, but he did the rest by himself
Although Millicent came to the party with an escort, she left by herself.

Also, see § Preposition—Expression with and § Preposition in Time Expression.

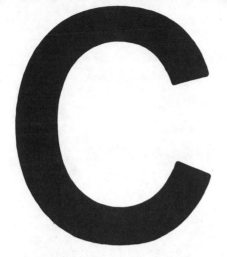

CAN VS. COULD VS. MAY VS. MIGHT   C.1

1. *Can, could, may,* and *might* are used as auxiliaries. They are used with subjects; they are not used as infinitives or participles. *Could* is the past form of *can,* and *might* is the past form of *may.*

2. A verb that follows *can, could, may,* and *might* does not have *to* before it.

> We can leave now.
> They could walk far.
> The child may have the toy.
> The teacher might get angry.

3. The word *not* follows *can, could, may,* and *might.*

> We can not leave now.
> They could not walk far.
> The child may not have the toy.
> The teacher might not get angry.

4. The *not* can be contracted with *can* and *could.* The contraction is customary in speech and informal writing. The *not* is usually not contracted with *may* and *might.*

> We can't leave now.
> They couldn't walk far.

5. In split word order, *can, can't, could, couldn't, may,* and *might* precede the subject.

> Can we leave now?   May the child have that toy?
> Can't we leave now?   May the child not have that toy?
> Can we not leave now?   Might the teacher get angry?
> Could they walk far?   Might the teacher not get angry?
> Couldn't they walk far?
> Could they not walk far?

6. *Can, could, may,* and *might* are used to express various notions such as ability, permission, uncertainty, request, prohibition, or unreality. Sometimes the auxiliaries are interchangeable; sometimes they are not.

a. *Can* and *could* are used to express ability. In this sense they are usually equivalent to the forms of "be able to." *Can* is used for present or future time; *could* is used for past time or for a future time in sequence to a past verb.

> I can speak Spanish.
> I am able to speak Spanish.
>
> When I was young, I could run very fast.
> When I was young, I was able to run very fast.
>
> I think now that I can go tomorrow.
> I think now that I will be able to go tomorrow.

> I thought yesterday that I could go tomorrow.
> I thought yesterday that I would be able to go tomorrow.

b. Could have and a past participle express a past possibility that was not fulfilled or achieved.

> You could have done much better yesterday. Why didn't you?
> That child could have been killed a few minutes ago. Fortunately, the driver stopped in time.

c. Can not and *could not* are used to express prohibition. *Can not* is used for present or future time; *could not* is used for past time or for a future time in sequence to a past verb.

> You can not smoke here. It is against regulations.
> Respectable women could not smoke in public a few years ago.
> The policeman says that we can not part near the hydrant.
> The policeman said yesterday that we could not park near the hydrant.

d. Can not seem is the equivalent of *it seems that . . . can not. Could not seem* is the equivalent of *it seemed that . . . could not.*

> I can't seem to understand that theory.
> It seems that I can't understand that theory.
>
> John couldn't seem to remember to hand in his homework.
> It seemed that John couldn't remember to hand in his homework.

e. May, might, and *could* are used to express uncertainty. All three are used for present or future time. In sequence of tense after a past verb, *might* is used for the same time or a future time. For an earlier time, *may* or *might* or *could* is used with *have* and a past participle.

> That explanation may be right.
> The check might come tomorrow.
> Jane could be waiting for us right now.
> The weatherman says it may (might, could) rain tomorrow.
> The weatherman said it might rain tomorrow.
> Mr. Ellis may have left his office by now.
> Your secretary might have misunderstood my message yesterday.
> Arnold could have taken the wrong train. That may be the reason why he has not arrived yet.

f. Can, could, may, and *might* are all used to express permission. *May* and *can* are used for present or future time; *might* and *could* are used for past time or for a future time in sequence to a past verb. In formal speech and writing, *may* and *might* are preferred in this sense.

> You may go now.
> You can go now.
> The teacher says we may (can) leave early tomorrow.
> The teacher said we might (could) leave early tomorrow.

g. *Can, can't, could, couldn't, may,* and *might* are all used with split word order in making a request for present or future action. Although negative in form, *can't* and *couldn't* are used with an affirmative intent for the sake of politeness.

Can   I have a conference with you now or tomorrow?
Can't   I have a conference with you now or tomorrow?
Could   I have a conference with you now or tomorrow?
Couldn't I have a conference with you now or tomorrow?
May   I have a conference with you now or tomorrow?
Might   I have a conference with you now or tomorrow?

7. *Can, could, may,* and *might* are used in clauses of purpose introduced by *so (that)* and *in order (that)*. *Can* and *may* are used for present or future time; *could* and *might* are for past time or a future time in sequence to a past verb.

Mrs. Hart works so that her husband may (can) go to school.
I left the room in order that Willis could (might) concentrate.

Also, see § Auxiliary, § Negative, and § Polite Expression.

CAPITALIZATION   C.2

1. Capitalize the first word of the following:

a. A sentence.

The boy looked at Sally for a moment. There was silence in the room.

b. A direct quotation.

"Are you coming?" he asked.
She shook her head and answered, "No, it's too late."
"That," he said bitterly, "is what you told me last time."

c. A line of poetry.

And the night shall be filled with music,
And the cares that infest the day
Shall fold their tents, like the Arabs,
And as silently steal away.—LONGFELLOW

Notice that if part of a line is run on beneath, it is indented (a few spaces on the typewriter).

And the night shall be filled
    with music,
And the cares that infest the
    day
Shall fold their tents, like
    the Arabs,
And as silently steal away.

C

When two or more lines of poetry are incorporated within a sentence, a slant line (a *slant* or *slash*) designates the beginning of each new line.

> My favorite poem is the one with "And the night shall be filled with music, / And the cares that infest the day . . . ."

d. A subdivision in an outline. The subdivision that you are reading right now is an example: the word after the *d.* is capitalized.

e. The complimentary close of a letter.

> Sincerely yours,   Yours very truly,   Cordially yours,

2. Capitalize the first and last word of the title of a composition, magazine article, poem, book, play, or movie, and capitalize all the other words in the title except short prepositions (e.g., *on, at,* and *by*), short conjunctions (e.g., *and, as,* and *but*), and the articles *a, an,* and *the.*

> *Index to Modern English*   "New Comforts for the Home"
> It Is Never Too Late to Try   *Storm and Stress*
> Learn by Doing   *The Thin Man*

3. Capitalize personal names.

> Elizabeth Barrett Browning   Roberto Maria Morales-Ocampo
> Tsai-Ho Chang   Henry Thornton

Modifiers which have become part of certain names are capitalized also. The word *the* is not capitalized.

> Alexander the Great   Ivan the Terrible
> Bloody Mary (Mary Tudor)   the Virgin Mary (the mother
> Elizabeth the Second (more often Elizabeth II)   of Christ)
> Honest Abe (Abraham Lincoln)   William the Conqueror

4. Capitalize titles preceding personal names. Some frequent titles are these:

Admiral	Colonel	Governor	Mother	Queen
Aunt	Commander	Grandfather	Pope	Senator
Brother	Cousin	Grandma	President	Sergeant
Captain	Dean	King	Prince	Sir
Chairman	Duke	Lady	Princess	Uncle
Chief	Father	Lieutenant	Professor	Vice-President

Have you seen Professor Kahrmann?
That picture was painted by Grandma Moses.
We are going to visit Sir William and his wife, Lady Mary.

A few titles are abbreviated when they precede a personal name. Notice that *Mr., Mrs., Prof.,* and *Dr.* have periods, but *Miss* does not.

> Dr. Hoffman was my teacher back in 1938.
> Miss Lindstrom came to the party, but Mr. and Mrs. Sherman did not.
> The course is taught by Prof. Charles Brown.

5. Capitalize a title when it is used alone either as a vocative in direct address or as a substitute for a personal name.

> But, Mother, you said last night that I could go.
> Can't you tell, Doctor, what's wrong with me?
> I will have to ask Father for permission to buy that suit.

a. The word *sir* is usually not capitalized when it is used alone. In the salutation of a letter, however, both *sir* and *madam* are usually capitalized.

> Pardon me, sir.   Dear Sir: Dear Madam:

b. A few terms are used very often as vocatives, but they are usually not capitalized. Examples are *dear, my dear, my dear sir, darling, fellows, honey, madam, ma'am, young man,* and *my friends.*

> Did you call me, dear?
> That, my friends, is all I have to say.

6. Do not capitalize a title word if it is used as a common noun.

> That man is a very good doctor.
> Mr. Greer is the president of our club.
> I went on a trip with my mother and one of my aunts last summer.

The word *president* is customarily capitalized when it refers to a specific president of the United States.

> Did you hear the President on the radio last night?

7. Capitalize abbreviated designations such as the following when they come after a name. Also, put a comma before them. Notice that there is no space between the first period and the following letter. See § Abbreviation.

> Jr. (Junior)   B.A. (Bachelor of Arts)   M.D. (Doctor of Medicine)
> Sr. (Senior)   M.A. (Master of Arts)   Ph.D. (Doctor of Philosophy)

> That popular new novel was written by William A. Owens, Ph.D.

8. Capitalize geographic names. The word *the* is used with many of these; see § Article—*The* vs. No *The,* and notice the examples below. The words *the* and *of* are not capitalized, but the other parts of the names are.

a. Continents, countries, states, and cities.

> Asia   the Union of South Africa
> the Dominion of Canada   New Jersey
> Italy   Paris
> the Philippines   Rome
> the United States   San Francisco

The names of the states are usually abbreviated after the names of cities.

> I have visited Chicago, Ill., Charleston, S.C., and Boston, Mass.

C

b. The words *East, Eastern, West, Western, North, Northern, South, Southern, Orient, Oriental, Occident,* and *Occidental* when they refer to a section of the United States or to a region of the world. Also, notice *the Middle West, the Far West, the Deep South, a Northerner,* and other similar expressions.

> The War Between the States was fought by the North and the South.
> Mr. Ferguson is interested in the conflict between Western attitudes and Eastern customs.

Do not capitalize the words *east,* etc., when they refer to directions.

> Canada is north of the United States and west of Europe.
> The wind is blowing from the east.

c. Oceans, seas, lakes, and rivers; mountains, peninsulas, islands, deserts, and valleys.

the Great Lakes	the Hawaiian Islands
the Mississippi	the Iberian Peninsula
the Pacific Ocean	Mount Everest
the Yellow Sea	the Rocky Mountains
Death Valley	the Sahara Desert

d. Streets, roads, squares, parks, zoos, bridges, and tunnels.

Columbus Avenue	Central Park
Forty-Second Street	the Cypress Gardens
Roosevelt Drive	the Bronx Zoo
U.S. Route 65	the Brooklyn Bridge
Herald Square	the Lincoln Tunnel

The abbreviations *St.* and *Ave.* are customary only in addresses on letters.

Mr. Floyd Johnson	Dr. Robert H. Jenkins
1927 Livingston St.	33–42 Marquardt Ave.
New Hope, N.J.	Evanston 5, Mich.

9. Capitalize a well-known substitute for the name of the Deity or any part of the Trinity, a personal name, or a geographic name.

the Almighty (God)	the Continent (Europe)
the Lord (God)	the Dark Continent (Africa)
the Prophet (Mohammed)	Dixie (the South)
the Savior (Christ)	the Eternal City (Rome)
Old Hickory (Andrew Jackson)	the Great White Way (Broadway)

10. Capitalize derivatives which are still associated with personal or geographic names.

Elizabethan literature	a native New Yorker
an Indian princess	a Roman villa
Italian history	Shakespearean drama

Derivatives such as the following are not capitalized because they are no longer associated with the originating name:

| china(ware) | pasteurize | volt |
| italicize | quixotic | utopian |

11. Capitalize the names of organizations, companies, colleges, stores, hotels, specific buildings, and specific rooms.

the Associated Press	Yale University
the Democratic Party	the A & P
(but: a democratic form of government)	the Capitol
the United Nations	the Empire State Building
the Macmillan Company	Morgan Library
Montgomery-Ward	the Sistine Chapel
the Pennsylvania Railroad	South Hall
Dartmouth College	the White House
the University of Arizona	Room 507

Capitalize *Congress* when it refers to the Congress of the United States.

Senator Williams has been absent from Congress for two weeks.

12. Capitalize the names of ships, trains, airplanes, and similar vehicles. These names are usually italicized in print and underlined in manuscript.

| the *Queen Mary* | the *Twentieth Century* |
| the *United States* | the *Columbine* |

13. Capitalize the names of newspapers and magazines. If the word *the* is part of the title, capitalize it. These titles are usually italicized or underlined.

| *The New York Times* | *The Saturday Evening Post* |
| *Popular Photography* | *Scientific America* |

14. Capitalize the names of particular college courses.

| Comparative Literature 183.BL | Humanities 145 |
| G. S. English A3 | Philosophy 22.16 |

15. Capitalize the pronoun *I.*

16. Capitalize words referring to specific groups of people and to languages.

Caucasian	Japanese	Negro	Slavonic
Gothic	Jewish	Old English	Spanish
Italian	Moorish	Slav	Teutonic

Did you know that French, Italian, Spanish, Portuguese, and Romanian are derived from the Latin language?

17. Capitalize religious terms such as the following:

Buddhist	Protestant	the Holy Ghost	the Old Testament
Catholic	Catholicism	the Messiah	the Talmud
Methodist	Christianity	the Bible	the Ten Commandments
Mohammedan	God (but: a god)	the Koran	the Lord's Prayer

18. Capitalize dates:

a. Months: January, February, etc.

b. Days of the week: Monday, Tuesday, etc.

c. Holidays and holy days such as the following:

Bastille Day	the Fourth of July	Halloween	Passover
Christmas	Girl's Day	Holy Week	Ramadan
Christmas Eve	Good Friday	New Year's	Yom Kippur

d. Historic epochs and events such as the following:

the Middle Ages	the Renaissance	the Second World War
the Reign of Terror	the Battle of the Bulge	World War I

e. Do not capitalize the names of the seasons: spring, summer, fall, autumn, and winter.

19. Prefixes to capitalized words have hyphens but are not capitalized unless the compound is part of a proper name.

pre-Christian   un-American

The Roman Empire began in pre-Christian times.
The members of the Un-American Activities Committee were discussing un-American acts.

20. Do not capitalize words like the following when they are used in an abstract or general sense:

city	government	literature	union
engineering	history	mathematics	university

I am going to take a course in history next semester.
That country has not produced much literature.
David is against all kinds of government.
Mr. Gordon has a good job with the government.
New York is a large city.
The workers in that plant have their own union.

-CI-, -SI-, AND -TI- WORDS   C.3

1. Words with the following endings are stressed on the vowel preceding those endings:

-cial	-sian	-tial
-cian	-sion	-tian
-cience		-tience
-ciency		-tient
-cient		-tion
-cion		-tional
-cious		-tious

2. With few exceptions, the *-ci-, -sci-, -si-, -ssi-,* and *-ti-* in those words are all pronounced the same way: [ʃ]. Don't pronounce the *i* separately in those combinations.

official	Russian	essential
musician	extension	Egyptian
conscience	discussion	patience
proficiency		patient
efficient		action
suspicion		national
precious		cautious

3. The *-ti-* is pronounced [tʃ] if it is preceded by an *s:*

Christian	question
combustion	suggestion

4. The *-si-* is pronounced [ʒ] if it is preceded by a vowel or *r:*

confusion	occasion
decision	Persian

CLAUSE   C.4

Before reading the following paragraphs, you should be sure that you have read § Subject and Simple Predicate.

1. A clause is a group of related words which contains a subject and a simple predicate. It may be composed of only the subject and the simple predicate, or it may have additional words such as complements, interpolations, and conjunctions. The only kind of clause without a subject is an imperative.

2. A clause may be either one of these two kinds:

a. A dependent clause, which is a part of another clause

b. An independent clause, which is not a part of another clause

C

Let's consider some model examples.

Model 1   What happened?

3. In Model 1, the word *what* is the subject of the simple predicate *happened*. The two words make up a clause. The clause is independent because it is not part of another clause. The independent clause is also a sentence. A sentence which is composed of one independent clause and no dependent clauses is called a *simple sentence.*

Model 2   He understood it.

4. In Model 2, the word *he* is the subject of the simple predicate *understood*. The word *it* is the complement (direct object) of *understood*. The three words are, therefore, related. The three words make up an independent clause, which is also a simple sentence.

Model 3   He understood what happened.

5. In Model 3, *he* is the subject of the simple predicate *understood,* and the word *what* is the subject of the simple predicate *happened*. Therefore, there are two clauses in that sentence. The clause *what happened* is used syntactically in the same way that the word *it* is used in Model 2: *what happened* is the direct object of *understood*. Since the clause *what happened* is syntactically part of another clause, it is a dependent clause. The whole sentence "He understood what happened" is an independent clause. The whole sentence "He understood what happened" is an independent clause composed of the subject *he,* the simple predicate *understood,* and the direct object *what happened*. A sentence which is composed of an independent clause including one or more dependent clauses is called a *complex sentence.*

6. Notice that neither Model 2 nor Model 3 has a comma after *understood*. A rule of punctuation is this: don't separate a verb and its complement with a comma.

Model 4   It was hard to explain.

7. In Model 4, the word *it* is the subject of the simple predicate *was*. The whole sentence is an independent clause because it is composed of a subject and a simple predicate and the related words *hard to explain*. The sentence is also a simple sentence.

Model 5   What happened was hard to explain.

8. In Model 5, the clause *what happened* has a subject, *what,* and a simple predicate, *happened*. That clause is used syntactically as the subject of the following simple predicate *was* just as the single word *it* is used in Model 4. The clause *what happened* is, therefore, a part of another clause: it is a dependent clause. The whole sentence of Model 5 is an independent clause which contains a dependent clause. It is also a complex sentence.

9. Notice that neither Model 4 nor Model 5 has a comma before *was*. A rule of punctuation is this: don't separate a subject and its simple predicate with a comma.

Model 6   He understood it, but it was hard to explain.

10. Model 6 has two independent clauses joined by the conjunction *but.* Neither clause is syntactically part of the other. A sentence containing two or more independent clauses is called a *compound sentence.*

11. Independent clauses are usually joined by the coordinating conjunctions *and, but, for, or,* and *nor.* Put a comma before a coordinating conjunction joining two independent clauses. Doing so will help your reader. Read the following examples, and mentally remove the commas.

> I do not like ham, and eggs make me sick.
>
> The matter creates some difficulty, for present-day scholars are not in accord on it.

12. You can use a semicolon (;) instead of *and* between two closely related independent clauses.

Model 7   He understood it; his sister did, too.

13. You can use a semicolon instead of *but, or,* or *not,* but you usually need a "transition expression" such as *however* or *else* to show the relationship between the two classes.

Model 8   He understood it; however, it was hard to explain.

See § Transition Expression.

14. You can use a colon (:) instead of *for* between two closely related independent clauses.

Model 9   He had difficulty: the event was hard to explain.

15. If two independent clauses are not closely related in meaning, make them separate sentences.

16. The use of a comma between independent clauses without a coordinating conjunction is called a *comma fault* or *comma splice;* it should be avoided.

Model 10   He understood what happened, but it was hard to explain.
Model 11   He understood it, but what happened was hard to explain.

17. Both Model 10 and Model 11 contain two independent clauses. The first independent clause in Model 10 contains a dependent clause, and the second independent clause in Model 11 contains a dependent clause. The term for such sentences is *compound-complex.*

18. Why do you need to know these things? You need to know the terms primarily to understand teachers and textbook writers who use them in giving you directions for improving your writing. You need to know the principles which the terms represent so that you can improve your writing yourself.

For instance, a teacher may tell you, "You must learn how to punctuate." Scattered throughout this discussion are a number of rules of punctuation.

A teacher may tell you, "Write complete sentences; don't write fragments. You have written a dependent clause." A dependent clause is a fragment because, as you have seen, it is a part, not a whole.

A teacher may tell you, "You use too many simple sentences. They are monotonous; vary them." You can use some compound sentences, but a compound sentence is only two simple sentences put together. You can use some complex sentences.

A teacher may tell you, "Subordinate some of the ideas." You subordinate an idea when you express it in less than an independent clause: you express it in a word, a phrase, or a dependent clause. Let's go back to Model 3. Which idea is subordinate? The *happening* is because it is in the dependent clause. The same is true in Model 5. Now look at Model 6. If we wish to subordinate the *understanding*, we can put it in a dependent clause like this:

Model 12   Although he understood it, it was hard to explain.

If the *explaining* is to be subordinated, we can express it in a dependent clause:

Model 13   He understood it although it was hard to explain.

By the way, grammatical subordination does not imply that a subordinated idea is unimportant; as a matter of fact, subordination presents the idea more succinctly and, therefore, more emphatically.   ·

Now you may ask, "How can I make a clause dependent?" There are various ways. I will discuss them in greater detail later, but now I will give you some of the principal ways.

19. Many dependent clauses are introduced by the following subordinating conjunctions:

after	before	provided	than	until
although	if	providing	though	whereas
as	lest	since	till	whether
because	once	so	unless	while

There are a few groups of words which can be classed as phrasal subordinating conjunctions:

as if	in case	provided that
as though	in order that	providing that
even if	in so far as	so that
even though	in that	
inasmuch as (or in as much as)	now that	

The words in the two lists above are subordinating conjunctions when they are immediately followed by a subject and a simple predicate.

INDEPENDENT CLAUSE	DEPENDENT CLAUSE
Jimmy woke up	before his alarm rang.
He could not go back to sleep	once he had opened his eyes.
He glanced out of the window	as he usually did.
He did not get out of bed	until his mother came in.

INDEPENDENT CLAUSE	DEPENDENT CLAUSE
She scolded him	because he was not ready for school.
She stayed in the room	so that he would not go back to sleep.
She made the bed	while the boy dressed.

Some of those words may at times be used as other parts of speech such as adverbs and prepositions.

I have never seen him before. [*Before* is an adverb.]
We should wait until morning. [*Until* is a preposition.]

20. The word *that* is often a subordinating conjunction. It will be discussed in ¶ 23 and later sections.

21. Many dependent clauses are introduced by the *wh* words *who, whom, whose, which, what, when, where, why,* and *how.* Those words can also begin independent clauses used as questions. For that reason they are sometimes referred to as the *interrogative words* or the *question words;* however, since those terms are misleading, I recommend that you not use them.

INDEPENDENT CLAUSE
Who complains all the time?
Why does he do that?
What does he want?
Where is he going now?
What time is it?

When a *wh* word is used in a dependent clause, that dependent clause has primary word order, and a question mark is not used unless the entire sentence is a question.

INDEPENDENT CLAUSE	DEPENDENT CLAUSE
I do not like a person	who complains all the time.
I have no idea	why he does that.
Can you guess	what he wants?
Let's ask him	where he is going now.
Do you know	what time it is?

22. A dependent clause may have no introductory word; in that case, the subject of the dependent clause nearly always begins the clause.

Mary took the book	you wanted.
She said	she needed it for a few minutes.

23. The word *that* often begins a dependent clause.

a. That may be the subject of the dependent clause.

Bob said	that was good.

b. That may modify a noun of the dependent clause.

Bob said	that statement was good.

c. ***That*** may be an alternate for a *wh* word.

| I do not like a person | that complains all the time. |

That use of *that* will be discussed in greater detail later.

d. ***That*** may be a subordinating conjunction or the last member of a phrasal subordinating conjunction.

| She said | that she needed it for a few minutes. |
| She stayed in the room | so that he would not go back to sleep. |

In its use as a subordinating conjunction, *that* may usually be omitted.

| She said | she needed it for a few minutes. |
| She stayed in the room | so he would not go back to sleep. |

However, *that* is not omitted when it is part of the phrasal subordinating conjunction *in that.*

| The student was at fault | in that she had not done her homework. |

The conjunctive *that* is also not omitted in a dependent clause used as an appositive or as a subject or complement beginning an independent clause.

Paul's excuse—that he had not had time to do his homework—was not accepted by the teacher. [***That he had not had time to do his homework*** is the appositive to ***Paul's excuse.***]

| That I am not always right | is quite obvious. [***That I am not always right*** is the subject of the simple predicate *is.*] |
| That I am not always right | I will freely admit. [***That I am not always right*** is the direct object of the verb *admit.*] |

Conjunctive *that* should not be omitted if the omission may cause your reader any difficulty.

| He understood his favor. | that the terms of the contract agreed upon were in |

If you omit the *that* in the above example, your reader may be momentarily confused when he comes to *were.*

24. Now let's look at the places in a sentence where a dependent clause may go. The dependent clause is at the end of its independent clause in nearly all the models and examples given above. It is at the beginning of its independent clause in Models 5, 11, and 12 and in the two next-to-last examples in ¶ 23. It is within its independent clause in the fourth-from-last example in ¶ 23. We see, therefore, that a dependent clause may appear at the beginning of, within, or at the end of the independent clause it is part of. However, the position of a dependent clause is not arbitrary. Like most components of English syntax, dependent clauses have relatively fixed positions.

25. The position and punctuation of a dependent clause depend upon whether the dependent clause is used like a noun, an adjective, or an adverb.

26. The position of a dependent clause used like an adjective is fixed: it follows the word or group of words it modifies. I will compare that position with those of adjectives.

27. An adjective sometimes precedes and sometimes follows the word or words it modifies.

> **Model 14**   The lazy student told me something strange.

In Model 14, the word *lazy* is an adjective preceding the word it modifies: *student.* *Strange* is also an adjective, but it follows the word it modifies: *something.*

28. If we substitute dependent clauses for those adjectives, the dependent clauses will take only one of the adjectival positions: after the word or words they modify.

> **Model 15**   The student   who is lazy   told me something   that was strange.

The first dependent clause—*who is lazy*—modifies the *student,* and the second dependent clause—*that was strange*—modifies *something.* Those two dependent clauses are used like adjectives.

29. An adjectival dependent clause has another characteristic: it may be introduced by one of four kinds of words:

a. A *wh* word

b. A movable preposition whose object is or begins with a *wh* word

c. *That*

d. Its own subject

The following examples give you an illustration of the possible beginnings of adjectival dependent clauses. Notice that a preposition belonging to the dependent clause may start the dependent clause or be moved to another part of the dependent clause.

The letter	for which he had been waiting	finally arrived.
	which he had been waiting for	
	that he had been waiting for	
	he had been waiting for	
The woman	for whom we ordered the dress	does not like it.
	whom we ordered the dress for	
	that we ordered the dress for	
	we ordered the dress for	
The house	in which he lived last year	has been sold.
	which he lived in last year	
	that he lived in last year	
	he lived in last year	
The boy	about whom I spoke to you yesterday	is absent.
	whom I spoke to you about yesterday	
	that I spoke to you about yesterday	
	I spoke to you about yesterday	

C

30. The punctuation of an adjectival dependent clause depends upon whether or not that adjectival dependent clause is needed by the reader to restrict the meaning of the word or words it modifies. In the next section, § Clause—Adjectival, restrictive and nonrestrictive adjectival clauses and their punctuation (or lack of it) are discussed in detail. In the present section the main points are summarized.

Here are your rules for punctuating adjectival dependent clauses. Notice that each rule contains a negative, which is italicized.

a. A restrictive adjectival clause is *not* marked off by punctuation.

b. A *non*restrictive adjectival clause is marked off by punctuation.

Commas are usual punctuation for marking off nonrestrictive dependent clauses, but dashes are sometimes used for long, internally punctuated clauses.

For illustration of the rules, I will take a dependent clause—*who is constantly busy*—and use it in one sentence for restriction and in another sentence solely for additional information.

A man		who is constantly busy		has no time to complain.
My father	,	who is constantly busy	,	has no time to complain.

In the first example, do I need to restrict the words *a man?* Yes, I do since I am not talking about any man but about a constantly busy man. In the second example, do I need to restrict the words *my father?* No, I do not since the word *my* restricts the word *father.* However, I can give additional information about my father by using the dependent clause.

31. Nonrestrictive adjectival clauses differ from restrictive adjectival clauses in the kinds of words that may begin the clauses. A restrictive clause may begin with any of the four kinds of words listed in ¶ 29. Nonrestrictive clauses, however, begin with only two of those four kinds of words:

a. A *wh* word.

b. A movable preposition whose object is or contains a *wh* word.

A nonrestrictive clause, therefore, does not begin with *that* or a subject other than a *wh* word. For practice, pick out all the instances of adjectival clauses in this discussion, and notice their punctuation and introductory words.

32. Dependent clauses may be used like nouns. They may be subjects, complements (direct objects, indirect objects, predicate nominatives, or predicate objectives), objects of prepositions, or appositives. Their position in a sentence is that of subjects, complements, etc.

33. The first word of a noun clause is usually either *that* or a *wh* word. The *wh* word is often compounded with *-ever* (e.g., *whoever* and *whatever*), less often with *-soever* (e.g., *whosoever* and *whatsoever*). The *that* may be omitted unless the dependent clause begins the larger clause it belongs to or is marked off by punctuation. The only kind of noun clause that is marked off by punctuation is one used as a nonrestrictive appositive.

34. Here are some examples of a noun clause, *what is known,* used in the same functional ways as a noun, *information.*

a. As subject of a verb

Information	is valuable.
What is known	is valuable.

b. As direct object of a verb

Students acquire	information.
Students acquire	what is known.

c. As indirect object of a verb

Students should give	information	their undivided attention.
Students should give	what is known	their undivided attention.

d. As object of a preposition

Students become acquainted with	information.
Students become acquainted with	what is known.

e. As predicate nominative

The accumulation of facts is	information.
The accumulation of facts is	what is known.

f. As predicate objective

Should we call wisdom	information?
Should we call wisdom	what is known?

g. As appositive

Students seek the accumulation of facts—that is,	information.
Students seek the accumulation of facts—that is,	what is known.

35. A noun clause has one use that a single noun does not have: a noun clause may be a restrictive appositive to the word *it* which precedes. (That appositive to *it* must contain a verb form and is not marked off by a comma.)

	NOUN-CLAUSE APPOSITIVE TO *it*
It was John	who told me
I thought it strange	that they had left without their friend.
Paul saw to it	that I understood what he meant.

36. Dependent clauses may also be used like adverbs. Their position is the least fixed of all dependent clauses: they may begin, come in the middle of, or end the clause they belong to.

37. Here is your general rule for punctuating adverbial dependent clauses: do not mark them off with punctuation if they end their clause; otherwise, mark them off.

38. The rule in ¶ 37 above is intended to help your reader. Quite frequently, when an adverbial clause begins or comes within a sentence, a word or group following the clause can be misinterpreted as being part of the dependent clause; a comma at the end of the dependent clause will obviate that interpretation. In the following examples, mentally remove the commas, and see what confusion can result for your reader.

> While we were cooking, the pig wandered away.
> That kind of conduct, as you know, thoroughly deserves praise.
> As you said, that poem was beautiful.
> When I arrived, there was no one in sight.
> As soon as the woman came to, the doctor lifted her from the floor.

Of course, not all adverbial dependent clauses are potentially ambiguous at the beginning or in the middle of a sentence, but if you form the habit of marking them off, you will prevent instances of ambiguity that you may not be aware of.

The exception to the above punctuation rule for adverbial clauses is an opinion-formula dependent clause at the end of its clause; mark it off with a comma.

> New York is too busy, I think. [*I think* is an opinion-formula clause.]

39. The easiest way to describe an adverbial clause is to say that it is not used like a noun or an adjective.

40. The best test for distinguishing the three kinds of dependent clause is that of substitution. A noun clause may have as its substitute one of the personal pronouns—*he, him, it, they,* etc. An adjectival clause modifies a word or group that can have the personal pronouns as its substitute. An adverbial clause can usually have as its substitute one of the *th* words *there, then, therefore,* or *thus.* Some adverbial clauses can not have one of those *th* words as a substitute, but those adverbial clauses also do not pass the substitute tests for adjectival and noun clauses.

41. The examples of clauses given in this discussion have been fairly uncomplicated. In nontextbook writing, however, sentences may have multiple clauses. Of the following three sentences from current publications, the first has six clauses, and the other two each have seven. Each clause is enclosed in brackets and labeled with its number at its beginning and its end.

> [1 [2 If that is so 2], somebody should tell them [3 that the quantity of Americans [4 who are impressive experts in [5 what we must do to be saved 5] 4] is already so tremendous [6 that they would face the most appalling sort of competition here 6] 3] 1].
> [1 This technicism is more and more pervasive 1]: [2 in every area methodology replaces substance 2]; [3 technical proficiency is valued over final excellence 3]; [4 the analysis of philosophical questions substitutes for their resolution 4]; [5 "know-how" supplants wisdom 5]; [6 "Whither?" has become archaic 6], [7 but "How?" is on every man's lips 7].
> [1 I have argued [2 that the positive and negative components of myth are related much as the constructive and destructive sides of an individual's fantasy life 2] 1]: [3 [4 if one dominates 4], it usually indicates [5 that the

other has been driven underground, [6 where it continues to exist [7 until it can be reintegrated into consciousness and given coherent form 7] 6] 5] 3].

These sentences, by the way, are not extreme examples of prose by any means.

Now continue with the following sections: § Clause—Adjectival, § Clause—Noun, and § Clause—Independent and Adverbial.

CLAUSE—ADJECTIVAL
C.5

After you have mastered the most frequent simple-sentence patterns, you can vary your writing by using clauses. Read § Clause for a discussion of the structure and kinds of clauses. In this section I will show you how you can combine related sentences by converting one of them into an adjectival dependent clause.

1. An adjectival clause is a dependent clause that adds information about a noun, pronoun, or noun phrase in the same sentence.

> EXAMPLE   My father, who works in a large city, is a lawyer.

The dependent clause *who works in a large city* adds information about the noun phrase *my father.*

2. Two sentences which make statements about the same person or thing can be put together by the use of a relative word: the *wh* words *who, whom, whose, which, where, when, why,* and *how* and *that.*

> EXAMPLE   My father is a lawyer. He works in a large city.

The personal pronoun *he* refers to *my father.* We change the *he* to *who* and place the resulting dependent clause next to *my father.* We then get the sentence that is used as the first example in this section:

> **Model 1**   My father, who works in a large city, is a lawyer.

The clause *who works in a large city* now "modifies" *my father:* it adds information about the words *my father.*

3. The rule for putting together sentences such as those in the above example is as follows:
   If the subject of one sentence is a personal pronoun (*I, we, you, he, she, it,* or *they*) which refers to a word or phrase in the other sentence, that personal pronoun can be changed to *who* for persons or to *which* for things, and the resulting dependent clause is placed in the other sentence after the word that the original personal pronoun referred to.

4. In the remainder of this discussion I will use two terms quite frequently: *restrictive* and *nonrestrictive.* Both are applied to adjectival clauses. The two types of clause, however, are punctuated differently, as I pointed out in the briefer discussion in § Clause.

All adjectival clauses add information about the words they modify, but some adjectival clauses distinguish the words they modify from all other uses of those same words: they restrict the meaning of the words they modify. Such adjectival clauses are called *restrictive,* and all other adjectival clauses are called *nonrestrictive.*

As an example I will take the clause *who need food* and have it modify the word *men* in two sentences:

| **Model 2** | Men | who need food | are hungry. |

In Model 2 the clause *who need food* distinguishes the word *men* from all other uses of the word *men:* the clause is, therefore, restrictive. Because of that clause your reader knows that you are talking about, not "all men" or "men in general," but just a restricted group of men. Notice that there are no commas around the clause.

| **Model 3** | Men, who need food, are like all other living beings. |

In Model 3 the clause *who need food* does not restrict the meaning of *men* although it does add information about *men:* the clause is nonrestrictive. In that sentence *men* means "all men" or "men in general." Notice that there are commas around the clause.

5. Here are your rules for punctuating adjectival clauses. To help you remember, notice that each rule has one negative element: the first rule has *not;* the second has *non-.*

a. Restrictive clauses are *not* marked off by commas.

*b. Non*restrictive clauses are marked off by commas.

Now look back at Model 1. The commas around the adjectival clause *who works in a large city* tell the reader that the clause is nonrestrictive. It adds information about *my father,* but it does not restrict those words. As a matter of fact, it is the word *my* that restricts the meaning of the word *father.*

Remember that the presence or absence of commas with adjectival clauses actually tells the reader something. For example, how many brothers does the writer of the following sentence have?

| My brother | who lives in Chicago | has six children. |

How many brothers does the writer of the next sentence have?

| My brother | , | who lives in Chicago | , | has six children. |

The writer of the first sentence has more than one brother; the writer of the second sentence has only one brother.

In speech a nonrestrictive clause usually has a slight pause before and after it. In writing, a comma before and after a nonrestrictive clause serves the purpose of that speech pause. A restrictive clause is usually not set off by such speech pauses. Listen to other people to see if you can punctuate their adjectival clauses.

6. We can make another variation with the example we used before.

| EXAMPLE | My father is a lawyer. | He works in a large city. |

We can make the second sentence modify *a lawyer* instead of *my father* by adding it after *a lawyer.* The adjectival clause then becomes restrictive: it distinguishes the words *a lawyer* from all other uses of the same words.

| **Model 4** | My father is a lawyer | who works in a large city. |

The clause is not marked off by a comma because it is restrictive.
We have the possibility of still another variation on the example.

| **Model 5** | My father is a lawyer | that works in a large city. |

In a restrictive clause the word *that* can be used instead of *who* and most other *wh* words. You should know, however, that some people do not like to use *that* to refer to human beings.

7. For practice we can add some more sentences to the first example in this section, "My father, who works in a large city, is a lawyer."

| EXAMPLE | The name of the city is Caracas. *It* is in Venezuela. |

The pronoun *it* can refer to either *city* or *Caracas.* Therefore, we have two possible models:

| **Model 6** | The name of the city, which is in Venezuela, is Caracas. |
| **Model 7** | The name of the city is Caracas, which is in Venezuela. |

In neither model does the adjectival clause *which is in Venezuela* serve the purpose of restricting the words it modifies even though it gives the location. *City* has already been mentioned in the preceding sentence (Models 4 and 5, "... in a large city"); in Models 6 and 7 the word *the* before *city* indicates that the reference is being continued. Since the adjectival clause in both models is nonrestrictive, *which,* not *that,* is used, and the clause is marked off by commas.

8. Proper names do not customarily need to be restricted: their uniqueness is indicated by their capitalization and lack of an article. If they are modified by a dependent clause, that clause is usually nonrestrictive and, consequently, is marked off by commas. See Model 7 above. Here are some other examples:

> Dante, who was born in the thirteenth century, was an outstanding Italian poet.
> There was friction between James, who believed in thrift, and Howard, who never thought about the future.

At times, however, bearers of the same names need to be distinguished. In such a case, an article is used, and an identifying dependent clause is restrictive and is not set off by commas.

| The John Smith colonist. | that the lecturer was discussing | was an early Virginia |
| The Samuel Johnson the Samuel Johnson | who wrote the first modern dictionary who was a president of Columbia University. | was not |

Now I will point out some other kinds of sentences that can be put together.

9. If the personal pronoun of the sentence that is to be made into an adjectival clause has its object form (*me, us, you, him, her, it,* or *them*), it is changed

C

CLAUSE—ADJECTIVAL

to *whom* for persons or to *which* for things and placed at the beginning of the adjectival clause. The clause is placed after the word or group it modifies.

a. A nonrestrictive clause is marked off by commas, and a *wh* word is used. The word *that* is not used, and the *wh* word is not omitted.

EXAMPLE	My father is in Venezuela. I have not seen him for a year.
Model 8	My father, whom I have not seen for a year, is in Venezuela.

b. In a restrictive clause, either a *wh* word or *that* may be used, or the relative word may be omitted. No commas are used.

EXAMPLE	I am reading a book.	I like it very much.
Model 9	I am reading a book	which I like very much.
		that I like very much.
		I like very much.

c. If the personal pronoun is the object of a preposition, the preposition may be placed at the beginning of the clause or be left in its original position.
Two arrangements are possible for a nonrestrictive clause.

EXAMPLE	Paris is beautiful. I lived in it for a short time.
Model 10	Paris, in which I lived for a short time, is beautiful.
	Paris, which I lived in for a short time, is beautiful.

Four arrangements are possible for a restrictive clause.

EXAMPLE	A girl got the job. Lew had spoken about her.		
Model 11	A girl	about whom Lew had spoken	got the job.
		whom Lew had spoken about	
		that Lew had spoken about	
		Lew had spoken about	

Some people prefer the first arrangement of Models 10 and 11, which has the preposition preceding the *wh* word. In formal writing, also, the first arrangement is customarily used.

d. However, if the personal pronoun is the object in a prepositional phrase which is a modifier in the subject of the original sentence, that pronoun is converted to *whom* or *which* in the dependent clause, but the word order is not changed.

EXAMPLES	I have many friends. Some of them are businessmen.
	Foreign students are numerous at that college. The majority of them are from Europe.
Model 12	I have many friends, some of whom are businessmen.
	Foreign students, the majority of whom are from Europe, are numerous at that college.

The prepositional phrase may also be placed at the beginning of the adjectival clause.

Model 13   I have many friends, of whom some are businessmen.

Foreign students, of whom the majority are from Europe, are numerous at that college.

e. It is appropriate at this point to mention the difference between speech and writing in the use of *who* and *whom* as objects. In speaking, most people, including the educated, use *who* at the beginning of a clause. However, in writing, *whom* is the standard form as an object.

10. If the sentence which is to be made into an adjectival clause has a genitive adjective (*my, our, your, his, her, its,* or *their*) which refers to a word or group in the other sentence, that genitive adjective can be converted to *whose,* and the *whose* and the word it modifies are placed at the beginning of the clause.

EXAMPLES   Miss Binet was born in Tokyo. Her parents were originally from France.

I recently met a Belgian scientist. A society is financing his research.

Mr. Brace collects coins. I was at his house last night.

Venezuela is in South America. Its capital is Caracas.

Model 14   Miss Binet, whose parents were originally from France, was born in Tokyo.

I recently met a Belgian scientist whose research a society is financing.

Mr. Brace, at whose house I was last night, collects coins.

Mr. Brace, whose house I was at last night, collects coins.

Venezuela, whose capital is Caracas, is in South America.

If the genitive adjective is *its* or *their* referring to inanimate objects, some writers prefer to use *of which* instead of *whose.*

Venezuela, the capital of which is Caracas, is in South America.

Venezuela, of which the capital is Caracas, is in South America.

Now I will give you some variations for some of the adjectival clauses discussed above.

11. If a preposition (usually *at, in,* or *to*) and *which* express place, the preposition and the *which* can be converted to *where.*

EXAMPLE   Paris, in which I lived for a short time, is beautiful.

Model 15   Paris, where I lived for a short time, is beautiful.

12. If a preposition (usually *at, in, on,* or *during*) and *which* express time, they can be converted to *when.*

EXAMPLE   My vacation, in which I can get some rest, is coming soon.

Model 16   My vacation, when I can get some rest, is coming soon.

13. The preposition *for* and *which* referring to *reason* can be converted to *why*. As a matter of fact, *why* is more frequent than *for which*.

EXAMPLE	I know the reason	for which John left.
Model 17	I know the reason	why John left.

14. Furthermore, in restrictive clauses *when* can be replaced by *that* or omitted; *why* can be replaced by *that* or omitted; and *where* can be omitted.

Model 18	I know the time	when John left.
		that John left.
		John left.
Model 19	I know the reason	why John left.
		that John left.
		John left.
Model 20	I know the place	where John lost his book.
		John lost his book.

15. Now here is a summary of the rules for adjectival clauses:

a. Adjectival clauses follow the word or group they modify.
b. A restrictive clause restricts the meaning of the word or group it modifies.
c. A nonrestrictive clause adds information about the word or group it modifies but does not serve to restrict the word or group.
d. Restrictive clauses are not marked off by commas.
e. Nonrestrictive clauses are marked off by commas.
f. The *wh* words may be used in both restrictive and nonrestrictive clauses.
g. The word *that* may be used in restrictive clauses except immediately after a preposition.
h. The relative word may be omitted in restrictive clauses if it is not the subject or part of the subject of the dependent clause.

CLAUSE—INDEPENDENT AND ADVERBIAL   C.6

1. Related simple sentences can be put together into a compound sentence. Each simple sentence is then an independent clause in that compound sentence. See § Clause for a general discussion of clauses and sentences.

The easiest way to make a compound sentence is by using the coordinating conjunction *and.* The following example has two simple sentences:

EXAMPLE	My father is a lawyer. He works for the government.

Those two simple sentences can be joined by the coordinating conjunction *and* and converted into independent clauses in a compound sentence:

Model 1	My father is a lawyer, and he works for the government.

Notice that a comma is used before the coordinating conjunction joining the two independent clauses of the compound sentence.

a. Both simple sentences may be negative.

> EXAMPLES   My father is not a doctor. He does not live in this city.
> My father is not a doctor. My grandfather was not a doctor.

Those two sentences may be joined in a number of ways:
The two sentences may be joined by *and.*

> **Model 2**   My father is not a doctor, and he does not live in this city.
> My father is not a doctor, and my grandfather was not a doctor.

The word *either* is frequently added to the end of the second clause, particularly in speaking.

> **Model 3**   My father is not a doctor, and he does not live in this city, either.
> My father is not a doctor, and my grandfather was not a doctor, either.

Instead of *either,* the word *neither* may be used. It is placed after the *and* and is followed by split word order (auxiliary + subject + main verb) or inverted word order (main verb + subject). No other negative word is used in the second clause.

> **Model 4**   My father is not a doctor, and neither does he live in this city.
> My father is not a doctor, and neither was my grandfather.

Instead of *and neither,* the coordinating conjunction *nor* may be used. It too is followed by split or inverted word order.

> **Model 5**   My father is not a doctor, nor does he live in this city.
> My father is not a doctor, nor was my grandfather.

Of those variations, Models 3 and 4 probably occur more frequently in speaking, and Model 5 occurs more frequently in writing.

b. A semicolon can be used instead of *and* between two independent clauses.

> **Model 6**   My father is a lawyer; he works for the government.
> My father is not a doctor; he does not live in this city.
> My father is not a doctor; he does not live in this city, either.
> My father is not a doctor; neither does he live in this city.
> My father is not a doctor; neither was my grandfather.

c. A number of transition words and phrases can be used with the semicolon replacing *and.* Notice that they are marked off by commas. See § Transition Expression.

> **Model 7**   My father is a lawyer;   *besides,* he works for the government.
> My father is a lawyer;   *in addition,* he works for the government.
> My father is a lawyer;   he works for the government, *moreover.*

Other similar transition expressions are *by the way, furthermore, incidentally,* and *similarly;* they are customarily marked off by commas. When *also* and *too* are so used at the beginning of an independent clause, they are followed by a comma; when they are so used at the end of an independent clause, they are preceded by a comma.

| Model 8 | My father is a lawyer; | also, he works for the government. |
| | My father is a lawyer; | he works for the government, too. |

2. Two simple sentences may express contrasting or opposing ideas.

| EXAMPLE | I am lazy. I must work. |

Those two sentences can be put together in a variety of ways.

a. The sentences can be joined as independent clauses with the coordinating conjunction *but.* A comma is used before the *but.*

| Model 9 | I am lazy, but I must work. |

b. You can use a semicolon and a transition expression of contrast. The transition expression is marked off by commas. *Yet* and *still* usually come after the semicolon; *though* usually comes at the end of the second clause; *however, on the contrary, nevertheless,* and *on the other hand* may vary in their positions: they may come before the subject, after the subject, or at the end of the second clause.

Model 10	I am lazy;	still, I must work.
	I am lazy;	I must work, though.
	I am lazy;	I, nevertheless, must work.

The transition expressions *all the same* and *just the same,* which have an informal flavor, are usually marked off by commas when they begin or interrupt the second clause.

Model 11	I am lazy;	all the same, I must work.
	I am lazy;	I must, just the same, work.
	I am lazy;	I must work just the same.

c. One of the contrasting ideas can be subordinated by the use of the phrases *in spite of the fact* and *despite the fact,* which is usually followed by the word *that.* The sentence that is subordinated becomes a dependent clause in a complex sentence; the phrase and the dependent clause are used like an adverb and, therefore, can take varying positions in the sentence. Do not mark them off with commas if they come at the end of the sentence; otherwise, mark them off.

| Model 12 | In spite of the fact that I am lazy, I must work. |
| | I must work   despite the fact I am lazy. |

d. Instead of *in spite of the fact* or *despite the fact (that),* the subordinating conjunction *although* or *though* may be used; the conjunctions *whereas* and *while* are used less frequently. Set off the dependent clause with commas unless it comes at the end of the sentence.

| Model 13 | Although I am lazy, I must work. |
| | I must work   though I am lazy. |

Be careful about the words *though* and *although:* if they come before a subject, they are subordinating conjunctions and are not marked off by a comma. As a conjunction, *though,* but not *although,* is often preceded by the word *even.* In addition, *though* may be used as a transition word in other positions; then, it is marked off by commas. *Although* is not used as a transition word.

> Though I am lazy,   I must work.
> I must work   although I am lazy.
> I must work   even though I am lazy.
> I must work;   I am lazy, though.

e. *Even if* may interchange with *even though.*

Model 14   Even if I am lazy, I must work.

f. Sometimes the predicate adjective or noun of the dependent clause is placed before the conjunction *though.* In that position the predicate noun does not have an article.

Model 15   *Lazy* though I am, I must work.
    Murderer though he was, his wife did not forsake him.

g. With a fronted predicate adjective or adverb of manner the words *as . . .as* may substitute for the *though.* The first *as* may also be omitted.

Model 16   As lazy as I am, I must work.
    Lazy as I am, I must work.
    As much as he likes her, he does get irritated with her.
    Much as he likes her, he does get irritated with her.

h. Similarly, the word *however,* may be used before a fronted adjective or adverb.

Model 17   However lazy I am, I must work.
    However much he likes her, he does get irritated with her.

For another use of *however* at the beginning of an adverbial clause, see § Clause —Noun, ¶ 10.

i. Also, the words *no matter* may be used with a *wh* word in the dependent clause.

Model 18   No matter how lazy I am, I must work.
    Do not believe that rumor no matter who tells it to you.

Also, see § Opposition Expression.

3. Two simple sentences may express an alternative or choice.

EXAMPLE   People eat. They starve.

a. Those two sentences can be joined by *or* and a comma. The word *else* is often added after the *or*, particularly in speaking.

Model 19   People eat, or they starve.
    People eat, or else they starve.

b. The two sentences can be joined by a semicolon without the *or* if *else* or the transition word *otherwise* is used. *Otherwise* usually follows the semicolon and is marked off by a comma.

Model 20   People eat;   else they starve.
    People eat;   otherwise, they starve.

4. One sentence may express a condition, and another may express the result of that condition.

EXAMPLE   Study hard. You will learn.

That condition may be converted into a dependent clause with the subordinating conjunction *if* and placed either before or after the result. If the condition comes first, put a comma after it.

Model 21   If you study hard, you will learn.
            You will learn   if you study hard.

Other words may be used instead of *if* to introduce the condition: *in case (that), on condition (that), provided* or *providing (that), so* (or *as*) *long as,* and *suppose* or *supposing (that).*

Model 22   Provided you study hard, you will learn.
            You will learn   so long as you study hard.

The subordinating conjunction **unless** may be used in place of *if . . . not.*

Model 23   Unless you study hard, you will not learn.

The conditional construction is discussed in detail in § Conditional Sentence.

5. One sentence may give the cause of the action or state expressed in another sentence.

EXAMPLE   He felt cold. He built a fire.

There are numerous ways of joining those sentences.

a. The two sentences may be joined with a semicolon and the transition word *therefore, consequently, accordingly,* or *hence.* The transition word is marked off by commas.

Model 24   He felt cold;   consequently, he built a fire.
            He felt cold;   he built a fire, therefore.

b. In conversation the two clauses are frequently joined by the word *so.*

Model 25   He felt cold, so he built a fire.

Many people consider the above construction to be childish in writing. I advise you to use the other constructions when you write.

c. If you modify an adjective or adverb in the cause clause with the word *so* meaning "to such a degree," you can add the dependent clause either with or without the word *that.* Do not use any commas.

Model 26   He felt so cold   that he built a fire.
            He felt so cold   he built a fire.

Nobody objects to that kind of *so.*

d. If the adjective in the cause clause is followed by a noun, you use *such* instead of *so.*

| **Model 27** | There were such cold winds | that he built a fire. |
| | There were such cold winds | he built a fire. |

e. You can also shift the position of the two clauses: you can put the cause clause second. The simplest way of doing that is by using a colon between the two independent clauses.

| **Model 28** | He built a fire: he felt cold. |

f. Instead of the colon, a comma and the coordinating conjunction *for* may be used before the cause clause.

| **Model 29** | He built a fire, for he felt cold. |

g. The cause may be put into a dependent clause by using the subordinating conjunction *because, as,* or *since.* Less frequently the phrases *inasmuch as* (or *in as much as*) and *in that* are used. The dependent clause may be put first or last in the sentence. If the dependent clause comes first, put a comma after it.

Model 30	He built a fire	because he felt cold.
	He built a fire	since he felt cold.
	As he felt cold, he built a fire.	

h. If the cause clause has a predicate nominative, the predicate nominative can be fronted and followed by *that.* No article is used.

Chemist that he is, Charles is suspicious of all doctors' prescriptions.
Fool that she was, Betty did not accept Bert's proposal.

6. One sentence may express an action, and another sentence may express the purpose of that action.

| EXAMPLE | He built a fire. He would be warm. |

a. Those two sentences may be joined by the words *so* or *in order* before the purpose clause. The word *that* may be added after the *so* and is always used after *in order.* The purpose clause usually has the auxiliaries *can, could, may, might, will,* or *would,* and it may be moved to the beginning of the sentence. In that position, it is followed by a comma.

Model 31	He built a fire	so that he would be warm.
	He built a fire	so he would be warm.
	In order that he would be warm, he built a fire.	

b. In rather formal writing, the word *lest* is sometimes used instead of *so . . . not* or *in order . . . not.* Do not use *that.* After *lest,* the verb in the purpose clause usually has its uninflected form; sometimes it has *should.*

| **Model 32** | He built a fire | lest he be cold. |
| | He built a fire | lest he should be cold. |

c. Some people have trouble distinguishing between the purpose *so* clause and the *so* clause used after a cause. The two kinds of clause are different in four ways: unlike the other clause, (1) the purpose *so* clause may be shifted to the beginning of the sentence; (2) it is marked off by a comma only if it begins the sentence; (3) the *so* may be followed by *that;* and (4) nobody objects to a purpose *so* clause in writing.

Here are some more examples with a purpose clause. Notice the punctuation.

> He built a fire   so he would not be cold.
> So that he would be warm, he built a fire.
> Night classes are given   so working people may get an education.
> Give the boy a dime   so he will leave us alone.
> I gave the girl the package   so that she could wrap it.
> In order that the girl might wrap the package, I gave it to her.
> In order that a hospital might be built, Fisher donated a million dollars.

7. Two sentences may express a comparison.

> EXAMPLES   Mary works hard. Sally does, too.
>   Robert is tall. John is taller.

For an equal comparison the two sentences are joined by *as . . . as,* and the *too* is omitted. For an unequal comparison the first sentence is joined to the end of the second with the subordinating conjunction *than,* and the term of comparison is not repeated. No commas are used. Also, see § Verb—Not Repeated.

> **Model 33**   Mary works   as hard as Sally does.
>   John is taller   than Robert is.

If no ambiguity is likely to result, the auxiliary or main verb after the second member of the comparison may be omitted.

> **Model 34**   Mary works as hard as Sally.
>   John is taller than Robert.

In sentences such as those in Model 34 ambiguity will result if the verb has an object: your reader will not be sure whether the comparison is between the subject or the object and the second member.

> EXAMPLE   Mr. Russo treats his car better than his wife.

To prevent ambiguity, state the subject and the auxiliary for the second member of the comparison.

> **Model 35**   Mr. Russo treats his car better than *his wife does.*
>   Mr. Russo treats his car better than *he does* his wife.

Your reader can then see clearly what you are comparing.

a. Two *the*'s are used in a set pattern of comparison: *the* (comparative) . . . , *the* (comparative). . . .

> **Model 36**   The more I earn,   the more I spend.
>   The bigger they are,   the harder they fall.
>   The more attention he gets,   the less effort he makes.

The first *the* introduces a dependent clause which is used like an adverb and is, therefore, marked off by a comma. Some grammarians call the clauses in sentences like these *interdependent clauses*. See § Comparison for additional examples.

b. The words *as if* and *as though* introduce comparison clauses which contain expressions of opinion. See § *As if* and *As though.*

Also, see § *As* vs. *Like* and § Comparison.

8. Two sentences that have a time relationship may be put together.

> EXAMPLE   She listens to the radio. She cleans the house.

Very frequently, when you join such sentences, you must make changes in verb forms. However, in most of the following models there are no such changes.

a. If the two times are simultaneous, the subordinating conjunctions *when, whenever, while,* and *as* or phrases like *during the time that, each time (that),* and *every time (that)* may be used. The dependent clauses beginning with the conjunctions are adverbial. The dependent clauses following *time* are adjectival, but together with the preceding phrase they form adverbial clauses. *That* is often omitted after *each time* and *every time.*

> **Model 37**   She listens to the radio   when she cleans the house.
> Whenever she cleans the house, she listens to the radio.
> While she cleans the house, she listens to the radio.
> She listens to the radio   as she cleans the house.
> During the time that she cleans the house, she listens to the radio.
> She listens to the radio every time she cleans the house.

When the dependent clause expressing time comes first in the sentence, put a comma after it.

b. If the time relationship is that of a series, the two sentences can be put together to form a compound sentence with time-sequence words like *first, next, later,* and *then* to indicate sequence.

> **Model 38**   First, she cleans the house,   and then she cooks the meal.
> She first cleans the house,   and she later cooks the meal.
> She cleans the house; next,   she cooks the meal.
> She cleans the house;   she cooks the meal afterwards.

Notice that the time-sequence word is not marked off by commas unless it is the first word in its clause.

c. One of the sentences can be converted into a dependent clause with the subordinating conjunction *before* or *after* or with a phrase like *before the time (that).* The clause can come at the beginning, in the middle, or at the end of the sentence. Set it off with commas unless it comes at the end.

Model 39 After she cleans the house, she cooks the meal.
She cooks the meal   after she cleans the house.
Before she cooks the meal, she cleans the house.
She cleans the house   before the time that she cooks the meal.
Before the time she cooks the meal, she cleans the house.

d. Sometimes the time of one sentence marks the end of the time of the other sentence.

EXAMPLE   He worked hard. He died.

The subordinating conjunction *until* or *till* can be used to convert the time-end sentence into a dependent clause. You can also use phrases like *until the day (that)* and *up to the time (that)*.

Model 40 He worked hard   until he died.
Till he died, he worked hard.
He worked hard   until the day he died.

e. Sometimes one sentence marks the beginning of the time period of the other sentence.

EXAMPLE   Columbus set sail. He had many difficulties.
You begin to watch television. Time flies.

You can convert the time-beginning sentence into a dependent clause with the conjunction *once* or phrases like *as soon as* or *from the time (that)*.

Model 41 From the day Columbus set sail, he had many difficulties.
Once you begin to watch television, time flies.

f. If the time period begins in the past and continues into the present, you use *since, ever since,* or phrases like *since the time (that)*.

EXAMPLE   I came to this college. I have broadened my horizon.

Model 42 Since I came to this college, I have broadened my horizon.
I have broadened my horizon   ever since I came to this college.
Since the moment I came to this college, I have broadened my horizon.

Notice that in the dependent clause the simple-past form of the verb is used and in the other verb the perfect-present tense denotes time from the past up to the present.

9. One sentence may express a statement, and another sentence may make a comment about it. The verb of the second sentence is one either of reporting (e.g., *say, state, exclaim*) or of mental activity (e.g., *know, believe, hope*).

EXAMPLE   Production was increasing. Mr. Lewis said so.
Marcus will win. I believe that.

The second sentence, without the words referring to the first (that is, *so, that,* etc.), may be placed either within the first, usually after the subject, or at the end of the first. It is marked off by commas.

| Model 43 | Production , Mr. Lewis said , was increasing. |
| | Marcus will win , I believe. |

This construction is similar to the ones discussed in § Clause—Noun.

10. Here is the summary of the punctuation rules of this section:

a. A comma is used to separate independent clauses that are connected by the coordinating conjunctions *and, but, or, nor,* and *for.*
b. A semicolon is used to separate independent clauses that could but do not have *and, but, or,* or *nor.*
c. A colon is used to separate independent clauses that could but do not have *for.*
d. An adverbial clause is customarily marked off by commas unless it comes at the end of the clause it belongs to.
e. A transition word or phrase is usually marked off by commas.
f. A time-sequence word is usually not marked off by commas unless it begins its clause.

Also, see § Clause—Noun, ¶ 10, for adverbial dependent clauses beginning with *whenever, wherever,* and *however.*

CLAUSE—NOUN C.7

1. A noun clause is a dependent clause that functions just like a noun, pronoun, or noun phrase in a sentence. It may be a subject, direct object, indirect object, object of a preposition, predicate nominative, predicate objective, or appositive. The noun clause customarily begins with a *wh* word or *that.* Its substitute is usually the word *it,* less often *he, him, she, her, they,* or *them.* A description and examples of noun clauses are given in § Clause.
In § Clause—Adjectival, I showed you how you could make adjectival clauses from sentences. Now I will show you how you can make noun clauses from sentences and other clauses. In certain instances I will give you examples of adverbial clauses that are alternates of noun clauses.

2. Two sentences can be put together if in one sentence the word *this, that, it,* or *so* refers to the whole of the other sentence.

EXAMPLES	"I will go." She says that.
	He has seen the woman. I believe it.
	Can war be stopped? The group thinks so.
	Men must die. This is a fact.

In the paragraphs that follow I will show you how pairs of sentences like those in the above example can be put together.

C

3. Quoted sentences can be used as noun clauses replacing *that, this, it,* or *so.*

a. A direct quotation can be added with a comma and quotation marks to verbs of reporting like *say, exclaim,* and *ask.*

Model 1	She says, "I will go."

In Model 1 the direct quotation, "I will go," functions as the direct object of the verb *says.*

The original second sentence, "She says that," has now become a *dialog guide.* As such, it can vary its position: it may introduce, go at the end of, or interrupt the quoted sentence. Notice the punctuation.

Model 2	"I will go," she says.
	"I," she says, "will go."

b. If the quotation marks are not used, the quotation becomes an *indirect quotation.* The conjunction *that* may be used before the indirect quotation, but no comma is used. It may be necessary to make changes in pronouns, verb forms, and other words.

Model 3	She says	that she will go.
	She says	she will go.

It is particularly in this kind of sentence where sequence of tense operates. As a general rule, if the verb before the indirect quotation has a past-tense form, the verb in the indirect quotation will also have a past form.

Direct:	She said	,	"I will go."
Indirect:	She said	that	she would go.
	She said		she would go.

c. If the direct quotation is a question that begins with a *wh* word, the conjunction *that* is not used before the indirect quotation. The *wh* word comes first in the dependent clause, and the dependent clause has primary word order (subject before the simple predicate). Notice that a question mark is not used for the indirect quotation.

Direct:	I asked her	,	"What will you do?"
Indirect:	I asked her		what she would do.

d. If the direct question does not begin with a *wh* word, the conjunction *whether* or *if* is used with the indirect quotation.

Direct:	I asked her	,	"Do you like him?"
Indirect:	I asked her	whether	she liked him.
	I asked her	if	she liked him.

e. The word *question* in a sentence affects the patterning somewhat. Notice that no comma is used in the following examples.

Direct:	The question is	"Should she go?"
Indirect:	The question is	whether she should go.

If the indirect quotation comes immediately after the word *question*, the word *of* is usually inserted.

The question of	whether she should go	must be answered.
The discussion failed to answer the question of	who would do the work.	
A "mother machine" raises the question of	how necessary a mother is.	

Here is a list of verbs of reporting which may have clauses as their direct objects:

acknowledge	confess	hint	own	reply	swear
add	confide	indicate	plead	report	tell
admit	contend	inform	point out	retort	vow
allege	declare	inquire	profess	reveal	whisper
announce	demand	insinuate	promise	say	yell
answer	deny	maintain	propose	scream	
ask	discuss	mention	protest	shout	
assert	emphasize	murmur	remark	sigh	
aver	exclaim	mutter	remind	state	
avow	explain	notify	repeat	suggest	

See § Direct vs. Indirect Speech and § Sequence of Tense for other details on direct and indirect quotations. Also, see § Verb—Uninflected in Dependent Clause for direct-object clauses after verbs like *advise* and *suggest*.

4. Just like the verbs of reporting (*say, ask,* etc.), verbs of mental activity like *know, notice, hope, believe, see,* and *think* can have noun clauses as their direct objects replacing *this, that, it,* or *so.* No commas are used before the noun clauses. Just as with an indirect quotation, the conjunction *that* may be used before the noun clause unless the noun clause begins with a *wh* word or *whether* or *if.*

EXAMPLES	He has seen the woman.	I believe it.
	She would go.	We knew that.
	Can war be stopped?	The group thinks so.
Model 4	I believe	that he has seen the woman.
	We knew	she would go.
	The group thinks	that war can be stopped.

Remember that there are no commas before dependent clauses like those in Model 4. One of the major punctuation rules is this: do not separate a verb and its direct object with a comma. The principal exception to that rule is with direct quotations, which is stated in ¶ 3, *a*, above.

Here is a list of verbs of mental activity which may have clauses as their direct objects:

assume	expect	guess	observe	recognize	suspect
believe	fancy	hear	perceive	regret	think
consider	fear	hope	presume	remember	understand
decide	feel	imagine	pretend	resent	wonder
discover	figure out	know	prove	see	
divine	find out	learn	realize	suppose	
doubt	forget	notice	recall	surmise	

5. The verbs of mental activity and their subjects in Model 4 may shift their position and become *opinion formulas.* The conjunction *that* is not used. The opinion formulas are marked off by commas.

Model 5	He has seen the woman, I believe.
	She, we knew, would go.
	War can, the group thinks, be stopped.

Such opinion formulas are classified as adverbial clauses modifying the rest of the sentence. See § Interpolation.

Note that one sentence may express a question beginning with a *wh* word or phrase (*who, why, how often,* etc.), and another sentence may ask for someone's opinion. The second sentence begins with *what* and has a verb of supposition (e.g., *think, suppose, believe*).

EXAMPLES	What did she do?	What do you think?
	Who was crying?	What did they suppose?
	Whom will they elect?	What does the columnist believe?
	How often has he tried that?	What do you imagine?

The second sentence, without its *what,* may be added at the end of the first with a comma, or it may be inserted without commas after the *wh* word or phrase of the first. The second sentence then becomes an opinion-asking formula.

Model 6	What did she do,	do you think?
	Who	did they suppose	was crying?

If the formula precedes the subject of the original first sentence, the original first sentence takes primary word order (subject before simple predicate).

Model 7	Whom	does the columnist believe	they will elect?
	How often	do you imagine	he has tried that?

Notice that the insertion of the formula, since it is parenthetical, does not change the form *who* or *whom* of the original first sentence. Also, see § Word Order—*Wh* Word.

6. In the second of a pair of sentences a *this, that,* or *it* referring to the first sentence may be the object of a preposition, or it may be followed by a predicate adjective or noun phrase.

EXAMPLES	Nothing will be done. You may depend upon this.
	Bob swam in deep water. We thought that dangerous.
	Mary could not go. I considered it a shame.

The *this* or *that* in the second sentence is customarily changed to *it* (an *it,* as in the third example, is retained), and the first sentence is added at the end of the second sentence, usually with the conjunction *that.*

Model 8	You may depend upon it	that nothing will be done.
	We thought it dangerous	that Bob swam in deep water.
	I considered it a shame	that Mary could not go.

In Model 8 the noun clauses beginning with the conjunction *that* are restrictive appositives to the preceding *it*'s. No comma is used before such dependent clauses.

a. The original second sentence may have the *this, that,* or *it* as the object of a preposition (usually *about* or *of*) following an adjective or past participle expressing an emotion—for example, *glad, sorry, angry, sure, amazed, excited, delighted, grieved, embarrassed,* or *convinced*

EXAMPLES	Nothing will be done. You may be sure of this.
	Bob swam in deep water. We were alarmed about that.
	Mary could not go. I was sorry about it.

In combining such a pair of sentences, both the preposition and the *this, that,* or *it* are omitted, and the first sentence is added after the adjective or past participle. The conjunction *that* may be used before the resulting dependent clause; it is nearly always used after the past participles.

Model 9	You may be sure	nothing will be done.
	We were alarmed	that Bob swam in deep water.
	I was sorry	Mary could not go.

The dependent clauses in Model 9 are not noun clauses but adverbial clauses since they modify adjectives and past participles used as verbal adjectives. Notice that no commas are used.

7. If the word *this, that,* or *it* which refers to the other sentence is a subject, two arrangements are possible in putting the two sentences together.

EXAMPLES	Men must die. This is a fact.
	She had married twice. That was true.
	Father did not scold me. It surprised me.

a. The conjunction *that* is added before the first sentence, and the word *that, this,* or *it* is eliminated from the second sentence.

Model 10	That men must die	is a fact.
	That she had married twice	was true.
	That Father did not scold me	surprised me.

In Model 10 the original first sentence has become a noun clause, subject of the original second sentence. Model 10 is one of the few patterns in which the conjunction *that* can not be omitted. Notice that there are no commas in Model 10. A comma between the dependent clause and the following verb of which it is the subject would violate one of the principal rules of English punctuation: do not separate a subject from its verb with a comma.

b. Model 11 shows the other possible arrangement: the word *it* is used first, and the noun clause is shifted to the end of the sentence. The conjunction *that* can be either used or omitted.

Model 11	It is a fact	that men must die.
	It was true	she had married twice.
	It surprised me	that Father did not scold me.

In the sentences in Model 11 the *it* is the subject of the verb *is, was,* or *surprised,* and the noun clause that the *it* refers to (e.g., "that men must die") is a restrictive appositive. No commas are used.

8. Here is a pointer on clarity.

As you know, the word *that* can function in three ways: as an adjective (e.g., "That man is tall"), as a pronoun (e.g., "That is true"), and as a conjunction (e.g., "I know that he went"). The word *that* may be either a source of or a safeguard against ambiguity. For an example, let's take the first sentence in the preceding Model 11 and change *men* to *man:*

It is a fact that man must die.

The new sentence is ambiguous since the *that* can be interpreted either as an adjective or as a conjunction. Each of the interpretations can be expressed unambiguously, however. For the first interpretation two *that's* may be used; the first *that* will be interpreted as a conjunction, and the second *that* as an adjective:

It is a fact that that man must die.

For the second interpretation no *that* should be used:

It is a fact man must die.

Ambiguity is possible whenever *that* is followed by a singular noun in a position where the *that* may be interpreted either as an adjective or as a conjunction. Look back at the third sentence in Model 4, "The group thinks that war can be stopped." That sentence is ambiguous. The ambiguity may be eliminated by either adding another *that* for one interpretation or by having no *that* for the other interpretation. The second interpretation may also be expressed by making war plural; the *that* may then be used or omitted:

The group thinks	that that war can be stopped.
The group thinks	war can be stopped.
The group thinks	wars can be stopped.
The group thinks	that wars can be stopped.

Now I will take up clauses that can be converted into noun clauses. Notice that the resulting clauses all begin with *wh* words.

9. Certain restrictive clauses may be turned into noun clauses by omitting the word or group that the clauses modify.

a. Before the appropriate *wh* word, these words or their equivalents may be omitted: *the person(s), the reason(s), the time(s),* and *the place(s).*

		ADJECTIVAL CLAUSE
EXAMPLES	I know the person	who wrote that book.
	I know the persons	whom you saw.
	I know the reason	why John left.
	I know the time	when John left.
	I know the place	where he lost his book.
		NOUN CLAUSE
Model 12	I know	who wrote that book.
	I know	whom you saw.
	I know	why John left.
	I know	when John left.
	I know	where he lost his book.

Look at the form *who* in the first example in Model 12. It is used because it is the subject of the verb *wrote*. In the second example *whom* is used because it is the direct object of *saw*. The fact that the two dependent clauses are used as direct objects of *know* has nothing to do with the forms *who* and *whom*.

b. The words *the thing(s)* or their equivalents may be omitted and *what* used instead of *which* or *that*.

		ADJECTIVAL CLAUSE
EXAMPLES	I know the thing	which happened.
	I know the things	that he told you.
		NOUN CLAUSE
Model 13	I know	what happened.
	I know	what he told you.

Look very hard at the above example and model. Remember that the word *that* is used only when there is no antecedent. See § *What* vs. *That* and *Which*.

c. The words *the means, the way(s), the method(s),* and *the manner(s)* or their equivalents may be omitted and the appropriate preposition (usually *by* or *in*) and *which* converted to *how*.

		ADJECTIVAL CLAUSE
EXAMPLE	I know the means	by which he won the contest.
		NOUN CLAUSE
Model 14	I know	how he won the contest.

10. Instead of the compounds or phrases with *any* meaning "without exception" or "it does not matter" followed by adjectival clauses, the compounds with *-ever* may be used to begin noun or adverbial clauses.

		ADJECTIVAL CLAUSE
EXAMPLES	Invite *anyone*	*who* is a friend of yours.
	Invite *anybody*	*whom* you like.
	He took *anything*	*that* he wanted.
	See me *any time*	*when* you are not busy.
	You can phone *any place*	*where* you see that sign.
	He will do it *any way*	*that* you want.
		NOUN OR ADVERBIAL CLAUSE
Model 15	Invite	*whoever* is a friend of yours.
	Invite	*whomever* you like.
	He took	*whatever* he wanted.
	See me	*whenever* you are not busy.
	You can phone	*wherever* you see that sign.
	He will do it	*however* you want.

In the first three sentences of Model 15 the dependent clauses are noun clauses. In the last three sentences they are adverbial clauses: their substitutes are *then, there,* and *thus,* not *he, him, she, it, they,* or *them,* which are the usual substitutes for noun clauses. However, all the dependent clauses in Model 15 can be derived in the same way.

11. In most of the preceding models the clauses are used as direct objects of verbs. Here are some examples of other uses of noun clauses:

a. As objects of prepositions

	PREPOSITION	OBJECT OF PREPOSITION
She tells that story	to	whoever will listen.
His life is an example	of	what can be done by effort.
They showed no concern	about	what she had said.
I understood his explanation	about	how the machine worked.
He wrote an article	on	why the project had failed.

No commas are used: do not separate a preposition from its object with a comma. Notice in the first example above that *whoever,* not *whomever,* is used because it is the subject of *will listen.*

b. As predicate nominatives

	VERB	PREDICATE NOMINATIVE
The topic of discussion	was	what had caused the wreck.
The mystery	is	how it all came about.

No commas are used: do not separate a verb from its complement with a comma.

c. As subjects of verbs

SUBJECT	VERB	
Who told me the news	was	John.
Whom you saw	was	my mother.
Who steals my purse	steals	trash.
Whoever is not with me	is	against me.
What I saw at the fair	made	me start thinking.
Whatever concerns you	concerns	me.
When he told me the news	was	last week.
Where he lost it	was	near the river.
Why John left	is	quite clear.
How he won the contest	is	a mystery.

No commas are used: do not separate a subject from its verb with a comma.

12. It is possible to vary some of the sentences in the preceding section: you can use the word *it* in the subject position before the verb *be* and move to the end of the sentence the noun clauses which begin with *who, whom, when, where, why,* and *how.* (The clauses beginning with the other *wh* words are not frequently used in this pattern.)

SUBJECT	*be*		NOUN CLAUSE
It	was	John	who told me.
It	was	my mother	whom you saw.
It	was	last week	when he told me the news.
It	was	near the river	where he lost it.
It	is	quite clear	why John left.
It	is	a mystery	how he won the contest.

As you can see, the above sentences are similar to those in Model 11 because they have an *it* as the subject and a dependent clause used as a restrictive appositive at the end.

COGNATE WORD   C.8

1. English has many words which are similar in origin to those in other languages. The English meaning, spelling, and pronunciation of those words are sometimes quite close to those of their cognates in other languages; sometimes, however, they are very different. Therefore, foreign-language speakers should be cautious about assuming knowledge of such words. An all-English dictionary is the safest guide, but even it may be misleading because it may list obsolete, archaic, or rare definitions without labeling them. Since the *American College Dictionary* (ACD) usually places the modern or most frequent definition first and is generous with labels such as "British" and "colloquial," it is probably the most reliable reference book for cognates. Although *Webster's New Collegiate Dictionary* also labels definitions, it does not do so as extensively as the ACD does, and it usually places first the oldest meaning, which may be completely obsolete nowadays. For the difference in their treatment, look up *nice* and *silly* in the ACD and Webster's.

2. Some words which may deceive you are listed below with some of their most common meanings.

acre, a measure of land: 160 square rods

action, deed

actual, real

actually, really

agony, intense pain

alley, narrow, back street

also, too, in addition

assist, help

attend, be present at

become, grow to be; be suitable for

billet, lodging for a soldier

billion, 1,000,000,000

blame, lay the responsibility for an error on

brave, courageous

brief, short

capacity, power of receiving or donating; volume

caution, carefulness, prudence; foresight

chef, cook

closet, small room or cabinet for clothing, food, etc.

competent, adequate; properly qualified

concurrence, agreement

confectionary, candy store

conjunction, combination, union; one of the parts of speech

consequently, therefore, for that reason

content, happy, satisfied

control, govern

cure, treatment for a disease; restoration to health

demand, ask with authority or force

divert, draw one's attention away

effective, producing the desired result

elaborate, done with great care

eventually, finally; ultimately

existence, being; state or fact of being alive

experience, encounter

experiment, test

famous, well known

fatal, causing death

feast, large meal, banquet

C

figure, form, shape
flesh, meat of a human body
genial, cheerfully friendly
gymnasium, place for exercise or sports
hell, place of torment
hello, a greeting: good day
homely, not good-looking, ugly
ideal, perfect
ignore, pay no attention to
impair, hurt
infant, young child, baby
involve, include, usually with complications or embarrassment
lecture, speech
loyal, faithful
map, a representation of a part or of the whole of the earth's surface
mean, signify
million, 1,000,000
minister, clergyman
mist, fog
notorious, well known for a bad reason
novel, unfamiliar; a long piece of prose fiction
outspoken, frank, unreserved in speech
overhear, hear without the speaker's intention or knowledge
overreach, reach too far
parent, father or mother
particular, excessively careful; special
pathetic, causing pity

pension, allowance, periodic payment
plump, somewhat fat
popular, favorite, liked by many people
positive, sure, confident
primitive, of an early era or development
principal, chief
process, series of related actions; procedure
realize, understand
record, register, put down in writing
reform school, prison for young criminals
response, answer
résumé, summary
schmaltz, excessive sentimentality
self-conscious, excessively aware of oneself, with embarrassment
sensible, intelligent; reasonable
serious, sincere; important
so, therefore
solid, not hollow; without a break
spiritual, pertaining to the soul
suite, set of rooms; kind of musical composition
sympathy, sharing another's feeling, usually sorrow
undertaker, one who prepares a dead person for burial
wagon, four-wheeled vehicle, usually drawn by horses
will, be going to

3. Some cognates are deceptive in pronunciation, particularly as to the location of stress. A list of them is given in § Stress—Word.

4. The number of English words whose spelling is similar to that of their cognates in other languages, particularly French and Spanish, is almost infinite. A great number of them are listed in § Spelling—Words Frequently Misspelled.

COLON

C.9

1. A colon (:) is like an equals sign (=): what follows the colon is equal to one or more words before the colon. It indicates an elucidation or explanation. It is very often used before a list.

> The countries which participated in the conference were the following: Peru, Yugoslavia, Jordan, and Greece.
> Directions: Copy the following sentence, adding necessary commas.
> Something must be disturbing Jules: he seems a little despondent.

Also, see § Appositive and § Clause—Independent and Adverbial.

2. The colon is used after the salutation in a formal or business letter.

> My dear Mr. Lansdowne: Dear Sir:

3. The colon is used in writing clock time.

> 9:20 a.m.   1:05 p.m.

The even hours are customarily written out.

> I woke up this morning at nine o'clock although I usually get up at seven.

4. The colon is used to introduce a long, formal quotation. The quoted passage is set off from the rest of the writing by indention on both the left and the right side, and no quotation marks are used. Also, see §Quotation Mark.

> Writing in *The Decline and Fall of the Roman Empire,* Edward Gibbon observed:
>
> > The various modes of worship which prevailed in the Roman world were all considered by the people as equally true; by the philosopher, as equally false; and by the magistrate, as equally useful.

COMMA   C.10

The following is a summary of the uses of the comma. Some of the rules given here are not observed by all writers, but if you follow all the rules, your writing will be consistent and clear.

1. The purpose of punctuation is to help your reader understand the expression of your thought. The use of both too little and too much punctuation can defeat that purpose.

2. In general, use a comma as a signal of interference in the customary word order of a clause: in effect, the comma says that the preceding word or group and the following word or group do not have a customary word-order relationship.

On the other hand, do not put a comma between two parts of a clause which have their customary relative positions. The customary word order of the parts of a clause is outlined in detail in § Word Order—Clause. Here is a simplified version of the diagram: conjunction + transposed + complement + subject + simple predicate + complement.

I will begin with negative rules. These have to do with the customary word order of the parts of a clause. Under the rules I will point out related rules for commas or other punctuation.

3. Do not set off a conjunction, particularly *but* and *although,* with a following comma.

> I called Jim, but   he did not hear me.
> Although   Sue works hard, she is not learning very fast.
> Sue is not learning very fast although   she works hard.

4. Do not put a comma between a subject and its verb.

> The speaker's statement   astounded the audience.
> What the speaker said   astounded the audience.

5. Do not put a comma between a verb and its complement.

> The boy asked   if he might leave.
> What   did Robert say?
> Burton remained   loyal for the rest of his life.

a. The exception to this rule occurs with a dialog guide, which has a direct quotation as its complement. Remember that commas come before the quotation marks.

> The boy asked, "May I leave now?"
> "Certainly," his father answered.
> "If you come in late," his mother added, "be sure to lock the door."

b. Do not put a period at the end of a quotation if the dialog guide follows.

> "I'll be back before you go to bed," the boy replied.

c. If an exclamation mark or a question mark precedes the dialog guide, do not use a comma.

> "May I leave now?" the boy asked.
> "Certainly!" his father answered.

6. Do not use a comma before a coordinating conjunction joining two parallel parts within an independent clause. In other words, do not separate a pair of words, phrases, or dependent clauses joined by *and, but, or,* or *nor.* Also, see § Parallelism.

> The two boys   and their father stood in the doorway.
> Their voices were low   but clear.
> Neither the men   nor their wives were happy about the result.
> You can keep your promise   or resign your position.
> Do not make any noise when you leave   or when you come back.

a. Use a comma between coordinate adjectives which are not joined by a coordinating conjunction. The positions of the coordinate adjectives may be reversed, or *and* may be used instead of the comma.

The girl brushed her sleek, glistening hair.
The girl brushed her glistening, sleek hair.
The girl brushed her sleek and glistening hair.
Their house has a spacious, comfortable living room.
Their house has a comfortable, spacious living room.
Their house has a spacious and comfortable living room.

b. Use a comma before the repetition of an adjective or an adverb. Such a repetition usually indicates emphasis.

Long, long ago an old, old man told a story.

7. Do not use commas in a series of three or more words, phrases, or dependent clauses if each member of the series is joined to the next by a coordinating conjunction.

The barn was dark   and warm   and damp.
Louis walked in the front entrance   and through the house   and out the back door.
That man will not hurry when he is working   or when he is eating   or when he is resting.

a. Use a comma between the members if there is only one coordinating conjunction in the series, and put a comma before the coordinating conjunction, which comes before the last member.

The barn was dark, warm, and damp.
Louis walked in the front entrance, through the house, and out the back door.
That man will not hurry when he is working, when he is eating, or when he is resting.

b. Treat a closely related pair like a unit in a series.

Alec is mixed up on nouns and pronouns, adjectives and adverbs, and prepositions and conjunctions.
Men seemed to Rachel to be either too young and inexperienced   or too old and tired.

c. Use a comma before the abbreviation *etc.* Do not use *and* before *etc.*

Vegetables are beans, peas, carrots, etc.

Now follow two uses of a comma to denote the completion of an independent clause.

8. Put a comma before the coordinating conjunctions *and, but, for, or,* and *nor* joining two independent clauses. The comma tells your reader that he has finished one complete clause and is beginning another.

His mother looked at him for a moment, and his father smiled.
The room was dark, but there was a grayness at the window.

a. Use a semicolon between two independent clauses which are not but could be joined by *and, but, or,* or *nor.*

> His mother looked at him for a moment; his father smiled.
> The room was dark; however, there was a grayness at the window.
> Vic had worked hard all day; he was tired, and he wanted to go home.

b. Use a colon between two independent clauses which are not but could be joined by *for.*

> Lila did not answer: she did not trust her voice.

9. Use a comma to set off a *question tag* from the rest of the independent clause. A question tag signals that the preceding clause is a question.

> I can't go, eh?
> That's good, huh?

A question tag is often composed of an auxiliary and a personal pronoun, which are related to the subject and simple predicate of the independent clause.

> Ivan didn't take it, did he?
> You will come tonight, won't you?
> Those boys know that they're wrong, don't they?

Here are the rules for words or groups which are outside or break into the customary word order of a clause.

10. Use commas to separate interjections from the rest of the sentence.

> *Yes,* that is correct.
> *Well,* I must be leaving.
> *Say,* what have you got there?
> I want to go to the party, but, *goodness gracious,* I haven't got anything to wear.

a. If an interjection expresses strong feeling, use an exclamation mark instead of a comma after it.

> Ouch! That hurt.
> Hurrah! We won.

11. Use commas to set off vocatives—that is, names or equivalents of persons addressed—from the rest of the sentence.

> *Mother,* may I leave now
> That, *my dear,* is up to Father.
> What do you think he will say to me, *Mr. Graham?*

a. Use a comma after the salutation in an informal letter.

> Dear John,
>   Your letter arrived this morning. . . .

b. Use a colon after the salutation in a formal or business letter.

> My dear Mr. Jackson:
>   In reply to your letter of August 15. . . .

12. Use commas to set off transition words or phrases from the rest of the sentence.

> The course is very interesting. *However,* the reading is heavy.

13. Use commas to set off *opinion-expressing* clauses such as *I think* when they come within or at the end of the sentence.

> You, I believe, are the best person for the position.
> Education is a wonderful thing, you know.
> Mr. Pickwick, it appeared, was no man to trifle with.

14. Use commas to set off opinion-expressing phrases such as "according to him (Mr. Richards, etc.)" and "in his (my, etc.) opinion" and "needless to say" and "what is worse."

> That, in my opinion, was a shameful thing to do.
> According to Gertrude, everything was going to be all right.
> The candidate's speech was full of platitudes, needless to say.

15. Use a comma to set off an *opinion-asking* formula such as *do you guess* when it comes at the end of the clause.

> What will happen next, do you suppose?
> Will she do that, do you think?

a. No commas are used if the opinion-asking formula follows a *wh* word or phrase within the clause.

> What   do you suppose   will happen next?

16. Use commas to set off a title or degree following a personal name.

> Johnson's predecessor was William Nolan, Jr.
> George Thompson, LL.D., wrote the preface to the final volume.

17. Use commas to set off a nonrestrictive ("nonidentifying") adjectival clause. Notice that such a clause is similar in function to a title or degree following a name in that it gives additional information about the word or group it modifies.

> Mr. Plant's wife, who had been listening silently, suddenly spoke.

18. Use commas to set off a nonrestrictive appositive which does not have internal punctuation. Such an appositive is similar in function to an adjectival clause. In writing, a nonrestrictive appositive sometimes precedes the word or group it is in apposition to.

> Betty's father, a strict disciplinarian, governed his family through fear.
> A strict disciplinarian, Betty's father governed his family through fear.

> Mr. Trollope wrote a long article about Jack Dempsey, the heavyweight boxing champion in the early twenties.
> My vacation begins next Tuesday, when I will leave for Florida.

a. Use a comma after an introductory word for an appositive or an example (e.g., *namely* and *for example*). The entire appositive or example is marked off with dashes or parentheses.

> The instigator of the plot—namely, Vega—was executed.
> Certain English words (for example, *climb, debt,* and *subtle*) have an unpronounced *b.*

b. Do not use a comma after words like *especially, chiefly,* and *particularly* when they introduce an addition.

> I hate to get up early, particularly on Sunday.

19. Use commas to set off a nonrestrictive participial phrase used adjectivally or adverbially.

> Bored with his work, he thought of going home early.
> The minister, shaking his head, stood up and departed.
> He walked slowly, stopping frequently to rest.

20. Use commas to set off an adjective or adjectival group which is not in one of the customary positions of adjectives. Participles and participial phrases are often put in such a position.

> Angry, the composer refused to say another word.
> Smiling, her father handed Irene the package.
> Accused of a crime he had not committed, Seymour reacted violently.
> The winner, hot and tired, was in no mood for speeches.
> "Why is that?" Mr. Williams asked, astonished.

All the remaining rules for commas serve the purpose of preventing misinterpretation or confusion.

21. Use a comma to separate the day of the week from the day of the month and the day of the month from the year.

> Richard was born on Friday, May 10, 1957.
> The inspection was made again on July 18, 1961.

a. If only the month and the year are given, the comma may be omitted.

> War broke out in September   ,   1939.
> War broke out in September   1939.

b. Do not put a comma in the year.

> Hopkins was traveling through Belgium in 1959.

22. Put commas between units in an address or location.

Mr. Peterson lives in Apartment 2B, 511 West Tenth Street.
My class meets in Room 422, Sterling Hall.
James comes from Portland, Maine.

a. When an address is arranged on separate lines, as on an envelope, a comma is not needed at the end of a line.

Dr. William Quesenberry	Mr. Joseph E. Daniels
Office of the Registrar	817 Woodlawn Drive
315 University Hall	New Zion 8, N.J.
Peterson College	
Desdemona 27, N.Y.	

b. Do not put a comma in the street number or between the street number and name.

The bookstore is at 2960   Broadway.
I am going to 427   Park Street.

c. Do not put a comma between the city and the zone number, but do put a comma between the zone number and the state.

Baltimore 32, Md.

23. Put a comma after digits indicating thousands, millions, and billions in sums with more than four digits.

There were 18,298 specimens in the box.
The total attendance was 3,182,759 persons.

a. A comma may be used or omitted in a sum with four digits.

The store sold 1,872 dresses in one month.
The store sold 1872 dresses in one month.

b. A period is used to indicate a decimal in a sum. No commas are used to the right of the decimal period.

The square root of 14 is 3.7416574.

24. Use a comma after an introductory adjectival or adverbial construction containing a verb form. Notice that this rule is a partial restatement of the rules in ¶ 19 and ¶ 20.

Noticing Dr. Clark's impatience, I said goodby quickly.
After having gone that far, George did not want to turn back.
In order to operate, a car has to have gasoline.
To be a doctor, one must go to school for many years.
To tell you the truth, I was very frightened.

25. Use a comma or commas to set off an adverbial clause that is not at the end of the clause it belongs to.

> When the bell rings, go to your next class.
> Although Peter had tried hard, he failed to win a prize.
> Black's speech, though he read it fervently, made no impression.
> George's response, when I questioned him, was a shake of his head.

a. If the adverbial clause immediately follows a conjunction, use a comma only at the end of the adverbial clause.

> I want you to play *because*   when you do, I feel relaxed.
> If you like me, you will go away, *and*   if you love me, you will stay away.

26. Use commas to set off an *absolute phrase*. An absolute phrase is a modifier, either adjectival or adverbial, which is composed of a noun or pronoun or noun phrase followed by a participle or a prepositional phrase.

> *All things considered,* I am glad we lost.
> Paul arose, *his hat in his hand.*

27. Use commas to set off "generalizing" or "summarizing" expressions such as *after all, in brief, in effect, in general, as a general rule,* and *on the whole.* Most of them would be sources of ambiguity if the commas were not used.

> After all, the men had done their best.
> Houses, on the whole, are necessities.
> Mr. Pope's remarks were, in general, pertinent.

28. Use a comma to separate an introductory word or construction if the sentence might be misread or hard to read without the commas.

> From April on, the calendar will have pictures of outdoor scenes.

However, do not overuse this rule. For instance, introductory adverbial expressions of place and time seldom need a comma. Two major uses for the rule are the following:

a. Put a comma between a transposed complement ending with a proper name and a subject beginning with a proper name.

> To John, Henry was an idol.

b. Put a comma between an introductory *-ly* adverb modifying the whole clause and a following word or group which that adverb might be incorrectly taken to modify.

> Unfortunately, small countries tend to be dominated by big countries.

29. The following final rule is a warning: do not use a comma for a period, question mark, semicolon, or colon. Such a use is called a *comma fault* or a *comma splice.*

> You stay here. I won't be gone long.

Wake up. It's half-past eight.
Where is the postman? Why hasn't he come?
Some people like to watch wrestling on television; others prefer plays.
I could not see the horses: the trees hid them from my sight.
We had a valuable custom in our high school: the teachers took us on a long
trip every year.

COMPARISON C.11

1. The three degrees of comparison in English are shown in the following examples:

a. The simple degree: John is *as studious as* Bill.

b. The comparative degree: John is *more studious than* Henry.

c. The superlative degree: Saul is *the most studious* of all the boys.

2. If the simple degree is preceded by a negative word, *so* is often used in place of the first *as.* However, *as* is all right.

Henry is not so studious as John.	No other boy is so studious as Saul.
Henry is not as studious as John.	No other boy is as studious as Saul.

3. The first *as* in the simple-degree construction is sometimes omitted in poetry for metrical purposes.

A poem [no *as*] lovely as a tree—KILMER

However, you should not omit that *as* in your customary writing.

4. Be sure to spell *than* correctly. Do not confuse it with the different word *then.*

5. After the superlative, the word *of* occurs very frequently. However, the word *in* is used with an expression of place. Also, see § Intensifier.

Robert is the most studious of all the boys.
Robert is the most studious in the class.

6. Most words of one syllable add *-er* for the comparative and *-est* for the superlative, and they are not preceded by the words *more* or *most.*

Godfrey is younger than Frank.	Egbert is the smartest boy in my class.
Hugh works harder than Fritz.	Nathan works the hardest of all.

7. Two-syllable words which end in *-y* and *-ow* usually add *-er* and *-est* and are not preceded by *more* or *most.* Two-syllable words which end in *-le* add *-r* and *-st* and are not preceded by *more* and *most.* For the spelling of the comparative and superlative forms of words whose simple form ends in *-y,* see Rule 4 in § Spelling —Words with Suffix.

Forty-Third Street is narrower than Broadway.
The sick man had the yellowest face I had ever seen.
Brutus was the noblest Roman.
Jasper is the laziest man in the world.
The man is even busier than he was yesterday.
Gladys gets up earlier than I do.

8. Most other words have *more* for the comparative and *most* for the superlative.

Jasper is the most unindustrious man in the world.
The man is even more occupied than he was yesterday.

9. A few words have irregular comparative and superlative forms. Those forms are not preceded by *more* or *most*.

SIMPLE	COMPARATIVE	SUPERLATIVE
bad	worse	worst
badly	worse	worst
good	better	best
well	better	best
far	farther, further	farthest, furthest
little	less	least
much	more	most
many	more	most

Julia writes as badly as her brother. She writes worse than her sister.
Tom spends as little money as he can. He spends less than any other person.

a. *Much* is used with uncountable and mass words, which are grammatically singular, and *many* is used with plural words. *Little, less,* and *least* are similarly used with singulars, and *few, fewer,* and *fewest* are used with plurals. See § *Many* vs. *Much* and § *Few* vs. *A Few.*

Cy bought as much bread as he could. He bought as many loaves as he could.
Even though I have fewer classes, I have less time than I used to.

More meaning "additional" occurs after both *many* and *much.*

There is not much more time before our vacation.
There are not many more days before our vacation.

b. The word *far* has two comparative forms—*farther* and *further*—and two superlative forms—*farthest* and *furthest.* Although many people make no distinction between the two alternatives, some people use *farther* and *farthest* in expressions of physical distance and *further* and *furthest* in all other kinds of expressions. Only *further* is used with the meaning of "additional."

Stephen ran farther than Philip.
Marcia sat in the farthest corner.
Mr. Carter will investigate further.
His answer was the furthest from the truth.
I will send you further details.
Have you anything further to say?

10. Comparison is shown by the words *alike, different, equal, inferior, like, same, similar, superior,* and *the way.* The verb *prefer* also is used to indicate comparison.

a. The word *same* is preceded by *the. As* is used before the second member of the comparison.

> Mary got the same grade as Henry.
> Mary and Henry got the same grade.
> Mary's and Henry's grades were the same.

b. The word *like* is used before the second member of a comparison. Grammatically, it is a preposition, and the second member is its object.

> Irving's book is like mine.   Sam talks like his father.
> My brother looks like me.   Like his father, Sam speaks well.

c. The word *alike* is used after verbs.

> Our books are alike.
> My brother and I look alike.
> Sam and his father talk alike.

d. The words *the way* and *as* are used before a subject and a verb.

> Sam talks the way his father does.
> That pie tastes sweet, the way [*or* as] a dessert should.
> Don't do as I do.

e. The word *different* usually has *from* before the second member of the comparison. Some people use *than* instead of *from.* I recommend that you use *from.*

> Norman's voice is different from his father's.

f. The words *equal, inferior, junior, prior, senior, similar,* and *superior* have *to* before the second member of the comparison.

> Harry's strength is equal to his brother's.
> Jennie's paintings were judged inferior to Wanda's.
> Will's voice is similar to his father's.
> The Crawfords think they are superior to other people.

g. The verb *prefer* also has *to* before the second member of the comparison.

> I prefer reading books to watching television.

In the above example *to* is a "true preposition," but notice that *to* may be part of the infinitive form of a verb following *prefer:*

> I prefer to read books rather than watch television.

Also, see § *Rather* and § Preposition—Expression with.

11. The set expression "as good as" means "virtually; practically; nearly."

> That used car is as good as new.
> The office boy does not know it, but he is as good as fired right now.

12. The comparative degree is sometimes shown as in the following examples. Notice the use of the articles *the* and *a.*

> Frederick is the taller of Mrs. Ross's two sons.
> Henry has a more nervous way of speaking than James.
> I have never read a more interesting book.

13. The pattern "*the* (comparative) . . . , *the* (comparative) . . ." occurs frequently and involves two comparative constructions. The first comparative construction states a condition, and the second comparative construction states its result. Notice the position of the comparatives and the punctuation.

> The longer you work, the more you will earn.
> The sooner Lester gets started, the sooner he will finish.
> The farther the explorers walked, the more confused they got.
> The more the teacher talked, the less I understood.
> The more courses you take, the more hours you will have to study.
> The more beautiful a girl is, the more necessary it is for her to appear intelligent.

One instance of that pattern is expressed in four words:

> The more, the merrier. ["The more people there are, the merrier the party will be."]

14. *Any, much,* and *no* often modify adjectives and adverbs in the comparative degree. *Any* occurs in questions or with negatives. Also, see § Intensifier.

> Is Hugh doing any better in his class?
> He is working much harder than he used to.
> I can expect no more effort from him.

15. .The superlative degree occurs very frequently after the words *one of, some of,* and so forth. The superlative construction with countable nouns is grammatically plural.

> Paul is one of the nicest boys I know.
> One of my most horrifying experiences was in an airplane.
> Sarah lived in one of the most crowded sections in the city.
> New York and Boston are two of the busiest seaports in the world.

a. If the subject of a following clause refers to the plural superlative construction, the verb in that clause is also plural.

> Mr. Blake is one of the best teachers that have ever been in this school.
> That teacher is one of the best that have ever been in this school.

b. If the subject of a following clause refers to the *one* before the superlative construction, then the verb in that clause is singular.

> Rachel was the only one of the youngest girls who was afraid to go.

16. Be sure to use enough words to make the comparison clear. The italicized words in the following examples are needed to prevent possible misunderstanding.

Mr. Tracy likes his dog better than his wife *does.*
Mr. Tracy likes his dog better than *he does* his wife.
Herbert studies harder than any *other* student in the class.
Professor Graham prefers Shakespeare to any *other* writer.
Myra's voice is as sweet as *that of* a bird.
Myra's voice is as sweet as a bird*'s.*

17. Do not use *more* or *-er* for *most* or *-est* in a superlative construction.

Of my three courses, history requires the most reading.

18. Put an adverb of comparison after a direct object.

I like New York better than Boston.
Leo likes history best of all studies.
Ada wanted wealth more than health.
Dot kept the ring longer than the pin.
Francis recited the poem the most clearly of all the students.

Also, see § Adjective vs. Adverb, § Clause—Independent and Adverbial, and § Word Order—Emphatic Adverb.

COMPLEMENT   C.12

1. *Complement* is the term used to refer to the word or words which complete the grammatical construction of a verb. A complement may include objects, a predicate nominative, and one or more modifiers.

Louis saw Sylvia. [*Sylvia* is the complement to *saw;* it is the direct object.]
I gave him money. [*Him money* is the complement to *gave; him* is the indirect object, and *money* is the direct object.]
The group elected Alfred chairman. [*Alfred chairman* is the complement to *elected; Alfred* is the direct object, and *chairman* is the predicate objective.]
My closest friend was Robert. [*Robert* is the complement to *was;* it is the predicate nominative.]
Simpson works slowly. [*Slowly* is the complement; it is an adverb modifying *works.*]
Alice is young. [*Young* is the complement to *is;* it is a predicate adjective.]

Also, see the sections in this book on the different types of complements and on word order, particularly § Word Order—Adverb Modifying Verb and § Word Order—Clause.

COMPOSITION   C.13

Following are general guides to writing of compositions. If your teacher gives you different ones, follow his.

1. Type or write in ink.

2. Use large (8½ by 11 inches) notebook paper, with lines if you write in ink, without lines if you type.

3. Have the wide, unlined margin at the top.

4. Write your name in the upper right corner.

5. Write the title of the composition on the first line, not below the first line.

6. Space the title so that it is in the center of the first line.

7. Try to make the title brief, accurate, and interesting.

8. In the title, capitalize the first and last words and all other words except short prepositions, conjunctions, and articles (*a, an, the*).

9. Do not put quotation marks around the title.

10. Do not underline the title.

11. Do not print the title.

12. Do not put a period at the end of the title.

13. Use a question mark at the end of the title if the title is a question.

14. Skip a line between the title and the body of the composition.

15. Indent the first word of each paragraph.

16. At the beginning of the composition, do not refer to the title with words such as *it, this, that, these, those,* or *such a thing.* The title is not part of the body of the composition, and you are supposed to pretend that the title is not at the top.

17. Leave a margin on each side of the page. If the left side has a ruled line, write up to that.

18. Write on alternate lines of the paper so that the teacher may have space for corrections and comments. Write on every line when you copy a corrected composition.

19. Do not divide words at the end of a line. The rules of syllabication are complicated, and you do not need to memorize them. If you do divide a word, put a hyphen at the end of the first line. Do not put a hyphen at the beginning of the next line.

20. Write complete sentences. Later on, when you have mastered sentence structure, you can write sentence fragments naturally and effectively.

21. Draw a line through mistakes. Do not use parentheses to indicate that a word should be canceled.

22. Make each composition at least two pages in length unless you are instructed otherwise. You may write on the back if the paper is thick. Do not write or type on the back if the words show through.

23. Write as legibly as possible. Remember that you are writing something to be read by somebody else.

COMPOSITION TOPIC   C.14

Here is a list of composition topics. These are topics, not titles; try to make your title short, accurate, and attractive to your reader. The first topics are grouped according to the verb forms that you will probably use most often in the composition.

PRESENT
1. Your usual day
2. Your hobby
3. Your present job
4. Your pet economy
5. The thing you dislike most of all
6. Your home, apartment, or room
7. Your home town
8. Saturday afternoon in your home town
9. A holiday
10. Your favorite animal
11. The problems of an only child
12. Your big (little) brother (sister)
13. Your father's favorite sayings
14. Your father's sense of humor
15. Are summer camps good for children?
16. Do children need discipline?
17. Are murder mysteries (detective stories) bad for children?
18. The causes of juvenile delinquency
19. Why you are in school
20. Your favorite subject (teacher, classmate) at school
21. What education means to you
22. Are examinations necessary?
23. Government aid to education
24. Life in a college dormitory
25. Differences between high school and college

26. The importance of sports in college
27. Education outside the class room
28. Your best friend
29. Your worst enemy
30. An interesting person you know
31. The strangest person you know
32. A character in fiction that you would like to meet
33. Who makes the best cars?
34. Are used cars good?
35. Traffic problems
36. Traffic cops are nuisances
37. Your feeling about outdoor advertising
38. The best kind of vacation
39. Why you like (do not like) television
40. What makes a good movie?
41. Popular music versus classical music
42. Milk versus wine
43. Hospital insurance—Federal or private
44. Small towns versus big towns
45. The high cost of living

PAST
46. A frightening experience
47. Your most embarrassing moment
48. Your first date

49. How you met your wife (husband, sweetheart)
50. Your biggest surprise
51. What you did last weekend
52. An untrue story you told
53. Your most interesting trip
54. Your first long trip
55. An important event in your life
56. A punishment you deserved
57. One time when you were misunderstood
58. A misconception
59. Why you decided to come to this school or city
60. The most important event in history
61. A famous inventor (musician, statesman, etc.)
62. A great man
63. A famous woman
64. A folk tale
65. The most unforgettable character in your childhood
66. A story or incident you think could be made into a play or movie
67. A movie or play you enjoyed (did not enjoy)
68. A case of injustice

FUTURE

69. The world in the year 2000
70. What will probably happen in the next six months
71. Things you intend to do
72. What you will probably do tomorrow
73. Your plans for a vacation
74. Your plans for next weekend (next year)
75. Your greatest ambition
76. The plans you have for your children or your grandchildren

SHOULD OR IMPERATIVE

77. How to be a good tourist
78. Travel tips
79. An efficient kitchen
80. How to bake a cake (a pie, etc.: recipe and instructions)
81. How to make a model airplane (a kite, etc.: instructions)
82. The proper colors for rooms
83. Students should be dignified
84. Should married women work outside the home?
85. Should young adults serve in the armed forces?

CONDITIONAL

86. If you had a million dollars
87. If you had three wishes
88. If you governed the world
89. If you had not come to this school
90. If you knew you had only two weeks to live
91. If there were no elevators
92. If the wheel had not been invented
93. If there were another Ice Age
94. What the Americas would be like right now if Columbus or somebody else had not discovered them
95. How you would teach English
96. How you would keep peace in the world
97. What you would say if you dared to be completely frank
98. What you would have done if you had been elsewhere this past Christmas (Easter, New Year's, etc.)
99. The changes you would make in this city
100. What you would be doing if you were not writing this composition
101. If you were the last person alive
102. What would happen if we lost all our mechanical devices

DIRECT AND INDIRECT SPEECH

103. The first conversation you remember
104. A conversation you had this morning
105. A conversation you overheard

126

106. An imaginary dialog between two famous persons
107. An argument you had or overheard
108. An interview for a job
109. What you would tell a person who is going abroad for the first time

MISCELLANEOUS

These are on very broad subjects. If you write on one of these, you should limit the topic: you should discuss a small, specific aspect of it.

110. Family
111. Home life
112. Childhood
113. Friends
114. Neighbors
115. Enemies
116. Memories
117. Ambitions
118. Personal habits
119. Education
120. University education
121. Studying
122. Fraternities or sororities
123. Manners
124. Customs
125. Social classes
126. Marriage and divorce
127. Race prejudice
128. Clothes
129. Religion
130. Holidays
131. Attitudes
132. Ways of thinking
133. Language
134. Amusements
135. Hobbies
136. Avocations
137. Reading
138. Sports
139. Nature
140. Radio
141. Television
142. Movies
143. Plays
144. Publications
145. Organizations
146. Business
147. Mass production
148. Labor relations
149. Atomic energy
150. Working conditions
151. Labor laws and regulations
152. Advertising
153. Civic problems
154. Government policies
155. Nationalism
156. Censorship
157. The Supreme Court
158. The Constitution
159. Foreigners
160. Going abroad
161. Tourists
162. Transportation
163. Animals
164. Farming
165. Food
166. Health
167. Medicine
168. Money
169. Weather
170. Satellites
171. Planets
172. Science fiction

CONDITIONAL SENTENCE

C.15

1. Verb forms express many concepts other than time. For one instance, the *-s* inflection of the third person singular of the present tense expresses agreement with the subject (e.g., "*He* sing*s*"). For another instance, in the operation of sequence of tense the past forms in dependent clauses express relationship with the main verb (e.g., "He *said* he *would* go tomorrow"). For a third instance, verb forms express reality or unreality. The expression of the last two concepts by verb forms is seen most clearly in conditional sentences.

C

2. A conditional sentence is an utterance (proposition) expressing a result expected from a condition, proviso, or requirement. In the *opinion* of the maker of the proposition, the proposition is either *real* or *unreal*. The maker expresses his opinion by means of the verb forms he uses.

There are many ways of constructing a conditional sentence, but only four of the most frequent ways are described in detail in the next few paragraphs. Each condition is stated in a clause beginning with the word *if*.

3. If the maker of the proposition believes that the proposition is possible or is likely to be fulfilled, he will probably use the following pattern:

Pattern 1   real, present

CONDITION	RESULT
a. If John hurries,	he will catch the bus.
b. If all students are serious,	their teachers are happy.
c. If the judge asks you,	tell him the truth.

4. Notice that the verb in the result may be future (*a*), present (*b*), or imperative (*c*). Nevertheless, each *if* clause has the present-tense verb form. We can say that the *time* of the whole proposition is *present* because the maker believes **right now** in the validity of the statement.

5. If the maker of the proposition feels that the proposition is not possible or is not likely to be fulfilled, he will probably use the following pattern:

Pattern 2   unreal, present

CONDITION	RESULT
a. If John hurried,	he would catch the bus.
b. If all students were serious,	their teachers would be happy.

6. Notice that *would* is used in the result and the simple-past verb form is used in the *if* clause. (Example *c* of Pattern 1 can not be shifted into an unreality.) We can say that the time of the whole proposition is present because the maker does not believe right now in the validity of the statement: he believes that it is impossible or unlikely that John will hurry, and he believes that not all students are serious.

7. A mnemonic aid that may be useful is this:

For Pattern 1: If something *is* possible in the opinion of the maker, the present-tense form *is* used in the *if* clause. The result may be either present or future.

For Pattern 2: If something *is not* possible in the opinion of the maker, the present-tense verb form *is not* used in the *if* clause: the verb form is shifted to the past form. The result has *would* + the uninflected form of a verb.

8. To express a proposition that was real in the past, the same relationship in the verb forms is used:

Pattern 3   real, past

CONDITION	RESULT
a. If John hurried,	he caught the bus.
b. If all students were serious,	their teachers were happy.

128

9. In Pattern 3, according to the maker, the proposition was fulfilled or had the possibility of fulfillment: in *a*, it was very likely that John did hurry; in *b*, all students were serious. (In *b*, the *if* could be replaced by *when* or *whenever*, but the sentence then would not be conditional.)

10. To express a proposition that was not real in the past, the verb forms are very special:

Pattern 4   unreal, past

CONDITION	RESULT
a. If John had hurried,	he would have caught the bus.
b. If all students had been serious,	their teachers would have been happy.

11. Notice that *have* is the second of the three verbs in the result in Pattern 4.

12. In Pattern 4, according to the maker, the proposition was not fulfilled or had no possibility of fulfillment: John did not hurry, and not all students were serious.

13. A mnemonic aid for the past propositions is this:
For Pattern 3: Use the simple-past tense for both verbs to show reality in the past.

For Pattern 4: Since the simple-past tense is used to show reality in the past, it can not be used to show unreality in the past; therefore, shift the verb form in the *if* clause to the more distant verb form (the past perfect: *had* + the past participle), and use *would have* + the past participle in the result.

14. A diagram outlining the verb forms in the four patterns is this:

OPINION	CONDITION		RESULT	
	PRESENT TIME	PAST TIME	PRESENT	PAST
Real	Present form	Past form	Future form Present form Imperative form	Past form
Unreal	Past form	Past perfect form	Past future form	Past future-perfect form

15. For illustration, we can fill in the places of the diagram with forms of the verb *study* in the condition and with forms of the verb *learn* in the result:

OPINION	CONDITION		RESULT	
	PRESENT TIME	PAST TIME	PRESENT	PAST
Real	study	studied	will learn learn(s) learn	learned
Unreal	studied	had studied	would learn	would have learned

Now consider the following sentences with those forms of *study* and *learn.*

> If you study, you will learn.
> If students study every day, they learn a lot.
> If you study, learn [= remember what you read].
> If you studied last night, you learned something. [I am sure of that.]
> If you studied, you would learn. [I think you do not study.]
> If you had studied last night, you would have learned something. [You did not study; therefore, you did not learn.]

16. Here are your punctuation rules for conditional sentences:

a. If the condition precedes the result, put a comma after the condition.

b. Do not use a comma if the condition follows the result.

17. For Pattern 2, the verb *be* has *were* for all persons, both singular and plural, in the *if* clause.

> If I were you, I would study hard.
> If Ann were invited, she would go.
> Alfred would tell you the truth if he were here.

18. Here are some examples of conditional sentences; the number of the pattern is given in the parentheses. Notice that the *if* clause may come before or after the result.

> If it rains tomorrow, the streets will be wet. (1)
> I would buy a car immediately if I had a lot of money. (2)
> If you meant to say that, I misunderstood you. (3)
> You would have seen the parade if you had come earlier. (4)
> If another war comes, many people will be killed. (1)
> There was no cure for a person if he got typhus in the Middle Ages. (3)
> If anybody calls, ask him to leave his telephone number. (1)
> Mother would have baked a cake if she had known in advance about your arrival. (4)
> If you buy a car, you have to get a license. (1)
> Dan said he was going to the party, but if he was there, I did not see him. (3)
> If it is cold tomorrow, we will postpone our trip. (1)
> A man does not have any money if he is poor. (1)
> If you had been born two hundred years ago, you would have lived in the eighteenth century. (4)
> I was always able to get my former teacher angry if I explained a rule in my own words. (3)
> If you try, you will succeed. (1)
> I did not hear William if he said that. (3)

Now I will go into some additions to the four basic patterns. However, you should try to understand the basic patterns thoroughly before proceeding further.

19. If the condition comes first, then the result frequently begins with the word *then.* Put a comma before but not after the *then.*

> If you believe that, then you are mistaken.

20. A condition may cover two or more results.

> If I were you, I would not work so hard, and I would get more sleep.
> If I had a million dollars, I would do a lot of things. I would. . . .

21. Patterns 1 and 3 may be combined. For instance, the *if* clause may express past reality, and the result may express present or future reality.

> (3) If Paul mailed the letter yesterday, (1) it will be delivered tomorrow.
> (1) I am sorry   (3) if I made Cy unhappy last night.

22. Patterns 2 and 4 may be combined. For instance, the *if* clause may express past unreality, and the result may express present or future unreality.

> (4) If Paul had received six more votes in the last election, (2) he would be our present chairman.
> (2) Sue would be alive today   (4) if the doctor had come sooner last night.
> (2) I would go on a vacation next month   (4) if I had earned some money last summer.

23. Sequence of tense operates in dependent clauses which are part of the condition or the result.

> I would not worry if I knew right now that I *were* not going to live much longer.
> If Anthony had been asked, he would have said that he *could* not go tomorrow.

The *were* in the first example illustrates the operation of sequence of tense: the past form *were* is used because of the influence of the past form *knew;* the verb *were* is used instead of *was* because of the influence of the *if* condition (see ¶ 17 above). (The clause "that I *were* not going to live much longer" is a noun clause of condition beginning with *if* and ending with *longer.*) Similarly, the *could* in the second example shows the influence of the past form *would have said.*

24. The operation of sequence of tense may change the verb forms in indirect speech.

Pattern 1	Mary said,	"If John *hurries,* he *will catch* the bus."
	Mary said that if John *hurried,* he *would catch* the bus.	
Pattern 2	Mary said,	"If John *hurried,* he *would catch* the bus."
	Mary said that if John *had hurried,* he *would have caught* the bus.	
Pattern 3	Mary said,	"If John *hurried,* he *caught* the bus."
	Mary said that if John *had hurried,* he *had caught* the bus.	
Pattern 4	Mary said,	"If John *had hurried,* he *would have caught* the bus."
	Mary said that if John *had hurried,* he *would have caught* the bus.	

As you can see, the conversion causes the verb forms of Patterns 1 and 2 in indirect speech to be the same as those of Patterns 2 and 4 in direct speech. No change occurs in the conversion of Pattern 4.

25. An imperative in direct speech is converted to an infinitive form in indirect speech. See § Direct vs. Indirect Speech for further details.

> Mr. Sams said, "*Give* me the answer if you know it, Mary."
> Mr. Sams told Mary *to give* him the answer if she knew it.

26. Other auxiliaries besides *will* and *would* may be used in conditional sentences. Generally you will have no problems with them except with *should*. In the following paragraphs I will discuss *should* and some uses of other auxiliaries in conditional sentences.

27. The auxiliary *should* may be used in the *if* clause to express future possibility with a degree of doubt. In this use, *should* does not imply obligation as it sometimes does. The result may have either *will* or *would*.

> If Mr. Lawrence should call, what will you say?
> If Mr. Lawrence should call, what would you say?

28. Do not use *should* as the equivalent of *would* in the result. Use *should* in the result only to express obligation.

> If I were you, I would do it.
> We would have made better grades if we had studied harder.
> If I had more money, I should be happier, but I probably would not be.

29. Like *should, were to* is often used in the *if* clause to express doubt. However, the result always has *would*.

> If Mr. Lawrence were to call, what would you say?

30. The auxiliary *will* can be used in the *if* clause of Pattern 1 to express the idea of willingness. It is usually a polite expression equivalent to *please* or *be kind enough to.*

> If you will play the piano, John will sing.

If the *will* in the condition is emphasized, the meaning is changed to "insist on" or "be foolish enough to."

> If you *will* play the piano, John will sing. [= If you insist on playing the piano, John will sing.]

31. The auxiliary *would* is also used in the *if* clause to express the idea of willingness. The result then takes the verb form of Pattern 2, but it expresses reality. The following example means the same as the first example in ¶ 30 above.

> If you would play the piano, John would sing.

32. The auxiliaries *would have* in the *if* clause express willingness which did not occur. The result, therefore, has the verb form of Pattern 4 and shows past unreality.

If you would have played the piano, John would have sung. [You did not play; John did not sing.]

I suggest that you avoid using that construction. Use *had been willing to* instead.

If you had been willing to play the piano, John would have sung.

33. If the condition has *were, had, should,* or *could,* the *if* is sometimes omitted, and the *were, had, should,* or *could* is placed at the beginning of the dependent clause. The condition is always unreal, or, with *should,* doubtful.

Were I you, I would study hard.
Were all students serious, their teachers would be happy.
Were Mr. Lawrence to call, what would you say?
John would have caught the bus had he hurried.
Should Mr. Lawrence call, what would [will] you say?
Could the dead man have spoken, he would have identified his murderer.

34. In a negative condition, the contraction *-n't* is not used with a fronted *were, had, should,* or *could;* the full form *not* is used.

Had the captain not foreseen the danger, the troop would have been ambushed.

35. The condition is sometimes introduced by words other than *if: in case (that), in the event that, on condition (that), provided* or *providing (that), as long as, so long as,* and *suppose* or *supposing (that).* The verb forms are the same as those after *if.*

Katie will lend you the money on condition that you return it tomorrow.
I will tell you the secret provided that you promise not to repeat it.
Supposing you had been the burglar, what would you have done?
The boy can stay in the room so long as he keeps quiet.
The game will be postponed in case it rains.

36. The word *unless* is the equivalent of *if . . . not* in the condition.

If John does not hurry, the bus will leave him.
Unless John hurries, the bus will leave him.

37. The condition may be expressed in a word or phrase. A frequent phrase is *if so* or *if not.*

Do you want to go? If so, I will go with you [*If so* = "If you want to go"]
Do you want to go? If not, I will go alone. [*If not* = "If you do not want to go"]

Other similar phrases often begin with the words *with* or *without.* Sometimes the condition is expressed by *otherwise.*

With a little help, Armand will succeed.
Without music, the world would be a dull place.
What would you do with a million dollars?
People in New York would be inconvenienced without the subway.
I am glad I studied. Otherwise, I would have failed.

38. Frequently a condition is indicated only by the verb forms in a result clause.

> I could continue talking about this, but we must go on to the next topic. ["If I had time" is indicated by the *could continue* in the result clause "I could continue talking about this."]
> Tim would have explained everything, but nobody paid any attention to him. ["If he had been permitted" is indicated by *would have explained*.]

39. The word *if* does not always indicate a condition. In the phrasal conjunction *even if*, it introduces a contrast, and in the phrasal conjunction *as if*, it introduces a comparison. The word *though* may alternate with the *if* in both phrasal conjunctions.

> Johnny could not learn even if [*or* even though] I helped him.
> Marian looked as if [*or* as though] I had insulted her.

Also, see § *As if* and *As though.*

Another noncondition function of *if* is to introduce a noun clause used as a direct object after verbs like *know, say,* and *wonder.* In that use, *if* may alternate with *whether.* See § Clause—Noun.

> Mrs. Steward does not know   if [*or* whether] her cousin will go.
> Did Sydney say   if [*or* whether] he liked the gift?
> I wonder   if [*or* whether] my answer was correct.

40. Now we can go back to *was* versus *were* with *I, he, she,* and *it* after *if.* The paragraph above gives you one helpful clue: if you can substitute *whether* for *if,* then choose *was,* not *were.*

> The tourist wanted to know if I was the manager of the hotel.
> The young girl would not say if she was angry about my remark.

Now let's review Pattern 2, in which *were* occurs, and Pattern 3, in which *was* occurs. In Pattern 2 you use *were* because the condition is unreal or impossilbe *now.* In Pattern 2 you use *was* with *I, he, she,* and *it,* because the condition was real or possible *then.*

> If he were here now, he would explain everything.
> If he was here last night, I saw his twin brother at Mary's party.

41. You will sometimes encounter uninflected *be* as the first verb after the subject in the *if* clause. That is an old-fashioned usage; don't imitate it. In 1765 Patrick Henry said, "If this *be* treason, make the most of it." If he were alive today, he would probably say, "If this *is* treason, make the most of it."

Also, see § *Wish* vs. *Hope* vs. *Want* vs. *Would Like* and § Verb Uninflected in Dependent Clause.

CONJUNCTION C.16

The conjunctions are discussed in detail under § Clause and § Part of Speech—Conjunction and Preposition. Also, see § Opposition Expression.

1. For stylistic reasons you should be cautious about beginning sentences with the conjunctions *and* and *but.* Frequent use of those words in that way is usually a sign of careless or immature writing. For variation, use some of the words and phrases listed under § Transition Expression.

2. In writing, do not use *also* after *and; also* is not necessary.

Leonard was an excellent student in grammar school and   in high school.

COUNTABLE WORD C.17

1. A *countable* word is a word that may be preceded by *one* (or *a* or *an*), *two, three,* etc. An *uncountable* word is one that can not be preceded by a cardinal number. The meaning of a word as it is used in a sentence determines whether that word is countable or uncountable. The form of a word—that is, its pronunciation or spelling—does not determine whether it is countable or uncountable. For instance, the word *hair* in the sentence "She has long hair" is an uncountable, but in the sentence "There is a hair on your coat" *hair* is a countable. In the sentence "Life is beautiful" *life* is an uncountable, but in "He had an interesting life" *life* is a countable. The matter of countables and uncountables is discussed under §§ Article, § Singular vs. Plural, § *Amount* vs. *Number,* § *Few* vs. *A Few,* § *Many* vs. *Much,* and § *Such* vs. *Such a.*

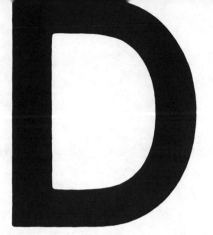

DASH

1. Use a dash (—) to indicate that a sentence has been interrupted or broken off. Be sure to use a pair of dashes if the break occurs within the sentence.

> During my vacation—I must have been insane—I decided I would ski.
> Jule said threateningly, "If you don't tell me—"

2. I advise you to be careful about using a dash in your writing. Frequent use of dashes is a characteristic of immature writing and can become very annoying to your reader. If you compose your thought before you begin writing a sentence, you will rarely have need for a dash.

3. Use a dash to set off an appositive that has internal punctuation. If such an appositive comes at the end of the sentence, either a colon or a dash may be used before it. See § Appositive.

> Money, fame, power—none of those things is important without health.
> All Mr. Gray's belongings—his house, his car, and even his clothes—were
>   seized by his creditors.
> Give your secretary what she needs—pencils, paper, and a good typewriter.
> Give your secretary what she needs: pencils, paper, and a good typewriter.

4. A dash is longer than a hyphen. In typing, you may use two hyphens (--) to indicate a dash.

DESIRE

1. When the word *desire* is used as a verb, it is followed directly by its object, which may be a noun, pronoun, or infinitive phrase.

> Lee desired success.
> Lee desired it.
> Lee desired to be successful.

2. When *desire* is used as a noun, it is customarily followed by *for* and an object. However, *for* is not used if an infinitive comes next.

> Lee's desire for success caused him to work hard.
> Lee's desire for it caused him to work hard.
> Lee's desire to be successful caused him to work hard.

Also, see § Infinitive vs. Gerund, § *Like*—Verb, and § *Wish* vs. *Hope* vs. *Want* vs. *Would Like.*

DIRECT VS. INDIRECT SPEECH

1. If we wish to report what somebody has said or thought, we may do so in two ways. The first way is *direct speech:* we give the exact words of the speaker or thinker in the form in which he expressed them. In writing, we designate direct speech by putting quotation marks around the speaker's words.

> Mr. Roosevelt said, "The only thing we have to fear is fear itself."
> My teacher says over and over, "English is difficult, but even a child can learn it."
> The director announced, "The class will go to the museum next Thursday if it doesn't rain."

2. Words like "Mr. Roosevelt said" and "My teacher says over and over" and "The director announced" in the preceding examples are called *dialog guides.* The dialog guide may come at the beginning, in the middle, or at the end of the quoted matter.

> "The only thing we have to fear," Mr. Roosevelt said, "is fear itself."
> "The class will go to the museum next Thursday if it doesn't rain," the director announced.

3. Direct speech is stylistically vivid. Writers should cultivate its use, but with a firm knowledge of necessary punctuation, capitalization, and paragraphing.

4. Quotation marks are written above each end of the quoted matter.

5. If more than one sentence is contained within the quoted matter, put quotation marks at the beginning of the first sentence and at the end of the last sentence.

> Mrs. Lister said, "I'll be home late. Don't wait for me."

6. If the quoted matter begins a line, put the first set of quotation marks before it on the same line, not at the end of the preceding line.

7. If the quoted matter ends a line, put the second set of quotation marks after it on the same line, not at the beginning of the next line.

8. Commas and periods are placed to the left of the quotation marks.

9. A question mark or an exclamation mark is placed to the left of the quotation mark if the quoted matter itself is a question or an exclamation. Otherwise, the question or exclamation mark is placed to the right of the quotation mark. Notice that a period or a second question mark is not used.

> The sick man asked, "Has my wife come yet?"
> Elizabeth screamed, "Help!"
> Did the teacher say, "Study the next lesson"?
> Did the teacher say, "Did you study the next lesson?"

10. A comma, not a colon, is the customary punctuation mark used to set off the dialog guide from the quoted matter. Notice the examples above.

11. If a dialog guide is inserted within the quoted matter, put quotation marks before and after the dialog guide.

> "English is difficult," my teacher says, "but you can learn it."

12. If a dialog guide is attached to the end of a quoted sentence, a comma is used at the end of the quoted sentence unless the quoted sentence ends with a question mark or an exclamation mark. Notice the lack of a comma at the end of the second and third quoted sentences below.

> "I simply don't believe you," Julia answered.
> "Has my wife come yet?" the sick man asked.
> "Help!" Elizabeth screamed.

13. Be careful about the punctuation around a dialog guide between two quoted sentences. Test your punctuation by mentally removing the dialog guide.

> "I'll be home late," Mrs. Lister said. "Don't wait for me."
> "I'll be home late   . Don't wait for me."

See § Quotation Mark for further details on punctuating direct speech.

14. The other way of reporting a person's words is *indirect speech* or *indirect discourse*. Quotation marks are not used in indirect speech, and the verb or verbs in the reported matter follow the rule of sequence of tense by taking the form which shows relation to the *time of the reporting.* See § Sequence of Tense.

The following examples mean the same thing as the examples in ¶ 1, but notice the differences in verb forms and other words.

> Mr. Roosevelt said *that* the only thing we *had* to fear *was* fear itself.
> My teacher says over and over *that* English is difficult but even a child can learn it.
> The director announced *that* the class *would* go to the museum *the following* Thursday if it *did* not rain.

15. A comma is not used before the quoted matter in indirect speech. Notice all the preceding and following examples.

16. In direct speech the connective word *that* is not used. In indirect speech it may be omitted if it is not needed for clarity.

> I said, "He can come."
> I said that he could come.   *or*   I said he could come.
> The girl repeatedly said that the poem she had memorized was beautiful.

If the *that* is omitted in the last example above, the reader, on first glancing at the sentence, may think that the girl recited the poem, and he may, therefore, be confused when he comes to the words "was beautiful."

17. In converting direct speech into indirect speech, certain other changes or additions may be necessary for clarity:

a. In nouns and pronouns.

> Mary remarked to John, "I like you."
> Mary remarked to John that she liked him.
> Robert said to Jim, "I've lost your watch."

> Robert told Jim that he had lost his watch. [Unclear: who lost whose?]
> Robert told Jim that the former had lost the latter's watch. [Clear but stilted]
> Robert said that he had lost Jim's watch. [It is clear that Robert did the losing, but whom did he tell? Of the four sentences, the first is the clearest.]

b. In time expressions, including verb forms.

> Last week Mary asked John, "*Are* you going *tomorrow?*"
> Last week Mary asked John if he *was* going *the next day.*
> John exclaimed, "I *have* to go right now!"
> John exclaimed that he *had* to go right *then.*

c. In imperatives. An imperative in direct speech is usually converted into an infinitive with *to* in indirect speech. The person spoken to is expressed and comes before the *to.*

> My father commanded, "Go to school."
> My father commanded me to go to school.
> "Call the police, Mary," Mr. Locke ordered.
> Mr. Locke ordered Mary to call the police.

Notice the conversion of a negative imperative.

> Marie said, "Don't go."
> Marie told me not to go.
> Saul begged, "Never do that, Sam."
> Saul begged Sam never to do that.

d. In dialog guides.

1. Reported statements should be clearly attributed to the speaker.

> Emily said, "Tim won't study. He's lazy."
> Emily said that Tim would not study because he was lazy.
> Emily said that Tim would not study. According to her, he was lazy.

2. The verb in the dialog guide may have to be changed.

> Mr. Dunn *exclaimed,* "Give me that book, Helen."
> Mr. Dunn sharply *told* Helen to give him that book.
> Mr. Dunn *ordered* Helen to give him that book.

18. The verbs *say, tell,* and *ask* have different uses in reported speech.

a. In direct speech *say,* not *tell,* is used in a dialog guide, and the preposition *to* is used if the hearer is mentioned.

> William said, "I'm leaving at once."
> Mr. Loggins said to his secretary, "I'll be gone for a few days."
> Mr. Dunn said to Helen, "Give me that book."

b. In indirect speech *say* is used if the person to whom the words were spoken is not mentioned; *tell* is used if the hearer is mentioned.

William said that he was leaving at once.
Mr. Loggins told his secretary that he would be gone for a few days.
Mr. Dunn told Helen to give him that book.

c. Say or *ask* may be used in a dialog guide for a question in direct speech, but *ask* is used with a question in indirect speech. Notice that a question mark is not used for an indirect question.

Henry said, "Where is Muriel?"
Henry asked, "Where is Muriel?"
Henry asked where Muriel was.

19. Contrary to some pronouncements you may encounter, usage sanctions *if* as well as *whether* for questions in indirect speech. The words *or not* may be added according to one's desire.

I asked Sue if she liked my new hat.
I asked Sue whether she liked my new hat
I asked Sue if she liked my new hat or not.
I asked Sue whether she liked my new hat or not.
I asked Sue whether or not she liked my new hat.

Word order in reported speech has definite patterns. A brief review of word order may be helpful.

20. In most statements, primary word order (subject before verb) is used.

He gets up early.
The man is coming.

21. In direct questions, split word order (auxiliary + subject + main verb) or inverted word order (main verb + subject) is generally used.

Does he get up early?	She asked, "Does he get up early?"
Is the man coming?	She asked, "Is the man coming?"

22. If one of the *wh* words (*who, whom, whose, which, what, when, where, why,* and *how*) is used, it is placed first in a direct question.

When does he get up?	She asked, "When does he get up?"
Why is the man coming?	She asked, "Why is the man coming?"
What did he say?	She asked, "What did he say?"

23. If the *wh* word is the subject or part of the subject, it is followed by the verb or verbs of the simple predicate. However, the question auxiliary *do, does,* or *did* is not used.

Who gets up early?	She asked, "Who gets up early?"
Which man is coming?	She asked, "Which man is coming?"

24. In indirect speech, a *wh* word is placed first in the dependent clause, but the subject comes before the verb, and there is no question auxiliary.

143

> I will ask him how early he gets up.
> He will not tell you when he gets up.
> Did you ask her which man was coming?
> Did she tell you what the man said?
> She asked who got up early.

25. Remember: Dependent clauses customarily have primary word order whether or not they are in a question—that is, they have the subject before the verb.

> Please tell me when the train arrives.
> Do you know when the train arrives?
> I want to find out when the train arrives.

For more details, see § Word Order—*Wh* Word, § Word Order—Primary, and § Word Order—Split.

DO—AUXILIARY

D.4

1. The verb *do,* with its inflected forms *does* and *did,* has varied uses as an auxiliary verb.

2. *Do* is used in direct questions which do not contain another anomalous finite (e.g., *can, ought*) or the words *who, what, whose,* or *which* used as the subject or part of the subject. For a list of the anomalous finites, see § Auxiliary.

Do you want to go with us?	Who wants to go with us?
Does Alec work downtown?	Is Alec going to work now?
Did she say she'd go with us?	Who said she'd go with us?
When do we start?	Is it too early to start now?
Why does she always come late?	Why is she always late?
What did he get on the test?	What happened to him?
Which book do you want?	Which book seems the best?

3. *Do* is used with *not* in negative sentences which do not contain another anomalous finite or another negative word like *nobody* or *nothing.* It is used with the verb *be* and *not* usually only in the imperative (however, see § Polite Expression). In speech and in informal writing the word *not* is usually contracted and joined directly to *do, does,* or *did.* The contracted form of *not* is written *n't.* Also, see § Word Order—Adverb Modifying Verb and § Negative.

I do not want to go with you.	I was not invited.
I don't want to go with you.	I haven't finished studying.
Doesn't he work downtown?	Isn't his job downtown?
We don't start until eleven.	Nobody starts before eleven o'clock.
Why does she not come earlier?	Why is she not more prompt?
Why doesn't she come earlier?	Why isn't she more prompt?
What didn't he answer correctly?	What was not correct?
Who did not understand?	Who understood nothing?
Who didn't understand?	Who couldn't understand?
Don't be lazy.	I am not lazy.

4. *Do* is used for emphasis in affirmative statements which do not contain another anomalous finite. It often indicates denial of something that has been stated or suggested. It is used with the verb *be* for emphasis usually only in the imperative.

> "Why didn't you tell me?"   "But I did tell you."
> The baby is generally healthy, but every now and then he does catch a cold.
> Lying is very bad, but many people do lie.
> My teacher thinks I am lazy, but I do try.
> I can't understand why Abe is late. He did tell me to meet him here.
> Do be quiet. I told you I had a headache.

Also, see § Verb—Not Repeated, § Word Order—Emphatic Adverb, § Word Order —*Wh* Word, and § Word Order—Split.

DO **VS.** *MAKE*   D.5

1. The verbs *do* and *make,* which have similar lexical definitions, can not usually be interchanged. Very often *do* has the meaning of "perform a routine or assigned activity," but *make* has the meaning of "produce" or "create." Study the examples in the following paragraphs to see how many of them conform to those meanings (not all of them do, unfortunately). One expression has both verbs: *make do,* "manage (with what is available)"—as in "The shop did not have exactly what I wanted, but I bought something I can make do with."

2. The verb *do* is used in the following phrases:

> *do one's assignment* or *lesson.* I try to do my assignments with care.
> *do one's best.* It is not perfect, but I did my best.
> *do business with.* Our company does business with that store. Mr. Pearson is so irritable that nobody likes to do business with him.
> *do the cleaning* (or *the sweeping, the ironing, the washing,* etc.). The Adamses have a maid who does the cleaning.
> *do* ("wash") *the dishes.* Does your father do the dishes at your home?
> *do one's duty.* Don't blame the guard for refusing you. He was just doing his duty.
> *do an exercise.* Be sure to read the explanation before doing the exercise.
> *do a favor.* Do me a favor, please: lend me your book until tomorrow.
> *do one's homework.* I will go with you after I have done my homework.
> *do a job.* Elmer is dependable: he does every job promptly and well. When I write a composition at home, I think I can do a better job.
> *do the laundry.* Mrs. Cole bought a new machine to do her laundry.
> *do research.* A graduate student is supposed to do a lot of research.
> *do one's work.* Don't copy other people's exercises. Do your own work.

3. *Do* is used with *what* in questions for the meaning "have as one's occupation."

> "What does your father do?" "He's a doctor."
> What are you going to do after you graduate from college?

4. The verb *make* is used in the following phrases:

make an attempt. The prisoner made an attempt to escape.

make ("behave") *as if* (or *as though*). Sally made as if she were surprised.

make a bargain. I will make a bargain with you. If you wash the dishes, I will dry.

make believe, "pretend." The baby makes believe he can not walk, but he really can.

make a change. A person should always be ready to make a change in his habits.

make a comparison. It is not possible to make a comparison between unlike things.

make a decision. You must make a decision about your future work.

make a discovery. Columbus made a discovery that people are still talking about.

make a donation. Mr. Calhoun made a donation to the scholarship fund.

make an effort. You will not succeed if you never make an effort.

make an error. Don't worry about making an error; go ahead and try.

make a face, "distort one's facial expression," usually signifying pain or displeasure. Mr. Lucas made a face when he heard his mother-in-law was coming to visit.

make a fool of. Don't let that young girl make a fool of you.

make friendships. In college we often make friendships that last indefinitely.

make friends with. Tracy gets along with everybody; he could make friends with a statue.

make fun of. It is not polite to make fun of physically handicapped persons.

make good. That man has certainly made good in his job: he is a success. I am sorry that check was worthless; I will make it good.

make improvement. You are making a great deal of improvement in your writing.

make a mistake. In surgery a doctor can not afford to make a mistake.

make money. Mr. Ford made a lot of money in his business. How much (money) do you make in that job? Do you make fifty dollars a week?

make a noise. Please don't make a noise if you come in late.

make peace. Utopia made peace with Erewhon.

make a plan. Harry makes a lot of plans, but he never carries them out.

make progress. If you keep trying, you will make progress.

make a promise (or *resolution* or *vow*). If you make a promise, you should fulfill it.

make a speech. The governor made a short speech at the dinner.

make a statement. My roommate made a statement with which I disagreed.

make a try. Don't be discouraged; go ahead, and make another try.

make a turn. Drive to the next intersection, and make a left turn.

make war. Utopia made war on Erewhon.

5. The verb *make* is frequently used in the pattern "*make* + a noun or pronoun + an adjective." See § Predicate Adjective.

Mr. Lord often makes his wife nervous.

Lois's rudeness certainly made me angry.

For *make* with a predicate objective, see § Predicate Objective.

Also, see § *Do*—Auxiliary, § Infinitive vs. Gerund, and § Preposition—Expression with.

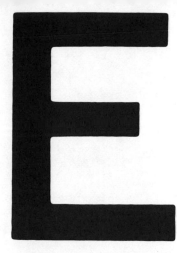

EACH VS. EVERY VS. ALL   E.1

1. The words *each* and *every* are singular. For plurals, *all* is used.

2. *Each* and *all* can be used without a following noun; *every* can not.

> Fifteen children came to the party. All were there promptly at three o'clock. Each was dressed very neatly.

3. Both *each* and *every* may be used when the members of a known group are considered separately. *All the* can be used similarly.

> Each child at the party received a present.
> Every child at the party received a present.
> All the children at the party received a present.

4. For the members of an indefinite or universal group, use *every* or *all* (without *the*).

> Every child likes a surprise.   You can get every kind of food there.
> All children like a surprise.   You can get all kinds of food there.

5. *Each other* refers to two or more members already mentioned.

> Mr. Shannon's children always help each other.

The expression *one another* is sometimes used in that way.

> Mr. Shannon's children always help one another.

6. *Every other* excludes the member or members already mentioned.

> Marie made a perfect score. Every other student had at least one error.

Every other also means "each alternate."

> Write on every other line of the paper. [Leave a line blank between two lines of writing.]
> The students sat in every other seat. [No student sat next to another.]

7. To refer to the remaining members of a known group, *all the other* is used before a plural noun, and *all the others* is used when no noun follows.

> Marie made a perfect score. All the other students had at least one error.
> Only one student made a perfect score. All the others had some errors.

8. To refer to the remaining members of an indefinite or universal group, *all other* is used before a plural noun, and *all others* is used when no noun follows.

> Only one person has ever made a perfect score on that test. All other foreigners have had at least one error.
> Only one foreigner has ever made a perfect score on that test. All others have had at least one error.

Also, see § *All* vs. *Whole* and § *Another* vs. *Other*.

e

1. The following adjectives, which are spelled with the letters *-ed*, end with unstressed [ɪd].

hundred	naked	rugged	wicked
kindred	ragged	sacred	wretched

2. The adjective *beloved* is usually pronounced [bɪˈlʌvɪd], sometimes [bɪˈlʌvd].

3. The following also have the final *-ed* pronounced [ɪd] when they are used as adjectives:

aged	crooked	jagged
blessed	dogged	learned

Similarly, in compounds with *one-*, *long-*, etc., the word *legged* is pronounced with final [ɪd].

Bob is a long-legged boy. A grasshopper is a six-legged creature.

4. When *aged*, *blessed*, etc., are used as verbs, the *-ed* is pronounced in accordance with the rules given under § Suffix *-ed.* For instance, *aged* is pronounced [edʒd], and blessed is pronounced [blɛst].

ENOUGH

1. The word *enough* follows the adjective, adverb, or verb it modifies.

You are not careful enough.
The soil is fertile enough to support extensive farming.
The conductor did not speak slowly enough for me to understand.
Do you really study enough?

2. *Enough* either precedes or follows the noun it modifies. It seems to precede more often than follow, but its position does not affect the meaning.

I wanted to buy you a present, but I did not have enough money.
"I'm going to the movies." "Do you have money enough?"
There is just enough time to catch the train.
There was cake enough for everybody to have a piece.

3. *Enough* combines with some adverbs into phrases which are used as modifiers of sentences or clauses. Notice the punctuation.

Interestingly enough, you can find mutually contradictory proverbs.
Maria was angered by Pete's attempt at kindness, strangely enough.
I offered to help, but, oddly enough, the stranger refused.

Also, see § Negative and § Infinitive vs. Gerund.

EXCLAMATION MARK   E.4

1. Use an exclamation mark (!) after an expression of strong feeling. The mark should be used sparingly; overuse of it is a sign of immature writing.

> I have lost everything!
> How dare you say that!

2. Use an exclamation mark after an expression imitative of a loud, violent, or sudden sound.

> Zing! The lightning ripped through the sky. Crash! The thunder pounded immediately afterward.

3. Notice the punctuation in the following examples with quotation marks. Neither a period nor a comma is used after an exclamation mark.

> She screamed, "Help! Save me!"
> "Help!" she screamed. "Save me!"
> "Help! Save me!" she screamed.
> That is pure "schmaltz"!

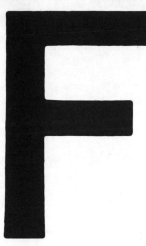

FEW **VS.** *A FEW* F.1

1. The word *few* conveys a more negative idea than *a few* does. *Few* draws attention to what is lacking; *a few* draws attention to what is present. The items are not interchangeable. They are used with countables. See § Countable Word.

> That tyrant has few friends, if any at all, but there are a few men who flatter him for their own advancement.
> Conrad improved his knowledge of English greatly in a few years.

2. The same implications exist with *little* and *a little,* used with uncountables.

> Helen has little money. Don't ask her to help you.
> Peter has a little money. Ask him to help you.

3. *Fewer* and *fewest* are used with countables, and *less* and *least* are used with uncountables.

> I have fewer friends here than in my own country because I have less time to socialize.

4. *Quite a few* is practically the equivalent of *many. Quite a little* is practically the equivalent of *much.*

> A good student spends quite a few hours in studying, and a good teacher spends quite a little time in preparing a lesson.

Also, see § *Many* vs. *Much,* § *Many a,* and § Singular vs. Plural.

FOR—PREPOSITION F.2

Some of the uses of the preposition *for* are discussed below.

1. *For* indicates the person or persons (*a*) to whom an action brings advantage or disadvantage or (*b*) to whom a thing or quality applies.

> The clerk gave a demonstration for us.
> Mr. Hamilton made a new toy for his children.
> The salesman left a message on the table for Mrs. Lewis.
> Let me lift that box for you.
> Mr. Foster works for a large newspaper.
> That suit is too big for that little boy.
> This lounge is for the students.

See also § Word Order.

2. *For* sometimes expresses such relationships with inanimate objects.

> The glazier made a frame for the picture.
> There are three chairs for each room.
> The movie actor posed for a picture.

3. *For* in the same way is used before the expressed subject of an infinitive. See § Infinitive vs. Gerund.

> It is difficult for foreign students to understand idioms.
> It became inconvenient for people to exchange commodities directly.
> Your mother is planning for you to take Martha to the dance tonight.

4. *For* indicates purpose or reason.

> My secretary has gone to the post office for some stamps.
> The Burkes built a roof on their plaza for protection against rain.
> The child stayed close to his new friend for comfort.
> There used to be a special room for parties.
> You had better buy a fire extinguisher for emergencies.
> Mr. Walsh was arrested for speeding.
> The time for reading a book is a long winter evening.
> We bought the refrigerator for fear that prices would go up.
> For some reason or other, Walter did not attend the meeting.
> For no apparent reason, the wall collapsed.

5. *For* indicates equivalence or compensation. Here, *in place of* and *in exchange for* are common alternates.

> Louisa paid fifty dollars for that dress.
> The Hawkinses bought a house for $12,459.
> The owners sold the old building for twenty thousand dollars.
> The young man thanked the old woman for the gift.
> Lou had to use an old can for a soap container.
> For stationery, the freshmen used wrapping paper.
> French has a different expression for the same idea.
> Writing is a substitute for speech.
> We substitute writing for speech.

6. *For* indicates intended destination. It is frequently used with the verbs *head, leave, sail, set out,* and *start.*

> The boat sailed for Europe last Saturday.
> Mr. Chapman started for the West Coast yesterday.
> Mrs. White leaves for Brazil tomorrow.

7. *For* indicates distance when the distance can be replaced by a period of time. *For* may usually be omitted in such an instance.

> The boys walked for a mile before they came to a house.   *or*   The boys
>   walked for an hour before they came to a house.
> The two friends rode together on the bus for six blocks.
> We drove for miles before we found an exit.

For *for* in time expressions, see § Preposition in Time Expression. Also, see § Preposition—Expression with, § *What for,* and § Word Order— Preposition.

Some of the uses of the preposition *from* are discussed below.

1. *From* indicates the source or origin of people, things, qualities, or conclusions. Note the two positions of the preposition in the eighth and ninth examples below. Also, see § Word Order—Preposition.

> Manuel and Oscar are from South America.
> The big ship from England was at the dock.
> We heard a broadcast from Paraguay last night.
> Philip graduated from Purdue University.
> I learned that trick from my father.
> The company received a letter of protest from Mr. Petty.
> It looked like a part from a car motor.   *or*   It looked like part of a car motor.
> I do not know from which room that noise is coming.
> I do not know which room that noise is coming from.
> Do you know where Mr. Hansen comes from?
> From my own experience I know that it is difficult to learn a new language.

2. The verb *be* or *come* is used with *from* to denote the birthplace or nationality of persons. The simple present tense is used for living persons, and the simple past tense for dead persons.

> Manuel and Oscar are from South America.
> Emily Waters comes from Boston.
> Caruso was from Italy.
> Shakespeare came from Stratford-on-Avon.

3. In the sense of source, *from* and *of* are usually interchangeable immediately after a proper noun. Note that the rule applies to business connection, too.

> Bill Johnstone from Chicago was at the meeting.
> Bill Johnstone of Chicago was at the meeting.
> Mr. Adams of the Bell Telephone Company spoke about the matter.
> Mr. Adams from the Bell Telephone Company spoke about the matter.

4. *From* in some cases makes source, means, and instrumentality closely allied. *From* and *by* are interchangeable in the following examples:

> We could tell from the clouds that it was going to snow.
> The picture hung from a nail in the wall.
> Judging from Mike's appearance, I would say that he is not happy.

5. *From* indicates the starting point (*a*) of a measure of distance (often *away from*), as in the first five examples below, or (*b*) of some action, as in the last four examples.

> The safe stood three feet from the wall.
> Ralph lives just a few blocks from me.

At eight o'clock we were still twenty miles from Duluth.
The traveler felt very far from home.
When he was far away from the city, he began to relax.
From our seats we could see the stage perfectly.
This machine is still a long way from being perfected.
The cars came from our left.
The driver pushed the stalled car from the rear.

6. *From* indicates contrast, difference, or separation.

Today's weather is different from yesterday's.
This is a change from the weather we had last week.
The final plan differed greatly from the original one.
You must be careful to distinguish that sound from the other.
It is difficult to tell one twin from the other.
The mountain climber had a narrow escape from death.
The leave was a welcome relief from the terrible business of fighting.
We could hardly keep from laughing at the expression on George's face.

7. *From* indicates cause.

The explorers got dysentery from the water.
The Arabic boys suffered from the cold.
We were tired and nervous from the constant tension.
Mr. Hart became deaf from the explosion.
Mr. Warren died from the explosion.   *but*   Mr. Ryan died of cancer [or any other disease].
Anthony's eyes were red from excessive reading.
The little boy's clothing was torn from climbing over the sharp rocks.

8. *From ... to* indicates movement or progression. *From ... on up to* is an alternative to *from ... to* that may be used with big differences in numbers, quantities, or grade. If two geographical locations are involved, the pattern *from ... to* can be reversed (*to ... from*) as in the first two examples below. Notice the lack of the definite article in the fourth, fifth, and sixth examples.

Mr. Hicks traveled from Chicago to New York last week.
Charles makes frequent trips to England from his office in Newark.
The inspectors moved from one building to the next.
The salesmen traveled from city to city.
The boat rocked from side to side.
The police searched the house from top to bottom.
The visitor saw everybody from the freshmen to the president.
Dogs usually eat from three to four times as much as cats.
The men's ages ran all the way from nineteen and twenty on up to fifty-five and sixty.

9. *From* occurs in combination with other prepositions.

We could hear loud voices from across the hall.
Three men stepped from behind the bar.

The bridal party had just come from inside the church.
The Persian cat strolled out from under the table.

For *from* in time expressions, see § Preposition in Time Expression. Also, see § Preposition—Expression with.

-FUL **ENDING** F.4

1. Be careful about the spelling of words which end in the sound [fʊl]. Examples are *beautiful, faithful, handful, thoughtful, useful,* and *wonderful.*

2. The spelling is also *ful* in *fulfill.*

GENDER

GERUND

GET

GIVE

GENDER   G.1

1. A noun, a noun group, or a pronoun is classified in one of three grammatical categories called *genders:* masculine, feminine, or neutor. The gender of a word or group determines which personal pronoun or adjective is used to refer to it or to substitute for it. A singular masculine word or group has as its substitute or reference *he, his, him,* or *himself.* A singular feminine word or group has as its substitute or reference *she, her, hers,* or *herself.* A singular neuter word or group has as its substitute or reference *it, its,* or *itself.* See § Agreement—Pronoun.

GERUND   G.2

1. A *gerund* is the term applied to the *-ing* form of a verb (e.g., *walking, loving*) when it is used as a noun. A gerund can be referred to by the word *it.*

> Walking is good exercise. It is one of my recreations.
> Children need loving. It is a basic requirement.
> Swimming develops the muscles. It tones up the whole body.

For a discussion of the gerund, see § Infinitive vs. Gerund. Also, see § Article—*The* vs. No *The.*

GET   G.3

1. The verb *get* is frequently followed by either an adjective or a participle (a *predicate adjective*). In such constructions *get* indicates the idea of "become" or "grow." Some people object to that use of *get* in writing and substitute the verb *be* or *become* for it.

> Mrs. Anderson got angry when I asked her a question.
> New York gets hot in the summer.
> The book got interesting toward the end.
> If you work very hard, you will get tired.
> Almost everybody gets lost the first time he tries to use the subway.
> I can not remember if they have just got engaged, got married, or got divorced.
>   They change their minds constantly.

2. *Have got* is frequently used as an equivalent of the simple present tense of *possess.* In spoken English the *have* or *has* is usually unstressed so that they sound like *ve* and *s.* Some persons object to the construction in writing and substitute *have* for it.

> I have got a present for you.
> Mary has got her notebook in her hand.
> Have you got a cigaret?
> Has the boss got time to talk now?
> Hasn't Bruce got his tie on?
> They haven't got what I want.

3. *Have got to* is frequently an equivalent of *must.* See § *Must* vs. *Have to* vs. *Have Got to.*

4. In writing, you will sometimes see *got* as the equivalent of *have got.* I advise you not to imitate that usage.

> I got a present for you. [Unless you are using *got* as the past tense of *get,* use *I have, I have got,* or *I've got....*]
> I got to leave now. [Avoid this; use *I have, I have got,* or *I've got....*]

5. Either *got* or *gotten* is used as the past participle of *get* except in the constructions meaning "possess" or "must." Then, only *got* is used.

GIVE   G.4

1. The verb *give* is used in the following phrases:

> *give dictation.* Do not interrupt the teacher while he is giving dictation.
> *give an impression.* Mr. Cole gives the impression of a man who cares for his clothes. He is always neatly dressed.

Also, see *give* in § Preposition—Expression with.

H- INITIAL   H.1

1. The letter *h* at the beginning of a word is usually pronounced. The article *a*, not *an*, is used before such words.

2. The major exceptions are *heir, honest, honor, hour,* and their derivatives such as *heiress, honesty,* and *honorable:* the initial *h* is not pronounced. *An*, not *a*, is used before them.

3. In ordinary speech, the words *he, him, his,* and *her* are usually not stressed. They usually do not have the [h] sound, but when they are at the beginning of a sentence or are emphasized for contrast, the *h* is always pronounced.

HAD BETTER   H.2

1. The expression *had better* is frequently used in conversation in giving or seeking advice.

> You had better study your lessons.
> You had better see a doctor soon.
> Allan had better stop staying up late. He looks tired.

2. The *had* is customarily reduced in speech.

> You'd better study your lessons.
> You'd better see a doctor soon.

At times you will see the expression written without the *had*. I advise against imitating that usage.

> You better study your lessons. [Avoid this; use *You had better study . . . .*]
> You better see a doctor soon. [Avoid this; use *You had better see . . . .*] ·

3. The negative form is either *had better not* or *hadn't better*.

> You had better not stay up late.
> You hadn't better stay up late.

4. Notice the question forms.

> Had I better tell him the news?
> Hadn't I better tell him the news?

Also, see § Auxiliary, § *Must* vs. *Have to* vs. *Have Got to*, and § *Ought* vs. *Should.*

HANDWRITING   H.3

1. Learning how to write is a waste if nobody can read your handwriting. If your present handwriting is hard to read, I recommend that you take time to practice forming letters in the way indicated by the little arrows in the following hand-writing guide.

HANDWRITING GUIDE

Small letters

a	an	ran Maria
b	boy	ebb rib
c	cut	act sac
d	do	edge did
e	ear	let apple
f	fit	effect tiff
g	go	regular egg
h	hat	light high
i	ice	site Hi!
j	just	adjoin Taj
k	kind	like ink
l	last	elevate kill
m	me	theme mom
n	new	any men
o	out	look bingo
p	pie	apple cap
q	quiet	equal coq
r	run	earn err
s	sun	test express
t	to	little sit
u	use	run Hindu
v	very	live flav
w	we	owe raw
x	x-ray	exit tax
y	you	eye boy
z	zoo	fuzzy buzz

Capital letters

a	Γ o a a	All
B	1 Γ P B B	Bees
C	Γ C C	Can
D	1 $\mathcal{d}$ L D D D	Do
E	c E E	Exit
F	$\overline{}$ T T F or	Fred
F	1 Γ F	Fred
G	1 γ γ $\mathcal{G}$ G G or	Go
g	Γ o g g g	Go
H	$)$ $)$ $)$ H H H	How
I	1 0 $\mathcal{I}$ $\mathcal{I}$	I'm
J	Γ o g J J	Just
K	1 K K	Kites
L	$\sim$ $\mathcal{L}$ L L L	Let
m	γ γ n m m m	My
n	γ γ n n	New
O	Γ O O O	Over
P	1 Γ P P	Put
q	Γ o g q q or	Queen
Q	Γ C O Q	Queen
R	1 Γ P R	Red
S	1 1 $\mathcal{S}$ $\mathcal{S}$ $\mathcal{S}$	Send
T	$\overline{}$ T T or	Too
T	1 T	Too
U	1 U U U	Usually
V	1 V	Very
W	1 U U W	Well
X	1 2 X	X-ray
Y	1 U y y y	You
Z	Γ 0 $\mathcal{z}$ $\mathcal{z}$ $\mathcal{z}$	Zoo

Numerals and punctuation marks

$1\ 2\ 3\ 4\ 5\ 6\ 7\ 8\ 9\ 0 \qquad 8,629,704,931$

.	period and decimal mark	I am. Dr. $1.50
?	question mark	Is he going?
!	exclamation mark	Hello!
,	comma	December 4, 1937
:	colon	Dear Sir :
;	semicolon	He came; I left.
( )	parentheses	Poe (1809–1849)
[ ]	brackets	"o'er [over] the waves"
' '	single quotation marks	He asked, "Did she say, 'I can go'?"
" "	double quotation marks	He said, "I can't go."
'	apostrophe	it's
-	hyphen	self-government
—	dash	My friends—John, Paul, and George—are coming.

HAVE H.4

1. In American English *do, does,* or *did* is customarily used (*a*) in a question if *have* is the main verb and the tense is simple present or simple past and (*b*) with *not* or *-n't* in either questions or statements under the same conditions. British English customarily does not use *do, does,* or *did* with *have* under those conditions.

AMERICAN ENGLISH	BRITISH ENGLISH
Do you have a cigaret?	Have you a cigaret?
The shop did not have shoes.	The shop had not shoes.
He doesn't have time now.	He hasn't time now.
Didn't he have a tie on?	Hadn't he a tie on?

Some Americans sometimes use the British constructions, and some Britishers sometimes use the American constructions.

2. The verb *have* is used in the following phrases:

> *have a celebration.* The city is going to have a celebration in honor of the hero.
> *have fun.* Did you have fun at the party last night?
> *have an idea.* I have an idea how to solve that problem.
> *have a good (nice, bad, etc.) time.* I certainly had a good time at that party.
> *have a hard time.* In winter, animals have a hard time finding anything to eat.

Also, see § Auxiliary, § *Get*, § *Must* vs. *Have to* vs. *Have Got to*, § Tense—Perfect Present, § Tense—Continuous Perfect Present, and § Preposition—Expression with.

HOME   H.5

1. For the meaning "at or to my (our, your, his, etc.) dwelling place," the word *home* may be used alone after the verbs *be, remain,* and *stay,* after verbs of motion like *come, go, hurry, run,* and *walk,* and after the word *way.*

> I will be home this afternoon.
> Paula will remain home over the weekend.
> Why didn't you stay home yesterday?
> When is your brother coming home?
> I have got to hurry home after class.
> Peter walked home with Wilma.
> We talked all the way home.
> I met Jack on my way home.

a. *At home* may be used for the same meaning after *be, remain,* and *stay.*

> I will be at home this afternoon.
> Paula will remain at home this weekend.
> Why didn't you stay at home yesterday?

b. *At home* may also mean "comfortable; at ease."

> Mr. Perkins is at home anywhere.
> Luella made me feel at home very soon.

c. *At home (to)* sometimes has the meaning of "ready or willing to receive as guests."

> Mrs. Rose is always at home to her friends.
> If Arthur calls, tell him I am not at home.

2. *Home* is used for the meaning "to my (our, etc.) dwelling place" after verbs like *bring, carry, follow, see* ("accompany"), *send,* and *take* when they have a direct object.

> Did you bring your books home?
> Elizabeth carried the kitten home.
> The stranger followed Lydia home.
> The teacher sent the boy home.
> I will take (or see) you home after the party.

3. *Home* is used alone with the meaning "from my (our, etc.) dwelling place" after the verb *leave.*

> When did you leave home today?
> George left home at fifteen and got a job.

HOMOGRAPH

1. A homograph is a word which has the same spelling as another word but has a different meaning. An example is *fair,* which may mean either "just" or "exhibition." English has a great number of homographs.

2. Most homographs have the same pronunciation, but a few do not. Here are some examples of those which have different pronunciation: *bow* ("front part of a ship" and "instrument for shooting arrows"), *lead* ("guide" and "kind of metal"), *minute* ("one sixtieth of an hour" and "very small"), and *tear* ("rip" and "eye water").

HOMOPHONE

1. There are groups of words which are spelled differently and have different meanings but are pronounced the same. Such words are called *homophones* or *homonyms.* Some of them are the following:

ail – ale	colonel – kernel	lain – lane
air – heir	dear – deer	leased – least
aisle – isle – I'll	die – dye	lessen – lesson
aloud – allowed	doe – dough	loan – lone
altar – alter	earn – urn	made – maid
ate – eight	fair – fare	mail – male
aye – eye – I	fir – fur	massed – mast
B – be – bee	flea – flee	meat – meet
ball – bawl	flew – flu – flue	miner – minor
bare – bear	flour – flower	missed – mist
beat – beet	foul – fowl	one – won
beau – bow	groan – grown	packed – pact
berry – bury	guessed – guest	pail – pale
berth – birth	hail – hale	pain – pane
blew – blue	hair – hare	pair – pare – pear
bough – bow	hall – haul	peace – piece
brake – break	heal – heel	plain – plane
buy – by	hear – here	pole – poll
C – sea – see	heard – herd	pray – prey
cell – sell	higher – hire	profit – prophet
cellar – seller	him – hymn	rain – reign – rein
cent – scent – sent	hole – whole	rap – wrap
cereal – serial	hour – our	right – rite – write
cite – sight – site	knew – new	road – rode
coarse – course	know – no	role – roll

rose – rows	son – sun	threw – through
sail – sale	stair – stare	to – too – two
scene – seen	steal – steel	vale – veil
seam – seem	suede – swayed	wade – weighed
serf – surf	suite – sweet	waist – waste
sew – so – sow	T – tea – tee	wait – weight
shone – shown	tacked – tact	way – weigh
side – sighed	tail – tale	weak – week
soar – sore	Thai – tie	wood – would
some – sum	their – there	

HUNDRED **VS.** *HUNDREDS OF*   H.8

1. The word *hundred* usually does not have an *-s*, and it is usually not followed by *of*. The same is true of the words *dozen, million, score,* and *thousand.*

> Only a hundred people were in the audience although two hundred and fifty had bought tickets.
> Paula has seen that movie a dozen times.
> That store sells several thousand dresses every month.
> The population of New York City was nearly two million in 1880.

2. The sum *100* may be expressed either as *a hundred* or *one hundred*. *A hundred* is customary; *one hundred* is used in consecutive counting or in contrasting. The same distinction holds for *a thousand* versus *one thousand,* etc.

> Mrs. Neustadt bought a hundred bars of candy for the children.
> Les was counting to himself, "Ninety-nine, one hundred, one hundred and one."
> I wanted one hundred pieces, not two hundred.

3. To express a large but inexact number, we add *-s* to the word *hundred, dozen, million, score,* or *thousand.* If a noun follows, that noun is plural and is preceded by *of.* Such an expression is frequently used in emphatic utterances.

> "How many people were there?" "Oh, hundreds!"
> Thousands of letters are never delivered because the addresses are incorrect.
> Scores of persons were hurt in the accident.

4. Similar expressions are *tens of thousands* and *hundreds of thousands* and *thousands upon thousands.*

> Tens of thousands of buffaloes used to roam the prairie.
> The human body is composed of hundreds of thousands of cells.
> Thousands upon thousands of scallops appear off Long Island in the fall.

5. A dollar bill is frequently referred to only by the number in its numerical value. Then, the plural form of the number is used for two or more bills of the same denomination.

> When Mr. Austin cashed his check for two thousand dollars, the teller gave him three five-hundred-dollar bills, eight fifties, four tens, four fives, eight twos, and twenty-four ones.

h

1. A hyphen (·) is a mark of union. It indicates that words or parts of words belong together. Do not confuse it with the longer dash (—); see § Dash.

2. Use a hyphen if you write part of a word at the end of a line and the rest of that word at the beginning of the next line. Use only one hyphen, and put it after the first part of the word, not at the beginning of the next line. Do not put it below the line, and do not put it high above the line.

> Yesterday afternoon some young boys from the village went out to gather mush-
> rooms and nuts in the forest.

The acceptable ways of dividing words are quite complicated. I recommend that you avoid breaking a word. If you must divide, consult a standard dictionary. Never divide a word so that only one letter appears by itself.

3. Use a hyphen in compound numerals from *twenty-one* to *ninety-nine* and *twenty-first* to *ninety-ninth*. Do not use a hyphen with *hundred, thousand*, etc.

> There were thirty-six members of the class present.
> Two hundred people had been invited.
> Oscar rode from Forty-Second Street to Ninety-Sixth Street on the subway.

a. A number composed of one or two words is usually written out in letters. A number composed of more than two words is usually written in figures. However, if the number is at the beginning of a sentence, write it out in words, or rewrite the sentence so that the number is not at the beginning. See § Number.

> Four hundred and thirty-four students had registered before eight o'clock.
> Before eight o'clock 434 students had registered.

b. Years are usually written in figures; for example, *1929*. In very formal announcements or invitations they are sometimes written in letters.

4. Use a hyphen in expressions of clock time such as *one-fifteen* and *six-thirty*. Expressions of more than two words are usually written in figures.

> I got up at seven-thirty this morning.
> The class begins at 8:25 p.m.

5. In ranges of inclusive dates and inclusive figures a hyphen is used in typing; this is often printed as a short dash (–).

> Nathan was in Albania during the First World War (1914–1919). [Read "from
> 1914 to 1919."]
> The theory is described on pages 25–37. [Read "on pages 25 through 37."]

6. Most words with a prefix like *pre-*, *re-*, *anti-*, and *un-* do not have a hyphen.

extraordinary	coeducation	exchange
intramural	unnatural	semiformal

However, certain kinds of compounds with prefixes do have a hyphen.

a. Use a hyphen if a prefix is joined to a proper name.

> pre-Columbian   pro-Roosevelt   un-Christian

b. Use a hyphen if the last letter of the prefix is a vowel and is the same as the first letter of the word that the prefix is joined to.

> anti-intellectual   pre-existing   re-elect
> pre-eminent   re-educate   semi-illiterate

c. Use a hyphen with *ex-* meaning "former."

> ex-serviceman   ex-President   ex-wife

d. Use a hyphen if a compound has a meaning different from that of a common word spelled without a hyphen.

> *co-op,* "co-operative organization," is different from *coop.*
> *re-collect,* "collect a second time," is different from *recollect.*
> *re-cover,* "cover again," is different from *recover.*
> *re-tire,* "put a new tire on," is different from *retire.*

7. Use a hyphen in compounds with the following elements: *-in-chief, -in-law,* long- and *self-.* Also, see ¶ 10.

> The President is Commander-in-Chief of the Army.
> Cy was editor-in-chief.
> I got a long-distance call last night.
> Elephants are long-lived.
> Jack likes his father-in-law.
> The youth was obviously self-conscious.
> The island wants to be self-governing.
> Modern cars have self-starters.

8. Use a hyphen in compounds with *great* denoting a family relationship. However, the words *grand* and *step* are usually joined with the words *father, mother,* etc.

> Your grandfather's father is your great-grandfather.
> When Jane's father married again, she acquired a stepmother.

9. Use a hyphen to indicate that a letter or group of letters is being referred to as a part of a word or a phrase. Those letters are usually underlined or italicized.

> A number of words beginning with *a-* never precede a noun—for example, *alone* and *afraid.*
> The suffix *-ed* is used to indicate past time.

10. Use hyphens in preposed modifiers which are constructions themselves. The hyphen is a reader-helping device since it indicates that the preceding word and the immediately following word make a construction. In the examples below, see if ambiguity or momentary confusion might result if you removed the hyphens.

h

I will enumerate kinds of constructions that are used as noun-preceding modifiers and should be hyphenated (some of the groups overlap: some examples apply to more than one group).

a. A reciprocal construction. The modifiers in the construction jointly apply to the following noun or noun construction.

> A new British-American treaty has been signed. [The treaty is jointly British and American.]
> The workers installed some telephone-telegraph poles. [The poles are for both telephones and telegraphy.]

b. A measurement construction. Often, the first member of the construction is a number, and the last member is an uninflected noun.

> I want a twenty-inch board.
> Mrs. Jay has a six-foot husband. ·
> Paul is taking a ten-day cruise.
> Visitors marvel at the 102-story building.
> The traveler demanded first-class accommodations.
> Ben received a twelve-volume set of detective stories for Christmas.

Such a construction can often be expanded into a longer group with the words *broad, deep, high, long, old, tall,* or *wide* and placed after the modified noun; the noun in the measurement construction is then inflected for number.

> I want a board twenty inches wide.
> Mrs. Jay has a husband six feet tall.
> Paul is taking a cruise ten days long.
> Visitors marvel at the building 102 stories high.

Some such constructions can be postposed with words like *having, of,* and *with.*

> Visitors marvel at the building with 102 stories.
> Ben received a detective-story set having twelve volumes.
> The traveler demanded accommodations of the first class.

c. A comparison construction. The last member of the construction is frequently a term of measurement such as *high, deep,* and *long.* The construction can often be postposed into a comparison with *as.*

> The ship wallowed in mountain-high waves. ["... in waves as high as a mountain."]
> That was an all-day job. [" ... a job as long as a day."]
> Alice wore a lily-white dress. ["... a dress as white as a lily."]

d. A degree construction. The first member is frequently a degree word like *dark, far, fast, full, half, hard, light, little, much, never, part,* or *well;* the last member may be a noun, adjective, or verb. However, do not use a hyphen with an *-ly* adverb or *very, quite,* and *rather.*

> The room had dark-brown paneling.
> The news had far-reaching effects.

> Wingate is a fast-growing lad.
> I get up at half-past seven.
> Bost is a much-admired actor.
> The team enjoyed the hard-won game.
> Bob used to have a part-time job, but now he has a full-time one.

A number of rather stereotyped phrases belong to this category.

> The Grand Canyon is a never-to-be-forgotten spectacle.
> Gracie's dress was made of a hard-to-get material.

e. A predicate-complement construction. The construction is made up of a verb form and a preceding complement. Some of the examples in ¶ *d* above illustrate the construction: *far-reaching, fast-growing, half-past, much-admired,* and *hard-won.*

The construction is often composed of a participle and its preceding direct object or predicate adjective.

> The old man told a heart-breaking story. [*Heart* is the direct object of *breaking.*]
> Advertisers look for attention-getting devices. [*Attention* is the direct object of *getting.*]
> The sick boy had to take some foul-tasting medicine. [*Foul* is the predicate adjective of *tasting.*]
> Mr. Evans's Steinway is a beautiful-sounding piano. [*Beautiful* is the predicate adjective of *sounding.*]

The last member often has the past-participle inflection *-d, -t,* or *-n.* Very frequently, however, the form to which the inflection is added is not ordinarily a verb (e.g., *old-fashioned;* similar terms are *-headed, -hearted,* and *-minded.*) The first term is usually an adjective form or a noun form. The construction can usually be postposed with a preposition such as *by, of,* or *with.*

> A long-legged boy is a boy with long legs.
> A self-satisfied man is a man satisfied with himself.
> A self-taught person is a person taught by himself.
> A feeble-minded child is a child with a feeble mind.
> A man-made satellite is a satellite made by man.
> A Paris-bound traveler is a traveler bound for Paris.
> Old-fashioned manners are manners characteristic of old fashions.

f. A construction of origin, location, material, composition, purpose, or destination. The construction can often be postposed with words such as *composed of, for, from, having, in, made of,* and *to.*

> The marooned man lived on a coral-reef island.
> The agency undertook a house-to-house canvass.
> Susan is studying sixteenth-century authors.

g. A stereotyped construction. Some phrases have been used so often that they have virtually become one word. Many of them contain a preposition.

> The headline was a tongue-in-cheek contribution by the editor.
> Mr. Plyler's proposal was a castle-in-the-air scheme.
> The judge was surprised at the counselor's matter-of-fact attitude.

h

11. Write the following -*self* compounds and generalizing words without a hyphen or a space:

himself	anybody	anything	whatever
herself	everybody	everything	whenever
itself	nobody	nothing	wherever
myself	somebody	something	whichever
oneself	anyone	anywhere	whoever
ourselves	everyone	everywhere	whomever
themselves	someone	nowhere	whosoever
yourself		somewhere	
yourselves			

a. Everybody and *everyone* both mean "every person"; they are the spellings you need most often. *Every body* usually means "every corpse." *Every one* means "each" and is usually followed by a phrase beginning with *of.*

Everybody needs a friend.
Every body was buried in a common grave.
Everyone was happy about the prize.
Every one of the boys was punished.

12. Write the following words without a hyphen or a space:

airplane	homesick	somewhat	widespread
another	household	subway	bathroom (but: living room)
baseball	instead	therefore	bedroom (but: dining room)
basketball	nowadays	throughout	everyday ("usual; ordinary")
football	praiseworthy	today	maybe ("perhaps")
goodby	roommate	together	sometimes ("at times")
highway	skyscraper	tomorrow	

13. Do not use a hyphen within a proper name or its derivative.

Robert Frost is a New Englander.
He is said to have a New England conscience.
Do you like the Radio City flower displays?
I read *The New York Times* every morning.
Brazil is the largest South American country.
Trudy is working in a Seventh Avenue drugstore.

14. Do not join these words:

all right	every day ("each day")	no one
any more	in fact	of course
any place	in spite of	some times ("some periods")

Everything is all right now.	We do not go there any more.
I see Boyd almost every day.	I will meet you any place you name.
Some times are better than others.	Bob is industrious in spite of his age.

Also, see § Word Order—Adjective before Noun.

-IC, -ICS, -ICAL, **AND** *-ICALLY*   I.1

1. Almost all words which end in *-ic, -ics, -ical,* or *-ically* have their primary stress on the vowel preceding those endings. Some examples are the following:

Atlantic	economics	mathematics	practically
chemical	enthusiastic	music	sympathetic
critical	frantically	picnic	tropics
democratic	garlic	political	typical

2. The major exceptions are these, all stressed on the first vowel: *Arabic, Catholic, lunatic, rhetoric,* and *politics.*

3. *Arithmetic* usually has primary stress on the first *i.* When it is used in phrases such as "arithmetic progression" and "arithmetic mean," it has primary stress on the *e.*

4. Adverbs which are related to words ending in *-ic* or *-ical* have the ending *-ically.* The only exception is *publicly,* and that has the stress on the *u.*

5. A *k* is added after the *-ic* before a suffix beginning with *e, i,* or *y.*

picnic – picnicker	mimic – mimicking	panic – panicky

IN—PREPOSITION   I.2

Some of the uses of the preposition *in* are discussed below.

1. *In* indicates confinement, containment, or general location within. Note the two positions of the preposition in the sixth and seventh examples. Also, see § Word Order—Preposition.

> The tourists ate their dinner in the large dining room.
> Carl was waiting for Millicent in the car.
> The miners were standing waist-deep in water.
> There was a large hole in the ground.
> There are not many students in our class.
> I did not know in which house Mr. Snodgrass lived.
> I did not know which house Mr. Snodgrass lived in.
> Mr. Whipple was carrying a letter in his hand.
> Martin was in the army for five years.
> The marines looked handsome in their colorful uniforms.
> The rascal was known in the region as "Crying" Kelly.
> Mr. Yarborough will be in town next week. [The meaning of *in town* here is "present, here, or available."]

2. *In* indicates location within continents, countries, states, and cities. Note that usage requires *arrive in* and *come to* for such locations, but *arrive at* for a place within such a location.

France is in Europe.
The Adamses stayed in France for several months.
Mark's home is in Michigan now.
Horace went to school at Harvard University in Boston.
Lionel arrived in New York yesterday.
Lionel came to New York yesterday.
Lionel arrived at the airport.

3. *In* expresses state, condition, or manner.

The beggar was dressed in rags.
The movie was in technicolor.
Howard spoke in a low voice.
Max spoke to the stranger in English.
Shoes are always sold in pairs.
I asked for change in one-dollar bills.
Irene writes in a conventional style.
We order from that company in large amounts.
We looked at the man in wonder.
Can you define it in a general way?

4. Note that *in* is written together with *stead* in the word *instead.*

Why don't you use the large book instead of the small one?

For *in* with time expressions, see § Preposition in Time Expression. Also, see § Article—*The* vs. No *The,* § Infinitive vs. Gerund, § Intensifier, and § Preposition —Expression with.

INFINITIVE VS. GERUND   I.3

1. The terms *infinitive* and *gerund* are applied to certain forms of verbs. The infinitive is that form which is customarily preceded by the word *to* (e.g., *to love*), and the gerund is the form which has the suffix *-ing* (e.g., *loving*) and which is used like a noun. The gerund is identical in form with the present participle, which is used as a modifier. (The gerund and the present participle are sometimes referred to together as "the *-ing* form.")

She wants to read. [*To read* is used as a noun, the object of the verb *wants.*]
Singing is enjoyable. [*Singing* is used as a noun, the subject of the verb *is.*]

The infinitive and the gerund may have modifiers and complements. A modifier that precedes a gerund usually has its adjective form; a modifier that follows a gerund usually has its adverb form.

Harmonious singing is enjoyable. [*Harmonious* modifies *singing.*]
Singing harmoniously is enjoyable. [*Harmoniously* modifies *singing.*]
She wants to read it. [*It* is a complement, the object of *read.*]

The infinitive and the gerund may have an expressed subject which precedes

182

the infinitive or gerund. When a personal pronoun is the subject of an infinitive, the pronoun has its object form. The subject of a gerund has its genitive form.

> She wants John to read. [*John* is the subject of *to read.*]
> She wants him to read. [*Him* is the subject of *to read.*]
> John's singing is enjoyable. [*John's* is the subject of *singing.*]
> His singing is enjoyable. [*His* is the subject of *singing.*]

When the subject of a gerund is a word group, the sign of the genitive ('s or ') is often omitted.

> She remembered the children's talking about the accident.
> She remembered the children in the school talking about the accident.
> She remembered their talking about the accident.

Sometimes there is no subject immediately before an infinitive or a gerund. In that case, the *contextual subject* for the infinitive or gerund is supplied from the context; it may be specific or generalized.

> She wants to read. [*She* is the contextual subject of *to read.*]
> Singing is enjoyable. [The contextual subject of *singing* is generalized: it may be anybody or anything.]

The expressed subject of an infinitive is usually preceded by the word *for* except after the verbs discussed in ¶ 11 (for example, *want*). Notice the difference in meaning in the following pairs of sentences.

> I signed the paper to get the license. [*I* is the contextual subject of *to get.*]
> I signed the paper for him to get the license. [*Him* is the expressed subject of *to get.*]
> Is there anything to eat? [*Anybody* is the contextual subject of *to eat.*]
> Is there anything for me to eat? [*Me* is the expressed subject of *to eat.*]

2. Sometimes the infinitive is interchangeable with the gerund; usually, however, it is not. Here is a summary of the places to use the gerund rather than the infinitive:

a. As a modifier of the adjective *worth*

> That shirt is not worth saving.

b. As an object of a preposition

> Charles finds relaxation in swimming.

c. As an object of a separable two-word verb

> Charles gave up swimming   *or*   Charles gave swimming up.

d. As a direct object of certain verbs, listed in ¶ 11

> Charles enjoys swimming.

e. As any other kind of complement (predicate nominative, indirect object, or predicate objective) expressing a continuing act, an action that has some duration

> Charles's favorite recreation is swimming. [*Swimming* is the predicate nominative of *is.*]
> Charles gives swimming his undivided attention. [*Swimming* is the indirect object of *gives.*]
> Do you call that swimming? [*Swimming* is the predicate objective of *call.*]

In contrast, the infinitive is timeless: it does not suggest duration.

> Charles's aim is to win. [*To win* is the predicate nominative of *is.*]

For the use of the gerund as a subject, see ¶ 5 below.

3. In other places, use the infinitive instead of the gerund, particularly to show purpose or reason. Usually, *in order* may be inserted before an infinitive expressing purpose or reason.

> They hurried to be on time. [They hurried in order to be on time.]
> Most people work to earn money. [. . . in order to earn . . .]
> She came here to study, not to have a good time. [. . . in order to study, not in order to have . . .]

4. The infinitive is often used after a noun or pronoun to express purpose or reason.

> Renee bought a book *to read* on the plane.
> Give me something *to remember* you by.

The following sections take up the uses of the infinitive and the gerund in detail.

5. Here are three complementary rules that apply to the infinitive and the gerund:

Rule 1: An infinitive is rarely used as a subject before a verb. You may sometimes encounter such a construction in writing, but I advise you to avoid using it.

Rule 2: A gerund is often used as the subject before a verb.

> Smoking is forbidden.
> Walking is good exercise.
> Learning takes time.
> Studying is not easy.

The gerund may have a complement, and it may have an expressed subject.

> Smoking in this room is forbidden.
> Walking dogs is good exercise.
> Children's learning takes time.

However, sometimes it seems very awkward or unnatural to have a long gerund construction as a subject. It is better to follow Rule 3 below when there are subjects and complements.

Rule 3: Very often a "filler *it*" or "preparatory *it*" is placed before the verb, and the *real subject* (often called the *delayed or deferred subject*) is expressed as an infinitive after the verb and its complements. Grammatically, the *it* is the subject, and the real subject is an appositive to the *it.*

It takes time to learn.
It is not easy to study.

It is often a good idea to use Rule 3 if the real subject contains more than one word.

It is forbidden to smoke in this room.
It costs ten dollars to fly to Rollins.

a. The word *for* is used before an expressed subject of the infinitive.

It is forbidden for students to smoke in this room.
It is not easy for me to study.

b. After *cost* and *take* with preparatory *it,* two constructions are possible: (1) the subject of the infinitive may be expressed with *for,* or (2) the subject of the infinitive may be placed after *cost* and *take* without *for.* The second construction is probably the more frequent.

It takes time for children to learn.
It takes children time to learn.
It costs ten dollars for a person to fly to Rollins.
It costs a person ten dollars to fly to Rollins.

c. After adjectives expressing judgements, *of* is used if the judgement is made about the subject of the infinitive, and *for* is used if the judgement is made about the action expressed by the infinitive.

It was good of you to help that old woman.
It was good for you to take that medicine.
It is absurd of you to believe that.
It is all right for you to leave now.
It was very kind of you to lend him some money.
It seemed cruel of the boy to kill the insect.
It appeared silly for us to have to wait in the outer office.

See ¶ 7 for a list containing adjectives of judgement.

6. Almost any adjective modified by *too* or *enough* may be followed by an infinitive.

That package is too big to carry.
The child is too young to go to school.
I am too tired to play any more.
Would you be kind enough to help me?
She was silly enough to cry.
He was angry enough to throw things.

If the subject of the infinitive is expressed, it is preceded by *for.*

> That package is too big for me to carry.
> That shirt is clean enough for you to wear.

7. Even when they are not modified by *too* or *enough,* certain adjectives are often followed by an infinitive. Those adjectives can be grouped in two general classes: (a) adjectives expressing judgements, and (b) adjectives expressing an emotion or desire. Those two classes include participles used like adjectives.

Here is a list of common adjectives expressing a judgement or an emotion or desire:

able	desirous	intelligent	rude
absurd	difficult	kind	shocked
afraid	disappointed	liable	silly
amazed	eager	likely	slow
anxious	easy	lucky	smart
apt	embarrassed	mortified	sorry
bold	excited	naughty	spiteful
bound	fair	nice	stupid
brave	fit	painful	suitable
bright	foolish	pleasant	sure
careless	fortunate	pleased	surprised
certain	glad	polite	thoughtful
civil	good	possible	thoughtless
clever	gratified	presumptuous	thrilled
considerate	grieved	prompt	welcome
content	happy	proud	wicked
courageous	hard	qualified	willing
cowardly	heartless	quick	wise
crazy	honest	rash	wonderful
cruel	horrified	ready	wrong
decent	impatient	reluctant	
delighted	impudent	right	

To this list can be added derivatives of those adjectives such as *dishonest, easiest, impolite, inconsiderate,* and *unwise.*

> The boy is able to walk again
> Mr. Cole is pleasant to work with.
> I was glad to see the policeman.
> Sam felt afraid to ask for a raise.
> The directions are easy to follow.
> The witness became reluctant to talk.
> Sally got impatient to start.
> Mazie was brave to express her feelings
> Paul's handwriting is hard to read.
> The player was clever to stop right then.
> Mrs. Cox looked desirous to help.
> I am surprised to hear your excuse.
> I grew anxious to know the result.

Tim stands ready to answer all questions.
Pearl seemed unwilling to reply.
Sal was foolish to take his advice.
I am eager to leave.
Mr. Allen was sorry to know the truth.

If the subject of the infinitive is expressed, it is preceded by *for.*

I am eager for Gertrude to leave.
He was sorry for her to know the truth.

8. Other adjectives are customarily followed by a preposition and a gerund. A large number of them are listed under § Preposition—Expression with.

Mr. Whitcomb is capable of committing any crime.
The Brewsters are intent on getting all they can.
Bob was successful in asking for a raise.

Some of the adjectives of judgement and emotion which are listed in ¶ 7 are also often followed by a preposition and a gerund. Sometimes the meaning is the same; sometimes it is different.

Aren't you afraid of getting wet?
Elaine was proud of getting an *A.*
My wife is not good at cooking.
Cy is happy about finding his lost pen.
Arnold is excited about going.
Miriam is careless about answering notes.

9. Another general rule is that a gerund is used after a preposition.

Lucas thought about quitting.
You should rely on studying, not guessing.
You can count on our helping you.
That child is in danger of falling.
Rowing is different from swimming.
I feel like crying.

Certain words are frequently followed by a preposition and a gerund. Consult the list in § Preposition—Expression with. Also, see § Preposition in Time Expression, and § Two-word Verb.

a. The word *to* may function either as a *true* preposition or as the *sign of the infinitive.* Here is a test that is sometimes helpful: replace the verb form by a noun which does not end in *-ing:* if the *to* is not retained, it is the sign of the infinitive; if the *to* is retained, it is a true preposition.

Roger wanted food.
Roger wanted to eat. [The *to* is the sign of the infinitive.]
Ralph objected to the trip.
Ralph objected to going. [The *to* is a true preposition.]

b. The words *used* and *accustomed* may be troublesome to many of you in this respect. Use the gerund after *accustomed.*

> Mr. Warren is accustomed to wearing good clothes.
> I have become accustomed to speaking English.
> Have the Barbours got accustomed to having less money?

For *used,* try this test: in an affirmative statement, if *used* is immediately preceded by a subject, use the infinitive; otherwise, use the gerund. Turn a question into a statement, and then apply the test.

> I used to think English was easy.
> Did you use to think English was easy? [You used to think. . . .]
> He did not use to think English was easy. [He used to think. . . .]
> We are used to seeing beautiful women in advertisements.
> Are you used to riding the subway? [You are used to riding. . . .]
> José became used to hearing people mispronounce his name.
> Have you got used to drinking American coffee? [You have got used to
>   drinking. . . .]

10. The gerund is used as the object of a separable two-word verb. See § Two-word Verb for a detailed discussion of those verbs and § Preposition—Expression with *for* a list of numerous two-word verbs; in that list those which are separable are marked by (S). Remember the test of a separable two-word verb: a short pronoun object comes between the verb and the participle.

> He gave up smoking. *or* He gave smoking up. *but* He gave it up.
> Don't put off studying. *or* Don't put studying off. *but* Don't put it off.

If the gerund is modified or has a complement, put the particle next to the verb.

> Don't put off your studying for the final examination.

11. It is necessary to learn whether an infinitive or a gerund follows certain verbs.

a. Certain verbs are ordinarily followed only by the gerund or only by the infinitive.

b. Certain other verbs are ordinarily followed by the infinitive, but *for* is not used before the expressed subject of the infinitive.

c. Still other verbs are similarly followed by the infinitive, but the word *to* is not used before the infinitive.

d. A few verbs may be followed by either the gerund or the infinitive. Sometimes there is a difference of meaning; sometimes there is not. If there is no difference in meaning and the verb ends in *-ing,* it is stylistically better to follow it with the infinitive, not the gerund—for example, "They are are beginning *to talk* about something else."

All of those verbs occur in one or more of the following four patterns:

Pattern 1	SUBJECT +	VERB +	GERUND
	He	enjoyed	dancing.
	They	have finished	studying.

In Pattern 1, the subject of the gerund is not expressed. It is usually but not always the same as the subject of the verb. For clarity, the subject may be expressed, but in that event Pattern 2 is used.

Pattern 2	SUBJECT +	VERB	+ SUBJECT OF GERUND +	GERUND
	He	enjoyed	Pavlova's	dancing.
	They	have finished	their	studying.

In Pattern 2, the subject of the gerund is expressed. (See § Predicate Adjective for another pattern which appears to be similar to Pattern 2. Here are some examples: "He left them crying" and "She caught them cheating.")

Pattern 3	SUBJECT +	VERB	+ INFINITIVE
	I	want	to go.
	They	have agreed	to stop.

In Pattern 3, the contextual subject of the infinitive is the same as the subject of the verb.

Pattern 4	SUBJECT +	VERB +	SUBJECT OF INFINITIVE +	INFINITIVE
	I	want	them	to go.
	They	warned	him	to stop.

In Pattern 4, the subject of the infinitive is expressed.

A number of the verbs described above also occur in two other patterns with the infinitive. In those patterns the *wh* words (*what, when, where, which, who, whom, whose, why,* and *how*) and *whether* and *if* (meaning "whether") are used.

Pattern 5	SUBJECT +	VERB	+ WH WORD +	INFINITIVE
	I	know	how	to dance.
	He	can't decide	when	to leave.

In Pattern 5, the contextual subject of the infinitive is the same as the subject of the verb. The exceptions are *tell, explain,* and similar verbs of reporting: the subject of the infinitive is generalized: it may be anybody or anything; for example, "The book tells how to use that word." Pattern 5 is also used with certain other expressions; see *figure out* and *find out* under § Preposition—Expression with and *have an idea* under § *Have.*

Pattern 6	SUBJECT +	VERB	+ NOUN OR PRONOUN +	WH WORD +	INFINITIVE
	We	showed	him	how	to swim.
	He	told	her	which dress	to wear.

In Pattern 6, the noun or pronoun is the subject of the infinitive except after *ask.* The subject of *ask* is the contextual subject of the following infinitive in this pattern—for example, "The boys asked the policeman how to go to the stadium."

Following is a list of verbs which govern the use of the six patterns described above. The number following the letter *P* indicates which of the six patterns the verb occurs in. If the same example is given for two patterns, there is no difference in the meaning of the verb in those patterns. Notice that the infinitive and the gerund may be modified by a preceding *not* or *never.* The list does not include those verbs which are followed only by an infinitive expressing purpose or reason.

admit, **P. 1.** The thief admitted   entering the house.

admonish, **P. 4.** His mother admonished   him   to behave.

advise, **P. 1.** The doctor advised   taking exercise.

     P. 2. The doctor advised   my   taking exercise.

     P. 4. The doctor advised   me   to take exercise.

     P. 6. A broker will advise   you   how   to invest your money.

afford, **P. 3.** I can't afford   to buy a new car.

agree, **P. 3.** Nations often agree   to reduce armaments.

aim, **P. 3.** A good businessman aims   to please his customers.

allow, **P. 1.** Mrs. Green does not allow   smoking in her house.

     P. 4. Walter's mother will not allow   him   to attend the game.

appear, **P. 3.** Mr. Fisher appeared   to know nothing about the incident.

appoint, **P. 4.** (See ¶ 12) We appointed   him   to be our spokesman.

appreciate, **P. 1.** Most invalids appreciate   receiving flowers.

     P. 2. I appreciate   your   telling me that.

arrange, **P. 3.** I will arrange   to see him tomorrow.

ask, **P. 3.** The soldier asked   to be given leave for a few days.

     P. 4. Lester asked   me   to go with him.

     P. 5. The tourist asked   how   to get to Grant's Tomb.

     P. 6. You had better ask   him   where   to transfer for Boston.

attempt, **P. 1.** You should not attempt   climbing that mountain.

     P. 3. You should not attempt   to climb that mountain.

avoid, **P. 1.** Intelligent people avoid   getting involved in such matters.

be, **P. 3.** You are   to go with us tomorrow.

bear, "endure," **P. 1.** Some people can not bear   watching a bullfight.

     P. 3. Some people can not bear   to watch a bullfight.

beg, **P. 3.** Johnny begged   to go with us.

     P. 4. The host begged   the guests   to have more refreshments.

begin, **P. 1.** They began   talking about something else.

     P. 3. They began   to talk about something else.

believe, **P. 4.** (See ¶ 12) We believe   him   to be the instigator.

bother, "take the trouble," **P. 3.** Mr. Jenkins did not bother   to reply.

can, **P. 3.** (no *to*). You can   stay with us.

can't help, "can't avoid," **P. 1.** (used only as *can't help* or *couldn't help*).
     Martha can't help   crying at a sad movie.

care, **P. 3.** Would you care   to go to a show tonight?

cause, **P. 4.** The incident caused   him   to change his intention.

cease, **P. 1.** The girls ceased   chattering when their mother came in.

     P. 2. The girls ceased   their   chattering when their mother came in.

     P. 3. The girls ceased   to chatter when their mother came in.

challenge, **P. 4.** Mr. Malcolm challenged   me   to prove my statement.

chance, "risk," **P. 1.** We can chance   leaving without permission.

     "happen," **P. 3.** I chanced   to meet Mitchell in the drugstore.

choose, **P. 3.** I would not choose   to live in Alaska.

     P. 4. The scoutmaster chose   me   to go with him.

claim, **P. 3.** The braggart claimed   to know everything.
come: a. The infinitive expresses purpose.
    P. 3. (Usually with *to*).   Norman came   to see me.
    (Sometimes with *and* instead of *to*).   Norman came   and saw me
    (Sometimes without *to* immediately after the form *come*).   He will
    come   see me tomorrow.   *but*   He is coming   to see me tomorrow.
b. The infinitive expresses result.
    P. 3. The Indians came   to distrust the colonists.
command, **P. 4.** The officer commanded   him   not to leave his post.
commence, **P. 1.** The canary commenced   singing.
    P. 3. The canary commenced   to sing.
compel, **P. 4.** Martin's conscience compelled   him   to tell the truth.
complete, **P. 1.** Have you completed   packing your bag?
consent, **P. 3.** The soprano consented   to sing at the concert.
consider, **P. 1.** Murray would not consider   working without pay.
    P. 4. (See ¶ 12) The girls consider   him   to be their hero.
    P. 5. I considered   how   to explain the problem.
continue, **P. 1.** You should continue   learning as long as you live.
    P. 3. You should continue   to learn as long as you live.
dare, **P. 3.**   (sometimes without *to*).   I did not dare   to ask for more.
    I did not dare   ask for more.
    P. 4. Mildred dared   me   to ask for more.
decide, **P. 3.** My aunt decided   to stay at home.
    P. 4. (See ¶ 12) The election decided   me   to leave England.
    P. 5. We must decide   whether   to go or stay.
declare, **P. 4.** (See ¶ 12) The referee declared   him   to be the winner.
defend, **P. 2.** The lawyer defended   my   leaving the scene of the accident.
defer, **P. 1.** Michael always defers   doing his homework until the last moment.
delay, **P. 1.** A lazy person delays   starting a job.
demand, **P. 3.** My doctor demanded   to know what I had been doing.
deny, **P. 1.** The witness denied   having seen the accused man.
deserve, **P.1.** (gerund = *to be* + past participle). The killer deserves   hanging.
    P. 3. My associate deserves   to have a promotion.
desire, **P. 3.** Newlyweds frequently desire   to go to Niagara Falls.
    P. 4. The butler desired   me   to follow him.
despise, **P. 1.** Eliot despises   working hard.
determine, **P. 3.** Marcel determined   to study harder.
    P. 4. Marcel's low grade determined   him   to study harder.
detest, **P. 1.** Some teachers detest   correcting papers.
    P. 2. Louisa detested   his   asking her for advice.
discover, **P. 5.** Have you discovered   how   to live without working?
dislike, **P. 1.** Do you dislike   getting up early?
    P. 3. Do you dislike   to get up early?
dread, **P. 1.** Monroe dreaded   being examined.
    P. 2. Bessie dreaded   his   coming home.
drive, **P. 4.** Alexander's sense of guilt drove   him   to confess his crime.
enable, **P. 4.** The scholarship enabled   him   to go to college.
encourage, **P. 4.** Mr. Collins's wife encouraged   him   to try again.

endeavor, **P. 3.** The miser endeavored   to hide his money.

endure, **P. 1.** I can not endure   listening for another moment.

P. 2. Lucille could not endure   his   speaking to her like that.

enjoy, **P. 1.** Almost nobody enjoys   sitting through a movie twice.

P. 2. I certainly enjoy   Bob's   singing.

entreat, **P. 4.** Sylvia entreated   me   to stay a little longer.

escape, "avoid," **P. 1.** Mr. Carr could not escape   answering his wife's question.

excuse, **P. 2.** Please excuse   my   delaying you.

expect, **P. 3.** We expect   to leave early in the morning.

P. 4. The manager expected   us   to pay the bill.

explain, **P. 5.** The book explains   how   to solve that problem.

fail, **P. 3.** The driver failed   to see the other car in time.

fancy, "like," **P. 1.** I did not fancy   getting up at six o'clock.

P. 2. Emily did not fancy   my   telling her what to do.

favor, **P. 1.** I favor   waiting until we are sure the rumor is correct.

fear, **P. 1.** The diver feared   making another attempt.

P. 3. The diver feared   to make another attempt.

feel, **P. 4.** (without *to;* also, see ¶ 12). Can you feel   the floor   shake?

find, **P. 4.** (See ¶ 12) The jury found   him   to be guilty.

finish, **P. 1.** Have you finished   studying for your examination?

P. 2. Have you finished   your   studying for your examination?

forbid, **P. 1.** Mrs. Peabody forbade   smoking in her house.

P. 2. Paul's mother will forbid   his   going with you.

P. 4. Paul's mother will forbid   him   to go with you.

force, **P. 4.** Anita's father forced   her   to go to school.

forget, "not have in mind from the past," **P. 1.** Mill forgot   paying the bill before.

P. 2. She forgot   my   telling her about it.

"not have in mind for the future," **P. 3.** Don't forget   to come tomorrow.

P. 5. Don't forget   how   to do that.

get, "begin," **P. 1.** I told the driver to get   going.

"succeed," **P. 3.** Jack was so friendly that he soon got   to know everybody.

"cause," **P. 4.** I got   him   to tell me who the girl was.

give to understand, **P. 4.** Sam gave   me   to understand that he was angry.

go: a. The infinitive expresses purpose.

P. 3. (Usually with *to*).   Helen went   to see the play.

(Sometimes with *and* instead of *to*).   Helen went   and saw the play.

(Sometimes without *to* immediately after the form *go*).   She will go   see the play tomorrow.   *but*   She is going   to see the play tomorrow.

b. The gerund expresses a prolonged activity.

P. 1. The girls went   swimming (dancing, golfing, shopping, etc.) today.

guess, **P. 4.** (See ¶ 12) We guessed   him   to be the man we wanted to see.

P. 5. Can you guess   how   to say that in French?

happen, **P. 3.** I happen   to know the answer to your question.

hate, **P. 1.** George hates   admitting that his wife was right.

P. 2. Lucas hates   anybody's   knowing more news than he does.

P. 3. George hates   to admit that his wife was right.

P. 4. Lucas hates   anybody   to know more news than he does.

have, "must," **P. 3.** I have   to leave now.

"cause; order," **P. 4.** (no *to*). I will have   him   deliver the package tomorrow.

hear, **P. 4.** (no *to*). The teacher heard   him   mispronounce the word.

P. 5. That student did not hear   how   to prepare his homework.

help, **P. 1.** (See *can't help* above.)

P. 3. (with or without *to*). I will help   wash the dishes.
I will help   to wash the dishes.

P. 4. (with or without *to*). Won't you help   me   make up my mind?
Won't you help   me   to make up my mind?

hesitate, **P. 3.** An indecisive man hesitates   to take any kind of action.

hire, **P. 4.** Mr. Simpson hired   her   to answer his letters.

hope, **P.3.** We hope   to see you again soon.

imagine, **P. 1.** Matthew must have imagined   seeing her there.

P. 2. You imagined   my   going there; I have been home all day.

P. 4. (See ¶ 12) I imagined   him   to be different.

P. 5. I can not even imagine   how   to pronounce that word.

impel, **P. 4.** Justice impels   me   to speak in his behalf.

implore, **P. 4.** Mrs. Bailey implored   him   to stop.

induce, **P. 4.** The judge induced   them   to testify.

inform, **P. 4.** The letter informed   me   to appear at nine o'clock.

P. 6. The policeman informed   them   where   to go to find the subway.

inquire, **P. 5.** They inquired   how   to find the address.

instruct, **P. 4.** I instructed   him   to take the boxes away.

intend, **P. 1.** What do you intend   doing after graduation?

P. 3. What do you intend   to do after graduation?

P. 4. I intended   him   to get the money.

invite, **P. 4.** The hostess invited   them   to stay for lunch.

judge, **P. 4.** (See ¶ 12) I judge   him   to be a clever man.

keep, "continue," **P. 1.** Don't quit; keep   trying.

know, **P. 4.** (See ¶ 12) I did not know   him   to be a criminal.

P. 5. Jacques does not know   how   to speak English.

lead, "cause," **P. 4.** I led   them   to believe that Mae was coming.

learn, **P. 3.** Where did you learn   to speak English?

P. 5. You can learn   how   to type at that school.

let, **P. 4.** (no *to*). Sally will not let   me   help her.

like, **P. 1.** Do you like   swimming?

P. 2. I do not like   his   singing.

P. 3. Do you like   to swim?

P. 4. Florence liked   him   to help her.

listen to, **P. 4.** (no *to* before the infinitive). Listen to   them   yell.

long, "desire," **P. 3.** Do all girls long   to get married?

love, **P. 1.** Children love   listening to fairy tales.

P. 2. Johnny loves   my   telling him ghost stories.

P. 3. Children love   to listen to fairy tales.

P. 4. Johnny loves   me   to tell him ghost stories.

make, **P. 4.** (no *to*). I will make   him   go with me.

manage, **P. 3.** How did Susan manage   to marry that nice young man?

mean, "intend," **P. 3.** I did not mean   to make you angry.

    P. 4. Your father meant   me   to help you with the job.

    "involve; have as a result," **P. 1.** Your plan would mean   spending hours.

    P. 2. Your plan would mean   our   spending hours.

mind, "object to," **P. 1.** The teacher did not mind   explaining the problem again.

miss, "avoid," **P. 1.** You can't miss   seeing the statue on your way there.

need, **P. 1.** (gerund = *to be* + past participle).   Your shoes need   polishing.

    P. 3. You need   to see a doctor.

    P. 4. Morton needed   them   to help him.

neglect, **P. 1.** Mr. Shaw neglected   answering the letter right away.

    P. 3. Mr. Shaw neglected   to answer the letter right away.

notice, **P. 4.** (no *to*). Did you notice   him   hesitate for a moment?

notify, **P. 4.** The landlord notified   them   to vacate their apartments.

oblige, **P. 4.** My father obliged   me   to tell the truth.

observe, **P. 5.** Interns observe   how   to perform operations.

offer, **P. 3.** The stranger offered   to show me the way.

omit, **P. 1.** The contractor omitted   signing the paper.

    P. 3. The contractor omitted   to sign the paper.

order, **P. 4.** The officer ordered   them   to surrender.

ought, **P. 3.** You ought   to help that old woman.

overhear, **P. 4.** (no *to*). I accidentally overheard   him   tell her to go away.

perceive, **P. 5.** The student finally perceived   how   to solve the puzzle.

permit, **P. 1.** That teacher permits   smoking in his class.

    P. 2. That teacher permits   our   smoking in his class.

    P. 4. That teacher permits   us   to smoke in his class.

persuade, **P. 4.** I persuaded   him   to do what I wanted.

plan, **P. 3.** Mr. Russell planned   to leave the next morning.

pledge, **P. 3.** Have you ever pledged   to stop smoking?

postpone, **P. 1.** You should not postpone   doing your assignment.

    P. 2. Harold postponed   his   leaving until the next day.

prefer (also, see § *Prefer*), **P. 1.** I prefer   doing it my way.

    P. 2. Bert's mother prefers   his   staying at home.

    P. 3. I prefer   to do it my way.

    P. 4. Bert's mother prefers   him   to stay at home.

prepare, **P. 3.** I am preparing   to take the examination on Monday.

pretend, **P. 3.** Lucy pretended   to know the answer.

proceed, **P. 3.** Mr. Blivens proceeded   to explain the whole procedure.

promise, **P. 3.** Vernon promised   to return in an hour.

propose, **P. 1.** Lois proposed   doing it another way.

    P. 3. Lois proposed   to do it another way.

prove, **P. 3.** The horse proved   to be difficult to manage.

    P. 4. (See ¶ 12) Lawrence's research proved   me   to be wrong.

quit, "put an end to," **P. 1.** Sal quit   drinking coffee at the age of ninety.

    "change from doing something else," **P.3.** At noon the men quit   to eat.

recall, **P. 1.** Can't you recall   telling me that story last week?

    P. 2. I do not recall   his   asking that question.

refuse, **P. 3.** Conscientious objectors refuse   to fight in wars.

regret, **P. 1.** (Time of following verb is previous to *regret*) I regret   telling you that. *or* I regret   having told you that.

   P.3. (Time of following verb is same as or future to *regret*) I regret   to tell you this.

remember, "recall from the past," **P. 1.** Can't you remember   telling me that yesterday?

   "have in mind for the future," **P. 3.** You must remember   to leave tomorrow.

   P.5. Joe can't remember   how   to say "Thank you" in Dutch.

remind, **P. 4.** I reminded   him   to go to the meeting.

report, **P. 4.** (See ¶ 12) The doctor reported   him   to be very ill.

request, **P. 4.** The secretary requested   me .   to call again.

require, **P. 1.** (gerund = *to be* + past participle) His story requires   investigation.

   P. 4. The teacher required   the students   to write clearly.

resent, **P. 1.** Parsons resented   being told what to do.

   P. 2. Polly resented   my   insisting on promptness.

resist, **P. 1.** The comedian could not resist   imitating everybody he saw.

resolve, **P. 3.** People often resolve   to change their habits.

   P. 4. The minister's talk resolved   me   to try to change my ways.

resume, **P. 1.** We resumed   talking after the interruption.

   P. 2. We resumed   our   talking after the interruption.

risk, **P. 1.** I do not want to risk   losing my money.

rule, **P.4.** (See ¶ 12) The referee ruled   the game   to be a tie.

save, "eliminate the necessity of," **P. 1.** Foresight will save   doing the work over.

   P. 2. Foresight will save   our   doing the work over.

see, **P. 4.** (no *to*). Did you see   him   take the book?

   P. 5. I can not see   how   to make the work any easier.

seek, **P. 3.** The man sought   to blame his wife for his troubles.

seem, **P. 3.** That boy seems   to know what he is doing.

select, **P. 4.** (See ¶ 12) The freshman selected   her   to be May Queen.

send, **P. 4.** The company sent   a boy   to do a man's job.

serve, **P. 3.** Clarence's excuse only served   to enrage his boss.

shall, **P. 3.** (no *to*). I shall   tell Theodore tomorrow.

should, **P. 3.** (no *to*). You should   study very hard.

show, **P. 6.** The teacher showed   him   how   to improve his handwriting.

stand, "bear," **P. 1.** Willie can't stand   being in a closed room.

   P. 2. Estelle could not stand   his   getting ahead of her.

   P. 3. Willie can't stand   to be in a closed room.

   P. 4. Estelle could not stand   him   to get ahead of her.

start, **P. 1.** Where should we start   looking for the book?

   P. 3. Where should we start   to look for the book?

state, **P. 4.** (See ¶ 12) The company stated   his account   to be in error.

stop, "end," **P.1.** As long as you live, your heart never stops   beating.

   "stand still; change from doing something else," **P.3.** Mr. and Mrs. White stopped   to buy some groceries on their way home.

suggest, **P. 1.** Some doctors suggest   drinking milk for ulcers.

suppose, **P. 4.** (See ¶ 12) The villagers supposed   him   to be an honest man.

teach, **P. 4.** Miss Jenkins taught   him   to speak more clearly.

    P. 6. Charles taught   her   how   to dance.

tell, **P. 4.** The teacher told   me   to leave the room.

    P. 5. The instructions tell   what   to do next.

    P. 6. Mr. Brewster will tell   you   when   to come back.

tempt, **P. 4.** The reward tempted   him   to reveal his secret.

tend, **P. 3.** We all tend   to forget unpleasant incidents.

think, **P. 4.** (See ¶ 12) My mother thought   him   to be a nice man.

    P. 5. Can't you think   how   to spell that word?

train, **P. 4.** Sarah trained   them   to keep very quiet.

trouble, **P. 4.** May I trouble   you   to tell me where the office is?

trust, **P. 4.** You can certainly trust   him   to deliver the message.

try, "make an experiment with," **P. 1.** If you want to improve it, try   adding some salt.

    "make an attempt or effort," **P. 3.** The boy tried   to answer each question. (Sometimes with *and* instead of *to* after the form *try*) I want you to try   and answer.

understand, **P. 2.** I can't understand   your   thinking such a thing.

    P. 4. (See ¶ 12) I understood   him   to be your guardian.

    P. 5. I still can not understand   how   to divide a number by zero.

undertake, **P. 3.** The teacher undertook   to answer their questions.

urge, **P. 4.** I urged   him   to write the letter.

used, **P. 3.** I used   to like Paul, but now I don't.

venture, **P. 3.** Mr. Snodgrass did not venture   to express his opinion.

wait, **P. 3.** We are waiting   to hear from Oscar before we continue.

want, "desire," **P. 3.** Do you want   to hear the end of the story?

    P. 4. I want   him   to clean the windows.

    "need," **P. 1.** (gerund = *to be* + past participle) Your shoes want   polishing.

warn, **P. 4.** Jimmy's mother warned   him ′ to behave.

watch, **P. 4.** (no *to*). My maid just sits and watches   machines   do her work.

wish, **P. 3.** Many people wish   to inherit a million dollars.

    P. 4. I wish   him   to come to see me tomorrow.

wonder, **P. 5.** Philip wondered   where   to go for dinner.

would, **P. 3.** (no *to*). I would   like to see you later.

12. A number of verbs expressing an opinion or a mental perception fit into Pattern 4 discussed in ¶ 11: subject + verb + subject of infinitive + infinitive. Some of those verbs are the following:

appoint	declare	imagine	report	suppose
believe	feel	judge	rule	think
consider	find	know	select	understand
decide	guess	prove	state	

The infinitive in the pattern is *to be,* which is often omitted. However, if the infinitive expresses time prior to the verb, *to have been* is used and can not be omitted.

```
We believe        him       to be guilty.
We believe        him                guilty.
The agency reported      her      to be a good cook.
The agency reported      her              a good cook.
I judge      him      to be about sixty.
I judge      him              about sixty.
An umpire ruled   .   the game      to be a tie.
An umpire ruled       the game          a tie.
The court martial declared      them      to have been spies.
```

Instances of the verbs listed above are found in Pattern 4 more frequently in writing than in speaking. In conversation it seems to be more customary to use a dependent clause, either introduced by *that* or not, after those verbs in that meaning.

```
We believe        that he is guilty.
The agency reported      she was a good cook.
I judge      he is about sixty.
An umpire ruled       that the game was a tie.
The court martial declared      that they had been spies.
```

13. Pattern 4 of ¶ 11 and ¶ 12 can usually be converted into a passive construction. The subject of the infinitive is made the subject of a form of *be*, which is followed by the past participle of the verb and then by the infinitive.

```
Pattern 4:   Mrs. Jones invited      him      to stay.
Passive:     He was invited      to stay.
```

If the original subject of the verb in Pattern 4 is expressed in the passive construction, it becomes the *agent* and is preceded by the word *by.*

```
He was invited      to stay      by Mrs. Jones.
```

Here are some of the examples of Pattern 4 in ¶ 11 converted into the passive construction:

```
I was advised to take exercise.
Walter will not be allowed to attend the game.
I was asked to go with Lester.
The guests were begged to have more refreshments.
I was challenged to prove my statement.
I was chosen to go with the scoutmaster.
The soldier was commanded not to leave his post.
Mr. Collins was encouraged to try again.
We were expected to pay the bill.
Paul will be forbidden to go with you.
```

In the conversion, *to* is used before the infinitive after *felt, made,* and the other verbs which omit the *to* in Pattern 4.

```
The floor can be felt to shake.
He will be made to go with me.
He was noticed to hesitate for a moment.
```

Pattern 4 with the verbs in ¶ 12 can also be converted into a passive construction with or without *to be*. *To have been*, however, has to be expressed.

He is believed	to be guilty.
He is believed	guilty.
She was reported	to be a good cook.
She was reported	a good cook.
They were declared	to have been spies.

Pattern 4 is not customarily transposed into the passive construction if the verb is one of the following:

cause	get	hate	like	love	watch
decide	have	let	listen	stand	wish

Also, see § *-ing* Form vs. Infinitive, § Passive, and § *Rather.*

-*ING* FORM VS. INFINITIVE

1. The *-ing* form is the simple form of a verb with the suffix *-ing*—for example, *going, loving,* and *staying.* It is used sometimes as a gerund and sometimes as a present participle. For some of its uses, see § Infinitive vs. Gerund, § Preposition —Expression with, and § Word Order—Adjective after Noun and Pronoun.

2. The *-ing* form is a great source of puns because it is frequently ambiguous. A standard joke goes like this: "The customer asked for a reading lamp, but I told her all of ours were illiterate." The point of the joke, of course, lies in the fact that the *-ing* form *reading* here can mean either "which is reading" or "for reading."

An *-ing* form which is preposed to a noun is a modifier of that noun. However, it is customary to distinguish two kinds of such modifying *-ing* forms:

a. The *-ing* form is classified as a participle if it can be postposed after the words *who* (or *which*) *is* (or *are* or *was* or *were*). For instance, *crying* is a participle in "The crying boy left" since the sentence can be rephrased as "The boy who was crying left."

b. A preposed *-ing* form that can be postposed in other ways, principally after *for,* is classified as a gerund. For example, "I need an *ironing* board" can be rearranged into "I need a board for *ironing*." The preposed gerund functions in the same way as the *noun adjunct,* which is mentioned under § Part of Speech— Adjective.

3. Like the gerund, the infinitive without *to* also occurs as a preposed modifier to a noun. For example, *pull* is an infinitive in "The child played with his pull toy." Such an infinitive can frequently be transposed with *-ing* into a postposed gerund phrase—e.g., "The child played with his toy for pulling." The preposed infinitive usually lacks the ambiguity which seems inherent in the preposed *-ing* form. For example, "a dance hall" has only one possible interpretation ("a hall for dancing"), but "a dancing girl" may mean either "a girl who is dancing" or " a girl whose profession is dancing."

4. The *-ing* form sometimes occurs as a preposed modifier of an adjective. The *-ing* form functions like an adverb, but it does not have the *-ly* ending of an adverb as in "an *interestingly* told story." It usually expresses *degree* or *comparison*. Examples are in "The coffee was *boiling* hot" and "The man looked *fighting* mad." When the *-ing* form and its adjective are used as a preposed modifying construction, you should use a hyphen between them to denote their relationship—e.g., "She gave me some boiling-hot coffee" and "The fighting-mad man frightened me."

INTENSIFIER   I.5

1. Certain words and phrases are used to express emphasis or emotion. The most frequent "intensifier" is *very*, with the meaning of "to a high degree." Similar ones are *quite, certainly, exceedingly, extremely,* and *really.* They are used before descriptive adjectives, participles expressing judgements or emotions (see § Infinitive vs. Gerund), and adverbs.

> It is very hot today.
> It is quite hot today.
> The book was very interesting.
> The book was really interesting.
> John was very surprised.
> John was extremely surprised.
> The girl sang very beautifully.
> The girl sang exceedingly beautifully.

2. The words *awful, awfully, dreadfully, enormously, fearfully, good and, horribly, just too, mighty, most, real, so, such, sure, terribly, too,* and *utterly* are often used in conversation as intensifiers, some of them particularly by women. In writing, the words are used in dialog, in letters to close friends, and sometimes in informal essays. In other kinds of writing, they are customarily replaced by other intensifiers such as *very* and *extremely,* or they are omitted entirely.

CONVERSATIONAL	GENERAL
It is so hot.	It is very hot.
I had such an enjoyable time.	I had an enjoyable time.
The air was awfully refreshing.	The air was refreshing.
I am just too tired.	I am extremely tired.
The birds made the most fasci- nating sounds.	The birds made fascinating sounds.

3. Colloquially, *pretty* has the meaning of "moderately" if lightly stressed, of "very" if heavily stressed.

> Those tomatoes look pretty good.
> Bill seems pretty young.

4. *Fairly, rather,* and *somewhat* are used in the sense of "moderately."

> Yes, I am fairly tired.
> The girl is rather pretty.
> Mr. Smith is somewhat deaf.

5. Quite often *very* occurs as an intensifier with *own* after the genitive.

> I finally have my very own room: I do not have to share it.
> I finally have a room of my very own.

6. *The very* has the meaning of "exactly the" or "even the."

> The clerk found the very thing I wanted.
> The very thought of that job makes me tired.

The very idea is used as an expression of indignation.

> The very idea of his telling you that story!

7. *Quite* is also used for the meaning of "entirely," "completely," or "exactly." Before nouns, pronouns, and verbs and in negative sentences that is its customary meaning.

> Charles is quite a boy.
> I quite believe you.
> That is not quite what I meant.
> Nobody quite trusts that man.
> That light is not quite bright enough.

8. The verb forms *do, does,* and *did* are used as intensifiers before main verbs. They often indicate denial of something that has been stated or suggested. See § *Do*—Auxiliary.

> Do tell me your secret.
> I am not fond of Mr. Levers, but I do like his wife.
> John does study every night.
> We did see the movie, after all.

9. A number of adverbs of degree are used as intensifiers before main verbs. Two frequent ones are *certainly* and *really.* For a list of them and their positions, see § Word Order—Adverb Modifying Verb.

> The men have certainly worked hard.
> Jonathan really gave an outstanding performance.

10. The expression *at all* is used like an adverb of degree. It is used in questions and negative statements. It customarily follows the verb and its complement, if any.

> Does Francis Cunningham do any work at all?
> If you have insomnia, you can not sleep at all.
> Some people do not like New York at all.

Not at all is a polite way of answering someone who thanks you for doing him a favor.

> "That was very kind of you. Thank you very much." "Not at all."

11. The phrases *in the world, on earth,* and *under the sun* are frequently used after superlatives, *wh* words, and generalizing words like *anything, everybody,* and *nothing.* Note that *world* and *sun* are preceded by *the,* but *earth* is not.

I had the best mother in the world.
Why in the world did you say that?
May thinks you are the meanest man on earth.
Where on earth did you find that horrible tie?
I do not know who under the sun told Eva our secret.
Nobody under the sun would buy that car.

12. The phrase *by far* intensifies comparisons. It may precede or follow the comparative or superlative.

Paul is by far the better student.
Paul is the better student by far.

13. The words *whatever* and *whatsoever* are used as intensifiers after nouns and generalizing words like *anything,* customarily in questions or negative statements.

I have no confidence whatever in that boy.
Saul has not shown any improvement whatsoever.
Have you done anything whatever about the application?
I believe nothing whatsoever that that man tells me.

14. The words *no matter* with the intensifying meaning of "regardless of" precede *wh* words. See § Opposition Expression and § Clause—Independent and Adverbial.

I do not believe that story no matter who tells it.
No matter how often Tim practices, he forgets immediately.

15. The *-self* words (*myself, ourselves, yourself, yourselves, himself, herself, itself, themselves,* and *oneself*) are used as intensifiers or *emphatic reflexive* appositives. For their positions, see § Appositive.

I myself will ask him.
I am myself not quite ready.
You can do it yourself.

16. *By all means* and *by no means* are used as sentence modifiers. They may occur either at the beginning or end of a sentence or before or after the word or phrase that is being intensified.

By all means you should go.
You should go by all means.
Pat is by no means selfish toward his sister.
Pat is selfish by no means toward his sister.

When *by no means* begins a sentence, it is followed by split or inverted word order.

By no means should you do that.

17. A number of interjections like *goodness* and *hurray* are intensifiers since they are expressions of emotion. See § Part of Speech—Interjection for a list.

> Goodness, it's hot.
> Hurray! I passed the course.

18. Certain intensifiers like *damn* and *the hell* are classed as profanity or "curse words." Since they are offensive to many people, you should be careful about using them.

Also, see § *Any* vs. *Some*, § Comparison, and § Preposition—Expression with.

INTERPOLATION

I.6

1. An interpolation is anything that defers or is appended to the expression of a subject and its predication.

2. There are three major groups of interpolations: interjections, vocatives, and amendments.

3. Interpolations are customarily set off by commas or sometimes by other marks of punctuation such as exclamation marks, dashes, parentheses, or brackets.

4. An interjection is probably the easiest kind of interpolation to recognize simply because it is a conventionalized utterance. There are two kinds: *sentence starters* and *spontaneous reactions.*

a. The most frequent sentence starters are the "agreers" and "disagreers" *yes* and *no* and their fairly numerous variations such as *yeah, yep, all right, certainly, O.K., sure enough, very well, nah,* and *nope.* The first two and last two are used only in the most informal speech and in writing dialog. Other sentence starters are "calls for attention" such as *hello, hey, hi, listen, look, look here, say, tell me,* and *you know.* A few sentence starters are "silence fillers" or "hesitatives": they are sounds that a speaker utters to give himself time to order his thoughts; the most frequent are *well, oh, now,* and *uh.* They are very similar to spontaneous reactions. Sentence starters nearly always come at the beginning of a sentence and are marked off by commas.

> Yes, I will do what you want.
> No, that is not right.
> Hello, how are you?
> Well, that may be correct.

If a sentence starter must be interpreted as being expressed with strong feeling, an exclamation mark is used instead of a comma. However, an expert writer avoids the exclamation mark because he assumes that his reader can interpret the sentence starter and he knows that expert readers tend to be annoyed by exclamation marks.

b. Spontaneous reactions or *exclamations* are words or groups expressing a response to an emotion such as surprise, disbelief, reluctance, pain, disgust, anger, joy, or sorrow. Commas usually set them off, but exclamation marks are sometimes used. They make up a sizable list, but everyone recognizes them or at least the emotion they express. Some of them are the following: *ah, aw, come on, darn, dear me, fortunately, gee, goodness gracious, gosh, ha, heavens, holy mackerel, hurrah, hurray, indeed, luckily, now, oh, ouch, pshaw, well, why* (pronounced like the letter *y*), and *wow.* The so-called "swear words" or "curse words" are often spontaneous reactions, also.

> Ouch! I pinched my finger.
> Wow! Did you see that bolt of lightning?
> Why, that can't be true.
> Luckily, no one was hurt.
> Good heavens, I've lost my pen again.
> Indeed, you are absolutely wrong.

See § Part of Speech—Interjection for a list of interjections.

5. A vocative is the name of a substitute for the name of a listener or reader used in direct address. It may come almost anywhere in a sentence and is marked off by commas. Be sure to set off a vocative from an interjection when they come together. See § Capitalization for the capitalization of terms used in direct address.

> *Mary,* I need you.
> Hey, *Joe,* when did you come?
> What happened, *John?*
> Yes, *sir,* you are absolutely right.
> Come here, *you in the cap.*
> *Whatever your name is,* keep quiet.
> I am considering, *my dear Mr. Smith,* the feasibility of firing you.

6. There are two kinds of amendments: the kind that is added by the speaker or writer (I will call that an *author's amendment*) and the kind added by an editor.

7. An author's amendment is one of four kinds: an opinion formula, a question tag, a digression, and an addition marked by a transition expression. (I am using a digression right now, and there is another within the parentheses in the preceding paragraph.)

a. An opinion formula expresses someone's viewpoint. Two very frequent opinion formulas are *in my (his,* etc.) *opinion* and *according to him (Mr. Richards,* etc.). Others are *most important of all, naturally* (or *strangely* or *oddly* or *interestingly,* etc.) *enough, needless to say,* and *of course;* some are quite similar to spontaneous reactions. Opinion formulas are set off by commas wherever they occur.

> That was, in my opinion, a shameful thing to do.
> According to Mary, everything was going to be all right.
> Mr. Sprock regretted his hasty action, needless to say.
> Strangely enough, Mr. Hart refused to say where he had been.

Certain clauses (constructions made up of a subject and a predication) are often used as opinion formulas. As opinion formulas, such clauses occur within or at the end of a sentence. They are set off by commas. Some opinion-formula clauses are *I think, it appears to me, Laura hoped, we find, they trust,* and *John has always felt.*

> New York, I think, is too noisy.
> International relations were improving, it seemed to the diplomat.
> You, he believes, are responsible for the error.
> Mr. Pickwick was, it appears, no man to trifle with.

If those clauses begin the sentence, they are not classed as formulas and, therefore, are not set off by commas. Notice that the word *that* can be used after them when they are first in the sentence but it can not when they are elsewhere.

> I think   New York is too noisy.
> It seemed to the diplomat   that international relations were improving.
> He believes   you are responsible for the error.
> It appears   that Mr. Pickwick was no man to trifle with.

See § Clause—Noun and § Word Order—*Wh* Word for additional discussion of formula clauses.

b. A question tag is the second kind of author's amendment. It signals that the preceding utterance is a question. Put a comma before the question tag.

> I can't go, *eh?*
> You like that boy, *hm?*

A special kind of question tag is the *tag question.* It is a shortened clause composed of an anomalous finite and a personal pronoun, both of which are related to a preceding subject and verb. The shortened clause has inverted word order and is separated from the preceding clause by a comma. See § Auxiliary and § Verb—Not Repeated for a fuller discussion.

> You did not see him   , did you?
> It has been nice   , hasn't it?

By the way, *do you* is not a tag question in "I know him. Do you?" since the subject of the question is not the same as the subject *I* in the preceding sentence. Notice that there is a period, not a comma, before the question and that the question begins with a capital letter.

c. A digression is material which is not directly related to the structure of a sentence or paragraph. Parentheses customarily enclose it. If the digression comes within a sentence, the digression has no sentence-initial capitalization or sentence-final period though it may have other kinds of capitalization and punctuation. If the digression is not contained within a sentence, the digression has customary sentence capitalization and punctuation.

> Albert made a visit to the Spice Islands (officially called the Moluccas).
> A special kind of auxiliary is the anomalous finite (see § Auxiliary).
> Mrs. Jay cleaned her house thoroughly. (Her neighbor's insinuation had had its intended effect.)

When the definition of a word or phrase in a sentence is given as additional material, that definition is considered a digression. Put quotation marks around the definition, and enclose it in parentheses. Use a comma after the name of the language to which the term belongs if that language is given in the parentheses.

> Felipe was questioned by the *jefe* ("chief").
> The manager scribbled *N.B.* (Latin, *nota bene*, "note well") on the memorandum before giving it to his assistant.

Sometimes dashes are used to set off a digression that is completely unrelated to the sentence as in "I was going up the street—John, are you listening?—when I heard a loud noise." (When you type, use two hyphens (- -) for a dash. Customarily, there is no space before and after the dash.) However, parentheses are probably preferable for all digressions since dashes have a tendency to make an adverse impression on readers in the same way that exclamation marks do.

d. Additions marked by transition expressions are discussed in detail under § Transition Expression. Some examples of transition expressions are *furthermore, nevertheless,* and *in other words.*

8. An editor's amendment is a digression added to someone else's piece of writing. It is enclosed in brackets (or *square brackets*).

> In "Locksley Hall" Tennyson refers to ". . . a cycle of Cathay [China]."

See § Bracket for other examples of editor's amendments.

9. Here is a final piece of advice: whenever you can, avoid interpolations because they tend to distract your reader. If it is at all possible, revise your sentences so that the interpolations will become part of the subject or predication.

INTONATION   I.7

1. Intonation is the rising and falling of the pitch of your voice as you speak. It is very important for you to realize that your listener responds to your intonation. If you use the wrong kind, your listener may misinterpret your intention. He will certainly be confused, and he may even be insulted. Your intonation, for example, can signify that you are making a statement or that you are asking a question or that you have not finished speaking. I suggest that you follow three general rules in your intonation:

a. Let your voice fall to its lowest pitch at the end of statements and at the end of questions beginning with the *wh* words *who, whose, whom, which, what, when, where, why,* and *how.*

| It is blue. | Where is my book? |
| She's Spanish. | How did you know that? |

b. Let your voice rise to a high pitch at the end of a question which does not begin with one of the *wh* words.

Did you lose your book?   It's blue?
Is she Spanish?   Going home now?

c. Let your voice stay on a middle pitch if you pause before you have finished a sentence.

I bought a table,   a chair,   and a bookcase.
I didn't need them,   but they looked nice.

IT VS. *THERE* 1.8

The words *it* and *there* have uses that are sometimes confusing.

1. The word *it* has three main uses:

a. Most frequently, *it* is a substitute for a word or construction that has already been expressed.

Roger told Mary something. I do not know what it was. [*It* is a substitute for *something.*]
I have a dog. It is six months old. [*It* is a substitute for *a dog.*]
The teacher read what you wrote. He was amused by it. [*It* is a substitute for *what you wrote.*]

b. *It* is used as the subject of a number of *impersonal* expressions:

1. Concerning weather.

It rained very hard yesterday.
It was snowing in Detroit when we left.
It will be cold in January.
Have you ever seen it hail?

2. Concerning time.

It is Tuesday.
It gets dark early in winter.
It will be summer before we finish the job.

3. Concerning space measurement.

It is two miles from here to there.
"It's a long way to Tipperary."

c. *It* is used as a *filler* subject or complement which stands for a verb construction that is the *real* subject or complement. The verb construction, which comes at the end of the clause, is syntactically an appositive to the *it.*

It is nice to see you again. [*It* is the subject of *is* and stands for the verb construction "to see you again."]
It is a pity that John left school. [*It* is the subject of *is* and stands for the verb construction "that John left school."]

Sam made it clear that he did not like the girl. [*It* is the object of *made* and stands for the verb construction "that he did not like the girl."]

2. The word *there* has three main uses:

a. *There* is often an adverb meaning "at or in or to that place."

Charles was in class. I saw him there.
I am going to the post office. Are you going there, too?

b. *There* is often used as a *sentence starter* when the subject is something that has not yet been specified by the speaker or writer. This introductory *there* frequently occurs at the beginning of a conversation or a piece of writing. The following subject is a noun, pronoun, or noun phrase.

There is something I want to tell you.
There was a man here a few minutes ago.

The verb *be* is most often used after such an introductory *there*. The subject of the clause follows the verb. Also, see § Word Order—Inverted.

There will be many people at the party. [*Many people* is the subject and follows *be*.]
There seemed to be little food in the house. [*Little food* is the subject and follows *be*.]
There happens to be a definite answer to that question. [*A definite answer to that question* is the subject and follows *be*.]

The form of the simple predicate after introductory *there* is determined by the following subject.

There is a boy in the car. [The simple predicate is *is* because the following subject, *a boy*, is singular.]
There are two boys in the car. [The simple predicate is *are* because the following subject, *two boys*, is plural.]

Note that the personal pronouns used as subjects do not occur after introductory *there*. The reason is that the personal pronouns are not indefinite. However, they do occur after initial *there* meaning "at or in or to that place," and the clause has primary word order.

"Where is John?" "There he is."

c. Introductory *there* is frequently used in the answer to a question which has an indefinite subject and the verb *be*.

"Was a man mentioned in the story?" "Yes, there was."
"Is anybody living in that house?" "No, there isn't."

Also, see § Agreement—Verb.

1. Most words of more than one syllable which end in the sound [aiz] are spelled with the letters *-ize.* Here are some examples:

apologize	civilize	generalize	philosophize	standardize
authorize	criticize	hypnotize	realize	summarize
baptize	dramatize	italicize	recognize	symbolize
capitalize	emphasize	memorize	satirize	sympathize
characterize	equalize	naturalize	specialize	

2. A relatively few words have the ending *-ise.* You should memorize their spelling.

advertise	compromise	disguise	franchise	supervise
advise	demise	enterprise	improvise	surmise
arise	despise	excise	merchandise	surprise
chastise	devise	exercise	revise	

3. Three verbs have -yze: *analyze, catalyze,* and *paralyze.*

4. The words *concise, paradise,* and *precise* end in the sound [aɪs]. The word *promise* ends in the sound [ɪs].

LETTER

LIKE—VERB

-LIKE—SUFFIX

LITERARY TERM

LOOK AT VS. *WATCH*

1. Letters are divided into *business* letters and *personal* letters. Business letters are those which are sent to and from companies, organizations, or individuals for business reasons. Personal letters are those which pass between friends or acquaintances.

2. All letters should be written on unlined paper. For business letters, use white paper (approximately 8½ by 11 inches), unpunched. For personal letters, use either *club paper* (approximately 7¼ by 11 inches) or *notepaper* (a four-page sheet); the color is customarily white although some persons prefer a lightly tinted paper.

3. Letters may be either typed or handwritten in black or blue ink. Business letters are usually typed, and very formal personal letters such as invitations are usually handwritten.

The parts of a letter and their arrangement have been conventionalized. I will discuss the business letter first.

4. A business letter should be neat. If you make a mistake, do not cancel it; rewrite the whole letter. Center the letter on the page: have generous margins on all four sides. The diagram of a business letter is as follows:

	Sender's address
	Date
Receiver's address	
Salutation	
Body of message	
	Complimentary close
	Signature—handwritten
	Signature—typed

5. The following specimen illustrates the diagram. Notice the indention and the punctuation.

> 633 West 215 St.
> New York 38, N.Y.
> January 12, 1962
>
> Bureau of Motor Vehicles
> Department of Taxation and Finance
> 155 Worth St.
> New York 5, N.Y.
>
> Gentlemen:
>
> Please send me the blank form necessary for the registration of my car for the year 1961. The car was registered in New York in 1960. I enclose a stamped, self-addressed envelope for your reply.
>
> Yours very truly,
>
> *Vernon J. Scott*
>
> Vernon J. Scott

6. If you write to a specific person, put his name at the beginning of the receiver's address, and use either *Dear Sir* or his name with *Dear* in the salutation. Always prefix his name with *Mr.* or, if appropriate, *Dr., Prof.,* etc.

> Mr. Horace Roberts
> Longwear Hosiery
> 415 E. Lombard Ave.
> Duluth 8, Minn.
>
> Dear Mr. Roberts:

7. If the receiver is a woman, use either *Dear Madam* or her title and name with *Dear* in the salutation.

> Dear Madam: Dear Miss Whitehead: Dear Mrs. Akers:

8. If the receiver is a company or organization, use either *Gentlemen,* as in the specimen in ¶ 5, above, or *Dear Sirs* for the salutation.

9. I recommend that you always indent the beginning of each paragraph in the body slightly, about four or five typewriter spaces from the left margin. Only in typed letters is the indention sometimes omitted. If you type, single-space within paragraphs, and double-space between paragraphs.

10. For the complimentary close, use one of these formulas:

> Yours truly,   Very truly yours,
> Yours very truly,   Sincerely yours,

11. Capitalize the first word of the complimentary close, and put a comma at the end.

12. Always sign your name in ink.

13. If you write by hand, sign your name only once, writing (*Miss*) or (*Mrs.*) before your name if you are a woman.

James L. Newton	(*Miss*) *Amy Pearson*	(*Mrs.*) *Mary Appleton*

14. If you type, sign your name in ink above your typed name without **Mr., Miss,** or **Mrs.,** and, if you are a woman, type **Miss** or **Mrs.** in parentheses before your typed name.

R. L. Morris	*Juliet Sanders*	*Rosemary Clark*
R. L. Morris	(Miss) Juliet Sanders	(Mrs.) Rosemary Clark

15. A married woman may use her husband's given name, as in the following examples:

Rosemary Clark	*Mary Appleton*
(Mrs. John T. Clark)	(Mrs. Henry Appleton)

16. The form of a personal letter is similar to that of a business letter. The major differences are (*a*) the receiver's address is not put in the personal letter and (*b*) the signature is handwritten only.

17. Here is a specimen of a personal letter. Notice the indention and punctuation.

> 410 Lansing Ave.
> Jefferson 14, Md.
> August 15.
>
> Dear Mr. Parker,
>
> Thank you for writing the recommendation for my application to Princeton. It was very kind of you to take the trouble. The admissions office notified me today that I had been accepted. If you come up after I get there, let me know, and I'll show you around my alma mater.
>
> Sincerely,
> *Eliot Spenser*

18. The salutation is usually *Dear* with the receiver's name. Use his first name or his nickname if you are close friends; otherwise, use the family name with **Mr., Miss,** or **Mrs.** Salutations such as *My dear Mr. Norris* are rather formal.

19. The complimentary close is most often *Yours truly, Sincerely yours,* or *Sincerely.* A number of other formulas are in use, but their use depends upon the degree of intimacy between the correspondents.

20. Sign with only your first name if you are close friends and you are sure that the receiver will recognize that the letter is from you; otherwise, sign with your full name. A man does not use the prefix **Mr.** A woman almost never writes (*Miss*) or (*Mrs.*) before her signature: she does so only if she is quite sure that the receiver does not know whether she is married or not.

21. For both business and personal letters, write your name and address in the upper left corner on the front of the envelope. In the center of the envelope, write the receiver's title, full name, and address. Fold the letter twice across to fit a long envelope (approximately 4 by 9½ inches), or fold it once across and then twice to fit a small envelope (approximately 3¾ by 6¾ inches). The paper of the envelope and of the letter should match.

Vernon J. Scott
633 West 215 St.
New York 38, N.Y.

Bureau of Motor Vehicles
Department of Taxation and Finance
155 Worth St.
New York 5, N.Y.

Eliot Spenser
410 Lansing Ave.
Jefferson 14, Md.

Mr. Joseph M. Parker
49 Monument Lane
Fort Worth 18, Texas

For other details, see the introduction to *The American College Dictionary,* or consult *A Manual of Style,* The University of Chicago Press, Chicago.

LIKE—VERB L.2

1. The verb *like* is *personal,* not *impersonal* as its equivalent is in some other languages. The person who is pleased is the subject, and the person or thing which pleases is the object.

I like bananas very much.
Betty did not like the boy because he said unkind things to her.

2. *Like,* meaning "find pleasant," is not a synonym for *want, desire,* or *wish.*

I like to go to movies because they are entertaining.
I want to go to a movie right now.

3. *Would like* is an equivalent of the present tense of *want, desire,* or *wish.*

> I would like to go to a movie right now.
> We will show you whatever you would like to see.
> Would you like to dance?
> I would like a quart of milk, please.

Also, see § *Wish* vs. *Hope* vs. *Want* vs. *Would Like,* and § *Desire.*

-LIKE—SUFFIX   L.3

1. The suffix *-like* is usually joined directly to a word if the meaning of the compound is immediately clear.

> his childlike expression   her velvetlike gaze

2. A hyphen is used if the compound might not be immediately clear.

> his ape-like manner

LITERARY TERM   L.4

1. There are a number of terms used in reference to language which you should be familiar with. They are often called *literary terms* because they are employed in discussing writing or the *literary devices* which authors use in their writing. Many of them apply equally to classic and to modern literature in foreign languages as well as English. Moreover, the matters that some of them refer to also occur in speaking. Primarily, you should be aware of what the terms stand for so that you can improve your general comprehension of English. If you become alert to matters such as *figures of speech,* for instance, you can increase your speed in reading. Below, I will give you a definition and illustrations of some of those terms. You should also read § Word Order—Transposed for the pattern of "complement + subject + verb," which will occur quite often in what you read.

2. An *allegory* is a story which presents one subject under the guise of another so that, in addition to the literal level, there is a secondary level of meaning which is sustained throughout the work. Thus, John Bunyan's *Pilgrim's Progress* is an allegory: it depicts through the varied adventures of its hero the way to Heaven. Allegory frequently makes use of personification and abstractions; characters in *Pilgrim's Progress,* for example, are named Mr. Money-love, Little Faith, and Lord Hate-good. Jonathan Swift's *Gulliver's Travels* is another long allegory; Aesop's *fables* and the *parables* in the Bible are short allegories. Many legends, myths, and folk tales are considered to be allegories.

Closely related to allegory is the technique of *symbolism,* in which a particular *symbol*—an image, object, or idea—receives a suggestive and connotative value beyond its literal meaning. In Herrick's poem the rosebud is the symbol:

> Gather ye rosebuds while ye may,
>   Old Time is still a-flying,
> And this same flower that smiles today
>   Tomorrow will be dying.

3. *Alliteration* is the repetition of a sound, usually initial and usually of a consonant, in two or more words or stressed syllables placed close to each other. In the following examples the *h* sound is repeated:

> It is hot and humid.
> There was a haze on the horizon.

There are many *set expressions* in English which have alliteration.

> bed and board [a place to sleep and food to eat]

In some of those expressions the two alliteration words mean the same thing.

bag and baggage	hearth and home	might and main
hale and hearty	kith and kin	safe and sound

Advertisers use alliteration very often because of its rhythmic effect.

> If you see it in *The Sun* [a newspaper], it's so.

Also, see *assonance, consonance,* and *tongue twister* below.

4. *Assonance* is the repetition of a vowel sound in words placed close to each other. In the second line of the following quotation from Tennyson, the repeating of the *o* sound is an example of assonance:

> Break, break, break
> On thy cold gray stones, O Sea!

5. *Blank verse* is unrimed iambic pentameter (see *meter* below). Milton's *Paradise Lost* is composed in that kind of line. *Free verse* is also unrimed but has no regular meter or length of line. Much of Walt Whitman's poetry is in free verse.

6. *Consonance* is the repetition of a consonant sound in one or more lines of a poem. The following example has a repetition of *p*.

> And feed deep, deep upon her peerless eyes.

Alliteration (see above) is a special type of consonance.

7. The *denotation* of a word is the meaning which simply identifies the thing the word refers to. It is sometimes called the *dictionary* or *factual* or *core* or *central* meaning. The *connotation* is the associated meaning that a word has; quite often the connotation causes an emotional response, either of approval or disapproval. For example, *bucket* and *pail* have the same denotation: they both identify a kind of container that is used for carrying material such as water or sand. However, for some speakers the words have different connotations: *bucket* is a *normal* word, and *pail* is an *old-fashioned* or *poetic* word which they would not use in their customary writing or speaking; for other people the reverse is true.

As another illustration, the words *slender* and *skinny,* applied to a human being, both denote the absence of excess weight. However, *slender* connotes a graceful, attractive thinness, and *skinny* connotes an undesirable thinness.

216

Both the denotation and connotation of a word are important. Even though two words may have the same denotation, they can rarely be interchanged.

Sometimes a word is inappropriate in a particular context: it has a connotation that makes it wrong. For instance, *handsome* is appropriately applied to a man but not to a girl, and *beautiful* is appropriate for a girl but not for a man.

The only way to learn the connotation of a word is through observation: seeing and hearing it used. A small dictionary usually lists only the denotation, and although the large dictionaries give some usage labels which indicate connotation such as *archaic* and *slang*, they do not have the space to enumerate all the associations that a word has.

8. An *epigram* or *aphorism* is a statement, either in prose or in verse, which expresses a great deal in a few words. The language is often figurative. An epigram that becomes well known is a *saying* or *familiar quotation.* A saying whose origin is unknown is a *proverb* or *adage.*

> Haste makes waste.
> Time is money.
> Still waters run deep.
> Let sleeping dogs lie.
> A watched pot never boils.
> Too many cooks spoil the broth.
> A bird in the hand is worth two in the bush.
> A stitch in time saves nine.
> Don't put all your eggs into one basket.
> The pen is mightier than the sword.—BULWER-LYTTON
> The course of true love never did run smooth.—SHAKESPEARE
> The devil can quote Scripture for his purpose.—SHAKESPEARE
> I can resist everything except temptation.—WILDE

A special kind of epigram is a *paradox:* a statement which seems self-contradictory or is opposed to a commonly held point of view but contains an element of truth.

> All generalizations are false, including this one.—ANONYMOUS
> In married life three is company and two is none.—WILDE

An *oxymoron* combines incongruous or contradictory terms for a startling effect.

> Yet from those flames
> No light, but rather darkness visible.—MILTON

> And then there crept
> A little noiseless noise among the leaves
> Born of the very sigh that silence heaves.—KEATS

An epigram is often changed slightly to fit a particular situation. For instance, the proverb "Time and tide wait for no man" might be changed to "Trains and busses wait for no man." Frequently the change is intended humorously: "My wife and my children wait for no man, including me." Such a change for the purpose of humor is a *parody.*

There is a danger in familiar epigrams: they are often used to respond verbally to a situation without any real effort at thinking about it. See *trite expression* below.

9. *Exaggeration* or *hyperbole* is saying more than you really mean. It is not lying. Its intention is to emphasize a statement or a situation. It is often used in ordinary conversation.

> I am dead [= very] tired.
> The play bored me to death [= bored me very much].

10. A *figure of speech* is a general term for expressions such as a metaphor, simile, and personification, in which words are not used according to their literal or original or most customary meaning. We use words *figuratively* to reveal or suggest a resemblance or a mental image. See *denotation, metaphor,* etc.

11. *Irony* is saying one thing but meaning the opposite. For instance, when a person hears something that he does not like at all, he may exclaim, "A fine thing!" On a rainy, cold day, someone may say, "Lovely weather, isn't it?"

12. A *limerick* is a humorous poem of five lines, in which the first and second lines rime with the fifth line, and the third and fourth lines, which are short, rime with each other. The first line usually begins with the words "There was. . . ."

> There was a young man of Madrid
> Who imagined that he was the Cid.
>   When they asked him, "Why?"
>   He could only reply
> That he didn't know why, but he did. —ANONYMOUS

13. A *metaphor* is a word or phrase which is applied to something to which it is not literally applicable, in order to reveal or suggest a resemblance. English speakers are very fond of metaphors. Slang is often metaphorical. We use the word *head* metaphorically, but not slangily, when we talk about the "head" of a pin or the "head" of a corporation. (By the way, the word *corporation* itself is a metaphor since it is derived from the Latin word *corpus* meaning "body.") Similarly, we talk about the "bed" of a river, the "legs" of a chair, and the "eye" of a needle. Many of the *secondary* definitions of words in a dictionary have come about through metaphorical use.

> May's father boiled with anger.
> The police hounded the fugitive.
> The baby crowed with delight.
> The train snorted into the station.
> We were left in the dark about Mr. Markham's intentions.
> Poor Soul, the center of my sinful earth. —SHAKESPEARE
> Cape Cod is the bared and bended arm of Massachusetts. —THOREAU

Sometimes a metaphor is *extended:* the resemblance is continued through more than one expression. A well-known extended metaphor is this one by Shakespeare:

> All the world's a stage,
> And all the men and women merely players.
> They have their exits and their entrances,
> And one man in his time plays many parts,
> His acts being seven ages.

14. *Meter* is the arrangement of words into a determinable rhythm of stressed and unstressed syllables. To *scan* poetry, we mark the stressed syllables with ′ and the unstressed syllables with ‿ or ×. Each combination of stressed and unstressed syllables is called a *foot* and is marked with | .

The scansion of a line by Thomas Gray, "The curfew tolls the knell of parting day," would be diagrammed in the following way:

> The cúr | few tólls | the knéll | of pár | ting dáy
>
> *Or:* The cúr | few tólls | the knéll | of pár | ting dáy

That line has an *iambic* pattern of one unstressed and one stressed syllable to the foot, in that order; because the line contains five feet, it is called *pentameter.* Much English verse is in iambic pentameter. Other patterns are *anapestic* (two unstressed syllables and one stressed syllable, as in "Thĕy wĕre mén"), *trochaic* (a stressed syllable and an unstressed syllable, as in "Trúlў"), and *dactyllic* (a stressed and two unstressed syllables, as in "Cómfŏrt mĕ"), *spondaic* (two stressed syllables, as in "Ó Lórd"), and *pyrrhic* (two unstressed syllables, as in "tý | rănnў | ").

Other lengths of line are *dimeter* (two feet), *trimeter* (three feet), *tetrameter* (four feet), *hexameter* (six feet), and *heptameter* (seven feet). A *truncated* foot has only one stressed syllable, as in "Fár | frŏm jóy."

A *caesura* is a pause or stop within a line. It is marked with double bars, ‖ .

> I have had playmates; ‖ I have had companions
> All, ‖ all are gone

A line without a pause at the end is a *run-on* line. The use of run-on lines is termed *enjambement.*

> Or if Sion hill
> Delight thee more, and Siloa's brook, that flow'd
> Fast by the oracle of God.—MILTON

A line which has a grammatical or sense pause at the end is called an *end-stopped* line.

> All are but parts of one stupendous whole,
> Whose body Nature is, and God the soul.—POPE

Also, see *rime* below.

15. *Metonymy* is the use of the name of one thing for another which is often associated with it. This device occurs very frequently in English.

219

School [= education] is good for you.
The White House [= the President] announced a new project.
That man has no heart [= pity].

16. A *nursery rime* is a short, simple poem or song for children. It usually tells a story or describes an incident.

Mary had a little lamb;
Its fleece was white as snow,
And everywhere that Mary went
The lamb was sure to go.

Some are fantastic.

Hey, diddle, diddle!
The cat and the fiddle.
The cow jumped over the moon.
The little dog laughed to see such sport,
And the dish ran away with the spoon.

Allusions to or variations (*parodies*) on a nursery rime often occur in both speech and writing.

17. *Onomatopoeia* is the use of a word whose pronunciation imitates or suggests a natural sound. We employ onomatopoeic words when we say that bees *buzz,* horses *neigh,* cows *moo,* and noisy sleepers *snore.*

The murmurous haunt of flies on summer eves.—KEATS
The moan of doves in immemorial elms.—TENNYSON

18. *Personification* is the implying that an inanimate object or a quality is a human being or has human attributes. When people refer to a ship or an automobile as "she," they are indulging in personification.

The bright sunshine called me.
The poison worked stealthily.
The moon chased away the darkness.
Mrs. Prim's bed received her with a sigh.

With how sad steps, O Moon, thou climbst the skies!
How silently, and with how wan a face!—SIDNEY

19. A *pun* or *play on words* or *paronomasia* is the humorous or ironical use of words or phrases to convey a *double meaning.* For example, since the word *can* has the meaning not only of "be able" but also of "preserve," there is a pun in "We eat all the fruit we can, and what we can't we can." Also, since *bear* meaning "carry, keep" has the same pronunciation as *bare* meaning "reveal," a person can pun by saying, "You must bear your secret." A similar instance in German involves *ist* meaning "is" and *isst* meaning "eats": if the sentence "Man ist was er ist" is spoken, it may be interpreted to mean either "Man is what he is" or "Man is what he eats."
Punning is especially characteristic of English literature, both serious and hu-

morous. Since the comprehension of puns requires a deep knowledge of the language, a reader must be highly proficient to grasp an appreciable part of the message of English authors.

20. *Rime* (or *rhyme*) is the similarity of sound in two words from the stressed vowel to the end of each word: *part - start; pleasure - measure; relieve - conceive; commendable - expendable.* If there is no vowel sound after the stressed vowel, the rime is called *masculine: part - start; relieve - conceive.* If there is a vowel sound after the stressed vowel, the rime is called *feminine: pleasure - measure; commendable - expendable.*

Since rime concerns sound, words that have quite different spellings may rime: *could - wood; whose - shoes; moon - tune; aisle - mile; best - guessed.*

Sometimes a word rimes with a whole phrase: *fundamentalist - sent a list; merrier - bury her; carnivorous - deliver us.* Such riming is usually humorous.

At times a writer will employ *eye rime* or *sight rime*—that is, he will use two words which have similar spelling but do not rime: *love - prove; rough - though.*

The riming words usually come at the ends of lines: such lines have *end rime.*

> Tiger! Tiger! burning bright
> In the forests of the night.—BLAKE

Two consecutive riming lines compose a couplet, as in the above example from Blake.

Some lines have the riming words in the middle and at the end: such lines have *internal rime.*

> I bring fresh showers for the thirsting flowers.—SHELLEY
> For the moon never beams without bringing me dreams.—POE

The *rime scheme* is the pattern of arrangement of the riming words in a *stanza,* a group of related lines of a poem. In an analysis of the rime scheme the first set of riming words is marked with the letter *a*; the second set is marked *b*; etc. In the following stanza by Browning the rime scheme is *a a b c c b.*

Grow old along with me!	(*a*)
The best is yet to be,	(*a*)
The last of life, for which the first was made.	(*b*)
Our times are in his hand	(*c*)
Who saith, "A whole I planned;	(*c*)
Youth shows but half. Trust God; see all, nor be afraid!"	(*b*)

A limerick has a rime scheme of *a a b b a;* see *limerick* above.

Some frequent iambic stanzas are the following:

quatrain, riming *a b a b,* with four- or five-foot lines.
rime royal, riming *a b a b b c c,* with five-foot lines.
ottava rima, riming *a b a b a b c c,* with five-foot lines.
Spenserian stanza, riming *a b a b b c b c c,* with five-foot lines except a six-foot
    final line.

two-couplet stanza, riming *a a b b,* with four- or five-foot lines.
ballad stanza, riming *a b c b,* with alternate four- and three-foot lines.

21. A *simile* is the expression of a comparison between two unlike things. The word *as* or *like* is used. The simile is *figurative:* the resemblance is not really true or is only partly true. Also, see *metaphor* above.

My love is like a red, red rose.
A pretty girl is like a melody.
The angry man looked as black as a thunder cloud.
The opened umbrellas stood around the platform like mushrooms around a tree.

Life, like a dome of many-colored glass,
Stains the white radiance of Eternity
Until Death tramples it to fragments.—SHELLEY

22. A *sonnet* is a poem composed of a single stanza of fourteen lines, customarily in iambic pentameter. There are two main types of sonnet: (*a*) the Shakespearian or English, with a rime scheme of *a b a b c d c d e f e f g g* or *a b b a c d d c e f f e g g* (three quatrains and a final couplet), and (*b*) the Petrarchan or Italian. The Petrarchan is normally divided into two parts called the *octave* and the *sestet.* The rime scheme of the octave is always *a b b a a b b a,* but the rime scheme of the sestet may be *c d e c d e, c d c d e e, c d e e d c, c d c d c d,* or some other form.

23. In *synecdoche* a part of something is used to signify the whole, or the whole of something is used to signify a part.

The farm employs a hundred hands [= men].
The government [= the Congress] passed a new law.

24. A *tongue twister* is an utterance that is difficult to say without making a mistake. Some tongue twisters employ a great deal of alliteration.

Peter Piper picked a peck of pickled peppers.

Sometimes the tongue twister has two sounds or words used repeatedly but in different positions.

Shall she sell sea shells?
How much wood would a woodchuck chuck if a woodchuck would chuck wood?

25. A *trite expression* or a *cliché* is a figure of speech which has been used so often inappropriately that it has lost its effectiveness and has become annoying to an educated person. Many such expressions were imaginative when they were first used, and you will probably think they are quite vivid the first time you encounter them. Only by continued reading will you become impressed by the fact that such an expression is trite or *hackneyed* or *stereotyped.* At times, just because it is understood to be hackneyed, a cliché is used humorously or satirically. Some clichés that you should avoid, at least in serious writing, are the following:

abreast of the times, up to date	*member of the team,* coworker
in the arms of Morpheus, asleep	*nip in the bud,* stop at the beginning
beat a hasty retreat, go away quickly	*render a selection,* play the piano or
better half, wife or husband	sing a song
a bolt from the blue, something un-	*replete with interest,* very interesting
expected	*saw the light of day,* was born
the briny deep, the sea	*single blessedness,* bachelorhood
out of a clear sky, unexpectedly	*the table groaned,* there was a lot of
clinging vine, dependent person	food
downy couch, bed	*the weaker sex,* women
the fair sex, women	*wee small hours,* late at night
filthy lucre, money	*wend one's way,* go
the grim reaper, death	*wreak havoc,* cause great damage
by leaps and bounds, rapidly	
mad as a wet hen, very angry	

By the way, if you speak another language, you have a source of figures of speech that you may be unaware of: some of the trite expressions in that other language seem quite fresh in English when they are translated well. You might try using them.

26. *Understatement* is saying less than you really mean. For instance, you may say, "I'm a little tired" when you really mean that you are utterly exhausted. Very often we use the negative with the contrary of what we mean (the special term is *litotes*). For example, we may say, "She's not a bad-looking girl" when we really mean that she is very pretty.

> He was the mildest manner'd man
> That ever scuttled ship or cut a throat.—BYRON

LOOK AT **VS.** *WATCH*   L.5

1. The verb *watch* has the meaning of "look at (something that can move or be moved) for some length of time." You usually *look* briefly *at* things that either can or can not move.

> The tourists looked at the skyscrapers.
> The spectators watched the men building the skyscraper.

MANY VS. MUCH
MANY A
-MINDED
MOVIE VS. MOVIES
MUST VS. HAVE TO VS. HAVE GOT TO

1. The word *many* is used with things that are grammatically plural. The word *much* is used with things that are grammatically singular: it is used with *uncountables* and *mass words.*

Do you go to many concerts?	Many hours are wasted in that plant.
Alan does not have much money.	Much time is wasted in that plant.
Charles has many friends.	Fritz drank many bottles of wine.
Was there much rain yesterday?	Fritz drank much wine.

2. Certain expressions can be substituted for *many* and *much.*

a. For *many:*
  a great number (of). A great number of people do not approve of Dick.
  a large number (of). The teacher gave us a large number of examples.
  a good number (of). Although not everybody came, a good number showed up.

b. For *much:*
  a great quantity (of). A great quantity of ink is used in publishing.
  a large quantity (of). There was a large quantity of dust on the books.
  a good deal (of). Mrs. Dixon spends a good deal of her time worrying.
  a great deal (of). Edward studies a great deal.

c. For both *many* and *much:*
  a lot (of). Arnold certainly has a lot of friends.
  lots (of). Mr. Jensen has lots of money.
  plenty (of). Kay has given me good advice plenty of times.

Also, see § *Many a,* § Agreement—Adjective, § Article (*A, An, The*), § Negative, § Singular vs. Plural, and § Word Order—Adjective before Noun.

MANY A   M.2

1. The expression *many a* is used more in writing than in conversation. It is grammatically singular. Although the idea is plural, the phrase modifies only a grammatically singular, countable noun, which in turn calls for singular agreement in verb forms and reference.

Many a boy has lost his heart to Louise.

2. The two words can not be separated, but a modifier can be placed between the *a* and a following noun.

Many a true word is spoken in jest.
Like many another boy, Joe has charm.

3. *Many a* is grammatically different from *a good many* and *a great many.* The latter expressions call for plural agreement.

A good many boys have lost their hearts to Louise.
A great many true words are spoken in jest.

m

         M.3

1. The compound component *-minded,* meaning "having a certain kind of mind or disposition," combines with an adjective, not an adverb. In writing, a hyphen is used.

> Serious-minded students spend a lot of time on their assignments.
> If you are artistic-minded, you can go to the galleries; if you are literary-minded, you can go to the libraries.

MOVIE **VS.** *MOVIES*   M.4

1. *Movie* is used to refer to a motion-picture film. *The movies* is used to refer to a motion-picture theater or to the motion-picture industry.

> I want to see a movie tonight.
> I want to go to the movies tonight.
> I enjoyed the movie I saw yesterday.
> I was at the movies when you called.
> That actress has been in the movies for a long time.

MUST **VS.** *HAVE TO* **VS.** *HAVE GOT TO*   M.5

1. To express present or future necessity, *must, have to,* or *have got to* may be used. The customary pronunciation of *have to* with this meaning is ['hæftə] and of *has to* is ['hæstə].

> We must work to earn money.
> We have to work to earn money.
> We have got to work to earn money.
> The boy must leave tomorrow.
> The boy has to leave tomorrow.
> The boy has got to leave tomorrow.

2. Of the three expressions, *have got to* is the most frequent in speech, but *must* and *have to* are more frequent in writing.

3. The *have* or *has* with *got to* is usually reduced in speech, but the *have* or *has* with *to* is not.

> We've got to work to earn money.
> The boy's got to leave tomorrow.

4. At times you will see *got to* written without *have.* I advise you not to use that form.

> We got to work to earn money. [Avoid this.]

5. Future time may also be expressed by *will have to.*

> The boy will have to leave tomorrow.

6. To express necessity in the past, *had to* is customarily used. The *had* is not reduced.

> We had to work late last night.
> The boy had to work the next day.

In indirect speech, *must* is rarely used; *had to* is usually substituted for *must* in a past sequence.

> I must go tomorrow.
> I told him that I had to go the next day.

See § Sequence of Tense.

7. With split word order, *have to* is most frequently used; *do* and *does* are used with it for the simple present, and *did* for the simple past. *Must* is less often used in split word order, and *have got to* rarely is.

> Do we have to tell him?
> Does the boy have to leave tomorrow?
> Did you have to work last night?
> Will the boy have to leave tomorrow?
> Must we tell him?
> Have we got to tell him?

8. With *not*, the meaning of *have to* is different from *must*. *Must not* expresses a prohibition, and *do not have to* expresses a lack of necessity. *Have got to* rarely occurs with *not*, but when it does, it expresses a lack of necessity.

> You must not smoke in that room. Smoking is forbidden.
> You do not have to tell me if you do not want to.
> The boy does not have to leave tomorrow if he gets his visa extended.
> The boy will not have to leave tomorrow if he gets his visa extended.
> The boy did not have to leave the next day because he got his visa extended.

9. *Must* (but not *have to* or *have got to*) may also express a supposition or an assumption. For the past, *must have* is used with a past participle.

> There is somebody at the door. It must be the laundry man.
> Mr. Joyce must be at home. I see his car in front of his house.
> My dictionary is not on my desk. My wife must have moved it.
> Parsons did not answer his phone. He must have gone out for the evening.

Also, see § *Had Better* and § *Ought* vs. *Should.*

NEGATIVE

NOUN—NOT REPEATED

NUMBER

1. The *negative words* are the following:

neither	no	none	nor	nothing
never	nobody	no one	not	nowhere

Not more than one of those negative words is customarily used within the same clause:

Mr. Greer is not pleasant or helpful.
Nobody is an exception to that rule or its corollary.
Why doesn't either candidate promise to do something about housing?
We can not change our faces for either better or worse.
No one wanted to spend a day either on a beach or in the mountains.
I have never been to Asia or Africa or Australia.
Mr. Kerry knows almost nothing about Americans' culture or their history.
You can find that plant in Arizona and nowhere else.
Mrs. O'Leary invited the boys, but none could go.

a. The interjection *no* at the beginning of a clause may be followed by a negative word.

No, I didn't go.   No, nobody called.
No, neither boy is coming.   No, I want nothing else, thank you.

b. The words *neither* and *nor* may appear together in a clause, but do not use *not* in that clause.

Neither Paul nor Vera can go.
I want neither you nor Bill to do that.

2. To answer a question negatively, *no* is used alone or at the beginning of the reply. The form of the question may be either affirmative or negative. Notice that the reply may contain *not* also.

Do you live in New York?	No.
	No, I do not.
	No, I don't.
	No, I live in New Jersey.
Don't you live in New York?	No.
	No, I do not.
	No, I don't.
	No, I live in New Jersey.

3. *No* may customarily be used before a noun without an article (*a, an, the*) or before a noun preceded by an adjective except *much, many, enough, any,* or *some.*

Adam had no books.
Ely could give me no explanation.
No exact time has been set.
I said no such thing.
No really intelligent man thinks he knows everything.

4. *No* may be used before an adjective or adverb in the comparative degree and before *other* and *different.*

> The sick man felt no better.
> Toby could work no longer.
> That man is no different from his brother.
> Take that towel; I have no other.

5. *Not* may be used in nearly all other cases, particularly to make a verb negative. Instead of *no, not* is used with sentences containing *any, enough, many,* and *much.* Notice that *not* is used to make a phrase or part of a sentence negative.

> Adam did not have any books.
> Ely could not give me an explanation.
> An exact time has not been set.
> Not any exact time has been set.
> A really intelligent man does not think he knows everything.
> Not much time is left.
> Ray did not have many friends.
> I don't have enough money to buy a new suit.
> I don't have money enough to buy a new suit.
> Juan comes from Brazil, not Cuba.
> "Have the boys left?" "Not yet."

6. When *not* is used to make a verb negative, it ordinarily comes after the first auxiliary. The contraction *-n't* is attached to the first auxiliary. See § Word Order—Adverb Modifying Verb and § *Do*—Auxiliary

7. Certain other words carry a negative force; do not use a negative word to reinforce them. They are the following:

barely	hardly	scarcely	without
but ("only")	rarely	seldom	

> I hardly know that man.
> I can scarcely understand what he says.
> Bob seldom comes to class on time.
> Aly rarely expresses his thoughts well.
> We talked without arriving at any decision about the problem.
> The producers have been able to supply but a small part of our needs.

For further details, see § Word Order—Emphatic Adverb.

8. For politeness or modesty, speakers often use a negative even though their intention is affirmative. That use occurs frequently in questions; see § Polite Expression, § *Can* vs. *Could* vs. *May* vs. *Might,* and § *Ought* vs. *Should.*

> Can't I help you?
> Let's see if I can't answer your question.
> Don't you live in New York?
> Wouldn't it be nice to take a trip?

9. In rather rare instances two negatives occur together to express an affirmative.

> Nobody does not believe him. [= Everybody believes him.]

Also, see § *Any* vs. *Some,* § Parallelism, § *So*—Substitute, § *Such* vs. *Such a,* and § Verb—Not Repeated.

NOUN—NOT REPEATED N.2

1. Just as speakers of English tend to avoid repeating a verb or predication (see § Verb—Not Repeated), they tend to avoid repeating a noun or noun construction in the same sentence or a following sentence. There are four ways to avoid the repetition of that noun or construction (I will designate that repetition as the *second instance*).

a. We substitute a pronoun like *it, him, they, some,* or *any.*

> Where is my umbrella? Have you seen it? [*It* substitutes for *my umbrella.*]
> If you need advice, ask your counselor for some. [*Some* substitutes for *advice.*]

b. We substitute *kind* or *sort* for uncountable nouns.

> American food is not the same as the English kind. [*Kind* substitutes for *food.*]
> Slang disappears quickly, especially the juvenile sort. [*Sort* substitutes for *slang.*]

c. We substitute *one* or *ones* for countable nouns.

> I need a stamp. Do you have one? [*One* substitutes for *a stamp.*]
> The grocer sells ripe bananas, not green ones. [*Ones* substitutes for *bananas.*]

d. We omit the second instance without making a substitution for it.

> These pens are better than those. [There is no substitution for *pens* after *those.*]
> William's mother is older than John's. [There is no substitution for *mother* after *John's.*]

The four ways are not necessarily interchangeable. Below, I will list some of the times when we employ *c* and *d.* For *a,* see § Agreement—Pronoun and § Singular vs. Plural.

2. We can substitute *one* for both the second instance and the indefinite article *a* or *an.*

> Harry has a dog. Do you have one?
> There are plenty of apples. Take one.

3. Similarly, if preceded by a descriptive adjective, a singular second instance is replaced by *one,* and a plural second instance is replaced by *ones.* Notice that if *a* or *an* precedes the descriptive adjective, the *a* or *an* is retained.

> If you want to hear a joke, I will tell you a good one.
> These red apples look better than those green ones.
> Students, of course, prefer easy tests to hard ones.

4. However, if that descriptive adjective is preceded by *the,* the word *one* or *ones* may be omitted. The adjective may be a superlative or *next* and *last.*

> That blue pencil belongs to Jim. Mine is the pink one.
> That blue pencil belongs to Jim. Mine is the pink.
> Of all those sisters, Mary is the most beautiful one.
> Of all those sisters, Mary is the most beautiful.
> Let's finish this exercise so we can go on to the next one.
> Let's finish this exercise so we can go on to the next.
> If you offer Billy cookies, he will take a handful of the biggest ones.
> If you offer Billy cookies, he will take a handful of the biggest.

5. It is a good idea to use *ones* when the second instance is plural but not clearly so from the context.

> If you offer Billy cookies, he will take the biggest. [The hearer or reader will probably assume the number of *the biggest* to be singular.]
> If you offer Billy cookies, he will take the biggest ones. [The number here is clearly plural.]

6. Certain differences arise in sentences in which if the second instance were expressed, it would be preceded only by a demonstrative, a genitive, or a count word.

a. **This** and *that* may be used alone or with *one.*

> I like this picture better than that.
> I like this picture better than that one.

b. **These** and *those* are used alone.

> I like these pictures better than those.

c. Genitives formed with an apostrophe are used alone.

> Bill's car is newer than John's.
> Those are not your gloves. You have taken your sister's.

d. The genitive adjectives *my, your, our, her,* and *their* are replaced by *mine, yours, ours, hers,* and *theirs* (*his* and *its* are used without change) without *one* or *ones.* No distinction is made between singular and plural in these forms, just as in the genitives in *c* above. *Whose* is used similarly.

> I brought my book, but I forgot yours. [Singular.]
> I brought my books, but I forgot yours. [Plural.]
> That is a nice-looking coat. Whose is it?

e. **Own** is used alone. It is always preceded by a genitive word.

> Thank you for offering me your pen, but I prefer to use my own.

f. **Either, former, latter, neither,** and *which* may be used alone or with *one* or *ones.*

> Some of your answers were correct, but I do not remember which.
> Some of your answers were correct, but I do not remember which ones.

g. *Another* and *other* for a singular may be used alone or with *one.* For a plural, *others* or *other ones* may be used. Also, see § *Another* vs. *Other.*

If that hat does not fit, try another.
If that hat does not fit, try another one.
You can take this book. I will keep the other.
You can take this book. I will keep the other one.
You can take this book. I will keep the others.
You can take this book. I will keep the other ones.
As soon as you learn these dance steps, I will show you some others.
As soon as you learn these dance steps, I will show you some other ones.

h. The cardinal numbers (*one, two, three,* etc.) and the ordinal numbers (*first, second,* etc.) are usually used alone. You may sometimes see an ordinal number followed by *one* or *ones,* but you will probably be correct if you omit *one* or *ones.*

Henry carried six chairs, but Jones carried seven.
Shirley sits in the second row, and Seymour sits in the eighth.

i. If preceded only by *the,* a singular second instance can be replaced by *one,* and a plural second instance can be replaced by *ones,* but usually only if the *one* or *ones* is followed by a modifier. Such a modifier may be a clause, a prepositional phrase, or a participle. If the modifier can be clearly understood from the context, it may be omitted. Notice that the *the* is retained.

Of all Byron's poems, Miriam liked the ones that were concerned with love.
Do you see those three girls? I like the one in the middle.
Hand me my coat, please. It is the one hanging on the third hook.
Some student borrowed my pen. I think Joe was the one [who borrowed it].

NUMBER N.3

1. The general rule for expressing numbers in writing is this: spell out numbers that can be expressed in one or two words; otherwise, use figures.

There were six boys in the room.
There were thirty-six boys in the room.
There were 136 boys in the room.
The painting cost $247.59.
I get up at seven-fifteen.
My class starts at 8:25 a.m.
Mike is six feet two inches tall although he is only fifteen years old.

2. Use a hyphen in compound numerals from *twenty-one* to *ninety-nine* and from *twenty-first* to *ninety-ninth.* Do not use a hyphen after *hundred, thousand,* etc.

3. The major exceptions to the general rule are the following:

a. Do not begin a sentence with a figure. Spell out the number, or rearrange the words so that the number comes inside the sentence.

One hundred and thirty-six boys were in the room.
There were 136 boys in the room.

b. If a sentence or paragraph contains many different numbers some of which are more than ninety-nine, use figures for all.

That farm has 12,492 chickens, 2,835 ducks, 167 geese, 54 turkeys, and 8 cows. *but* Murray made a profit of eight dollars by buying the table for fifteen dollars and selling it for twenty-three.

c. Avoid writing two sets of figures next to each other: they may be confusing.

In 1934 twenty-two thousand voters registered. [*not* In 1934, 22,000. . . .]
Twenty-two thousand voters registered in 1934.

d. Use figures for house, apartment, or room numbers.

Jocelyn lives in Apartment 12 at 38 Cortland Street.
Our class meets in 332 Pupin Building.

e. Use figures for page, chapter, or section numbers or college course numbers when those numbers follow the words *page, chapter,* etc., or the course name.

For tomorrow, read page 8 and 17 (or Pages 8 and 17).
Read Chapters 1 and 2. *but* Read the first and second chapters.
I am taking G.S. English B23, Astronomy 41, and General Linguistics 207.

f. Use figures for dates. Do not use *-st, -nd,* or *-th* with the day of the month, and do not put a comma within the year.

The Markwardts' youngest child was born on May 24, 1956.

A day such as that in the example may be read "on May twenty-fourth," "on May twenty-four," or "on the twenty-fourth of May."

However, spell out the day of the month if it does not immediately follow the name of the month.

Even though Christmas was not going to arrive until December 25, George started celebrating on the twenty-first.

On formal invitations, acceptances, and announcements, dates are often spelled out.

4. The names of certain sums in English are the following:

SUM	AMERICAN ENGLISH	BRITISH ENGLISH
1,000	one thousand	one thousand
1,000,000	one million	one million
1,000,000,000	one billion	one thousand million *or* one milliard
1,000,000,000,000	one trillion	one billion

Also, see § *Hundred* vs. *Hundreds of.*

ONLY

OPPOSITION EXPRESSION

OUGHT **VS.** *SHOULD*

-OUS **WORD**

ONLY

1. In writing, put *only* before the word or group it specifically modifies.

> You live only once.
> I know only what I was told.
> That train carries only passengers.
> Only the doctor knew the remedy.

2. If *only* modifies a final word or phrase, it may either precede or follow that word or phrase.

> Mr. Ford told only Eleanor.
> Mr. Ford told Eleanor only.
> The company wants only trained men.
> The company wants trained men only.

3. Similarly, put the correlative expressions *not only ... but also* before the words they modify. Also, see § Parallelism.

> Not only the teacher but also the students objected to the change.
> Man needs not only food but also shelter.
> Geography plays a major role not only in the physical development of a country but also in its cultural advancement.

4. In spoken English, *only* frequently comes before the main verb and is stressed to show emphasis.

OPPOSITION EXPRESSION

Certain words are used to indicate that even though something is true, there are obstacles or opposing conditions.

1. *Despite, in spite of,* and *notwithstanding* are used as prepositions. *In spite of* is the most frequent.

> Mr. Mangum is very active despite his age.
> Mr. Mangum is very active in spite of his age.
> Mr. Mangum is very active notwithstanding his age.

Notwithstanding sometimes follows its object. The phrase is then marked off by commas.

> Mr. Mangum is very active , his age notwithstanding.
> His age notwithstanding , Mr. Mangum is very active.

2. The following are used as subordinating conjunctions:

although	even if	in spite of the fact (that)
despite the fact (that)	even though	though

Do not separate those conjunctions from the following words in the dependent clause by a comma.

> Although he was reluctant, Jane's father gave his permission.
> Despite the fact that they were tired, the soldiers continued.
> Even if Roscoe invites me, I will not go.
> Elizabeth did it even though I told her not to.
> Mr. Wright continues smoking in spite of the fact that it hurts him.
> Hemphill won the fight though his opponent seemed stronger.

3. *However* and *no matter* also introduce dependent clauses. *However* in that function precedes an adjective or an adverb, and *no matter* precedes a *wh* word (*who, when, how,* etc.).

> You can improve however good you think you are.
> However hard I work, my boss does not compliment me.
> No matter when I go to bed, I do not get enough sleep.
> That man ought to be polite no matter who he is.

4. These expressions are used as transition expressions:

however	nevertheless	though
just the same	still	yet

In that function they are marked off by commas. Their position within sentences varies.

a. However, just the same, and *nevertheless* come at the beginning of, within, or at the end of the opposition.

> I want to go. However, I must stay here.
> I want to go. I must, nevertheless, stay here.
> I want to go. I must stay here, just the same.

b. Still and *yet* come at the beginning of the opposition.

> Alicia works very hard. Still, she does not progress very much.
> Boyd seemed to be honest. Yet, I did not quite trust him.

c. Though comes within or at the end of the opposition.

> Clark's fever did not go down, though, even after he had taken the medicine.
> Helen is a pretty girl. I do not like her, though.

5. The variant spellings *altho* and *tho* for *although* and *though* have not yet been adopted by most writers.

Also, see § Transition Expression and § Clause—Independent and Adverbial.

1. In many of their uses, *ought* and *should* are interchangeable.

2. Both *ought* and *should* are used to express desirability or moral obligation.

> You should wear brown shoes with that suit.
> Theodore ought to help his mother with her chores.
> A student should not be late.
> Big boys ought not to tease little boys.

3. *Should* is used more frequently than *ought* to indicate a recommendation rather than an obligation. It is used particularly in asking for advice. In split word order *-n't* is usually affirmative in intent, and *not* is negative in intent.

> Should I tell Mr. Fredericks what his wife said?
> Shouldn't we leave before it gets dark?
> Should we not take the children to the play?

4. *Ought to have* and *should have* with a past participle indicate a past obligation or desirability that was not fulfilled.

> That boy ought to have written his assignment yesterday.
> You should have seen that movie last night.

5. *Ought not to have* and *should not have* with a past participle are used to indicate disapproval of something that was done in the past.

> You ought not to have told our secret to Mr. Hicks.
> The guests should not have left without saying goodby.

6. *Ought* and *should* indicate likelihood.

> Since Mark is an expert, he ought to be able to answer that question.
> If it is fair tomorrow, there should be a large crowd at the circus.
> You ought not to have much trouble in your interview next week.

7. In the condition of a conditional sentence, *should* but not *ought* is sometimes used to express future possibility with a degree of doubt. The condition may begin with *should* without *if*. See § Conditional Sentence.

> If Mr. Bennett should ask me, what will I tell him?
> Should Mr. Bennett ask me, what will I tell him?
> If the money should not arrive, how will we pay the rent?

8. Do not use *should* in the result of an unreal conditional sentence. Use *would*.

> If I were you, I would tell him.
> We would have got here sooner if we had not stopped for lunch.

9. In dependent clauses of indirect speech, use *ought* and *should* to express time the same as or future to the time of the main verb *say, think,* etc. Use *ought to have* and *should have* with the past participle to express earlier time.

> I said, "John, you ought to do it."
> I told John that he ought to do it.
> Bob thinks Mary should go tomorrow.
> Bob thought Mary should go the next day.
> I believe that John ought to have done it last night.
> Bob said last night that Mary should have gone the week before.

Also, see § *Had Better* and § *Must* vs. *Have to* vs. *Have Got to.*

-*OUS* WORD   O.4

1. A large number of words end in the letters *ous.* That ending is not stressed. It is pronounced [əs], like unstressed *us.*

2. Words with -*ous* are very regular in the location of stress. The addition of the -*ly* adverb ending does not change the place of stress. You can tell where the primary stress is from the spelling. Count the *vowel signs* before the -*ous.* A vowel sign is either a single vowel letter or a combination of vowel letters. The vowel letters are *a, e, i, o, u,* and *y* (except *u* after *q,* and *y* before a vowel).

3. Here are the rules:

a. If the word has only one vowel sign before the -*ous,* the stress is on that vowel sign. In the following examples, the stressed vowel sign is underlined:

famous	pompous	jealous
nervous	joyous	grievous

b. If the word has more than one vowel sign before the -*ous,* the stress is on the next to the last vowel sign. In the following examples, the stressed vowel sign is underlined:

curious	continuous	dangerous	monotonous
serious	spontaneous	humorous	villainous

There are no exceptions to the first rule. Rule *b* has relatively few exceptions, and all of those are stressed on the vowel sign before the -*ous.* Rather common exceptions are *desirous, enormous, disastrous,* and adjectives that end in -*endous* —e.g., *tremendous, horrendous,* and *stupendous.*

1. Two or more words, phrases, or clauses are *parallel* if they perform the same syntactical function in a sentence. Such words, phrases, and clauses are called *members of a parallelism* and are usually joined by the conjunctions *and, but, or,* or *nor.*

2. Do not use a comma before the conjunctions if they join two words, phrases, or dependent clauses.

3. In the examples below the parallel parts are arranged in a diagrammatic scheme.

George and Thomas went with us. [*George* and *Thomas* both function as subjects of *went:* they are parallel.]
```
George
  and        went with us.
Thomas
```

Bob sang and danced in the show. [*Sang* and *danced* both function as simple predicates of the subject *Bob:* they are parallel.]
```
          sang
Bob        and        in the show.
          danced
```

Bernice spoke loudly and clearly.
```
                  loudly
Bernice spoke      and
                  clearly
```

The children sang songs and played games at the party.
```
              sang songs
The children      and            at the party.
              played games
```

You can have the black kitten or the white dog.
```
              the black kitten
You can have        or
              the white dog.
```

Mr. Rogers looked for his watch but could not find it.
```
              looked for his watch
Mr. Rogers          but
              could not find it.
```

Mother complains before I leave the house and after I come home.
```
                  before I leave the house
Mother complains            and
                  after I come home.
```

4. Use a comma before *and, but, or,* or *nor* joining two independent clauses.

George went with us, and Thomas came later.
Mr. Rogers looked for his watch, but he could not find it.

5. Use a semicolon if the two independent clauses could be but are not joined by these conjunctions *and, but, or,* or *nor.*

> George went with us; Thomas came later.
> Mr. Rogers looked for his watch; he could not find it, however.

6. The expression *as well as* is also used for parallel constructions.

> Beatrice is taking a course in geometry as well as physics.

7. The expressions *both ... and, either ... or, neither ... nor, not (only) ... but (also),* and *rather ... than* often join the members of a parallelism. Put the first part of such an expression before the first member, and put the second part before the second member.

> Both George and Thomas went with us.
> You can either go or stay.
> Millie spoke neither loudly nor clearly.
> Jake would rather sleep than eat.
> The child seemed not stupid but exhausted.
> Henry not only returned the money but also paid interest.

8. If *neither ... nor* or *either ... or* is used for more than two members, put *neither* or *either* before the first member and *nor* or *or* before the other members. If you start with *neither,* remember to continue with *nor.*

> You can either see the agent or talk with the superintendent or write a letter to the landlord.
> Neither rain nor snow nor snarled-up traffic can deter those faithful letter carriers.

9. A series is an instance of parallelism.

a. Use no commas if each member of the series is joined to the next by a conjunction.

> The garden was filled with trees *and* flowers *and* birds.

b. Use commas between the members if there are no conjunctions. If there is a conjunction before the last member, put a comma before that conjunction.

> I enjoy walking, boating, *and* swimming.
> We shall fight them on the land, on the sea, *and* in the air.
> Mrs. Jones does not relax when she is working, when she is talking, *or* when she is watching television.

c. Treat a closely related pair like a unit in a series.

> The lecturer compared Molière and Racine, Goethe and Heine, *and* Dante and Petrarch.
> That actress can portray characters that are *either* young and innocent *or* mature and sophisticated.

d. Use a semicolon between units in a series when there is punctuation, particularly commas, within the units. However, avoid such a construction if there is a possibility that its elaborateness may distract your reader.

> Americans attach particular significance to three dates: October 12, 1492, for the discovery of America; July 4, 1776, for the Declaration of Independence; and November 11, 1918, for the armistice of World War I.

e. If the members of the series are independent clauses, use a semicolon between the clauses that are not joined by a coordinating conjunction.

> The big bear glared; the middle-sized bear shrieked, *and* the baby bear wept.

f. Use a comma before the word *etc.* Do not use *and* before *etc.*

> The school offers courses in economics, sociology, finance, etc.

10. A careful writer tries to make the members of a parallelism the same kind of syntactical unit. For example, he joins adjectives with adjectives, nouns with nouns, infinitives with infinitives, gerunds with gerunds, phrases with phrases, and clauses with clauses; he does not mix such units.

> McGraw is *athletic* and *scholarly.*   or   McGraw is an *athlete* and a *scholar.*
> Skippy talks *rapidly* and *loudly.*   or   Skippy talks *with rapidity* and *in a loud voice.*   or   Skippy talks with *rapidity* and *volume.*
> If *the rain stops* and *the field dries off,* we will play ball.   or   Should *the rain stop* and *the field dry off,* we will play ball.

11. Sometimes, in haste, you may fail to use the correct form for the second member of a parallelism. To test yourself, imagine that the first member is not there.

> Clem went with John and me. [If you omit the first member, you have "Clem went with me."]
> I enjoy seeing my friends and talking with them. [I enjoy talking with them.]
> Sarah has always admired Venice and wanted to go there. [Sarah has always wanted to go there.]
> Scheherazade decided to save the situation by marrying the caliph and trying to hold his interest. [. . . by trying to hold his interest.]
> Are you working as well as going to school? [Are you going to school?]

12. Be sure to use enough words to complete the parallelism. Be particularly careful about prepositions that vary with constructions.

> Johnny will not look *at* or speak *to* his little sister.
> A poem has both an interpretation *of* and an attitude *toward* its subject matter.

13. Be consistent in your parallelism. For instance, you may either repeat a word before all the members of a parallelism or use it only before the first member.

> Mr. Fowler left with *his wife* and *his daughter.*   or   Mr. Fowler left with *his wife* and *daughter.*

> Nathan likes *to swim, to play tennis,* and *to ride horseback.*   *or*   Nathan likes *to swim, play tennis,* and *ride horseback.*

However, repeat a word to eliminate any possibility of ambiguity.

> Stevens discussed the proposal with his partner and friend. [The partner and friend may be one person or two.]
> Stevens discussed the proposal with his partner and his friend. [The partner and the friend are clearly two different persons.]

14. Don't be redundant in a parallelism. For instance, don't use both *and* and *also.*

> Mrs. Daniels bought apples and oranges.
> We visited Thailand on our trip; we also stayed a short time in Laos.

15. Excessive parallelism can be confusing. Avoid, for example, joining a series of objects and a series of verbs; put them into separate sentences.

> In the morning I could smell the wood fire, boiling coffee, and frying bacon. I could see the bright sun and mountain peaks.
> I must make the most of my stay here. I must disregard the standards I have been accustomed to, the terms of comparison, the ideals, and the visions. I must learn to judge this new country on its own terms and take back with me memories of it as it is, not as I think it ought to be.

PARENTHESIS   P.2

1. Use parentheses ( ) to enclose explanatory or additional material which is not directly related to the structure of a sentence or paragraph. If the parentheses come within a sentence, the enclosed material has no sentence-initial capitalization or sentence-final period though it may have other kinds of capitalization and punctuation, and the sentence punctuation comes outside the parentheses. If the parentheses come outside a sentence, the enclosed material has customary sentence capitalization, and its final punctuation comes within the parentheses.

> The first company Marvin worked for was Century (now Appleton-Century-Crofts).
> The exercise was on the position of modifiers (adjectives and adverbs), verbs (auxiliary and main), and objects (direct and indirect).
> In my early childhood (that was many years ago), I decided not to grow up.
> The maid swept the room clean. (The condition of the room was clean as a result of her action.)

2. Use parentheses around the definition of a word or phrase in a sentence when that definition is given merely as additional material. Underline or italicize the word or phrase, and put quotation marks around the definition. Use a comma after the name of the language to which the term belongs if that language is given in the parentheses.

> French speakers are frequently misled by English words which have cognates

in their language—for example, *actual* ("real") and *assist* ("help"). Germans call such deceptive cognates *falsche Freunde* ("false friends").

Julio ended his letter with *gracias* (Spanish, "thanks").

3. Use brackets [ ], not parentheses, around an addition to someone else's piece of writing.

The beginning of Lincoln's Gettysburg Address is "Fourscore and seven years ago [1776] our fathers brought forth on this continent a new nation. . . ."

4. Do not use parentheses to cancel a mistake. Draw a line through the error in manuscript, or mark over it with *X*'s in typing.

It was a ~~wunderful~~ wonderful day.
It was a XXXXXXX wonderful day.

5. Remember that parentheses come in pairs. Each half of a pair is called a parenthesis.

PART OF SPEECH

1. *Part of speech* is a term given to a word in the analysis of a language. It tells you what the function of the word is. The traditional terms for the parts of speech are *noun, pronoun, adjective, verb, adverb, preposition, conjunction,* and *interjection.* The terms are employed for the same reason that symbols are used in chemistry or mathematics: to help people discuss matters in an area of study efficiently. Similarly, to make compounds in chemistry correctly, the student who is beginning his study of that science has to learn the simplest facts about the elements first. As he progresses in his knowledge of the science, he can investigate the more complicated phenomena. I will follow the same line of reasoning here: in this discussion I will confine myself to single words as parts of sentences. After you have finished reading the following sections, go on to § Phrase, in which more complicated matters are discussed.

2. A dictionary tells you what part of speech a word is and often gives more than one part of speech for the same word; that is, it gives you some of the meanings of a word when it is used as a noun, as a verb, etc. For example, the word *well* can be different parts of speech according to its use in different sentences:

The well is dry. [*Well* is a noun.]
Paul works well. [*Well* is an adverb.]
I do not feel well. [*Well* is an adjective.]
Tears often well up in her eyes. [*Well* is a verb.]
Well, I think so. [*Well* is an interjection.]

Even the familiar word *man* may be used as four different parts of speech:

Man needs food and shelter. [*Man* is a noun.]
Someone must man the boats. [*Man* is a verb.]
The restaurant has a man cook. [*Man* is an adjective.]
Man! That was good. [*Man* is an interjection.]

The ability to put "proper words in their proper places" is, of course, the thing you are striving to obtain. Practice in identifying words according to their use in a sentence can help you learn the patterns of structure (*syntax*) of English. The sections on word order in this book should aid you in your practice. However, remember that memorizing rules is valueless if you do not put the rules into practice when you speak and write.

In the following paragraphs I will give you various tests or "short cuts" to determine the use of a word, but it must be understood, unfortunately, that no test is infallible.

In identifying the parts of speech of the words of sentences, it is a good idea to look first for subjects and simple predicates and then note the relationship of the other words to them. Therefore, read § Subject and Simple Predicate before you read the sections below, in which the parts of speech are taken up in the following order: noun, pronoun, adjective, verb, adverb, interjection, and conjunction and preposition.

PART OF SPEECH—NOUN   P.4

1. A good test for a noun is this: as it is used, can it have as a substitute one of the personal pronouns *I, me, we, us, you, he, him, she, her, it, they,* or *them?*
Let's take a model sentence:

> Model: Mary gave John help on grammar after dinner.

The words in the original sentence which can have those substitutes are nouns: *Mary* [= *she*], *John* [= *him*], *help* [= *it*], *grammar* [= *it*], and *dinner* [= *it*].

2. The major functions of a noun in a sentence are these:

a. Subject of verb.
b. Predicate nominative.
c. Indirect object of verb.
d. Direct object of verb.
e. Predicate objective.
f. Object of a preposition.
g. Vocative.
h. Appositive.

3. A test for a subject is this: the subject of a verb is usually the word which can have as a substitute *I, we, you, he, she, it,* or *they* immediately before that verb.

> Mary gave John help.
> She gave John help. [*Mary* is the subject of the preceding sentence.]
> Help was given by Mary.
> It was given by Mary. [*Help* is the subject of the preceding sentence.]
> Will John give help?
> Will he give help? [*John* is the subject of the preceding sentence.]

Notice that in the last example the subject comes before the *main* verb, not before the auxiliary. See the various sections on word order, particularly primary, split, and inverted.

4. A predicate nominative is a noun in the predicate (that is, after the verb) which describes or identifies the subject. The verb is usually *be* or *become.* The personal-pronoun substitutes for a predicate nominative are the same as those for a subject: *I, we, you, he, she, it,* or *they.*

> His sister is Mary.
> His sister is she. [*Mary* is the predicate nominative in the preceding sentence.]
> Her gift will be money.
> Her gift will be it. [*Money* is the predicate nominative in the preceding sentence.]
> Mr. Adams became president.
> Mr. Adams became it. [*President* is the predicate nominative in the preceding sentence.]

For an extended discussion and a list of the special verbs which are followed by predicate nominatives, see § Predicate Nominative.

5. The indirect object of a verb is the word which can have as its substitute *to* or *for* + *me, us, you, him, her, it,* or *them* after a verb. The indirect object is the equivalent of both *to* or *for* and the personal-pronoun substitute.

> Mary told John the story.
> Mary told the story to him. [*John* is the indirect object in the preceding sentence.]
> Bob did Helen a favor.
> Bob did a favor for her. [*Helen* is the indirect object in the preceding sentence.]

Also, see § Word Order—Object of Verb.

6. The direct object of a verb is the word which can have as its substitute *me, us, you, him, her, it,* or *them* after the verb. Remember, however, that the verbs *be* and *become* and the others listed under § Predicate Nominative are not followed by a direct object.

> Mary gave help to John.
> Mary gave it to John. [*Help* is the direct object in the preceding sentence.]
> His mother sent Bill to school.
> His mother sent him to school. [*Bill* is the direct object in the preceding sentence.]

Also, see ¶ 8 below and § Word Order—Object of Verb.

7. The predicate objective is the word in the predicate which refers to the direct object. It follows the direct object and has *it* or *them* as its substitute. The special verbs which are followed by a direct object and a predicate objective usually have the meaning of "designate" or "cause to be." Some of them are *call, elect, make,* and *name.*

> We elected Kennedy president.
> We elected Kennedy it. [*President* is the predicate objective in the preceding sentence.]
> We call him Johnny.
> We call him it. [*Johnny* is the predicate objective in the preceding sentence.]

Also, see § Predicate Objective.

8. The object of the preposition is the word which can have as its substitute *me, us, you, him, her, it,* or *them* after that preposition.

> Mary told a story about Paul after school.
> Mary told a story about him after it. [*Paul* is the object of the preposition *about,* and *school* is the object of the preposition *after.*]

Notice that in the sentence "Mary told John a story" *John* is the indirect object of the verb *told,* but in the sentence "Mary told a story to John" *John* is the object of the preposition *to.* Also, see § Word Order—Preposition.

9. If you use the name or a substitute for the name of a person to whom you are speaking or writing, that name or substitute is classified as a *vocative.* It is always the equivalent of *you.* Notice that vocatives are set off in writing by commas.

> Then, Mary, what did you do? [*Mary* is a vocative.]
> Come quickly, Doctor. [*Doctor* is a vocative.]
> Friends, Romans, countrymen, lend me your ears. [That sentence has three vocatives: *friends* and *Romans* and *countrymen.*]

10. An appositive is a word which restates the content of another word or group in the same sentence. However, it is *not* a predicate nominative, a predicate objective, or a word used in direct address. An appositive usually comes immediately after the word or group that it is in apposition to.

> My eldest sister, Beatrice, left yesterday. [*Beatrice* is the appositive to *my eldest sister.*]
> Have you read anything by the poet Chaucer? [*Chaucer* is the appositive to *the poet.*]

Also, see § Appositive.

See § Part of Speech—Adjective for nouns which are used as adjectives. Also, see § Singular vs. Plural.

PART OF SPEECH—PRONOUN   P.5

1. A pronoun has the same uses as a noun in sentences, and the same tests may be applied to it. Some grammarians group nouns and pronouns together as *substantives.*

She told John a story. [*She* is the subject.]
My sister is she. [*She* is the predicate nominative.]
Mary told him a story. [*Him* is the indirect object.]
Mary told it after school. [*It* is the direct object.]
We elected Kennedy it. [*It* is the predicate objective.]
Mary told a story about him. [*Him* is the object of the preposition *about.*]
You, what is your name? [*You* is a vocative.]
Oh, yes, he spoke to some students, us. [*Us* is the appositive to *some students.*]

2. The difference between a predicate nominative and an object is important with certain pronouns. When they are used as a predicate nominative, those pronouns have the same form that they have as a subject. When they are used as an object, however, they have a different form. Those pronouns are the following:

Subject form: I, he, she, we, they, who.
Object form: me, him, her, us, them, whom.

3. Some of the words which are frequently used as pronouns are the following. Remember, however, that these words are pronouns only when they function as pronouns. For instance, some of them can immediately precede nouns, but when they do, they are probably adjectives.

all	hers	much	somebody	what
another	herself	myself	someone	whatever
any	him	neither	something	whatsoever
anybody	himself	nobody	that	which
anyone	his	none	thee	whichever
anything	I	nothing	theirs	who
both	it	one (two, etc.)	them	whoever
each	its	ones	themselves	whomever
either	itself	oneself	these	whomsoever
enough	least	other	they	whose
everybody	less	others	thine	whosoever
everyone	little	ours	this	ye
everything	many	ourselves	those	you
few	me	plenty	thou	yours
half	mine	several	thyself	yourself
he	more	she	us	yourselves
her	most	some	we	

Also, see § Agreement—Pronoun, § Noun—Not Repeated, § Two-word Verb, and § Part of Speech—Adjective, for words which may be either pronouns or adjectives.

PART OF SPEECH—ADJECTIVE

1. An adjective modifies a noun or pronoun. It ordinarily answers the question "Which?" or "Whose?" or "What kind of?" or "How many?" or "How much?" An adjective ordinarily occupies one of three positions in a sentence:

p

a. Before the noun or pronoun it modifies.

> Sarah likes pretty dresses. [*Pretty* is an adjective.]
> Walter has a new car, and I have an old one. [*New* and *old* are adjectives.]

See § Word Order—Adjective before Noun and § Noun—Not Repeated.

b. After the noun or pronoun it modifies.

> Kelly's cosmetics make girls happy. [*Happy* is an adjective.]
> Can't you say anything kind? [*Kind* is an adjective.]

See § Word Order—Adjective after Noun and Pronoun and § Predicate Adjective.

c. After certain verbs.

> The doctor was anxious about the child. [*Anxious* is an adjective.]
> Don't become old before you have to. [*Old* is an adjective.]
> The little boy got angry at his sister. [*Angry* is an adjective.]

See § Predicate Adjective.

2. There are special terms for certain kinds of adjectives:

a. Words like *both, those, all, his, her,* and *which,* which can function both as pronouns and as adjectives, are called *pronominal adjectives* when they occur as preposed modifiers of nouns (e.g., *both boys* and *those children* and *all food*).

b. The words *my, our, your,* and *their* are called *genitive adjectives,* and so are *her, his, its,* and *whose* when they occur as preposed modifiers of nouns (e.g., *her child* and *his house* and *its name* and *whose mother*).

c. Words like *college, ball,* and *chemistry* which can also function as nouns are called *nominal adjectives* or *noun adjuncts* when they occur as preposed modifiers of nouns (e.g., *college boys* and *ball games* and *chemistry course*).

d. Words like *washing* and *washed* (*gerunds* and *participles*) and *wash* (*infinitives*) which can also function as verbs are called *verbal adjectives* when they function as adjectives (e.g., *a washing machine* and *the washed clothes* and *a wash cloth*). See § *-ing* Form vs. Infinitive.

PART OF SPEECH—VERB   P.7

1. The major use of a verb in a sentence is as the simple predicate or part of the simple predicate. The simple predicate usually tells the *action* or *state* of the subject: "John *told* a story"; "Mary *is* my sister." The simple predicate may contain one verb, as in the preceding examples, or it may contain more than one verb, of which the last one is the *main* verb and the others are the *auxiliaries.*

> Wadsworth has a friend. [*Has* is the simple predicate; it is a verb.]
> Renee should have gone. [*Should have gone* is the simple predicate; *should* and
>   *have* are auxiliaries and *gone* is the main verb.]

Also, see § Subject and Simple Predicate, § Clause, § Phrase, § Auxiliary, § Infinitive vs. Gerund, §-*ing* Form vs. Infinitive, § *Do*—Auxiliary, § Part of Speech —Adjective, § Tense and Time and its following sections on tense, § Two-word Verb, and § Word Order and its following sections.

PART OF SPEECH—ADVERB   P.8

1. An adverb modifies a verb, an adjective, or another adverb. It customarily answers the question "How?" or "Where?" or "When?" or "Why?"

> Jennie spoke quite suddenly. [*Quite* modifies the adverb *suddenly*.]
> Henry is very tall. [*Very* modifies the adjective *tall*.]
> The travelers came here. [*Here* modifies the verb *came*.]
> The Crawfords arrived yesterday. [*Yesterday* modifies the verb *arrived*.]
> I, therefore, forbid it. [*Therefore* modifies the verb *forbid*.]

2. Adverbs modifying adjectives and other adverbs usually precede those words. See § Word Order—Adverb Modifying Adjective and Adverb.

3. The position of adverbs modifying verbs varies; see § Word Order—Adverb Modifying Verb and § Word Order—Emphatic Adverb.

The adverb is discussed further under § Adjective vs. Adverb, § Part of Speech— Conjunction and Preposition, § Transition Expression, and § Two-word Verb.

PART OF SPEECH—INTERJECTION   P.9

1. The interjection is probably the easiest part of speech to identify. An interjection is a conventionalized utterance which has no grammatical relationship to other words. Sometimes it is a spontaneous reaction expressing an emotion, and sometimes it is just a *sentence starter* or *attention attracter*. In writing, interjections occur chiefly in dialog and usually come at the beginning of a sentence, but they sometimes occupy other positions. Some words and phrases which are often used as interjections are the following:

ah	gosh	listen	pshaw
all right	gracious	look	say
aw	ha	look here	shoot
certainly	heavens	luckily	sure enough
come on	hello	my	tell me
darn	hey	nah	very well
dear me	hi	no	well
for the life of me	ho	nope	why (pronounced [waɪ])
fortunately	holy mackerel	now	wow
gee	hurrah	oh	yeah
goodness	hurray	O.K.	yes
goodness gracious	indeed	ouch	you know

The so-called "curse words" or "swear words" like *damn* and *hell* are often interjections.

2. Interjections are usually set off by commas. If they express a really strong feeling, an exclamation mark is used.

> Hey, you're sitting on my hat.
> Well, that may be correct.
> Goodness, the wind's very strong.
> No, I am not going.
> Oh, that would be nice.
> Now, what did I tell you yesterday?
> Why, that can't be true.
> Yes, I am going.
> Luckily, nobody was hurt.
> Say, what have you got there?
> Ouch! I caught my thumb in the door.
> Wow! Did you see that flash of lightning?
> I looked where she told me, and, sure enough, there was my lost book.

3. You should remember that literal translations of interjections such as *mon dieu* and *dios mio* are not socially acceptable.

Also, see § Interpolation.

PART OF SPEECH—CONJUNCTION AND PREPOSITION   P.10

1. Distinguishing between a conjunction and a preposition is hard because the two parts of speech seem to have similar functions and because many words may be used as either a conjunction or a preposition and sometimes as an adverb or some other part of speech.

2. *And, but, or, nor,* and *for* (the last when it is used as a conjunction) are called *coordinating conjunctions.* They join words, phrases, and clauses.

> Pete and Joe are studying. [*And* joins *Pete* and *Joe.*]
> Don't do it for me but for yourself. [*But* joins *for me* and *for yourself.*]
> You can go with them or stay here. [*Or* joins *go with them* and *stay here.*]
> I stopped, for I was tired. [*For* joins *I stopped* and *I was tired.*]
> Jack has not left, nor is he planning to leave. [*Nor* joins *Jack has not left* and *is he planning to leave.*]

3. When *both* is paired with *and, not* with *but, either* with *or,* and *neither* with *nor,* both members of the pair are called conjunctions. The special term for them is *correlative conjunction.*

> I saw both Pete and Joe
> Not Alice but Mary made the cake.
> Either Jane or her brother will help.
> Lionel will neither study his lessons nor do his homework.

4. All other conjunctions are called *subordinating conjunctions.* Some words which are usually subordinating conjunctions are *although, as, because, if, lest, than, unless,* and *whether.* They are followed by a subject and a simple predicate. See § Clause and the following sections.

> Victor bought the tie because he liked it.
> I do not know whether they want to go with us.

5. Like many verbs, prepositions have objects. A prepositional object is a word or group which is the pronoun *me, us, you, him, her, it,* or *them* or which can have one of those pronouns as its substitute.

> I looked at Arthur.
> I looked at him. [In the above sentence *Arthur* is the object of the preposition *at.*]
> The girls left with the boys.
> The girls left with them. [In the above sentence *the boys* is the object of the preposition *with.*]

These words are usually prepositions:

against	between	like	unto
amid	concerning	notwithstanding	upon
amidst	despite	of	via
among	during	onto	with
amongst	except	per	within
at	from	toward	without
beside	into	towards	

Prepositions customarily immediately precede their objects; however, see § Word Order—Preposition and § Opposition Expression.

6. A few combinations of words are often classed as *complex prepositions.* Some of them are the following:

according to	contrary to	instead of
ahead of	due to	on account of
apart from	in lieu of	out of
as to	in place of	owing to
back of	in regard to	up to
because of	in spite of	

Sometimes only the last word of the combination is classed as a preposition, and the other word or words are classed differently.

7. These words are usually either prepositions or conjunctions: *after, before, for, since, till,* and *until.* If they are followed by a subject and a simple predicate, they are probably conjunctions. If they are followed by a noun, a pronoun, or a phrase *but not by a simple predicate,* they are probably prepositions.

> We got there before anyone else had arrived. [*Before* is a conjunction.]
> We got there before anyone else. [*Before* is a preposition.]

8. These words are usually either prepositions or adverbs:

aboard	around	by	out	underneath
about	behind	down	outside	up
above	below	in	over	
across	beneath	inside	throughout	
along	besides	off	to	
alongside	beyond	on	under	

If those words are followed by a noun, pronoun, or noun phrase, they are probably prepositions; otherwise, they are probably adverbs.

> I looked at the sailor as he walked by me. [*By* is a preposition.]
> I looked at the sailor as he walked by. [*By* is an adverb.]

9. A few other words which may be other parts of speech sometimes function as prepositions—e.g., *minus, near, opposite, past, plus, regarding, round, save, through,* and *unlike.*

Also, see § Agreement—Pronoun, § Phrase from Clause, § Preposition—Expression with, and § Two-word Verb.

PASSIVE

1. The term *passive voice* is used to refer to two different things: (*a*) it is used to refer to a meaning, which I will call *passive meaning* in the following paragraphs, and (*b*) it is used to refer to a construction which is not always passive in meaning; I will refer to that construction as the *passive construction.*

2. A passive construction is a combination of a form of the verb *be* with the past participle of another verb.

> The man was killed by the lion. [*Was killed* is a passive construction.]
> They are interested in English. [*Are interested* is a passive construction.]

Both examples above have a passive construction. The first example has a passive meaning. The second example does not have a passive meaning.

3. A passive meaning occurs in an expression in which the subject of a verb is either the receiver or the undergoer of the action of that verb. In all three examples below, *the teacher* is the *performer* of the action of the verb; *John* is the *receiver;* and *a book* is the "undergoer."

> The teacher gave John a book. [*The teacher* is the subject.]
> John was given a book by the teacher. [*John* is the subject.]
> A book was given John by the teacher. [*A book* is the subject.]

The first example has an *active meaning* because the subject is not the receiver or the undergoer of the action of the verb. The other two examples of the group have a passive meaning because the subject is either the receiver or the undergoer. All three examples express the same thing.

In the following group of examples, *his father* is the performer; *the boy* is the receiver, and *that story* is the undergoer. The first example is active; the other two examples are passive in meaning.

His father told the boy that story. [*His father* is the subject.]
The boy was told that story by his father. [*The boy* is the subject.]
That story was told the boy by his father. [*That story* is the subject.]

When the performer of the action is mentioned in a passive-meaning sentence, it is called the *agent*. It is customarily preceded by the word *by*. In the first group of examples above, *the teacher* is the agent in the second and third example, and in the second group *his father* is the agent in the second and third example.

4. As you can see, active constructions can be turned into passive constructions with the appropriate form of the verb *be* in two ways:

a. An original direct object (an undergoer) can be made the subject.

Active: The lion killed the man. [*The lion* is the subject; *the man* is the direct object.]
Passive: The man was killed by the lion. [*The man* is the subject; *the lion* is the agent.]

b. An original indirect object (receiver) can be made the subject.

Active: The teacher gave John a book. [*The teacher* is the subject; *John* is the indirect object.]
Passive: John was given a book by the teacher. [*John* is the subject; *the teacher* is the agent.]

5. Sometimes a passive meaning is expressed in a phrase. In that event, a noun or pronoun outside that phrase is the receiver or undergoer of the action of the verb in the phrase.

Having been hurt before, the child was very careful. [The child had been hurt before.]
Upon being questioned by the police, the man confessed the crime. [The man was questioned.]

6. Sometimes there is no expressed receiver or undergoer of the passive meaning. In that event, the receiver or undergoer is *generalized:* everybody or anybody may be the receiver or undergoer.

Being ignored is often worse than being criticized.

7. A passive meaning is often expressed by a combination of a form of the verb *get* with the past participle of another verb.

A bystander got struck by a bullet.
Did your question get answered?
Nothing ever gets cleaned properly in that house.

8. As I said before, a passive construction does not always have a passive meaning. For instance, the past participle is sometimes used to express the state or condition of the subject, without reference to an action.

> I am determined to do that.
> Phil was tired when he came home.

Also, instead of *have,* the verb *be* is often used with *gone* and *finished* and with *done* meaning "finished" to express an active meaning.

> The visitor is gone. *or* The visitor has gone.
> I am finished studying. *or* I have finished studying.
> Bob said he would call when he was done. *or* . . . when he had finished.

9. Either of two passive constructions is often used with verbs of saying or believing. They are the equivalents of *generalized expressions* like "People say (think, believe) . . ." or "Everybody says . . ." or "Somebody says. . . ."

> People say   that Mr. Ross is very wealthy.
> It is said   that Mr. Ross is very wealthy.
> Mr. Ross is said   to be very wealthy.
>
> Everybody thought   war was inevitable.
> It was thought   war was inevitable.
> War was thought   to be inevitable.
>
> Somebody reported   that Jack was dead.
> It was reported   that Jack was dead.
> Jack was reported   to be dead.

Also, see § *By*—Preposition, § Infinitive vs. Gerund, § Predicate Adjective, § Predicate Objective, and § Subject and Simple Predicate.

PERIOD   P.12

1. The period has three main uses: (*a*) to indicate the end of a statement, (*b*) to indicate an abbreviation, and (*c*) to indicate a decimal. Other less frequent uses are pointed out below. By the way, the terms *stop* and *full stop*, which are customary with Englishmen, are not used very often by Americans. The term *point* is often used in reading a decimal sign; for example, the figure *2.5* may be read "Two point five."

2. Use a period at the end of a statement or request.

> I met Hank in Barcelona.
> Come along with me.

3. Use a period, not a question mark, at the end of a statement which contains a reported or *indirect* question.

> Sue asked Evan where he was going.
> I wonder who is coming with the girls.

4. Use a period with a complete statement inside parentheses unless the parenthetical statement comes within a sentence. (For examples, see § Parenthesis as well as this sentence.) If a sentence or only one word or a few are added in parentheses (as here) within a sentence, do not use a period with them.

5. Do not use a statement period with a question mark, an exclamation mark, or another period. Notice the place of punctuation in the following examples:

> Sally said, "I have to stay here."
> Did she say, "I have to stay here"?
> She said, "Do I have to stay here?"
> Did she say, "Do I have to stay here?"

6. A period is used with most abbreviations.

a. The initial letters of a person's given or first names are frequently used before his surname or family name—e.g., D. L. Clark and Roger S. Loomis. Less often, a shortened form of the given name is used—e.g., *Ed.* for *Edward* or *Edgar* and *Geo.* for *George*. Certain short forms or alternates for given names do not have a period—for example, *Bill* for *William, Bob* for *Robert, Dick* for *Richard, Dot* or *Dolly* for *Dorothy, Gus* for *Augustus, Jim* for *James, Joe* for *Joseph,* and *Tom* for *Thomas.*

b. Initials or abbreviations for the names of states are usual after the names of cities. In other uses the state names are spelled in full.

> San Francisco, Calif.   Charlotte, N.C.
> New Orleans, La.   Have you ever been to California?
> Boston, Mass.

c. In formal writing, use *U.S.* for *United States* only if it is part of a title such as *U.S. Steel* or *U.S. Department of Commerce.* Use *&* for *and* only in the most informal writing.

d. Many very common abbreviations are listed under § Abbreviation. Notice that a few of them do not have a period.

7. An abbreviation period is used with any mark of punctuation except another period.

> Roy grew up in Washington, D.C.
> Did Roy grow up in Washington, D.C.?
> Roy grew up in Washington, D.C., and went to Seattle at the age of twenty.

8. Use a period to designate a decimal, to separate dollars and cents in a sum, and to precede cents written alone.

> My books cost $25.85 altogether.
> A third is expressed by 33.3333%.
>
> $1.25 $10.45
>   .37   − .02
> ─────   ──────
> $1.62 $10.43

p

a. Use a comma, not a period, to mark off thousands, millions, billions, etc. See § Number.

> The store sold 15,457 copies of the bestseller.
> The assets of the company amounted to $3,822,751.21.

b. A comma is not used to the right of a decimal sign to mark off thousands, etc.

> Pi is equal to 3.141592+.

9. Use a period after a number or letter which heads a part of a list or outline. Each of the sections of this book has periods used in that way—for example, this paragraph has a period after the *9* at the beginning.

10. Use a series of three periods (an ellipsis mark) to indicate the omission of words from a quoted passage. The ellipsis mark is used in addition to the quoted punctuation and in addition to the punctuation at the end of a complete sentence.

> It is a sad reflection . . . that I knew almost as much at eighteen as I do now.
>   —SAMUEL JOHNSON
> Hail, Sabbath! . . . the poor man's day.—JAMES GRAHAME
> Do you know Hamlet's soliloquy beginning with "To be or not to be . . ."?

11. To suggest a pause, hesitation, or break in dialog, either an ellipsis mark or a dash is used.

> "I'll do what . . . what you want," Mrs. Arnold stammered, "but now. . . ."
> "I'll do what—what you want," Mrs. Arnold stammered, "but now—."

12. Frequent use of a dash or ellipsis mark is characteristic of immature writing. If you compose your thought before you begin to write, you will discover that you rarely need to use those marks.

13. Do not use periods with Roman numerals, chemical symbols, or names of broadcasting or television stations.

> Read Chapter III for tomorrow.
> Henry VIII had six wives.
> Be sure to distinguish between Co meaning "cobalt" and CO meaning "carbon monoxide."
> Did you listen to the symphony over WQXR last night?

PHONETIC SYMBOL   P.13

1. You know that there is little certain relationship between the spelling of an English word and its pronunciation. To compensate for the lack of phonetic spelling, we can employ various devices to demonstrate the pronunciation. The most frequent non-oral device is respelling a word according to a *phonetic alphabet.* In my opinion, the most useful phonetic alphabet is that one worked up by the International Phonetic Association (usually referred to as the IPA). In that system one symbol represents one distinctive sound, and each distinctive sound is represented by one symbol. Various systems with modifications of the IPA symbols are used, but, again, it is my opinion that it is wise to conform to the IPA Alphabet (also called IPA) because it is simple, quickly understood, and widely known and used.

2. An excellent book employing the IPA symbols is available: *A Pronouncing Dictionary of American English* by Kenyon and Knott, published by the G. & C. Merriam Company. Once a person has learned the sounds represented by the symbols, he can use the book independently. However, it gives only pronunciations, not definitions.

3. The IPA symbols are listed below. Brackets ([ ]) indicate that the writing inside them is in symbols, not in the ordinary English alphabet. The stress mark ['] is placed *before* the stressed syllable of a word—for instance, *money* ['mʌnɪ] and *along* [ə'lɔŋ]. For the explanation of *voiced* and *voiceless,* see § Voiced vs. Voiceless.

4. Vowels are voiced—that is, produced with vibration of the vocal cords.

[i] as in *see* [si], *key* [ki], *each* [itʃ], *leisure* ['liʒɚ], *scene* [sin], *chief* [tʃif], *machine* [mə'ʃin], *peas* [piz], *freed* [frid]

[ɪ] as in *sit* [sɪt], *Monday* ['mʌndɪ], *fear* [fɪr], *weird* [wɪrd], *been* [bɪn], *busy* ['bɪzɪ], *cottage* ['kɑtɪdʒ], *England* ['ɪŋglənd], *build* [bɪld], *myth* [mɪθ], *women* ['wɪmɪn], *movies* ['muvɪz], *carried* ['kærɪd]

[e] as in *take* [tek], *fail* [fel], *say* [se], *break* [brek], *gauge* [gedʒ], *prey* [pre], *neighbor* ['nebɚ], *days* [dez], *played* [pled]

[ɛ] as in *set* [sɛt], *bread* [brɛd], *many* ['mɛnɪ], *said* [sɛd], *friend* [frɛnd], *guess* [gɛs], *leopard* ['lɛpɚd], *bury* ['bɛri], *says* [sɛz]

[æ] as in *sat* [sæt], *laugh* [læf], *plaid* [plæd]

[ɑ] as in *top* [tɑp], *car* [kɑr], *father* ['fɑðɚ], *calm* [kɑm], *heart* [hɑrt]

[ɔ] as in *law* [lɔ], *call* [kɔl], *haul* [hɔl], *cost* [kɔst], *broad* [brɔd], *ought* [ɔt], *draws* [drɔz], *thawed* [θɔd]

[o] as in *low* [lo], *note* [not], *coal* [kol], *toe* [to], *sew* [so], *soul* [sol], *shows* [ʃoz], *flowed* [flod]

[ʊ] as in *pull* [pʊl], *took* [tʊk], *wolf* [wʊlf], *would* [wʊd]

[u] as in *pool* [pul], *group* [grup], *lose* [luz], *shoe* [ʃu], *rude* [rud], *threw* [θru], *glue* [glu], *fruit* [frut], *views* [vjuz], *chewed* [tʃud]

[ʌ] (always stressed) as in *sun* [sʌn], *flood* [flʌd], *rough* [rʌf]

[ə] (always unstressed) as in *alone* [ə'lon], *apartment* [ə'pɑrtmənt], *specimen* ['spɛsəmən], *gallop* ['gæləp], *Plymouth* ['plɪməθ], *jealous* ['dʒɛləs], *campus* ['kæmpəs], *sodas* ['sodəz]

[ɝ] (always stressed) as in *term* [tɝm], *first* [fɝst], *word* [wɝd], *turn* [tɝn], *heard* [hɝd], *journey* ['dʒɝnɪ], *occurs* [ə'kɝz], *stirred* [stɝd]

[ɚ] (always unstressed) as in *permit* [pɚ'mit], *similar* ['sɪmələ], *actor* ['æktɚ], *surpass* [sɚ'pæs], *sisters* ['sɪstɚz], *bothered* ['bɑðɚd]

5. All diphthongs are voiced—that is, produced with vibration of the vocal cords.

[aɪ] as in *mine* [maɪn], *cry* [kraɪ], *lie* [laɪ], *eye* [aɪ], *height* [haɪt], *buy* [baɪ], *flies* [flaɪz], *tried* [traɪd]

[aʊ] as in *loud* [laʊd], *how* [haʊ], *cows* [kaʊz], *allowed* [ə'laʊd]

[ɔɪ] as in *oil* [ɔɪl], *boy* [bɔɪ], *toys* [tɔɪz], *annoyed* [ə'nɔɪd]

p

6. The following nine consonants are voiceless—that is, produced without vibration of the vocal cords.

[p] as in *piece* [pis], *map* [mæp], *speech* [spitʃ], *hope* [hop], *happy* ['hæpɪ], *lips* [lɪps], *shopped* [ʃɑpt]

[t] as in *tea* [ti], *sight* [saɪt], *steal* [stil], *letter* ['lɛtɚ], *states* [stets], *lifted* ['lɪftɪd]

[k] as in *cold* [kold], *like* [laɪk], *custom* ['kʌstəm], *question* ['kwɛstʃən], *box* [bɑks], *rocks* [rɑks], *knocked* [nɑkt]

[f] as in *find* [faɪnd], *phrase* [frez], *half* [hæf], *life* [laɪf], *rough* [rʌf], *cuffs* [kʌfs], *coughed* [kɔft]

[θ] as in *think* [θɪŋk], *breath* [brɛθ], *nothing* ['nʌθɪŋ], *toothed* [tuθt]

[s] as in *say* [se], *city* ['sɪtɪ], *gas* [gæs], *miss* [mɪs], *last* [læst], *hits* [hɪts], *kisses* ['kɪsɪz], *guessed* [gɛst]

[ʃ] as in *ship* [ʃɪp], *dish* [dɪʃ], *machine* [mə'ʃin], *crashes* ['kræʃɪz], *rushed* [rʌʃt]

[tʃ] as in *cheap* [tʃip], *touch* [tʌtʃ], *match* [mætʃ], *catches* ['kætʃɪz], *reached* [ritʃt]

[h] as in *hate* [het], *hot* [hɑt], *ahead* [ə'hɛd], *who* [hu]

The following fifteen consonants are voiced—that is, produced with vibration of the vocal cords:

[b] as in *bite* [baɪt], *tub* [tʌb], *robber* ['rɑbɚ], *cabs* [kæbz], *globes* [globz], *rubbed* [rʌbd]

[d] as in *death* [dɛθ], *mad* [mæd], *ladder* ['lædɚ], *shady* ['ʃedɪ], *rides* [raɪdz], *needed* ['nidɪd]

[g] as in *go* [go], *bag* [bæg], *bigger* ['bɪgɚ], *legs* [lɛgz], *begged* [bɛgd]

[m] as in *make* [mek], *farm* [fɑrm], *bomb* [bɑm], *homes* [homz], *seemed* [simd]

[n] as in *night* [naɪt], *pain* [pen], *shine* [ʃaɪn], *sign* [saɪn], *manner* ['mænɚ], *know* [no], *joins* [dʒɔɪnz], *cleaned* [klind]

[ŋ] as in *hang* [hæŋ], *angry* ['æŋgrɪ], *thank* [θæŋk], *singer* ['sɪŋɚ], *finger* ['fɪŋgɚ], *brings* [brɪŋz], *banged* [bæŋd]

[v] as in *voice* [vɔɪs], *save* [sev], *heaven* ['hɛvən], *shaves* [ʃevz], *lived* [lɪvd]

[ð] as in *this* [ðɪs], *breathe* [brið], *bathed* [beðd]

[l] as in *late* [let], *meal* [mil], *cold* [kold], *silly* ['sɪlɪ], *hills* [hɪlz], *mailed* [meld]

[r] as in *red* [rɛd], *far* [fɑr], *berry* ['bɛrɪ], *cars* [kɑrz], *tired* [taɪrd]

[z] as in *zoo* [zu], *rose* [roz], *days* [dez], *quizzes* ['kwɪzɪz], *amazed* [ə'mezd]

[ʒ] as in *vision* ['vɪʒən], *pleasure* ['plɛʒɚ], *garages* [gə'rɑʒɪz], *rouged* [ruʒd]

[dʒ] as in *jam* [dʒæm], *German* ['dʒɚmən], *age* [edʒ], *edges* ['ɛdʒɪz], *caged* [kedʒd]

[j] as in *yet* [jɛt], *unit* ['junɪt], *beauty* ['bjutɪ]

[w] as in *wait* [wet], *away* [ə'we], *whirl* [hwɚl], *quit* [kwɪt], *once* [wʌns]

7. Here is the English alphabet in phonetic symbols:

a	[e]	e	[i]	i	[aɪ]	m	[ɛm]	q	[kju]	u	[ju]	y	[waɪ]
b	[bi]	f	[ɛf]	j	[dʒe]	n	[ɛn]	r	[ɑr]	v	[vi]	z	[zi] (American)
c	[si]	g	[dʒi]	k	[ke]	o	[o]	s	[ɛs]	w	['dʌblju]		[zed] (British)
d	[di]	h	[etʃ]	l	[ɛl]	p	[pi]	t	[ti]	x	[ɛks]		

Also, see § Pronunciation and its following sections, § *A* vs. *An*, § *H*- Initial, § Silent Letter, § Spelling—Word with Suffix, § Suffix *-ed*, and § Suffix *-s*.

1. You are aware that certain kinds of words frequently appear together in *units* or closely connected groups. Those units occur so frequently and regularly that you have developed a feeling that the words which compose them "go together." In speech, the related words usually occur in a *breath group;* that is, there may be a slight pause before and after the set of words. Such a unit is called a *phrase,* or group of related words.

> **Model 1**   The boy will leave in June.

In Model 1 all the words go together to express an idea. However, certain ones of the words have a particularly close relationship. The words *the* and *boy* are closely related, and so are *will* and *leave,* and so are *in* and *June.* Each of those groups is a phrase.

2. A phrase is classified in one of two ways. The first is the *formal* classification. It is made according to the kinds (or *forms*) of words which make up the phrase. It might also be called the *internal* classification because it is based on the words which occur *within* the phrase. Under the formal method the phrase is labeled according to a distinctive word or *head word* in the phrase. This is a matter of convenience. The phrase *will leave* is conveniently referred to as a *verb phrase* because it contains a form of a verb (*leave*) as its head word. The phrase *in June* is conveniently referred to as a *prepositional phrase* because it begins with the word *in,* which belongs to a small group of similar words usually called prepositions, such as *between* and *upon.* The phrase *the boy* is referred to as a *noun phrase.* Actually, the distinctive word in that phrase is the word *the,* but since it usually goes with words which are classified as nouns, we called the phrase by the name of the other word in the phrase.

3. For further illustration of the formal classification we will make a slight change in our model:

> **Model 2**   The boy will leave next June.

The meaning of Model 2 may be exactly the same as that of Model 1, but the phrase *next June* is formally a noun phrase because in this context the word *June* goes with *next,* which we recognize as the same kind of word as *the* in the phrase *the boy*—that is, a modifier.

4. A *noun phrase* is a group of related words containing a noun and its modifiers —in particular, adjectives. Those adjectives may also have modifiers; for instance, the word *very* is an adverb modifying the adjective *little* in the noun phrase *the very little boy* in the sentence "The very little boy will leave in June." Sometimes you may have a pronoun instead of a noun in a noun phrase; for instance, *someone remarkable* is a noun phrase composed of the pronoun *someone* and its adjective modifier *remarkable* in the sentence "I have just met someone remarkable." (If you want to be consistent and call the phrase a *pronoun phrase,* nobody will object.)

p

5. A *verb phrase* is a group of related words containing one or more verb forms and their modifiers and complements. In the verb phrase in Model 1, you have two verb forms, *will* and *leave*. In the sentence "Do you know the boy leaving now?" the verb phrase *leaving now* is composed of the verb form *leaving* and its adverb modifier *now*. In "Do you know the boy selling books?" the verb phrase *selling books* is composed of the verb form *selling* and its direct object (that is, complement) *books*.

6. A *prepositional phrase* is a group of related words containing a preposition and its object. In Model 1 the word *June* is the object of the preposition *in*.

7. In analyzing phrases formally, start with the smallest unit.

Model 3   He left before seeing his mother.

Model 3 contains three phrases. The smallest is *his mother*, a noun phrase containing a noun, *mother*, and its adjective modifier, *his*. The next phrase is *seeing his mother*, a verb phrase containing the verb form *seeing* and its direct object *his mother*. The third phrase is *before seeing his mother*, a prepositional phrase containing the preposition *before* and its object *seeing his mother*.

8. The second way of classifying a phrase is according to its use or function in its sentence. This is the *functional* classification. It may be called the *external* classification since it is based on the relationship of the phrase to words *outside* the phrase. For instance, in Model 1 the phrase *the boy* functions as the subject of the simple predicate *will leave*. We say that the phrase *the boy* "is used as a noun" simply because one of the most frequent uses of a single-word noun is as the subject of a simple predicate, just as the noun *John* is the subject of the simple predicate *will leave* in the sentence "John will leave in June."

Similarly, in Model 1 the phrase *will leave* functions as the simple predicate of the subject *the boy*. We say that the phrase *will leave* is "used as a verb" simply because one of the most frequent uses of a single-word verb is as a simple predicate, just as the verb *leaves* is the simple predicate in the sentence "He leaves in June."

The phrase *in June* functions as a modifier of the verb phrase *will leave* just as the single-word adverb *then* does in the sentence "He will leave then." Accordingly, we say that *in June* is "used as an adverb."

9. Phrases, then, may function as nouns, verbs, and adverbs. A phrase may also function as an adjective: it may modify a noun or pronoun.

Model 4   The boy from France will leave in June.

In Model 4 the phrase *from France* is used as an adjective modifying *boy* just as the single-word adjective *French* is used in the sentence "The French boy will leave in June."

10. In analyzing phrases functionally, start with the smallest unit. We can take Model 3 as a specimen again. It contains three phrases. The smallest phrase is *his mother*, which is used functionally as a noun, direct object of the verb *seeing*.

The next phrase is *seeing his mother,* which is also used functionally as a noun, the object of the preposition *before.* The third phrase is *before seeing his mother,* which is used functionally as an adverb, modifying the verb *left.*

11. It is regrettable that we do not have two complete sets of different terms for the two classification systems. The only term so far discussed that is distinctive is *prepositional phrase,* which is a formal designation. To indicate a distinction when you use the other terms, you have to say something like "That phrase is formally a verb phrase but functionally a noun phrase." However, the lack of distinctive terms is not really an inconvenience as long as you make clear which classification you are talking about.

12. For practice, we can analyze the following example both formally and functionally. Let me warn you that the analysis will be long.

Model 5   My oldest brother's wife, finally guessing the cause of the trouble, bought some cough medicine at the shop on the corner.

We will begin at the end. The phrase *the corner* is formally a noun phrase composed of the adjective modifier *the* and the noun *corner;* it is used as a noun, object of the preposition *on.* The next phrase, *on the corner,* is formally a prepositional phrase composed of the preposition *on* and its object *the corner;* it is used as an adjective modifying the noun *shop. The shop on the corner* is formally a noun phrase composed of the noun *shop* and its modifiers *the* and *on the corner;* it is used as a noun, object of the preposition *at.* The phrase *at the shop on the corner* is formally a prepositional phrase composed of the preposition *at* and its object, *the shop on the corner;* it is used as an adverb modifying the verb *bought.*

Cough medicine is formally a noun phrase composed of the noun *medicine* and its modifier *cough;* the phrase is modified by the adjective *some;* the noun phrase *some cough medicine* is used as a noun, direct object of the verb *bought.*

The phrase *bought some cough medicine at the shop on the corner* is formally a verb phrase composed of the verb *bought* and its direct object *some cough medicine* and its modifier *at the shop on the corner;* it is used as a verb, the predicate of the subject.

Our analysis of that specimen is less than half done. The phrase *oldest brother* is formally a noun phrase composed of the noun *brother* and the adjective *oldest.* That phrase is modified by the adjective *my.* The noun phrase *my oldest brother's* is used as an adjective modifying the noun *wife.* The apostrophe and *s* belong to the whole phrase, not just *brother.* The inflection *'s* signals a genitive relationship between the phrase *my oldest brother* and the noun *wife.*

The phrase *the trouble* is formally a noun phrase composed of the noun *trouble* and the modifier *the;* it is used as a noun, object of the preposition *of.* The phrase *of the trouble* is formally a prepositional phrase composed of the preposition *of* and its object *the trouble;* it is used as an adjective modifying the noun *cause.*

The cause of the trouble is formally a noun phrase composed of the noun *cause* and its modifiers *the* and *of the trouble;* it is used as a noun, direct object of the verb *guessing.* The phrase *finally guessing the cause of the trouble* is formally a verb phrase composed of the verb form *guessing* and the adverb modifier *finally* and the noun direct object *the cause of the trouble;* it is used as an adjective modifying the noun *wife.*

p

The phrase *my oldest brother's wife, finally guessing the cause of the trouble* is formally a noun phrase composed of the noun *wife* and the two adjective modifiers *my oldest brother's* and *finally guessing the cause of the trouble;* it is used as a noun, the subject of the simple predicate *bought.*

Now, returning to Model 3, you can see that that sentence really contains four phrases, not just three. They are (*a*) *his mother,* (*b*) *seeing his mother,* (*c*) *before seeing his mother,* and (*d*) *left before seeing his mother.* Phrase *d* is formally a verb phrase composed of the verb form *left* and its adverbial modifier *before seeing his mother;* it is used as a verb, the predicate of the subject *he.*

13. Some other terms that you will encounter are *infinitive phrase, participial phrase, gerund phrase,* and *absolute phrase.*

a. The first two are formal terms. An *infinitive phrase* is a verb phrase that contains an infinitive preceded or not by the word *to:* "We wanted *to help her*" and "He made her *leave the room.*" A *participial phrase* has a present or past participle of a verb: "I saw the boy *running down the street*" and "*Separated from his mother,* the young child became frightened."

b. *Gerund phrase* is a mixed term. Such a phrase formally contains an *-ing* form of a verb, and it is used as a noun: "*Driving a car* calls for concentration."

c. *Absolute phrase* is primarily a functional term: such a phrase is formally a noun or a pronoun followed by a participle or by a prepositional phrase, and it is said to be used *absolutely* or without a close syntactical connection with the rest of the sentence. However, most absolute phrases can be interpreted as being used either as adjectives or adverbs. For instance, in the sentence "The boy, his clothes in rags, was a pitiful sight," the absolute phrase *his clothes in rags* can be interpreted as being used as an adjective modifying the noun *boy.* Similarly, in "All things considered, you have made the right decision," the absolute phrase *all things considered* can be interpreted as an adverb modifying the verb phrase *have made.*

14. Another kind of group of related words is the clause. See § Clause.

PHRASE FROM CLAUSE

P.15

1. You can vary your sentences by using phrases instead of clauses. In § Clause —Adjectival, § Clause—Noun, and § Clause—Independent and Adverbial there are directions showing you how you can make clauses from simple sentences. You should read those sections before reading this. In this section I will show you how you can make phrases from dependent clauses.

The phrase not only gives variety to your style but also permits you to express information in a relatively small space: you can say in a phrase the content of a sentence.

Also, in your reading, you will very frequently encounter the kinds of phrases discussed here. If you understand the meaning of such phrases, you can greatly speed up your rate of reading.

2. The position of a phrase is very important. If you "misplace" a phrase, you can unintentionally misinform or confuse your reader. Sometimes you will unintentionally amuse him.

> Nonchalantly smoking a big black cigar, Mr. Ross picked up the tiny baby.

What would your reader think if you put the phrase "nonchalantly smoking a big black cigar" at the end of that sentence above? In that position you would have a *misplaced modifier.*

A misplaced modifier is an adjective, adverb, phrase, or dependent clause which is put in such a position that the reader understands it to modify something that the writer did not intend it to modify. In general, modifiers come next to the words they modify. The phrases that are discussed here are all used as modifiers. As you read the examples, see whether some of them could be taken to modify wrong things if they were put in positions other than those I recommend.

3. I will first discuss adjectival clauses that can be converted into phrases.

a. In an adjectival clause whose subject is *who, which,* or *that,* you can omit that subject and the words *am, is, are, was,* or *were* before a present participle, a past participle, or an adjective phrase. Notice that the punctuation of the clause is not affected.

> I know the men [who are] sitting in that car.
> My father, [who was] wearing his old blue suit, stalked into the room.
> The boys helped the people [that were] hurt in the accident.
> The problem [which is] bothering everybody is the lack of money.
> A man [who is] capable of doing that is capable of anything.
> The puppy, [which was] too excited to be calmed, barked furiously.
> We said goodby to Mrs. Long, [who was] still busy at her chores.

b. In a nonrestrictive adjective clause, you can omit the same words before a noun phrase. That noun phrase becomes an appositive. You keep the commas.

> Arthur Symons, [who was] a decadent, wrote about vampires.
> You should have a talk with Mr. Worth, [who is] the adviser to students.
> We finally reached Rio, [which was] the end of our journey.

c. You can substitute *with* for *who, which,* or *that* and the verb *has, have,* or *had* meaning "possess" in an adjectival clause. The punctuation is not affected.

> The company wants men who have experience.
> The company wants men with experience.
> Buy the machine which has a guarantee.
> Buy the machine with a guarantee.
> My father went up to the woman that had a book under her arm.
> My father went up to the woman with a book under her arm.
> Washington, which has a million inhabitants, does not have suffrage.
> Washington, with a million inhabitants, does not have suffrage.

d. Similarly, you can substitute *without* if the verb of the clause is negative. The punctuation is not affected.

> The company seldom hires men who do not have experience.
> The company seldom hires men without experience.
> Don't buy the machine which does not have a guarantee.
> Don't buy the machine without a guarantee.
> The teacher was looking for a rule that did not have an exception.
> The teacher was looking for a rule without an exception.
> Washington, which does not have suffrage, has a million inhabitants.
> Washington, without suffrage, has a million inhabitants.

e. If a nonrestrictive phrase modifies a subject, it can be placed before that subject. The phrase is marked off with a comma.

> Wearing his old blue suit, my father stalked into the room.
> Too excited to be calmed, the puppy barked furiously.
> A decadent, Arthur Symons wrote about vampires.
> With a million inhabitants, Washington does not have suffrage.
> Without suffrage, Washington has a million inhabitants.

4. Now I will take up the kinds of adverbial clauses that you can convert into phrases.

a. The subject of the adverbial clause must be the same person or thing as the subject of the main verb. The resulting phrase may assume three positions:

1. It usually comes before the subject of the main verb. There it is marked off by commas.
2. It sometimes comes immediately after the subject of the main verb. There it is marked off by commas.
3. It may come at the end of the sentence if there is no noun or pronoun before it which it might be taken to modify. There it is not marked off by commas unless it begins with a verb form.

You should be wary of the third position because there is where you can most often be guilty of a misplaced modifier.

b. You can omit the subject of the clause and the word *am, is, are, was,* or *were* if the clause begins with *although, if, though, until, when, whenever,* or *while.*

> When [he was] asked his opinion, Mr. Boyd remained silent.
> Mr. Boyd, when asked his opinion, remained silent.
> Mr. Boyd remained silent when asked his opinion.
>
> Until [you are] spoken to, you should not speak.
> You should not speak until spoken to.
>
> If [she is] in need, Gloria ought to ask her parents for money.

c. You can convert certain other adverbial clauses into phrases by changing the verb in the clause to a participle. With most of them you use the present participle—e.g., *studying*—if the time of the clause is the same as or future to the time of the main verb. You use the perfect participle—e.g., *having studied*—if the time of the clause is earlier than the time of the main verb.

d. In converting an adverbial *reason* clause beginning with *because, since,* or *as,* omit the conjunction and the subject, and change the verb to a participle. Here the customary position of the phrase is before the subject of the main verb. The phrase sometimes goes immediately after the subject. Notice that the punctuation conforms to the rules in ¶ 4, *a.*

> Mary sat down quickly because she suddenly felt dizzy.
> Suddenly feeling dizzy, Mary sat down quickly.
> Mary, suddenly feeling dizzy, sat down quickly.
>
> Since I had worked hard all day, I was ready for bed by nine o'clock.
> Having worked hard all day, I was ready for bed by nine o'clock.
>
> Mrs. Jay has opened a savings account since she is planning to buy a car.
> Planning to buy a car, Mrs. Jay has opened a savings account.
>
> As he was interested in science, Franklin made numerous experiments.
> Being interested in science, Franklin made numerous experiments.

The word *being,* as in the last example above, can be omitted if it is followed by a past participle, an adjective, or a noun phrase. As a matter of fact, the *being* is more frequently omitted than used in such a phrase.

> Interested in science, Franklin made numerous experiments.
>
> Because he was sure of his evidence, the detective accused Miss Perry.
> Being sure of his evidence, the detective accused Miss Perry.
> Sure of his evidence, the detective accused Miss Perry.
>
> Since he is an expert speaker, Jim knows how to influence an audience.
> Being an expert speaker, Jim knows how to influence an audience.
> An expert speaker, Jim knows how to influence an audience.

e. In converting an adverbial *time* clause, you can use a present participle and omit the conjunction and the subject if the time of that clause is the same as the time of the main verb.

> When he stood up, Lucas stretched and yawned.
> Standing up, Lucas stretched and yawned.
>
> Connie shouted to me as soon as she saw Bert.
> Seeing Bert, Connie shouted to me.
>
> A teacher must consider his students while he is giving instruction.
> Giving instruction, a teacher must consider his students.

You can use certain words before the participle to express clearly the time relationship between the phrase and the main verb.

1. Use *on* or *upon* to indicate that the time of the phrase is the starting point of the main verb.

> On standing up, Lucas stretched and yawned.
> Upon seeing Bert, Connie shouted to me.

2. Use *when, while,* or *in* to indicate that the time of the phrase continues throughout the time of the main verb.

> In giving instruction, a teacher must consider his students.

f. If the time of the dependent clause is different from the time of the main verb, you must use certain words before the participle to indicate the time relationship.

1. Use *since* to indicate that the time of the main verb began at the time of the phrase and has continued up to the present. Do not confuse this *since* with the one that is a synonym for *because.*

> Since I came here, I have seen many new things.
> Since coming here, I have seen many new things.

2. Use *before* to indicate that the time of the phrase is later than the time of the main verb.

> Before you leave the house, turn off the lights.
> Before leaving the house, turn off the lights.

3. Use *after* to indicate that the time of the phrase is earlier than the time of the main verb. Either the present participle or the perfect participle may be used.

> After she had closed the office, Mrs. Brown felt much relieved.
> After having closed the office, Mrs. Brown felt much relieved.
> Mrs. Brown felt much relieved after closing the office.

The *after* may be omitted if the perfect participle is used before the subject.

> Having closed the office, Mrs. Brown felt much relieved.

5. I have been warning you against moving a phrase away from the subject. However, a phrase quite often comes after a verb of saying. The phrase is marked off by commas.

> Mary, *thinking about her party*, said, "I should invite John."
> Mary said, *thinking about her party*, "I should invite John."
> "I should invite John," Mary said, *thinking about her party.*

Nevertheless, do not use that position if there is any possibility that the phrase may become a misplaced modifier—that is, be understood to modify the wrong word.

6. Here is a final warning: a modifying phrase must have something to modify. Otherwise, the phrase is a *dangler* because it is not *tied* to anything.

Sometimes you write down a phrase when you begin to compose a sentence, and then you decide to change the expression of your thought. If you are not careful about tying into the rest of your sentence the phrase that you have already written, your shift in construction may be confusing or unintentionally amusing to your reader.

As an example, let's begin a sentence with the phrase "thinking about her party," which occurs in the preceding subsection.

> Thinking about her party...

How should we continue? Would it be all right to finish the sentence with the words "it seemed a good idea to invite John"? No, it would not because there would be no word for the phrase to modify. We should finish the sentence by tying the phrase to Mary, who was doing the thinking.

Thinking about her party, Mary said she should invite John.

Very often it is necessary to rewrite a sentence completely in order to eliminate a dangling modifier.

POLITE EXPRESSION   P.16

1. *Please* is the word most frequently used for softening a command·or request. It is ordinarily placed before the main verb or at the end of the sentence. A comma is placed before *please* in the latter position.

Please tell me the answer.
Tell me the answer, please.

2. Two other polite expressions which take the same positions are *will you* and *won't you*. They are both affirmative in intent. *Please* may be added. Either a period or a question mark may be put at the end of the sentence.

Will you tell me the answer.
Won't you please tell me the answer?
Tell me the answer, won't you, please?

3. *Would you* and *could you* go before the main verb, and *please* may be added.

Would you tell me the answer?
Could you please tell me the answer?
Could you tell me the answer, please.

4. *I wish you would* also goes before the main verb, and *please* may be added.

I wish you would tell me the answer.
I wish you would please tell me the answer.
I wish you would tell me the answer, please.

5. Two other polite formulas are *Do you mind* and *Would you mind* followed by the *-ing* form of the main verb.

Do you mind telling me the answer?
Would you mind telling me the answer?

6. The formula *Why don't you* followed by the simple form of the main verb is quite frequently used. It is affirmative in intent. The verb *be* is often found in this construction.

Why don't you tell me the answer?
Why don't you study?
Why don't you be quiet?
Why don't you be reasonable?

p

7. The most frequent way of asking a person *not* to do something is *Please don't* or *Don't ... please.* (*Won't you* is not intended negatively.)

> Please don't tell me the answer.
> Don't tell me the answer, please.

8. The same negative request is made with five other formulas. The first three go before the simple form of the main verb, and the last two go before the *-ing* form. A period is the customary punctuation for the end of the sentence.

> Will you please not tell me the answer.
> Would you please not tell me the answer.
> I wish you would not tell me the answer.
> Do you mind not telling me the answer.
> Would you mind not telling me the answer.

9. Notice that the auxiliaries *will, would,* and *could* in all those expressions have little meaning other than politeness; they do not show time.

Also, see § *Can* vs. *Could* vs. *May* vs. *Might,* § Conditional Sentence, § Negative, § *Shall,* and § *Wish* vs. *Hope* vs. *Want* vs. *Would like.*

PREDICATE ADJECTIVE   P.17

1. The verbs *be* and *become* often occur in constructions with adjectives. The adjectives, which are called *predicate adjectives,* describe the subject of the *be* or *become.*

> Millicent is pretty. [*Pretty* is a predicate adjective.]
> The boy became famous. [*Famous* is a predicate adjective.]

2. A number of other verbs may be followed by a predicate adjective. The trouble is, however, that most of those verbs may also be followed by adverbs. A test to determine whether an adjective form or an adverb form should follow is this: if you can substitute *be, become,* or *seem to be* for the verb and have a sentence which is similar in meaning, then you need the adjective form. The substitute sentence does not have to mean exactly the same as the original sentence.

Test: Fill in the blanks with the adjective *rapid* or the adverb *rapidly.*

a. Your brother certainly grew ____. He was very small the last time I saw him. [*Was* or *became* can not be substituted for *grew* here and give a similar meaning. Therefore, the adverb form *rapidly* is needed in the blank.]

b. Your brother certainly grew ____ in his movements after the boss had spoken sharply to him. [*Became* can be substituted for *grew* here and give a similar meaning. Therefore, the adjective form *rapid* is needed in the blank.]

3. Some other verbs which may be followed by a predicate adjective are these:

act	blow	bulk	feel	fly	grow	look
appear	blush	continue	flame	get	keep	loom
bang	break	fall	flush	go	lie	make

play	remain	set	sound	taste	wear
prove	run	slam	stand	turn	work
rank	seem	smell	stay	wax	

4. Many of those verbs may also occur in predicate-adverbial constructions. Here are some paired sentences. The adjectival complements of those on the left are either adjectives or participles; the adverbial complements of those on the right are adverbs with the *-ly* inflection.

ADJECTIVAL COMPLEMENT	ADVERBIAL COMPLEMENT
Sue acts angry.	The doctor acted quickly.
My boss appears gruff.	The sun appeared briefly.
Those leaves will turn brown.	The pedestrian turned unexpectedly.
The door banged shut.	The policeman banged noisily.
The woman went insane.	The prisoner went reluctantly.
The man fell sick.	The man fell accidentally.
The sky looked foreboding.	The searchers looked thoroughly.
The grass grew green.	The grass grew rapidly.

By substituting the appropriate form of *be, become,* or *pretend to be* for each of the verbs in those sentences as an empirical test for adjectival use, you will observe that the sentences on the left will still have meaning but those on the right will not.

5. Another set of verbs that can occur with an adjectival complement includes most of those listed under § Predicate Objective as occurring with predicate objectives. The general meaning of those verbs is "designate" or "cause to be." Those verbs, if active, occur with both a direct object and a predicate objective. However, the list of verbs that can occur in the construction "verb + direct object + adjectival complement" is much longer. The general meaning of the adjectival complement is "the condition of the direct object in relation to the verb." Since the total list of verbs is too long to be given here, I will just give examples in paired sentences. The sentences on the left illustrate the meaning signaled by adjectives or participles in contrast to the meaning signaled by the adverbs in the sentences on the right.

ADJECTIVAL COMPLEMENT	ADVERBIAL COMPLEMENT
She sweeps the room clean.	She sweeps the room briskly.
That machine can cut bread thin.	That machine can cut bread rapidly.
The court declared the act illegal.	He declared his opinion vehemently.
He called his dog unfaithful.	He called his dog loudly.
The teacher caught the boy cheating.	The player caught the ball easily.

6. Now let's consider passive constructions. Let's convert the preceding examples into passives by making the direct object the subject and using a form of the verb *be* with the past participle of the main verb. Notice that an adjectival complement remains adjectival and an adverbial complement remains adverbial.

ADJECTIVAL COMPLEMENT	ADVERBIAL COMPLEMENT
The room is swept clean.	The room is swept briskly.
Bread can be cut thin.	Bread can be cut rapidly.

ADJECTIVAL COMPLEMENT	ADVERBIAL COMPLEMENT
The act was declared illegal.	His opinion was declared vehemently.
His dog was called unfaithful.	His dog was called loudly.
The boy was caught cheating.	The ball was caught easily.

Also, see § A- Words, § Adjective vs. Adverb, § Infinitive vs. Gerund, § Passive, and § Word Order—Adjective after Noun and Pronoun.

PREDICATE NOMINATIVE   P.18

1. Certain verbs occur in constructions with nouns or pronouns which are not their subjects or objects. The verbs are called *linking* or *copulative* verbs, and the nouns or pronouns are called *predicate nominatives.* The construction identifies or describes the subject of the linking verb.

2. The verb of a predicate-nominative construction may be one of the following:

act	be	continue	look	play	remain	seem
appear	become	feel	make	prove	turn	

In the following examples, the verb is italicized, and the predicate nominative is between vertical lines.

That man *is* |my teacher|.
The men *seemed* |enemies|.
Bruce intends to *be* |a lawyer|.
The cause of the blast *was* |a bomb|.
|Who| *is* that man?
Do you know |who| that man *is?*
|Who| could that caller have *been?*
|What| are you planning on *becoming?*
Mr. Lewis is thinking about *remaining* |the chairman of our club|.
Louisa will definitely *make* |a good nurse|.
I *felt* |a fool| when I could not answer the teacher's question.
Having *turned* |traitor|, the soldier refused repatriation.
Becoming |a doctor| requires years of study.

3. In formal writing and speech, the subjective forms *I, he, she, we,* and *they* are used for predicate nominatives, not the objective forms *me, him, her, us,* and *them.*

This *is* |he|.
The culprit *was* |I|.
The persons who should be blamed *are* |we|, not |they|.

4. Remember that the verb agrees with the subject, not the predicate nominative. See § Agreement—Pronoun.

It *was* |we| who did it.

PREDICATE OBJECTIVE

1. Certain verbs occur in constructions with nouns which are called *predicate objectives.* The verbs have the meaning of "designate" or "cause to be." The verb may be one of the following:

appoint	consider	designate	judge	name	term
brand	crown	elect	keep	nominate	think
call	declare	hold	label	pronounce	
choose	deem	imagine	make	prove	

2. If the verb is in an active construction, it has a direct object as well as a predicate objective. If the two complements follow the verb, the direct object precedes the predicate objective. In the following examples, the verb is italicized, the direct object is between brackets, and the predicate objective is between vertical lines. Notice that no article is used before the predicate objective if the designation denoted by the predicate objective is unique.

> We *elected* [Alice] |president of our class|.
> The committee *appointed* [me] |bookkeeper|.
> Mrs. Rawls *calls* [her son] |her little treasure|.
> The court martial will probably *pronounce* [the soldier] |a traitor|.
> The enemy intended to *keep* [Barsow] |a prisoner| indefinitely.

3. If either the direct object or the predicate objective is or contains a *wh* word, it is shifted to a position before the verb. Sometimes a direct object or a predicate objective without a *wh* word is similarly transposed for contrast.

> |What| did we *elect* [Alice]?
> [Whom] did we *elect* |president|?
> You can't guess [whom] the committee *appointed* |bookkeeper|.
> [Which soldier] will the court martial probably *pronounce* |a traitor|?
> Mrs. Rawls calls her son her little treasure; [her husband] she *considers* |her burden|.

If you are not sure which complement is the predicate objective, put both of them after the verb; the second will then be the predicate objective. For instance, take the first example above: "We *elected* [Alice] |what|?"

4. If the verb is converted into a passive construction, the direct object becomes the subject, but the predicate objective remains a predicate objective. The original subject of the active construction is often but not always converted into a prepositional phrase with *by.* In the following examples, the subject of the converted sentence is between parentheses. Also, see § Passive.

> (Alice) was *elected* |president of our class|.
> (I) got *appointed* |bookkeeper| by the committee.
> (Her son) is *called* |her little treasure| by Mrs. Rawls.
> (The soldier) will probably be *pronounced* |a traitor|.
> (Barsow) was intended to be *kept* |a prisoner| indefinitely by the enemy.

5. With the verb *make,* an alternative construction exists for the two complements: the predicate objective can be turned into a direct object, and the direct object can be turned into a prepositional phrase with *of* or *out of.*

The army *made* [John] |a man|.
The army *made* [a man] out of John.

PREFER   P.20

1. The verb *prefer* is used in the construction "*prefer* something *to* something else."

Mr. Brunner prefers chemistry to physics.

2. The *to* in the construction is a "true" preposition and, therefore, will be followed by an *-ing* form instead of an infinitive.

Joe prefers skating to skiing.
Bill preferred playing soccer to swimming.

3. A similar construction is "*prefer* something *rather than* something else."

Mr. Brunner prefers chemistry rather than physics.

4. In that construction the infinitive is used, not the *-ing* form.

Joe prefers to skate rather than ski.
Bill preferred to play soccer rather than swim.

Also, see § *Rather* and § Infinitive vs. Gerund.

PREPOSITION—EXPRESSION WITH   P.21

Probably one of the greatest difficulties in English is remembering how to use the words usually called prepositions: *at, by, in, to,* etc.

1. The list in ¶ 4 below contains examples of expressions with prepositions which have caused difficulty for students. The list treats as prepositions these words: *about, above, across, after, against, ahead, along, around, as, at, away, back, before, behind, below, by, down, for, forward, from, in, inside, into, like, of, off, on, out, outside, over, past, through, to, under, up, upon, with, within,* and *without.* Grammatically these words are not always prepositions: they are sometimes used as adverbs, conjunctions, or other parts of speech. Some grammarians call them *particles* or *function words.* Often they are part of a two-word verb (see ¶ 2 below). For the purposes of this list, however, they will be classified as prepositions even though in many of these expressions they do not have the function of prepositions.

The listing is according to the *head word* or most distinctive word of the expression. For instance, the expression *put up with* is alphabetically arranged with *put* as the head word, and *for the most part* is alphabetized under *part.* An expression is followed by a definition only if it has a special meaning. You probably know the definition of the other phrases but have trouble remembering which preposition is used. Each time you consult an entry, however, you should study the illustrative sentence to see if it expresses the meaning you want.

Many of the expressions include more than one preposition. In the illustrative sentences notice the prepositions and their relative positions. When a preposition is given in parentheses in the entry, that preposition is used when there is an addition to or expansion of the phrase. For example, when *fall out* has the meaning of "quarrel," it may be followed by *with* and then by either *about* or *over:*

> John and Paul fell out.
> John fell out with Paul.
> John fell out with Paul about the money.
> John fell out with Paul over the money.

2. The list has numerous *two-word verbs.* They are often included among the expressions which are called *idioms.* See § Two-word Verb for the characteristics of those combinations. The (S) in this list indicates that the phrase is a separable two-word verb and, therefore, most objects may come either before or after the preposition. However, a short, one-syllable pronoun object comes *before* the preposition of a separable combination. That pronoun object may be *me, you, him, her, it, us,* and *them.* For example, you may say with *find out,* "discover" (S), either "He found my secret *out*" or "He found *out* my secret," but with *it* instead of *my secret* you should say only "He found it *out.*"

In speech the two kinds of two-word verbs are usually distinguished by stress: the separable preposition usually has more stress than the verb, but the inseparable preposition usually has less stress than the verb. For instance, with *call for* meaning "come or go to get" the *call* has more stress than the *for,* but with *call up* meaning "telephone" (S) the *up* has more stress than the *call.*

3. Also, in the examples be sure to notice the form of the verb which comes either between or after the phrase. The use of the *-ing* form is very frequent with these expressions. Pay special attention to the expressions which have *to;* see § Infinitive vs. Gerund.

4. Here is the list of prepositional phrases. Read the illustrative sentences very carefully.

> *abide by.* Every member of the club must abide by the rules.
> *absent from.* Your friend has been absent from classes for three days.
> *acceptance of.* The conference recommended acceptance of the compromise.
> *acceptance of . . . for,* "on behalf of." The maid's acceptance of the package for her mistress will not make her responsible for the payment.
> *according to.* According to Mr. Pierson, the decision will be reached tomorrow.
> *account for.* No one can account for the man's strange disappearance.
> *accuse of.* The suspect was accused of murder. The headmaster accused the boy of stealing. The boy was accused of stealing by the headmaster.
> *accustom to.* The immigrant had to accustom himself to new social habits. Mr. Jones is accustomed to having his own way. I have not got accustomed to that food.

acquainted with. International House helps students get acquainted with American customs.

adapt to. Charles adapted the machine to his needs.

addition (to), (in). The Andersons have built an addition to their cottage. Sue is studying stenography in addition to statistics. What sport do you like in addition to skating? Jake is our gardener; in addition, he is a fine cook.

adequate for. Will that amount of money be adequate for all your needs?

adjust to. We all have to adjust to our environment.

advise ("inform") *of.* Have you advised the postman of your change in address?

advise ("counsel") *on.* The dean advised the students on their courses.

afraid of. Some people are afraid of cats and dogs.

agree with ... on (or *upon*). I agree with you on that matter. That food did not agree with Mr. Lewis; he felt ill.

agreeable to. Are you agreeable to the plan?

agreement (with), in. I am in agreement with you on that matter.

ahead of. The scout went ahead of the group. Johnny is ahead of his brother in reading ability.

all, at (an intensifier; used only in questions or after a negative). Does that boy study at all? Sally had nothing at all to do with the argument.

always, for. George promised to love her not for just a day but for always.

angry at ... about. She is angry at her sister about something or other.

anxious about (or *over*). I am very anxious about appearing in front of so many people. There's no reason to be anxious over such a small thing.

apologize to ... for. The teacher apologized to the class for his error. Have you apologized to Peter for scolding him?

apparent to. Their dissatisfaction was apparent to all of us.

apply to ... for. Paul applied to several schools for scholarships.

appropriate for. The lines the speaker quoted were appropriate for the occasion.

approve of. Did the director approve of your suggestion for a change?

argue (with) ... about (or *over*). I do not want to argue with you about the matter. Mr. Abbott argued about going, but he finally went. The motorist argued with the judge over paying the fine.

arrive (or *arrival*) *at* (any point or location other than a continent, country, state, or city). We arrived at the school promptly. Have you arrived at a solution to your problem?

arrive (or *arrival*) *in* (a continent, country, state, or city). When did you arrive in Paris? Paul was met by his father on his arrival in Africa.

ashamed of. He should be ashamed of himself. Aren't you ashamed of doing that?

ask for. The man asked for help. I asked my parents for some money.

attend to. Would you kindly attend to that matter as soon as possible?

attention to. Pay attention to your father. Pay attention to what he says. Please give your attention to me for a moment. Please give me your attention..

attraction for. A magnet has attraction for iron filaments.

attraction to. Iron filaments exhibit attraction to a magnet.

available to. The company does not make its annual report available to the public.

awake from. The baby is not awake from his nap yet.

aware of. We weren't aware of your strong interest in the subject.

back out (*of*), "withdraw from; fail to keep (a promise)." At first, John said he would join us, but then he backed out. Don't back out of a promise.

back up: a. "Support" (S). If you object, I will back you up.

    b. "Go or put (a car) in reverse" (S). Back up in that alley, and then turn left. Back the car up first.

bad (*with*), *in.* Laziness will get you in bad with your employer.

base on (or *upon*). Mr. Bryant's opinion of you is based on his acquaintance with you. That short story is based upon an incident in the author's life.

because of. The secretary is absent because of a cold.

become of. Where is George? What has become of him?

belong in (a container). The brush belongs in the chest, not in the closet. My little daughter thinks she belongs in the movies.

belong to. That car belongs to Paul. To whom does this belong?

benefit (*of*), *for the.* We are collecting money for the benefit of some orphans. I am doing this for your benefit.

blame for. I will take the blame for that blunder. Don't blame the child for saying what he did.

blow up: a. "Explode; destroy by explosion" (S). The engineers blew the old dam up.

    b. "Become greatly angered." Charles blew up when I told him my secret.

boast of (or *about*). Beowulf boasted of his exploits. Don't boast about getting the highest grade.

borrow from. Do you think you can borrow some money from your friend?

break down: a. "Stop functioning properly." Oil the pump so that it will not break down.

    b. "Lose one's composure or health" (S). The accused man broke down and confessed. If you do not rest enough, you will break down (or will have a breakdown).

    c. "Analyze" (S). Please break that bill down so that I will know the expense for each item.

break in: a. "Tame" (S). Cowboys break wild horses in.

    b. "Train" (S). I am breaking a replacement in for my job.

    c. "Make comfortable through use" (said of shoes) (S). You should break those new shoes in by wearing them only a few hours a day.

    d. "Put into operation gradually" (S). If you do not break that new motor in, it may smoke.

    e. "Enter illegally." Someone broke in last night and stole my watch.

break into. The thief broke into the museum and stole a painting.

break off, "stop; discontinue" (S). It is impolite to break a conversation off when someone comes in.

break out: a. "Escape." A prisoner has just broken out of jail.

    b. "Develop a rash or a similar physical ailment." The baby broke out, and we thought it was smallpox. Bob broke out into a sweat when he was called into his boss's office.

    c. "Arise; begin suddenly." World War I broke out in 1914.

break up, "put an end to" (S). The police broke up the demonstration.

bring about, "cause" (S). What brought about your change in plans?

bring on, "cause; produce" (S). Getting overheated can bring on a cold.

bring out: a. "Produce, display; reveal" (S). Sally brought out her new dress for

p

everybody to see. The lawyer's clever questioning of the witness brought the truth out.

    b. "Publish" (S). I am waiting for my publisher to bring out my new book.

    c. "Introduce into society" (S). That ball will bring sixteen debutantes out.

bring up: a. "Rear" (S). Lane's grandparents brought him up because his parents had died when he was six months old.

    b. "Introduce into a discussion" (S). Mr. Campbell brought your name up in the directors' meeting.

burn down, "burn completely" (used with buildings) (S). The Joneses' house burned down last night.

burn up: a. "Burn completely" (used with anything combustible) (S). All Mr. Bass's belongings burned up in the fire.

    b. "Anger" (S). The rumor about his daughter burned Mr. Simpson up.

business (with), in. Mr. Spotts has retired: he is no longer in business. Jack is in business with his uncle.

call down, "reprimand" (S). The teacher called Jane down for being unprepared.

call for: a. "Come or go to get." Bob will call for Mary on his way to the party. I will call for the laundry on my way home.

    b. "Require, demand." Nursing calls for patience and devotion.

call off, "cancel" (S). The chairman called the meeting off because there was no business to transact.

call on: a. "Go to visit." Mrs. Boggs serves tea when her friends call on her.

    b. "Ask to speak." You should be prepared when your teacher calls on you.

    c. "Appeal to; summon." Call on me whenever you need help. War calls on the loyalty of citizens.

call up: a. "Telephone" (S). Call me up after the meeting.

    b. "Make one remember" (S). That name always calls up my first day in school.

capable of. Don't take a job that you are not capable of doing.

care about. A kind man cares about other people.

care for: a. "Like." I do not care for oysters at all.

    b. "Tend; watch." A groom cares for the horses in a stable.

carry on, "continue the conduct of" (S). Mr. Smith carried on the business after his partner withdrew.

carry out, "fulfill; execute" (S). When you are assigned a task, you should carry it out.

carry over, "keep for a later time" (S). We will carry that topic over to the next meeting.

case, in any, "anyhow; under all circumstances." You may fail at times, but, in any case, you should not stop trying.

case of, in, "in the event of." I will help you in case of need. Pull the lever on the alarm box in case of fire.

catch on (to): a. "Understand." Geometry was mysterious to me at first, but I finally caught on. Did you catch on to that joke?

    b. "Become popular." Some songs of that new musical have already caught on.

catch up (with), "overtake." The boys have just left; if you hurry, you can catch up (*or* catch up with them).

center (of), in the. Write the title in the center of the first line.

certain of (or *about*). Is John certain of the facts? He seemed certain about them.

change from ... to. It is very difficult to change from a poor student to an excellent one overnight.

charge (of), in. Mr. Echols is in charge of the accounting department. When an officer is absent, the next in command is in charge.

clear to. After the teacher's explanation, everything was clear to us.

clear up: a. "Become fair weather." This rain won't last; it will clear up soon.

b. "Explain (a problem or mystery)" (S). The author cleared up the mystery at the end of the story.

collect from. They were unable to collect any money from the company.

come about, "happen." How did that accident come about?

come to: a. "Concern; be a question of." When it comes to having a reliable guide, I will choose Henry.

b. "Regain consciousness." Most people who faint come to in a short while.

come up, "arise." We will have to deal with that problem when it comes up.

command (of), in. On a ship the captain is in command. A general is in command of an army.

compete with ... for. The students competed with each other for the prize.

complain to ... about (or *of*). Complain to the landlord about the lack of heat.

composed of. The jury was composed of six men and four women.

conceal from. That movie actor does not try to conceal himself from his admirers. The witness concealed the truth from the lawyer.

conceited about. That boy acts conceited about winning the prize.

concentrate on. The government is concentrating on improving the southern part of the country. I can not concentrate on my reading in a noisy room.

concern about, "worry about; bother with." You should concern yourself about your studies. The girl showed no concern about her action.

concern with, "interest in; engage in." A doctor is concerned with life and death.

conclusion, come to (or *arrive at*) *a,* "decide." I have not yet come to a conclusion about your plan. Jackson arrived at the conclusion that he should change jobs.

confidence in. You should have confidence in your abilities.

confuse with. Be careful you don't confuse this word with that other one.

conjunction with, in. The police association works in conjunction with the rehabilitation society.

connect ("physically join") *to.* The hose is connected to the faucet.

connect with. The hose is connected with the faucet. Mr. Adams is connected with the company. I did not connect the stranger with the mysterious telephone call.

connection with, (in). The fire had no connection with the burglary. In connection with his main topic, the speaker mentioned a recent news event.

conscious of. Were you conscious of any change in their attitude?

considerate of. You should try to be considerate of people's feelings.

consist in, "be demonstrated by; have as a cause or essential nature." Unselfishness consists in demonstrable love.

consist of, "have as parts or ingredients." Cement commonly consists of clay and limestone.

consult about. The student consulted his adviser about the two courses.

p

contrast to, in. That boy is certainly in contrast to his sister as far as studiousness is concerned.

contribute to. Rogers contributes ten percent of his salary to charity. Parental neglect definitely contributes to juvenile delinquency.

convince of. It was impossible to convince them of the value of the plan.

cooperate with ... in. I refuse to cooperate with them in that matter.

count in, "include (in a project, game, etc.)" (S). Be sure to count me in when you want to have a ball game.

count on, "rely on." I need a secretary I can always count on.

count out, "exclude (from a project, game, etc.)" (S). I can not contribute any money to the undertaking; please count me out.

couple of, a. That student has come to class only a couple of times.

course, in due. If you practice conscientiously, you will be able to play the piano in due course.

course of, in the. In the course of events every man must make decisions.

critical of. The director was critical of the way we were doing the work.

cut in (on), "interrupt." It is usually impolite to cut in when two other people are talking privately. I must cut in on your talk to tell you some good news.

cut off: a. "Stop (someone who is speaking) abruptly" (S). Before I had finished my statement, the judge cut me off. The operator cut Helen and me off when we were talking on the phone.

    b. "Disinherit" (S). Fathers sometimes cut off sons who marry without their consent.

cut out for (or *to* + infinitive), *be,* "be disposed; have talent for." Helene feels that she is cut out to be a teacher, but she really is not cut out for that work.

danger (of), in. Call the police if you believe you are in danger. If you do not work hard, you are in danger of failing the course.

deal of, a great (or *a good*). I have a great deal of respect for that man. Susan had a good deal of trouble in her first job.

debt to ... for, in. Are you in debt? I am in debt to the bank for two thousand dollars. I feel in debt to you for your generosity.

decide on. The committee hasn't decided on a course of action yet.

dedicate to. The author dedicated his book to his teacher. The statesman dedicated his efforts to improving international relations.

depend (or *dependent*) *on* (or *upon*) ... (*for*). Children depend on their parents for support. Children are dependent upon their parents for support. You can depend on Albert: he is reliable.

deprive of. The captors deprived the prisoners of adequate food.

desire for. Our desire for adventure usually decreases as we grow older.

despair about, in. Robertson is in despair about his future.

detail, in. The witness described the accident in detail.

devote to. You should devote more time to studying. Ellen is devoted to her mother.

different from. That story is different from the one you told me yesterday.

difficult for. That work is too difficult for that child.

difficulty in. Did you have any difficulty in your last course?

direct to. Can you direct me to the information office? You had better direct your efforts to getting a good job.

disagree with ... on (or *about*). Dr. Peterson disagreed with me on my conclusion.

disapprove of. Everyone disapproved of John's supercilious attitude.

discourage by ... (*from*). Don't be discouraged by one setback from doing what you can.

disgusted with. I am disgusted with that woman's habit of gossiping.

dismiss from. We were dismissed from our classes early today.

distance, in the. From the Capitol you can see the White House in the distance.

distinct from. The customs in the southern part of the country are quite distinct from those in the northern part.

distinguish from. My sister can't distinguish one car from another.

do away with, "eliminate; discard." I am going to do away with all these old papers.

do in: a. "Exhaust, tire" (S). Does a long trip do you in?

   b. "Kill" (S). A heart attack did Mr. Long in.

do out of, "cheat" (S). That grocer did me out of seventy cents.

do over, "repeat, do again" (S). If you do not do that exercise correctly, the teacher will ask you to do it over.

do up: a. "Wrap and tie" (S). Have you done up your gift for your mother?

   b. "Comb and fasten (hair) with pins" (S). Many women do their hair up before going to bed.

   c. "Launder" (S). Why don't you have a laundry do your shirts up?

do without, "manage without." Can't you do without cigarets? If there's not enough pie, I will do without.

doubtful about (or *of*). I am doubtful about his ability to do it. The teacher was doubtful of the possibility of changing anything.

draw up, "compose; write" (S). The secretary is drawing up a proposal for the committee.

dream about (or *of*). I dreamed about my mother last night. I will bet that you are dreaming of your vacation right now.

drop in (*on*), "visit without prior notice." I do not get much work done when people drop in. Drop in on me whenever you are in town.

drop out (*of*), "leave; quit attending." Many students want to drop out of school; they should not drop out.

drunk on. Have you ever got drunk on beer? Bob is drunk on love.

eager for. Everyone is eager for news about the result of the election.

earnest, in. Believe what I say: I am in earnest.

earth, on (an intensifier; used after superlatives, *who, where, everything,* etc.). Mr. Richards is the kindest man on earth. Who on earth told you that?

eligible for. Are you eligible for membership in that honor society?

eliminate from. He eliminated several sentences from his original draft.

encourage in. All of the author's friends encouraged him in his work.

end of, at the. The solution of the crime comes at the end of the story.

end in. The Davises' marriage ended in divorce.

engage in. Dr. Smith engages in scholarly research. The members are engaged in a discussion right now.

engaged to. Miss Miller is engaged to Mr. Dowson; they will be married in June.

enter into (or, less frequently, *in*), "take part in; be a part of." Mrs. Smith entered into the spirit of the occasion. The matter of financing will enter into the discussion.

enter on (or *upon*), "begin." John has finally entered on a career. The company has entered upon a new selling campaign.

enthusiastic about (or *over*). He is enthusiastic about his new car. You have good reason to be enthusiastic over the possibilities.

equal to. The horsepower of this motor is not equal to the horsepower of the other motor.

equivalent to. Eight pesos are roughly equivalent to two dollars.

essential to. The teacher felt that good discipline was essential to the success of the class.

evident to . . . from. It was evident to us from his behavior that he was quite upset.

example, for. Certain vegetables have a large starch content—for example, potatoes.

exchange (for), in. I will give you a pack of cigarets in exchange for your handkerchief. Bill helped me a great deal; what should I give him in exchange?

excited about. The girls are excited about their vacation plans.

export to. That company exports farm machinery to South America.

expression to. A poet gives verbal expression to his emotions.

faith in. I do not trust Mr. Williams: I have no faith in him.

faith, in good (or *bad*). Courts expect contracts to be made in good faith. If you make a promise that you do not intend to carry out, you are acting in bad faith.

faithful to. Although treated badly, the dog remained faithful to his master.

fall back on, "use in an emergency." We have plenty of cold roast beef; we can fall back on that if they stay for lunch.

fall behind, "make less progress than expected." Attend classes regularly so that you won't fall behind.

fall in: a. "Collapse" (used with a building or a part of a building). That old house is going to fall in some day. The roof fell in when the house caught fire.

b. "Agree." If you explain your plan, the committee will fall in with it.

c. "Line up." The soldiers fell in after their meal.

fall off, "decrease." Trade falls off during the week after Christmas.

fall out (with) . . . (about or *over),* "quarrel; become unfriendly." Mr. Carlson fell out with his partner about the conduct of the business. The brothers fell out over the inheritance.

fall through, "fail." If you had followed my advice, your project would not have fallen through.

familiar to. That expression is not familiar to me.

familiar with. I am not familiar with that expression.

famous for. That artist is famous for his unusual methods of painting.

fashion, after a, "in one way or another but not very well." The mechanic repaired my typewriter after a fashion.

favor (of), (in). I am in favor of doing that. All in favor say, "Aye." Please do me the favor of being quiet.

figure on: a. "Intend." I am figuring on going to a movie tonight.

b. "Expect." I was figuring on your assistance tonight.

figure out, "solve; understand" (S). Have you figured that algebra problem out? Husbands sometimes say that they can not figure their wives out. I can not figure out how to treat my wife.

fill in: a. "Substitute." While Mr. Blake is on vacation, Mr. Topps will fill in for him.

b. "Complete (a document, etc.)" (S). Have you filled in the registration form for your license?

fill out: a. "Complete by writing in" (S). Have you filled out the registration form for your license?

b. "Complete" (S). When Mr. Johnson resigned from the Senate, another man was appointed to fill his term out.

fill with. The farmer filled the bag with apples. He was filled with pity for the orphan.

find out, "discover" (S). I hope nobody finds my secret out. When did you find out that you had lost the book? Did you find out how to register?

fond of. Uncle Joe is fond of his niece. Are you fond of visiting museums?

foreign to. The use of machinery is foreign to that culture.

forgive for. Please forgive me for saying that to you.

forward to, look. I am looking forward to my vacation. Aren't you looking forward to reading that new book?

friendly to. Arthur is friendly to almost everyone he meets.

front (of), in. The boy stood in front of the class and recited his poem. Mrs. Algood insists on sitting in front with the driver.

full, in. You do not have to pay the charges in full at once; you can pay them in installments.

full of. The room was full of smoke.

fun, in. When I made that remark, I was not in earnest; I said it in fun.

fun of, make, "ridicule." You should never make fun of anyone who is trying his best.

generous about. That man is very generous about making donations to charities.

generous with. That man is always generous with his money and time.

get along: a. "Manage." An old person usually needs only a little money to get along.

b. "Be congenial." Joe gets along with all his fellow workers.

c. "Be on one's way." It is getting late; I must be getting along.

get along in years, "grow quite old." Mrs. Slate is getting along in years.

get away (from): a. "Escape." The soldier managed to get away from his captors.

b. "Leave" (usually because of unpleasantness). Mr. Brown told the children to get away from the fire.

get back (to) . . . (from), "return." When did you get back to the office from your vacation?

get by: a. "Pass." Did the mailman get by our house without our seeing him?

b. "Manage; succeed" (usually not very well). My salary lets me get by.

get in: a. "Enter (a conveyance)." Mr. Ace got in the cab and rode away.

b. "Bring in" (S). You'd better get the milk in before it sours in the sun.

get in the way, "be obstructive or annoying." Parents should see to it that their children do not get in the way.

get off, "leave (a conveyance); dismount (a horse), etc." We will get off the train at the next stop. When the bus stopped, the passengers got off.

get on: a. "Enter (a conveyance); board (a ship); mount (a horse), etc." Bob got on the ship at Genoa.

b. "Progress." I am getting on in my studies very well.

c. "Be congenial." Those two brothers never got on very well. They never got on with each other.

d. "Be on one's way." You had better get on before your boss finds you talking.

get out (of): *a.* "Leave; be released from." Carl got out of his car and went into the house. When do you get out of school? I must go to class now; I will talk with you when I get out.

b. "Evade." Mark tries to get out of every assignment he is given.

get out of order, "stop functioning properly." Telephones used to get out of order very frequently. A teacher must not let his class get out of order.

get over (with): *a.* "Recover." Bea had pneumonia, but she got over it very quickly.

b. "Finish" (S). The best thing to do with an unpleasant job is to get it over. Let's get that job over with.

get through, "finish". Would you help me with my exercise when you get through with yours?

get to: *a.* "Reach, arrive at." When do you get to your office in the morning?

b. "Begin." When Mrs. Smith gets to talking about her ailments, she continues for hours.

get together (with), "bring together; unite" (S). We should get the other members together and plan the meeting. We should get together with the other members.

get up: *a.* "Stand up". Everybody got up when the national anthem was played.

b. "Awake, arise; make arise" (S). I usually get up at seven o'clock. When does your wife get you up?

c. "Organize" (S). Let's get a group up and plan the graduation ceremony.

give back, "return" (S). Please give that book back to me when you finish.

give in (to), "yield; give one's consent." Don't give in to temptation. If you keep asking him, he will probably give in.

give up: *a.* "Abandon" (S). Don't give up trying even if you do not succeed at first.

b. "Surrender" (S). The outlaw gave himself up last week.

c. "Admit failure (on)." This math problem is too hard; I am going to give it up.

glad about. Aren't you glad about Sam's promotion?

glad to. The salesman will be glad to help you select a gift.

glance at. The policeman glanced at the car which shot past him.

go back on, "fail to keep (a promise)." Once you make a promise, you must not go back on it.

go on (with), "continue." Are you going on with your studies next year? I think I ought to go on, but I am not sure now.

go out: *a.* "Leave" (usually temporarily). When did Sister go out?

b. "Cease burning." When the lights went out, someone screamed.

go out on (a date, trip, errand). George goes out on a date almost every evening. Six of us went out on a sight-seeing trip yesterday.

go over: *a.* "Look over; review." My mother went over my homework last night.

b. "Have success." His play went over in London but not in New York.

go through with, "complete, bring to an end." Whenever George begins a project, he always goes through with it.

go with: *a.* "Harmonize with." Your hat certainly goes well with your dress.

b. "Have dates with." Sam went with Mary for six months before they were married.

c. "Be a part of." The furnishings go with the apartment.

good at. I'm not good at solving crossword puzzles.

good for. Telling them the news would be good for their morale.

good (and all), for, "finally and permanently; forever." When Bob was eighteen, he left school for good. He left school for good and all.

good (of), for the. Congressmen are expected to work for the good of their country. You should study for your own good.

good (with), in. Robert is very likable: he gets in good with everybody.

good of. It was good of you to speak to the director on my behalf.

good to. The owner of that store is always good to his employees.

goodness' sake, for (a mild exclamation). For goodness' sake, why did you do that?

gossip about. That woman has a reputation for gossiping about people.

grateful to ... for. We are very grateful to you for your assistance.

half, in. My mother broke the candy in half so we each would have an equal part.

hand in, "give, submit" (S). You should hand your homework in when it is due. He handed in his resignation.

happy about (or over). He was happy about the decision. Our friends were happy over the results of the meeting.

haste, in. You are likely to make errors if you do your exercise in haste.

have on: a. "Be wearing" (S). Sam has his new hat on.

   b. "Have scheduled" (S). The boss can not see you at that time since he has a meeting on at three o'clock.

health, in good (or bad or poor). I hope you are in good health. I am worried about Mr. Quant: he seems to be in poor health.

help with. The man offered to help us with the work.

hide from. Why are you trying to hide the information from them?

hold on: a. "Wait." If that is Bill on the telephone, ask him to hold on until I can get there.

   b. "Grasp." You had better hold on to your hat when it is windy.

hold over: a. "Continue or keep until a later time" (S). The performer was so popular that the manager is holding him over for another week. This item on the agenda will be held over until the next meeting.

   b. "Use as a threat against." Blackmailers hold indiscretions over their victims.

hold up: a. "Rob" (S). A robber held two people up last night.

   b. "Delay; stop" (S). A strike is holding up work on that new building.

   c. "Endure, last." The new cars do not hold up as well as the old ones did. The wounded man will not hold up long.

homesick for. During the first few months of college Bob was very homesick for his family.

hope for. Mr. Stokes is hoping for a raise. There is no hope for the dying man.

hope (or hopes) of, in the. Kathy retraced her steps in the hope of finding her lost watch.

hopeful of. The man is hopeful of receiving a large inheritance from his uncle.

hurry, in a. People in New York always seem to be in a hurry.

identical to (or with). The second one he showed me was identical to the first. The fifth one was identical with the third.

p

illustrate by (or *with* usually). The article was illustrated by drawings.

illustrate by (an agent). The book was illustrated by a well-known artist.

immunity from. John thought a special license would give him immunity from arrest.

impermeable to. The geologic formation is impermeable to water.

import from. The Ajax Company imports silver from Mexico.

impose on. The legislature has just imposed another tax on merchandise. Don't impose on your friends by constantly borrowing from them.

impress by. The critic was impressed by the pianist's skill.

impression of. Mr. Joyce gave the impression of being unworried.

impression on (or *upon*). The applicant made a bad impression on the interviewer.

incapable of. The man seemed to be incapable of doing the work neatly.

independent of. That former colony is now independent of the empire.

inferior to. This car is quite clearly inferior to the other one.

inquire of . . . about. Let's inquire of the agent about the train schedule. Have you inquired about the subscription rates?

insist on (or *upon*). The child insisted on going with her brother. The teacher insisted upon our being quiet.

instance, for. A number of proper nouns end in *-ese*—for instance, *Chinese.*

instead of. Instead of studying, Percy went for a walk.

intent on (or *upon*). Samuel is intent on getting a promotion.

interest in. I am interested in learning Japanese. Bob is interested in tropical fish. Don't lose your interest in improving yourself. Toby wanted to interest me in his new toy.

interest of, in the. Everything the mayor does is in the interest of the city.

interfere with. Why should we interfere with their activities at all?

introduce to. The host introduced his friend to the guest of honor.

jealous of. Why is that man always jealous of his friends' success?

judge between, "make a choice between." You must judge between the two plans.

judge by (or *from*). You should not judge a book by its cover. Judging from what I know of the two men, I will say that Phil is probably right.

keep off, "stay away from (a piece of ground)." Don't walk where a sign says, "Keep off the grass."

keep on: a. "Continue wearing" (S). The boy kept his coat on because he was cold.

    b. "Continue" (a course; used with the words like *way, journey,* and verbs with *-ing*). I called Bob, but he kept on his way. Barbara kept on talking even after I asked her to stop.

keep up: a. "Maintain" (S). It takes time and money to keep a house up properly. Keep up your good work.

    b. "Maintain the same speed or level." Please don't walk so fast: I can not keep up. I can not keep up with you. If you keep up in your work, you won't have any trouble.

kind of: a. "Considerate of." It was kind of him to help that old lady.

    b. "Rather" (colloquial). It was kind of upsetting to hear him say that. That's kind of obvious.

    c. "Type of." What kind of impression did you get of him?

kind to. That woman is always kind to everyone.

known for. That university is known for its excellent medical school.

lack of, for. The play failed for lack of interest.

laugh at. You shouldn't laugh at them: it's not polite.

lazy about. Charles is lazy about paying bills.

lean on (or *against*). He leaned on the edge of the table. Please don't lean against the wall: it has just been painted.

leave out, "omit" (S). Be sure to invite Charles to the party; I do not want to leave him out.

lend to. No one around here cares to lend money to him any more.

liberal in. My friend is very liberal in his thinking about that subject.

liberal with. That teacher is always liberal with high grades.

lie on. The wounded man lay on the operating table.

lieu of, in. The stockholders accepted shares in lieu of a dividend.

life of one, for the (a mild interjection). For the life of me, I can not get interested in that book.

limit to. You must limit your composition to two pages. There is a limit to every man's patience.

listen for. Listen for the signal to begin. Don't start until you hear it.

listen to. The candidates listened carefully to the instructions. Just listen to that wind! The students listened to the speaker.

look after, "take care of." A secretary looks after Mr. Sloan's appointments.

look at. The boy looked at me in surprise. Barbara was looking at a magazine when I entered. Irma took a look at the picture.

look for, "search for." I must look for that book; I can not remember where I put it. Are you looking for a job?

look forward to, "anticipate" (usually with pleasure). Are you looking forward to your trip? Are you looking forward to going abroad?

look like. Bill certainly looks like his older brother. We had better hurry home: it looks like rain.

look out (for), "take care; be on guard (against)." Look out for cars when you cross the street. The guide warned us by shouting, "Look out!"

look over, "examine" (S). You should look your homework over before you hand it in.

look through: a. "Search." The secretary is looking through the files for the folder. Did you look through the newspaper for that advertisement?

b. "Look at without appearing to recognize." John's former friend looked through him when she passed him.

look up: a. "Search for" (S). When you do not know a word, look it up in a dictionary.

b. "Call; get in touch with" (S). Do you look your old friends up when you go back to your home town?

c. "Improving." Pete felt that his chances for finding a good job were looking up.

lot of, a. Paul has a lot of clothes. Cecil had a lot of courage.

lots of. Paul has lots of clothes. Cecil had lots of courage.

love (with), in. I think you are in love. Are you in love with that new girl?

loyal to. The soldiers remained loyal to their leader despite the circumstances.

mad at . . . about. Paul is mad at me about something or other.

made up of, "composed of." Your personality is made up of all your habits.

make head or tail of, "understand." Mr. Carr could not make head or tail of the painting.

make of: a. "Construct or compose of." Some tribes make their houses of mud and sticks. Those pans are made of copper.

b. "Understand to be (used in questions)." What did you make of Sam's message?

c. "Cause to be or seem." Persecution made a martyr of the rebel.

make off, "escape, run away." The thief made off when he heard the police siren. The bookkeeper made off with a thousand dollars.

make out: a. "Understand" (S). The letter was so illegible that I could not make it out.

b. "Manage; do; get along." How did you make out on that test?

c. "Complete (a form)" (S). Before you can enter the course, you must make an application out.

d. "Pretend." Joe made out that he could not understand the question.

e. "Construct." That carving is made out of a piece of hard wood.

make over: a. "Remake; alter" (S). Sue made her bridal gown over into an evening dress.

b. "Give legally" (S). Mr. Stone has made his business over to his son.

make up: a. "Compose" (S). Charlotte is making up the list of guests for the party.

b. "Invent" (S). Nana made up a bedtime story for the children.

c. "Become reconciled." That couple had an argument, but they have made up.

d. "Compensate for; prepare" (S). You should make up the assignments you missed.

e. "Apply cosmetics" (S). Betty made herself up in the bedroom. Betty made up in the bedroom.

make up one's mind, "decide" (S). I can not make my mind up whether to go or not.

matter, for that. George works very diligently, but, for that matter, so does his brother.

matter of fact, as a, "really, in truth." I do not feel very energetic; as a matter of fact, I feel ill.

matter to. The state of the world matters a great deal to all of us.

member of. Is that country a member of the world organization?

membership in. That new nation has requested membership in the United Nations.

middle (of), in the. The Christmas tree stood in the middle of the room. The men sat by the windows, and the woman sat in the middle.

midst (of), in the. Dr. Fitzgerald became confused in the midst of his lecture.

mind, in. The interviewer said he would keep me in mind for the next vacancy. What do you have in mind for me to do?

mind, in one's right, "sane." Sal was not in her right mind when she wrote that note.

mind, out of one's, "insane." Sal was out of her mind when she wrote that note.

need for (a requirement which is felt as a desire; also, used before the subject of an infinitive). He spoke of the need for leadership. There is no need for you to worry.

need (*of*), *in.* I am in need of money. The Salvation Army helps people in need.

need of. Bob has need of sympathy. Bob is in need of sympathy.

nothing, for: a. "Uselessly." You did all that work for nothing: it was the wrong assignment.

    b. "Without charge." The mechanic repaired my radio for nothing.

object to. Why does he object to your going? He doesn't object to it at all.

obtain from. My friend finally obtained the information from the agency.

occasion, on, "now and then; occasionally." We do not use our TV set very often; we turn it on only on occasion.

off and on, "irregularly." Pete does not attend classes every day; he goes off and on.

once and for all, (*for*), "definitively; now and never again." The judge settled the dispute for once and for all. Once and for all, I swear I did not do it.

once, for. For once Charles had had enough ice cream.

once, for this. I will let you drive my car for this once but not again.

one, for (a mild intensifier, usually after *I*). I, for one, don't believe that story.

opinion, in one's. In my opinion, Sampson's plan was the best.

opinion on (or *about*). What is your opinion on the suggestion? I really have no opinion about the matter.

order to, in. Mr. Seward put his glasses on in order to read the fine print.

own, for one's very. Tilly does not want to share a room; she wants one for her very own.

paper (or *papers*), *in the* (*paper* = "newspaper"). I saw that story in the paper this morning. Charles's picture was in the papers yesterday.

part, for one's (a mild intensifier). For my part, I think it was a great mistake.

part, for the most, "considering the greatest part; mostly." For the most part, his lecture was quite clear.

part, in, "partially." The girl's explanation was correct in part.

participate in. Lew participates in all the committee's discussions.

particular, in. I have nothing in particular against the boy; I just do not like him.

patience with. A clerk must have patience with all customers.

patient with. Some people are not patient with little children.

pay for. How much did he pay for the car? We paid the man for his help.

payment for, in. Mr. Wills sent her a check in payment for the work she had done.

perfect for. This small suitcase is perfect for weekend trips.

persist in. You must persist in your studies.

person, in. You have to make the application in person; no one else can do it for you. The movie star appeared in person in the theater.

pick out, "choose, select" (S). Do you like someone to go with you when you pick a suit out? The captain picked Otto out to do the job.

pick up: a. "Make orderly" (S). Mr. Willis leaves his clothes scattered all over the room; he never picks them up. The maid picked the room up in the morning.

    b. "Take (somebody) along in a car, ship, etc." (S). If you are going to the meeting, I will pick you up in half an hour.

    c. "Make active; increase" (S). The new interest rate should pick business up.

place, in, "in the proper location." In Mrs. Johnson's house everything is always in place.

place of, in. Mary used the new tablecloth in place of the dinner mats.

place, in one's. If I were in your place, I would accept the offer. Since John is ill, William will go in his place.

plan on. We're planning on speaking to Mr. Harris tomorrow.

pleased with (or *over*). We were pleased with the results. My friend is pleased over the good news.

plenty of. Flowers need plenty of water and sunshine. Laura gave me plenty of chances to change my mind.

point of. Alice finally reached the point of assenting to my proposal.

point of, on the, "about to; on the verge of." Mr. Allen was on the point of revealing his secret when his wife came into the room.

point out, "indicate" (S). When I could not find the right street, a policeman pointed it out to me.

polite to. A clerk should always be polite to customers.

positive of (or *about*). Are you positive of that? The man seemed to be positive about the information he had.

possession of, in. You should be in possession of all the facts before you make your decision.

prefer to. I prefer vanilla ice cream to chocolate. I prefer tennis to hiking.

preferable to. I think traveling by air is preferable to traveling by train.

preparation for. Have you made any preparation for your final examination?

prepare for. You should prepare for the examination. We are prepared for almost anything that might happen.

present at. Twenty guests were present at the party.

present, at. At present Mr. Lynch is in Honolulu, but he will return in a week.

prevent from. I want nothing to prevent you from getting an education.

prison, in. All of the rebels are now in prison.

private, in. I want to discuss the matter with you in private, not in front of other people.

probability, in all. In all probability, the mail will arrive before noon.

process of, in the. The committee members are right now in the process of voting.

produce from. Aluminum is produced from bauxite.

profit from. We can all profit from traveling. Did you make any profit from the sale?

prohibit from. Shyness prohibited Mark from speaking.

proper for. I want some stationery that is proper for social correspondence.

protect from. The heavy lining in the coat will protect you from the cold.

proud of. John's parents were proud of his good school record.

provide with. Arnold's parents provide him with everything he needs.

public, in. Most ladies do not apply cosmetics in public. That hermit has not been seen in public for years.

purpose of, for the. Mr. Sims wrote the editorial for the purpose of publicizing the needs of the inmates of the hospital.

purposes, for practical. The kitchen has been designed for practical purposes.

put off, "delay, postpone" (S). Since John can not come tonight, we are going to put the party off until next week.

put on: a. "Don" (S). George put his hat on when he left the house.

   b. "Assume falsely; be ostentatious" (S). Mr. Fox puts on an air of knowing more than he really does. Some people who rapidly become wealthy put on about their importance.

put out: a. "Extinguish" (S). When you go to bed, be sure to put your cigaret out before you put out the lights.

b. "Expel" (S). College students may be put out if they violate regulations.

c. "Annoy, irritate" (S). George certainly put Helen out when he told that story about her.

d. "Inconvenience" (S). Carl does not mind putting his friends out if he needs something from them.

put up with, "endure, tolerate." Mr. White is so easygoing that he will put up with anybody.

quarrel with . . . about (or *over*). That man constantly quarrels with his wife about money. Why should you quarrel over such a small point?

quibble over (or *about*). The staff quibbled over these three phrases.

read in. Did you read the news in the paper? I read that explanation in a book.

ready for. You should be ready for them when they come.

reality, in. Mr. Connors looks like an aggressive man, but in reality he is timid.

reason for. Do you have any reason for complaining about your grade?

reason, for no particular. Last week Jack gave up his job for no particular reason.

rebel against. The slaves finally rebelled against their masters. That child rebels against any form of discipline.

recommend to . . . for. The foreman recommended him to the boss for a promotion.

refer to. Refer to the instructions. The man didn't refer to his accident at all.

rely on. He's very dependable; we can rely on him to help us tomorrow.

remainder of, for the. After dinner we conversed for the remainder of the evening.

remind of. That boy always reminds me of his father at that age.

remove from. His name was removed from the list of members of the club when he did not pay his dues.

representative of. This short story is representative of the author's work.

repugnant to. The thought of war is repugnant to me.

reside in. The Joneses reside in a large house in Newark. The cause of the friction resides in the men's dislike for each other.

resistant to (less frequently, *against*). Some plastics are resistant to household acids.

respect for. Fred shows very little respect for his parents. I really respect that man for his honesty and willingness to defend his views.

respects, in all. That boy is commendable in all respects.

responsible for. Is a husband responsible for his wife's debts? The janitor is responsible for keeping the building clean.

rest of, for the. Mr. Able will be on vacation for the rest of the month.

result (verb) *from.* Tragedy can result from thoughtlessness.

result (verb) *in.* Thoughtlessness can result in tragedy.

result (noun) *of.* Tragedy can be the result of thoughtlessness.

return (for), in. Mother gave Jimmy a piece of candy in return for his good behavior. Clarke gave Louise a handbag, and she kissed him in return.

return to . . . from. When did Charles return to his home from the hospital?

rich in. Trinidad is rich in mineral resources.

rid of. You should rid yourself of that bad habit. You should get rid of that bad habit.

right away, "immediately." I want you to do that work right away.

ruins, in. The city was left in ruins by the conquerors.

run across: a. "Find unexpectedly; meet by chance." I ran across my high school diploma last night.

   b. "Convey by car" (S). The chauffeur will run you across to your office.

run down: a. "Say unkind things about, disparage" (S). Mrs. Bach enjoys running her friends down.

   b. "In bad physical condition." You catch cold easily when you are run down.

   c. "Stop" (used with a spring machine). If you do not wind your watch, it will run down.

   d. "Hit (with a car)" (S). If you drive fast, you may run a pedestrian down.

   e. "Find" (usually with some effort) (S). I have finally run down that poem you wanted.

run into: a. "Collide with." Mrs. Jellinson ran into a truck this afternoon.

   b. "Meet by chance." I ran into an old friend of yours today.

run out (of), "exhaust the supply (of)." I have only a little flour; I hope I do not run out while I am cooking.

run up: a. "Increase" (S). If you are not careful, you can run up your grocery bill very easily.

   b. "Raise (a flag)" (S). The janitor runs a flag up over the post office every morning.

rush, in a. New Yorkers always seem to be in a rush.

sake (of), for the. Millie kept quiet for the sake of keeping peace. For your own sake, you should not work so hard.

sale, for. That house you like is now for sale.

sale, on, "temporarily at a reduced price." The grocery has apples on sale today.

satisfactory for. That man should be satisfactory for the position.

satisfactory to. Does his writing appear satisfactory to you?

school, in. The children are all in school right now.

search for. I am searching for that book you want. Did you make a thorough search for your watch?

see about: a. "Consider." My father said he would see about getting me a bicycle.

   b. "Attend to, arrange." My landlady sees about my bed linen.

   c. "Consult about." I saw the mechanic about the knock in my car.

see to, "attend to." The housekeeper will see to the arrangements for the party.

self-defense, in. The girl claimed that she had killed the burglar in self-defense.

sense, in a. In a sense, your explanation is right, but there is a better one.

shop for. The two women went shopping for new spring hats.

short, in, "in a few words; in brief." The story, in short, is about a poor man who finally wins success.

short of. May I give you a check? I am a little short of cash.

shut off, "cause to stop operating; extinguish" (used with electrical or mechanical appliances) (S). Why don't you shut that motor off when you are not using it?

shut up: a. "Close" (S). It's five o'clock; let's shut up shop.

    b. "Stop talking" (this is usually an impolite expression) (S). The only person who can shut Hilda up is her mother.

sight (of), in. After six days the shore came in sight. We were finally in sight of land.

similar to. Isn't this example similar to the other one?

smell of. That closet smells of moth balls. It has a smell of moth balls.

smile at. Most clerks smile at customers.

solution to. Have you found the solution to that problem? Some people think that money is the solution to all difficulties.

sorry about. Harry said he was sorry about his mistake. Paul was sorry about forgetting the ice cream.

sorry for. Mr. Spencer felt sorry for the victims of the flood.

speak of, "mention." Mr. Lenz never speaks of his former wife.

speak on, "give a speech concerning." The professor spoke on metaphysics.

speak to . . . about (*about* is the most frequent and useful preposition meaning "concerning"; *on* and *of* have specialized uses). Did you speak to the newsboy about the paper? Mr. Snyder spoke about going. Mr. Lenz never speaks about his former wife. The professor spoke about metaphysics.

spite of, in. The traveler continued his journey in spite of the warning. In spite of the fact that he was afraid, Johnston volunteered for the assignment.

stand out, "be conspicuous or prominent." Mary's red hair makes her stand out in any group. Printers italicize words that they want to stand out.

stand up for, "defend; support." If you don't stand up for your beliefs, no one else will.

stock, in. The store has plenty of copies of that book in stock.

stop from. Nothing can stop Mary from saying what she believes.

style, in. That dress was in style ten years ago, but it is out of style now.

submit to: a. "Send to." The author submitted his short story to several editors.

    b. "Yield to." I refuse to submit to his authority.

substitute for. Since Perry is ill, we need a substitute for him. You can substitute garlic for onions in that sauce.

succeed in. You must work hard to succeed in your studies. Did the police succeed in catching the robber?

successful in. Were you successful in finding out the man's name?

succession, in. I have three meetings in succession this afternoon.

sudden, all of a, "suddenly." Mary Lou was sitting by the window when, all of a sudden, she screamed.

suffer from. Floridians suffer from the cold when they go to Maine. The crops are suffering from the drought.

suggest to. Why don't you suggest your plan to the members of the committee?

suitable for. Do you think this suit will be suitable for the occasion?

superior to. The lecturer claimed that Thackeray was superior to Dickens. The patricians felt superior to the plebeians. Do you think that skating is superior to skiing?

supply with. You should supply yourself with several pencils and plenty of paper before you go to the examination.

sure of (or *about*). Are you sure of your answers? It's hard to be sure about something like that.

surprise at. I am surprised at your statement. Mr. Payne showed great surprise at his wife's announcement.

susceptible to. Are you susceptible to colds?

suspense, in. Quickly! Tell me what happened; don't keep me in suspense.

suspicious of. The police were suspicious of the man's behavior.

swing, in full. When a party gets in full swing, everybody talks and has a good time.

take after: a. "Resemble (a parent)." Bob takes after his father, but his sister takes after her mother.

   b. "Follow the example of." Will took after his older brother and became a lawyer.

take back: a. "Return" (S). I am going to take these gloves back to the store; they do not fit.

   b. "Apologize for; retract" (S). What you said is not true; you had better take it back.

take care of. A mother has to take care of her children.

take for, "mistake for; assume to be." Many people take Mr. Sonoda for a Chinese, but he is Japanese.

take for granted, "assume to be true; accept without thought or question" (S). Don't take anything he says for granted; he is not truthful. Husbands sometimes complain that their wives take them for granted.

take in: a. "Bring from outside" (S). We can take in the "Vacancy" sign now.

   b. "Include" (S). We took a lot of plays in in our visit to New York. Our property takes in the woods and the streams.

   c. "Deceive" (S). Did that magician take you in with his tricks?

   d. "Make smaller" (S). If you go on a diet, you will have to take your dresses in.

   e. "Listen to; become absorbed in" (S). Mr. Burton took in every word of the President's speech.

take into consideration (or *account*), "consider" (S). Don't be impolite; you should take other people's feelings into consideration.

take off: a. "Remove" (used with clothes) (S). Mr. Smith took his hat off and sat down.

   b. "Leave the ground" (used with planes). The plane will take off at noon.

   c. "Not work" (for a period) (S). Carl took the day off and went to the dentist.

take on: a. "Hire" (S). That factory took on twenty workers yesterday.

   b. "Undertake to do" (S). I will take that part of the work on.

   c. "Assume." That rose takes on a yellowish hue when it is in full bloom.

   d. "Show great emotion." Mr. Hewitt took on about the loss of his job.

take out: a. "Remove; delete" (S). Don't leave the apples in the bag; take them out. Take your hands out of your pockets. Why don't you take that word out? It is not needed in the letter.

   b. "Have a date with" (S). Are you taking a girl out tonight?

   c. "Buy (insurance)" (S). You must take out insurance on your car.

   d. "Run." When the boys saw the policeman, they took out. He took out after them.

take over, "assume control or direction (of)" (S). Another director is going to take the program over next month.

take up: a. "Consider, discuss" (S). Congress will take the proposal up next week.

   b. "Begin; develop the habit of" (S). When did you take up smoking?

   c. "Shorten" (S). That dress is too long; you had better take the hem up.

   d. "Tighten" (S). If you take up the screw on the bottom, that lamp will stand straight.

   e. "Occupy; consume" (S). That huge bed takes up most of the room. I read to take up the time while I was waiting.

talent for. Julia shows great talent for acting.

talented in. Julia is very talented in that sort of thing.

talk to ... about. John talked to the man about plans for the summer.

taste, in good (or *bad* or *poor*). Mary's conservative clothes are always in good taste. Your cynical remark was in poor taste.

tear up, "rip into pieces" (S). Lucy tore the telegram up and put it in the basket.

tears over (or *about*), *in.* The child was in tears over the loss of her doll.

technique ("method") *for* (or *of*). The instructor devised a technique for explaining the problem.

technique ("skill") *in.* The artist shows good technique in shading.

tell by (or *from*), "recognize by." You can tell by the clouds that it is going to snow.

tell from, "distinguish between." Can you tell one twin from the other?

tell on: a. "Reveal secrets of." Children are likely to tell on their parents.

   b. "Produce noticeable or severe effects on." Age has started to tell on Mrs. Lynch. Mr. Hart's drinking certainly tells on him.

terms of, in. The committee discussed the proposal in terms of its real cost.

thank for. The officials of the school thanked the man for his generosity.

theory, in. Some suggestions that seem all right in theory are not good in practice.

think about: a. "Consider." I am thinking about taking a trip next month.

   b. "Be one's opinion" (in clauses beginning with *what*). What do you think about John? Have you found out what the boss thinks about your suggestion?

think of: a. "Remember." I will tell you that boy's name as soon as I think of it.

   b. "Consider." I would not even think of asking him for a loan.

   c. "Be one's opinion" (in clauses beginning with *what*). What do you think of John? I know what the boss thinks of your suggestion.

   d. "Have a mental image of." I think of Jespersen primarily as a grammarian.

   e. "Form (an idea or thought)." Can't you think of anything to write about?

thoughtful of. It was thoughtful of you to buy a gift for them.

time being, for the, "temporarily." For the time being, Jack is staying at a hotel.

time, in due. If you continue to practice, you will become expert in due time.

time for (or *time* + infinitive), *in,* "soon or early enough (to do something)." We got to the show in time for the beginning. We got to the show in time to see the beginning.

time (flat), in no, "quickly; very soon." The test was very easy; I finished in no time. The company answered my letter in no time flat.

tired from, "physically exhausted from." The maid is tired from ironing the clothes today.

p

tired of, "emotionally weary of." I am tired of that popular song. Mrs. Long never gets tired of talking about herself.

tired out, "completely exhausted." The candidate was tired out at the end of the election campaign.

tolerant of. You should try to be more tolerant of people's criticism.

transfer to . . . from. Mr. Pyles has been transferred to San Francisco from Miami.

transform into. Jim has transformed himself from a meek person into an extrovert. The group transformed the barn into a theater.

translate from . . . into. Do you still translate your thoughts from Japanese into English? Blanco translated Ibáñez's play into English from the original Spanish.

trouble (with), in. Mr. Lewis is in trouble with the bank. You look unhappy; are you in trouble? Did you have any trouble with the last assignment?

try on, "test for fitness or appearance" (S). Women love to try new hats on.

try out, "test for appropriateness" (S). The machine has a guarantee: you can return it if it does not work after you have tried it out for a week.

turn down: a. "Decrease the volume or brilliance of" (S). Please turn the radio down just a little bit. That lamp has three switches; you can turn it down if it is too bright.

b. "Reject" (S). The author was very unhappy when the company turned his novel down.

turn in: a. "Go to bed." I usually turn in at eleven o'clock.

b. "Submit" (S). Please turn your homework in at the beginning of the class.

turn into, "transform into." The mayor has turned that apartment building into a hospital.

turn off, "stop the operation of (an appliance)" (S). Did you turn the light off when you left that room? The cook forgot to turn off the oven at twelve o'clock.

turn on: a. "Begin the operation of (an appliance)" (S). I will turn the radio on.

b. "Become unfriendly or vicious toward." Sue is likely to turn on you if you tell that story about her. The mad dog turned on its owner and bit him.

c. "Depend on." The plot turns on the reaction of the girl to the proposal.

turn out: a. "Extinguish (an electric light)" (S). You forgot to turn the light out.

b. "Produce" (S). That author turns a novel out every year.

c. "Result." Have you discovered how the interview turned out?

d. "Expel" (S). The college will turn a student out if he makes poor grades.

turn out to be, "prove to be." Most rumors turn out to be false. That boy has turned out to be a very good student.

turn over, "give; relegate; transfer" (S). Mr. Brewster turns his salary check over to his wife every month. The mayor turned over the letter of complaint to his assistant.

turn up: a. "Appear; be found." The guest turned up an hour late. My missing umbrella turned up in the hall closet.

b. "Find" (S). The secretary has turned up the information you wanted.

two, in. The woodsman cut the bough in two with one blow.

typical of. His unkind remark was typical of an envious person.

understanding ("knowledge; comprehension; interpretation") *of.* The student showed no understanding of the problem. My understanding of the wording differs from yours.

understanding ("sympathy") *of* (or *about*). The nurse exhibited understanding of her patients' fears.

understanding ("agreement") *on* (or *about*). The factions reached an understanding on the terms.

understanding ("sympathetic") *with* (or *of*). The nurse is understanding with her patients.

unfamiliar with. I am unfamiliar with much of the current slang.

unfit for. In your present state of health, you are unfit for hard work of any kind.

upset about (or *over*). Mrs. Brown is upset about the loss of her purse. Students often get upset over their final grades.

used to: a. (Indicating a past habit.) Mr. Black used to teach, but now he does not. [*To teach* is an infinitive in this sentence.]

   b. "In the habit of; adjusted to." Are you used to getting up at seven o'clock? A soldier gets used to hardships. Eva has become used to eating Italian food. [*To* is a preposition in these sentences.]

useful for. The salesman said the device was useful for many things.

vain, in. All Mr. Jolson's efforts to rescue the child were in vain.

vary from...(to). The temperature of the water varies from sixty to eighty degrees in twenty-four hours. His method varies from mine a great deal.

view of, in. The mountain finally stood in view of the travelers. In view of your grades, I would say that you have not studied very much.

wait for. Let's wait for Bob; he will be finished in a few minutes. You can wait for a streetcar on that corner.

wait on (or *upon*), "serve." Salesgirls should wait on customers pleasantly. Jimmy waited on tables to earn his tuition.

want of, for. We watched television for want of something better to do.

warn about. He was warned about that several times. The teacher warned the student about his attitude.

watch for. Watch for that article when you look at the magazine.

way to, (on the). He met an old friend on the way to the office. The policeman showed me the way to the bank.

wear off, "decrease gradually." It will take about an hour for the anesthetic to wear off.

wear out: a. "Use until useless" (S). I have already worn these shoes out.

   b. "Exhaust" (S). Climbing stairs wears me out.

wonder about. Sometimes I wonder about him: he never seems to be concerned.

word for word, "literally; exactly." It is impossible to translate from one language to another word for word. The child repeated her parents' argument word for word.

word of mouth, by, "orally." Rumors usually spread by word of mouth.

words, in so many. Mr. Blake did not say he disapproved of Eva in so many words, but that was his intention.

work on. That famous author is working on another novel at the moment.

work out: a. "Solve" (S). Have you worked that puzzle out yet?

   b. "Devise" (S). The adviser worked out a schedule for my classes.

   c. "Prove to be satisfactory." Do you think your new secretary will work out?

p

> *world, in the* (an intensifier, used after superlatives, *who, where, everything,* etc.). Sarah thinks her husband is the nicest man in the world. Why in the world did you ask that question? Nothing in the world will please that woman.
>
> *worry about.* Don't worry about the test: I'm sure you did well.

Also, see § *As* vs. *Like,* § *Because* vs. *Because of,* § *Beside* vs. *Besides,* § *By,* § *Do* vs. *Make,* § *For*—Preposition, § *From*—Preposition, § *Home,* § *Hundred* vs. *Hundreds of,* § *In*—Preposition, § Infinitive vs. Gerund, § Intensifier, § Opposition Expression, § Preposition—Expression without, § Preposition in Time Expression, § Two-word Verb, § Word Order—Object of Verb, and § Word Order—Preposition.

PREPOSITION—EXPRESSION WITHOUT

1. Sometimes, of course, you have the problem of remembering whether or not a preposition should be used. A preposition is not used with the words listed below when those words occur with the meaning they have in the examples.

> *abuse.* The dictator abused his power.
>
> *answer.* I answered Mr. Hawkins's letter immediately.
>
> *applaud.* The audience applauded the speaker's statement.
>
> *approach.* The robber approached the house cautiously.
>
> *ask.* I do not know, but I will ask my teacher.
>
> *attend.* Are you attending your classes regularly?
>
> *believe.* Mr. Hamilton will not believe the truth.
>
> *change.* Alec changed his job last month.
>
> *concern.* That matter concerns us all.
>
> *contribute.* Mr. Foster contributed money to the program.
>
> *doubt.* At times my wife doubts my affection for her.
>
> *dozen.* I want to buy a dozen eggs.
>
> *encounter* (verb). I encountered Mr. Murray in Japan.
>
> *enjoy.* Mr. Williams certainly enjoys a good meal.
>
> *enter.* The doctor entered the room quietly.
>
> *escape,* "avoid." You can not escape punishment.
>
> *fit.* Mrs. Riley's sparkling eyes did not fit her old face.
>
> *fulfill.* Be sure to fulfill your obligations.
>
> *hundred.* The company employs a hundred people. Several hundred boys live in the orphanage.
>
> *influence.* The humidity influences our comfort.
>
> *lack.* An untrained worker lacks self-confidence.
>
> *let.* The nurses will not let anybody help them.
>
> *make.* The teacher's explanation made me realize my error.
>
> *marry.* Paulson married his first sweetheart.
>
> *match.* Ed's tie matches his suit.
>
> *meet.* I met Bill's mother yesterday.
>
> *near.* The Stewarts live near me. The accident happened near my house.
>
> *need.* Do you need my help?
>
> *obey.* Children should obey their parents.
>
> *oppose.* Johnson opposes all my suggestions.

> *reach.* The aviator has not reached his destination yet. The jury reached a verdict very quickly.
> *remember.* I remember my grandfather very clearly.
> *resemble.* My hometown resembles an Alpine village.
> *resist.* Wilde could not resist any temptation.
> *survive.* That fish is able to survive almost anything.
> *visit.* Mr. Powers made up his mind to visit Portugal.

Also, see § Preposition—Expression with.

PREPOSITION IN TIME EXPRESSION

P.23

1. The word *after* indicates the time following which an event takes place.

> After Tuesday we will begin our vacation.
> Mark got a job immediately after his graduation.
> Mark got a job immediately after graduating.

2. The word *at* precedes words expressing an exact moment of time. It is used with expressions of clock time and with single words denoting a part of the day: *dawn, daybreak, sunrise, noon, dusk, twilight, sunset, night,* and *night time.*

> Herbert came to see me at ten o'clock.
> School ends at 3:25 p.m.
> I must be there at a quarter to nine.
> Do you ever get up at dawn?
> Let's have lunch at noon today.
> It grows cold at night.

3. *At* is used in the following expressions of order or sequence of time:

> *at first.* At first, I did not like the idea, but now I do.
> *at last.* Otto has been working very hard, but he has finished at last.
> *at once.* Do that at once; don't delay.
> *at the beginning.* We got to the theater at the beginning of the play.
> *at the conclusion.* There was loud applause at the conclusion of his speech.
> *at the end.* Mrs. Erickson was exhausted at the end of the day.
> *at present.* At present I am living on Long Island, but I will move soon.
> *at the present time.* At the present time, Carl is working for his father.
> *at a (the) time when.* Rudy asked me for money at a time when I had none. That happened at the time when I was a graduate student.
> *at this time.* Mr. Wheeler has no definite plans at this time.
> *at that time.* At that time Miss Ross was living in Peru.
> *at no time.* Mr. Hanson has been away from home at no time.
> *at times.* At times Miss Dunn feels rather faint.
> *at all times.* Mr. Newton must stay in bed at all times.
> *at other times.* Sometimes Jack feels very ambitious, but at other times he feels quite lazy.
> *at various times.* I have seen Miss Shute at the office at various times.

4. The word *by* is used for the meaning "no later than" a specified time.

> You must be in the office by nine o'clock.
> Joe had finished his work by noon.
> Mr. Dutton should receive a reply to his letter by Tuesday.
> The building was completed by June.
> By the time I finished one chore, my wife had thought up three more.

5. The word *for* indicates duration of time. With the past tense, the period of time does not have the present moment as the end point (see the first example below). With the present perfect tense, the period extends from the past to the present moment (second example); see *since* in ¶ 20. With the future tense or the "future substitute" *be going to,* the period may commence either from the present moment (third example) or some time in the indefinite future (fourth example). *For* may be omitted in the first five and the seventh examples when the time phrase is at the end of the clause.

> Young lived in Chicago for five years.   *or*   He lived in Chicago five years.
> Manuel has lived in New York for two months.
> William is going to be here for three more years.
> Charlotte will be in Italy for three weeks.
> Mr. Green will be out of town for the next week or so.
> We did not hear from the official for days.
> The Dixons were in Portugal for a while last year.
> For a time we thought that Ellis had told us the truth.
> For a moment I was surprised to see Crawford there.
> For the present (*or* For now) I can use this instead of the other.

With *for,* the concern is about the *length of time,* but not any particular point. If the concern is about some action that will occur at the end point of a period in the future, the preposition *in* is used.

> I will be in Tokyo for two days. [I will stay there for two days.]
> I will be in Tokyo in two days. [I will arrive there at the end of two days.]
> Hubert will be in Italy for two years.
> Hubert will be back in New York in two years.
> The boat will not arrive for forty-eight hours.   *or*   The boat will arrive in forty-eight hours. [The two sentences have the same meaning.]

6. *For long* or simply *long* is a short form of *for a long time.* It usually occurs at the ends of sentences with a negative word.

> Cox did not stay in Peoria for long.   *or*   Cox did not stay in Peoria long.
> Amelia will not be here for long.   *or*   Amelia will not be here long.

7. The word *from* indicates the starting point of a time measurement. Either *to, until,* or *till* indicates the end point. Quite frequently an expression with *from...to* has no articles. The word *on* following the time expression indicates that the measurement has no end point. (See ¶ 14 below.)

> Mr. Sullivan will arrive a week from today.
> Mrs. Sullivan will arrive a week from tomorrow.

The tourists drove from eight o'clock to midnight.
Richard was in Canada from June until September.
From beginning to end, the play was a disappointment.
Allyson goes to Florida from time to time. [*From time to time* = occasionally.]
A mother never knows what to expect from day to day (*or* from one day to the next).
From now on, we will use a different method.
Mr. Griffin kept silent from then on.

8. The word *in* with the meaning of "some time within" is used with expressions of periods of time. However, it is not used with specific days.

In the past, I lived in Spain.
In the future, I will live in Morocco.
Ellen arrived here in 1950.
We will take our vacation in July.
The repairman arrived in the morning (*or* in the afternoon, in the evening).
Those flowers bloom in spring (*or* in the spring). [Similarly with *summer, fall, autumn,* and *winter.*]
Those flowers bloom in spring time (*or* in the spring time). [Similarly with *summer time* and *winter time.*]
Those flowers bloom in day time (*or* in the day time, *but* at night time).
That event happened in peace time. [Similarly, *in war time, in ancient times.*]
Milton lived in the seventeenth century.
Chaucer lived in the Middle Ages.
Shakespeare lived in the Renaissance.
In a few minutes my order was filled.

Compare this use of *in* with the similar use of *for* and *during*. Note that *in* and *for* are interchangeable in the fourth and fifth examples below. *In* and *during* are interchangeable in the next three examples. *In* or *during* is usually necessary where there are obviously definite limits in time: compare the third, fourth, and fifth examples. *In, when,* and *while* are interchangeable in the ninth example; also, see § Phrase from Clause.

In a few days everything became quiet again.
Every dictionary had been sold in a few days.
Harold had received two promotions in less than three months.
It was the first time I had seen him in (*or* for) three weeks.
It was the first time I had seen him in (*or* for) three years.
The worst moments in (*or* during) the whole occupation came in (*or* during) the third day.
Jacques had been in France in (*or* during) the last war.
The company often received as many as five hundred letters in (*or* during) one day.
In writing the book, the author neglected to include an introduction.

9. *In* expresses a particular moment or time in the future when some action will occur or some action will be completed. Equivalent expressions are *after* and *at the end of.* If the concern is about the length of time, *for* is usually the needed preposition.

The train will arrive in three hours.   *but*   The train will not arrive for three hours yet.

Richard will be back in a few minutes (*or* in a short time, in a minute or two, in a second, in a moment, in no time).

The station master said the train would arrive in six more hours.

10. Note the use of *in* in the following expressions of time:

in advance. I pay my rent a month in advance.

in the beginning. In the beginning I felt very lonesome in London.

in the end. We tried to avoid it, but in the end we had to face it.

in the first few days. In the first few days I did a lot of sightseeing.

in the future. You should try to be more careful in the future.

in the long run. In the long run your money will be more safely invested in bonds.

in the meantime (meanwhile). I have a class tonight; in the meantime I must study.

in the middle of. He interrupted me in the middle of a sentence.

in the nick of time. He caught the girl in the nick of time. If he had not, she would have fallen.

in no time (flat), "very quickly." The repairman will fix your radio in no time. The doctor got to the hospital in no time flat.

in the past. People used to do that quite differently in the past.

in [somebody's] time. Roland lived in Charlemagne's time. There were no automobiles in my great-grandfather's time.

in those days, "in that span or period of the past (or the future)" (the present equivalent is *nowadays* or *these days*). The Renaissance was a time of discovery. In those days people were adventuresome.

in time, "soon or early enough (to do something)." You are in time to have breakfast with me.

in a (little) while. Wait for me; I will be ready to go in a while. David just phoned; he will be here in a little while.

once in a (great) while. I watch TV only once in a while. Paul goes to the opera once in a great while; last year he went only twice.

11. The word *on* is used with days.

I can see you on Thursday.

Alex arrived on Christmas Day.

School ends on Friday afternoon.

Harris came to see me on Monday morning.

It got cold on Sunday night.

What do you do on a rainy day?

The Declaration of Independence was signed on July 4, 1776.

Dr. Barbour sends his bills out on the first of every month.

12. The *on* does not have to be used before specific days.

I can see you Thursday (*or* Christmas Day, Friday afternoon, Sunday night, July 4, the first of every month, etc.).

But   What do you do on a rainy day?
       On clear days I sit on the river bank.

13. *On* is used with the word *occasion.*

> At times I can not go to sleep at once. On such an occasion I read in bed.
> I regret that I was absent from school on that occasion.
> The nurse visited the patient's home on several occasions.

On occasion means "now and then; occasionally."

> Gertrude is extremely rude on occasion.

14. *On* following a time expression indicates that the measurement has no end point; see ¶ 7 above.

> *from now (today) on.* Please come to class on time from now on.
> *from then (that time) on.* From then on, William was a model student. From that time on, the teacher had no trouble with him.
> *later on.* I can not speak with you now, but I will later on.

15. *On* is used in the following expressions:

> *on and on.* That woman talks on and on: she never stops.
> *on* (or *at*) *a moment's notice.* Johnson is ready to go on a trip on a moment's notice.
> *on the spur of the moment.* Tom made his decision on the spur of the moment. He had not thought about the matter before.
> *on those days,* "on those specified days; on those occasions." Policemen are not fond of Memorial Day and the Fourth of July because on those days they have to work extra hours.
> *on time,* "punctually; on schedule; at the appointed time." My train arrived exactly on time.

16. Either *on* or *upon* is used with an *-ing* form of a verb expressing an exact moment of time. *Upon* is less frequent. See § Phrase from Clause.

> On arriving in New York, Richard was met by some friends.
> Upon leaving your room, please turn out the lights.
> On being introduced to each other, men should shake hands.

17. *On* or *upon* is similarly used with *arrival, departure,* and *return.*

> On his arrival in New York, Richard was met by some friends.
> Upon your departure, give your key to the desk clerk.
> On my return home, I was greeted by my sister.

18. *Once upon a time* is the conventionalized beginning of a story told to children.

> Once upon a time there was a beautiful princess....

19. *One* may be used without a preposition to refer to a particular day, morning, month, etc., that is not fully identified.

> I met Sam one Sunday last month.
> Mr. Evans called me one midnight.
> The couple's wedding took place one beautiful morning in May.

> One year when he was sick, Mr. Rogers stayed in Italy.
> *But* What do you do on a rainy day?
> That happened in the year I was ten. *or* That happened the year
> I was ten.

20. The word *since* marks the beginning of a length of time which extends from the past up to the present moment. Because it introduces an expression of time meaning "from . . . up to the present," *since* will accompany the present perfect tense in the principal verb; compare with *for* in ¶ 5. Notice the difference in meaning in the first two examples below:

> Since his graduation Paul has worked in New York. [He is working in New
> York now.]
> After his graduation Paul worked in New York. [He is not working in New
> York now.]
> The workers have been on strike since yesterday.

When *since* begins a dependent clause expressing time, the tense within that clause is usually simple past.

> Mr. Ross has kept pets   since he was fifteen years old.
> Since I saw you last, I have not done anything exciting.

Also, see § *Ago* vs. *Before,* § Preposition—Expression with, and § *Still* vs. *Any More* and *Any Longer.*

PRONUNCIATION

1. In the production of English sounds, these things are important: your breath, your vocal cords, the roof of your mouth, your tongue, your tooth ridge, your teeth, your lips, and your nose. With the exception of your breath, those things are called your *speech organs.*

2. Your breath is moved from your lungs out either through your mouth or through your nose. If a sound is made through your mouth, it is called an *oral* sound. If it is made through your nose, it is a *nasal* sound.

3. Your vocal cords are in the larynx, one part of which is the hard, angular piece of cartilage that sticks out on your throat. This cartilage is called your *Adam's apple.* It moves up and down when you swallow. You can feel it with your fingers. If your vocal cords vibrate when you make a sound, that sound is *voiced.* If the cords do not vibrate, the sound is *voiceless.* You can feel the vibration when you say a sound like [a] in *father* or [m] in *my.*

4. The roof of your mouth is your *palate.* Feel it with your tongue. The front part is *hard,* and the back part is *soft.* Your *velum* is that soft, back part of the roof of your mouth. The part that hangs down in the back of the throat is called the *uvula.* You can see it in a mirror. When you make an oral sound, the velum rises so your breath can not go up into your nose. When you make a nasal sound, the velum is lowered so that your breath can be expelled through your nose.

SPEECH ORGANS

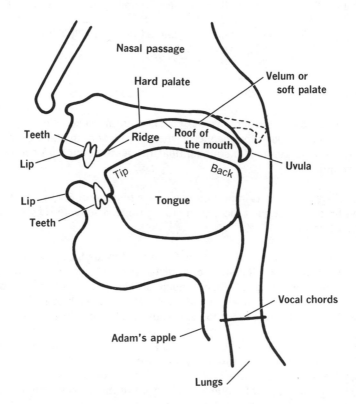

5. Your tongue is very active when you speak. You can raise it, lower it, move it front, and move it back.

6. Your tooth ridge is the hard projection above and behind your upper teeth. (You have a tooth ridge for your lower teeth, but it is not very important in the production of English sounds.) Put your tongue on the back of your upper front teeth, and then move it upward. Right above the teeth you will feel the ridge. Continue to move your tongue upward. It will suddenly go straight upward: it has left the tooth ridge.

7. Your teeth are important because you form certain sounds by putting your tongue or your lower lip near the teeth.

8. Your lips are important because you make a number of sounds by either closing your lips or putting them into varied positions.

In the next sections I will discuss the production of English sounds according to two groups: the consonants and the vowels. The symbols in brackets are the IPA symbols explained under § Phonetic Symbol. Also, see the following sections in this book: § *A* vs. *An*, § *-ace*, *-ess*, *-ice*, and *-is*, § *-age*, § *-ate*, § *-ci-*, *-si-*, and *-ti-*

Word, § Cognate Word, § -ed Adjective, § H- Initial, § Homophone, § -ic, -ics, -ical, and -ically, § Intonation, § -ize vs. -ise Ending, § -ous Word, § -ry Ending, § Silent Letter, § Spelling—Word with Suffix, § Stress—Group, § Stress—Word, § Suffix -ed, § Suffix -s, § -sure ending, § Syllabic Consonant, § T Intervocalic, § -ture Ending, § Voiced vs. Voiceless, and § X Word.

PRONUNCIATION—CONSONANT

In the following paragraphs the consonants are taken up in groups of sounds which are related in the manner of their production: tooth-ridge sounds, r sounds, nasal sounds, stops, lip sounds, near-the-teeth sounds, th sound, y sound, and h sound.

1. The tooth ridge is important because a number of English sounds are made by the tip of the tongue touching the tooth ridge. The *tooth-ridge* consonants are [l], [n], [d], and [t].

a. The sound [l] is made with the tip of the tongue touching the tooth ridge. Your breath comes over the sides of your tongue and out through your lips. You can continue the sound [l]. Take a deep breath of air, put the tip of your tongue against your tooth ridge, and then let all the breath out of your lungs slowly. Don't move the tip of your tongue. Your vocal cords vibrate: [l] is a voiced sound.

b. The sound [n] is made with the tip of your tongue touching your tooth ridge. Your breath comes out through your nose. Keep your lips open. The sides of your tongue press against the sides of your upper teeth. You can continue the sound [n]. Don't move your tongue until all your breath has come out through your nose. Your vocal cords vibrate: [n] is a voiced sound.

c. Both [d] and [t] are made by stopping the breath. You put the tip of your tongue on the tooth ridge and the sides of your tongue against the sides of your upper teeth just as you did for [n], but don't let the breath come out through your nose. The difference between [d] and [t] is that [d] is voiced and [t] is voiceless. Your vocal cords vibrate when you make [d], and they do not vibrate when you make [t].

Practice making the sound [o] followed by [l], then by [n], then by [d], and then by [t]. Next, practice making the sounds [lo], [no], [do], and [to].

Be sure to put the tip of your tongue on your tooth ridge, not on the back of your upper front teeth.

d. Another sound of English is made with the tip of your tongue *near* the tooth ridge. That sound is [r]. Put your tongue into the position of [n], and then bend the tip of your tongue backward just a little. Let your breath come out through your lips. Hold your tongue in that position: the tip close to the tooth ridge and the sides against the upper side teeth. Don't shake the tip. Don't make a shaking sound in the back of your mouth. Practice making the sound [o] followed by [n] and then [o] followed by [r]. Then, say [no] and [ro]. If you have trouble producing a distinction between [l] and [r], do this: move the tip of your tongue *down* quickly when you finish making [l]; move the tip *upward* quickly when you finish making [r].

Practice making these words which are different from each other only because of the tooth-ridge sounds:

[l]	[n]	[d]	[t]	[r]
lap	nap	...	tap	rap
law	gnaw	daw	taw	raw
lay	neigh	day	...	ray
lays	neighs	daze	...	raise
leap	...	deep	...	reap
led	Ned	dead	Ted	red
lent	...	dent	tent	rent
lest	nest	...	test	rest
lewd	nude	dude	...	rude
lice	nice	dice	...	rice
light	night	...	tight	right
limb	...	dim	Tim	rim
lime	...	dime	time	rhyme
line	nine	dine	tine	Rhine
lip	nip	dip	tip	rip
lock	knock	dock	tock	rock
loom	...	doom	tomb	room
lose	...	dues	two's	ruse
lot	knot	dot	tot	rot
low	know	dough	toe	row
dill	din	did	...	dear
file	fine	...	fight	fire
fill	fin	...	fit	fear
hill	...	hid	hit	hear
ill	in	id	it	ear
owl	...	...	out	our
till	tin	...	...	tear

Also, see § Syllabic Consonant

2. *r* sounds include [r], [ɜ], [ɚ]. To make the vowels [ɜ] and [ɚ] and the consonant [r], you do the same thing: you put the tip of your tongue near your tooth ridge and bend the tip backward; see ¶ 1, *d*, above.

Don't touch anything, and don't shake anything.

a. Make the sound [n]: touch your tooth ridge with the tip of your tongue. Now make [ɚ]: move the tip backward. Now, say the sounds one after the other: [n...ɚ...n...ɚ]. Now, say [d...ɚ...d...ɚ] and [t...ɚ...t...ɚ]. Finally, say [l...ɚ...l...ɚ]. Now pronounce the words *nerve* [nɜv], *dirt* [dɜt], *turn* [tɜn], and *learn* [lɜn].

p

b. Don't let the tip of your tongue shake when you make [r]: hold the tip back firmly; you can with practice. Pronounce *car* [kɑr], *here* [hir], and *war* [wɔr].

c. Don't let your uvula shake. Bend your head far back, and say [r]; then, with your head in its natural position, say [r]. If you hear a difference, you probably let your uvula vibrate with the second [r]. Pronounce [ɑ] and then [r]. Your breath should come out of your mouth in the same way: there should be no "rubbing" sound accompanying the [r].

d. The symbols [ɝ] and [ɚ] each represent one sound, and the symbol [r] represents one sound. The [ɝ] is used in a stressed syllable, and the [ɚ] is used in an unstressed syllable. In the word *fur* there are two sounds: [f] and [ɝ]. In the word *far* there are three sounds: [f] and [ɑ] and [r]. In each word in the first column of the following list, the letter *r* and the vowel letter or letters preceding it represent just one sound: [ɝ]. In the other columns, the vowel letter or letters before the *r* represent one sound, and the following *r* represents a separate sound. Two *r* letters together are pronounced like a single *r*.

ONE-SYLLABLE WORDS

[ɝ]	[ir]	[ɛr]	[ɑr]	[or]	[ʊr]
bird	beard	bared	barred	board	...
burn	...	...	barn	born	...
burr	beer	bear	bar	bore	boor
cur	...	care	car	core	...
curse	...	...	...	course	...
curd	...	cared	card	cord	...
dirt	...	...	dart	...	...
err	ear	air	are	or	...
firm	...	...	farm	form	...
fur	fear	fair	far	four	...
gird	geared	...	guard	gourd	...
heard	...	haired	hard	hoard	...
hearse	...	...	...	horse	...
her	hear	hair	...	...	...
hurt	...	...	heart	...	...
lurk	...	...	lark	...	...
per	peer	pair	par	pour	poor
pert	...	...	part	port	...
shirr	sheer	share	...	shore	sure
shirt	...	...	...	short	...
sir	sear	...	Saar	sore	sewer
spur	spear	spare	spar	spore	spoor
stir	steer	stare	star	store	...
turn	...	...	...	torn	...
were	...	wear	...	war	...
word	weird	...	...	ward	...
worm	...	...	...	warm	...
...	cheer	chair	char	chore	...
...	dear	dare	...	door	...

314

ONE-SYLLABLE WORDS

[ɝ]	[ir]	[ɛr]	[ɑr]	[or]	[ur]
...	fierce	...	farce	force	...
...	leered	...	lard	lord	lured
...	mere	...	mar	more	Moore
...	near	...	...	nor	...
...	rear	rare	...	roar	Ruhr
...	sneer	snare	...	snore	...
...	tear (eye water)	tear (rip)	tar	tore	tour

TWO-SYLLABLE WORDS

curtain	...	...	carton	...	...
further	...	...	farther	...	...
occurred	...	...	...	accord	...
person	Pearson	...	parson	...	...
...	...	...	ardor	order	...

You will hear differences among speakers in their pronunciation of stressed vowels before [r]. For example, for *beard* some people say [bird], and others say [bɪrd]. For *care* some say [kɛr], others [kær], and still others [ker]. For *board* some say [bɔrd], and others [bord]. For *boor* some say [bur], and others [bʊr].

3. The three sounds [m], [n], and [ŋ] are called **nasal** sounds because your breath comes out of your nose when you make them.

a. To make [m], close your lips, and let your breath come out through your nose. You had better keep the tip of your tongue down against your lower teeth.

b. To make [n], put the tip of your tongue against your upper tooth ridge, and let your breath come out through your nose. Don't close your lips.

c. The sound [ŋ] is the hardest nasal to feel. Put the back of your tongue against the roof of your mouth. Put the tip of your tongue against your lower teeth. Don't close your lips.

d. When you finish making a nasal, don't "explode": don't let your breath come out of your mouth with an audible noise. If you explode after [m], you will probably say [p]; after [n], you will probably say [t]; after [ŋ], you will probably say [k]. Don't explode.

Pronounce the following triplets. Don't explode after the nasal. The final letters *ng* represent [ŋ]; don't make a [g] or [k] after the [ŋ].

[m]	[n]	[ŋ]	[m]	[n]	[ŋ]
bam	ban	bang	rum	run	rung
bum	bun	bung	some	sun	sung
clam	clan	clang	tam	tan	tang
dim	din	ding	tum	ton	tongue
ram	ran	rang			

p

4. The sounds [b], [p], [d], [t], [g], and [k] are called *stop* sounds because they are made by stopping the breath.

a. [b] and [p] are made by closing the lips.

b. [d] and [t] are made by putting the tip of the tongue against the tooth ridge.

c. [g] and [k] are made by putting the back of the tongue against the roof of the mouth.

d. [b] and [d] and [g] are voiced, and [p] and [t] and [k] are voiceless.

e. If one of the stops is the first sound in a word, your breath is suddenly released from your mouth; there is an "explosion." If a stop is inside a word, your breath is suddenly stopped and then released. If a stop is the last sound in a word, your breath is stopped and is usually not released: there is no explosion.

f. Close your lips and keep them closed to prevent yourself from exploding a final [b] or [p]. Put the tip of your tongue on your tooth ridge and leave it there for a final [d] or [t](and don't close your lips). Press the back of your tongue against your velum and keep it there for a final [g] or [d](and don't close your lips).

Pronounce the following words. The differ from each other only in the first sound.

[b]	[p]	[d]	[t]	[g]	[k]
bad	pad	Dad	tad	gad	cad
bail	pale	dale	tale	gale	kale
been	pin	din	tin	...	kin
beer	peer	dear	tear	gear	...
bold	poled	doled	told	gold	cold

g. A vowel before a final *voiced* stop is usually pronounced *longer* than a vowel before a final voiceless stop. When you pronounce the following words, lengthen the vowel before the final [b], [d], or [g]. Give less time to the vowel before the final [p], [t], or [k]. Don't explode any of the final stops; don't release your breath at the end of the word with an audible noise.

[b]	[p]	[d]	[t]	[g]	[k]
gab	gap	gad	get	gag	...
lab	lap	lad	...	lag	lack
Rab	rap	Rad	rat	rag	rack
rib	rip	rid	Rit	rig	rick
tab	tap	tad	tat	tag	tack

h. A final stop is exploded if it follows another stop or a nasal—for example, in *stamp, land,* or *think.* The reason is that the breath has been stopped from coming out of the mouth by the preceding sound. If the final stop were not exploded, it would not be heard. However, do not explode such a final stop violently; explode

316

gently. Remember to have vibration with final voiced sounds, and remember that final *ng* represents only *one* sound. Similarly, final *mb* has no [b] sound—e.g., *bomb* and *thumb.*

5. Six consonants are made by action of the lips, to produce *lip* sounds: [m], [b], [p], [v], [f], [w].

a. The lips are closed for [m], [b], and [p].

b. The lower lip touches the edges of the upper front teeth for [v] and [f].

c. The lips are rounded for [w].

d. When you pronounce [m], [b], and [p], be sure to close your lips firmly.

e. The sounds [f] and [v] are distinguished from each other only by the presence or absence of vibration of your vocal cords. You make both sounds by lightly touching your lower lip against the tips of your upper front teeth. Your breath comes out through your mouth. Don't make your lips round. Keep the lower lip touching the upper front teeth. Do not close your lips. [f] is made with no vibration, and [v] is made with vibration of the vocal cords. Make [f] with much force; make [v] with little force. Shorten a stressed vowel before [f]; lengthen it before [v].

f. [w] occurs only before vowels. If you have difficulty with [w], you should practice making it by rounding and slightly extending your lips. Make sure that you do not suddenly pull your lower lip under the upper teeth. You can also practice by first pronouncing [u] and then adding another vowel—for example, [u . . . i], [u . . . e], and [u . . . o]. Now say them together, and stress the second vowel: [wi], [we], and [wo]. You have just said the words *we, way,* and *woe.*

The following words on each line differ from one another only in the first sound.

[m]	[b]	[p]	[v]	[f]	[w]
mail	bail	pail	veil	fail	wail
main	bane	pain	vain	fain	wane
mare	bear	pair	vair	fair	wear
mend	bend	penned	vend	fend	wend
mere	beer	peer	veer	fear	we're
merry	berry	Perry	very	fairy	wary
mile	bile	pile	vile	file	wile
mind	bind	pined	vined	find	wind

6. *Near-the-teeth* sounds, [s], [z], [ʃ], [ʒ], [tʃ], and [dʒ], are made by putting the tip of the tongue near the front teeth. Don't touch the teeth, however.

a. To make distinctions among the six sounds, try this: put the tip of your tongue close to your upper front teeth for [s] and [z], and put the tip close to your lower front teeth for [ʃ] and [ʒ]. You can also protrude your lips for [ʃ] and [ʒ].

b. You touch your tooth ridge when you make [t] and [dʒ]. Touch the ridge with your tongue tip and quickly move the tip downward.

c. The sounds [s], [ʃ], and [tʃ] are voiceless. The sounds [z], [ʒ], and [dʒ] are voiced. As an aid to your production of those sounds, think of the voiceless ones as "strong" and the voiced ones as "soft." Push your breath out strongly when you say [s], [ʃ], and [tʃ]; let it out gently when you say [z], [ʒ], and [dʒ]. As with the voiced stop sounds, lengthen a vowel that precedes [z], [ʒ], and [dʒ], and give less time to a vowel before [s], [ʃ], and [tʃ].

d. The sound [ʒ] occurs only inside or, rarely, at the end of words. Some examples are *vision, measure, pleasure,* and *usual.* It will be omitted from the groups below.

[s]	[z]	[ʃ]	[tʃ]	[dʒ]
Saar	czar	· · ·	char	jar
sack	Zack	shack	· · ·	jack
sear	· · ·	sheer	cheer	jeer
see	*z*	she	· · ·	*g*
seek	Zeke	sheik	cheek	· · ·
seep	· · ·	sheep	cheap	jeep
sees	*z's*	she's	cheese	*g's*
sews	· · ·	shows	chose	Joe's
sin	· · ·	shin	chin	gin
sip	zip	ship	chip	gyp
sown	zone	shone	· · ·	Joan
sue	zoo	shoe	chew	Jew
bass	· · ·	bash	batch	badge
mass	· · ·	mash	match	Madge

e. The letter *s* at the beginning of a word is nearly always pronounced voiceless [s]. The major exceptions are words beginning with *sh* and the words *sure* and *sugar,* which are pronounced with [ʃ]. *Sc* before the letters *e* and *i* is pronounced [s], but before other letters *sc* is usually pronounced [sk].

f. Be sure to make initial [s] voiceless before a following consonant. Don't substitute [ʃ] or [z], and don't put an [ε] before the [s]. Practice making [s] alone with much force and then adding the other consonant; for example, [s . . . m] in *small, smoke, smile,* and [s . . . l] in *slow, sleep, sling.* Here are a few more examples of words with initial [s]: *scale, slang, smell, snake, space, staff,* and *swallow.*

7. The *th* sounds are [ð], [θ]. Put the tip of your tongue lightly between your teeth for [ð] and [θ]. Don't stop the breath from coming out through your mouth, not even for a moment. For [ð], the vocal cords vibrate; for [θ], they do not. Pronounce [ð] with little force; pronounce [θ] with much force. Lengthen a stressed vowel before [ð]; shorten it before [θ].

In order to distinguish clearly between [d], [ð], and [z], and between [t], [θ], and [s], be sure that you stop your breath by putting the tip of your tongue against the tooth ridge for [d] and [t] and that you put the tip of your tongue close to your tooth ridge but do not stop your breath for [z] and [s]. Do not touch the back of your teeth, and do not stop your breath for [ð] and [θ].

[d]	[z]	[ð]	[t]	[s]	[θ]
bad	bass	...	bat	bass	bath
booed	boos	...	boot	...	booth
bowed	bows	...	boat	...	both
d	*z*	thee	tea	see	...
dank	...	...	tank	sank	thank
dare	...	there	tear	...	Thayer
deem	...	...	team	seem	theme
Dick	...	...	tick	sick	thick
die	...	thy	tie	sigh	thigh
din	...	...	tin	sin	thin
dough	...	though	toe	so	...
doze	...	those	toes	sews	...
d's	*z's*	these	tease	sees	...
fade	phase	...	fate	face	faith
ford	fores	...	fort	force	fourth
laid	lays	lathe	late	lace	...
load	lows	loathe	...	...	loath
mad	...	...	mat	mass	math
owed	owes	...	oat	...	oath
pad	...	...	pat	pass	path
reed	...	wreathe	...	Reece	wreath
seed	sees	seethe	seat	cease	...
she'd	she's	sheathe	sheet	...	sheath
sued	sues	soothe	suit	...	sooth
teed	tease	teethe	...	...	teeth

8. The *y* sound [j] occurs only before a vowel. It is usually spelled *y*, as in *yellow* and *yet*, but it is also frequently part of the sounds represented by the letter *u*, as in *unite* and *particular*.

a. The easiest way to make [j] is to pronounce it as though it were an unstressed [i] before another vowel. Practice these combinations, not stopping between the two sounds and putting extra stress on the second vowel: [ie], [ia], [io], and [iu]. You can do the same with [ii]: try *yeast* and *yield*.

b. If you have trouble distinguishing [j] and [dʒ], do this: put the tip of your tongue lightly against your *lower* front teeth when you begin to make [j]. For [dʒ], begin by pressing the tip of your tongue firmly against your *upper* tooth ridge.

No [j]	[j]	[dʒ]
ale	Yale	jail
am	yam	jam
ear	year	jeer
l (the letter)	yell	jell
oak	yoke	joke
ooze	use (verb)	Jews
s	yes	Jess

9. The *h* sound [h] occurs only before a vowel or [j] or [w]. The letter *h* at the beginning of a word or syllable is usually pronounced. The major exceptions are *hour, honor, heir, exhibit,* and *exhaust* and their derivatives. The *h* is often not pronounced in *he, his, him,* and *her* but is always pronounced when those words begin a sentence or are emphasized. Remember that the unstressed auxiliaries *have, has,* and *had* are customarily reduced to [v], [z] or [s], and [d]. Don't try to pronounce the *h* in *John, Sarah,* and *Utah.*

a. The combination [hw], spelled *wh,* as in *white, why, what, while,* and *when,* is frequently reduced to [w], particularly if the word in which it occurs is not stressed. If you stress the word, you had better pronounce the full combination. Don't forget that *who, whose, whom,* and *whole* do not have any [w] sound: [hu], [huz], [hum], and [hol].

b. If you have trouble making the English [h], try whispering. Start by whispering a vowel and then continue the vowel in your natural voice. Practice with [o]: [h . . . o]. However, don't make a rustling sound in the back of your mouth or throat.

You can practice these pairs with and without an [h]:

A – hey	arm – harm	ear – hear	ill – hill
air – hair	art – heart	eat – heat	it – hit
all – hall	ash – hash	Ellen – Helen	*l* (the letter) – hell
am – ham	ate – hate	I – high	old – hold

PRONUNCIATION—VOWEL

1. The position of your tongue in your mouth is very important in the production of the vowels. You can move your tongue front—that is, toward your lips. You can move it back—that is, toward your throat. You can move it high—toward the roof of your mouth. You can move it low—toward the bottom of your mouth.

2. These vowels are *front vowels:* [i], [ɪ], [e], [ɛ], [æ].

3. These vowels are *back* vowels: [u], [ʊ], [o], [ɔ], [ɑ].

4. To feel the movement of your tongue, say *he* [hi] and then say *who* [hu].

5. These vowels are *high vowels:* [i], [ɪ], [u], [ʊ].

6. These vowels are *low vowels:* [æ], [ɑ].

7. To feel the movement of your tongue, say *beam* [bim], and then say *bam* [bæm], *bomb* [bɑm], *boom* [bum]. As you say those words, feel your tongue move from **high front** for *beam,* to *low front* for *bam,* to *low back* for *bomb,* and to *high back* for *boom.* Also, notice that your lower jaw moves down when you go from high to low, and that it moves up when you go from low to high.

8. Between the high front vowels and the low front vowel there are the *mid front* vowels [e] and [ɛ], as in *mate* and *met.*

9. Between the high back vowels and the low back vowel there are the *mid back* vowels [o] and [ɔ], as in *so* and *saw.*

10. Now say the words in the following list. Your tongue gradually moves from high front to low front to low back to high back. Notice also that your lower jaw gradually goes down and then up. Your lips become more and more open as you progress from the high vowels to the low vowels. With the back vowels your lips become more and more round as you progress from low to high.

[i]	peel	feel	[ɑ]	poll	follow
[ɪ]	pill	fill	[ɔ]	Paul	fall
[e]	pale	fail	[o]	pole	foal
[ɛ]	pell	fell	[ʊ]	pull	full
[æ]	pal	fallow	[u]	pool	fool

11. Some persons have trouble distinguishing pairs of English vowels such as [i] and [ɪ], as in *feet* and *fit.* It may help to know that the difference between such pairs can be felt.

a. Some vowels are *tense*—that is, the muscles of the speech organs are relatively tight or tense when those sounds are made. You can feel the tenseness in your tongue and in the muscles along the lower part of your face. The tense vowels are [i], [e], [æ], [ɑ], [o], [u].

b. The other vowels are *lax*—that is, the muscles of the speech organs are relatively relaxed when those sounds are made. The lax vowels are [ɪ], [ɛ], [ʌ], [ə], [ɔ], [ʊ].

c. The most relaxed vowels are [ʌ] and [ə]. Your speech organs are in a neutral position: your tongue sits down, and it is not tense at all; your lips are relaxed; your lower jaw is in a middle position: it is not pulled either up or down. The difference between those two sounds is primarily a matter of stress: [ʌ] occurs in stressed syllables, as in *cut* [kʌt], and [ə] occurs in unstressed syllables, as in *sofa* ['sofə]. The word *above* has both sounds: [ə'bʌv].

Pronounce the following pairs. The vowel in the first word of the pair is tense, and the vowel in the second word is lax.

[i] – [ɪ]	[e] – [ɛ]	[o] – [ɔ]	[u] – [ʊ]
beat – bit	age – edge	boat – bought	cooed – could
feet – fit	date – debt	coat – caught	fool – full
leak – lick	late – let	low – law	pool – pull
seat – sit	main – men	so – saw	shooed – should
sheep – ship	taste – test	woke – walk	wooed – would

12. The low vowels [æ] and [ɑ] are both tense. For [æ], press the tip of your tongue against the gum below your lower front teeth. Keep the rest of the tongue as flat as you can. For [ɑ], pull your tongue back and down as far as you comfortably can. Now, as a contrast to those two low vowels, you can use [ʌ]. For [ʌ], be as relaxed as you can. Let your tongue rest. If you feel any tightness, you will not make the sound correctly. Pronounce the following triplets. For [æ] and [ɑ], make your tongue tense; for [ʌ], relax.

[æ]	[ʌ]	[ɑ]
backs	bucks	box
cap	cup	cop
cat	cut	cot
hat	hut	hot
lack	luck	lock

For the production of [ɝ] and [ɚ] see the *r* sounds, § Pronunciation—Consonant, ¶ 2.

13. The diphthongs are made by starting with the vowel in the first part of the diphthong and then moving the tongue. For [ɑɪ], put your tongue in the position of [ɑ] and then quickly raise it toward the front of your mouth. For [ɑʊ], move your tongue from [ɑ] upward and make your lips round. For [ɔɪ], raise your tongue from [ɔ] toward the front of your mouth.

[ɑɪ]	[ɑʊ]	[ɔɪ]
aisle	owl	oil
buy	bough	boy
sigh	sow	soy
vied	vowed	void

Here are some triplets that you can use for practice. Each word in a group is different from the other two words in that group only because of the vowel sound.

[i] – [ɪ] – [e]
bean – been – bane
beat – bit – bait
deal – dill – dale
ease – is – *A's*
feast – fist – faced
feel – fill – fail
feet – fit – fate
heel – hill – hail
keen – kin – cane
lead – lid – laid
leak – lick – lake
least – list – laced
meal – mill – mail
meet – mitt – mate
peat – pit – pate
peel – pill – pale
read – rid – raid

reason – risen – raisin
seat – sit – sate
seek – sick – sake
seen – sin – sane
sheep – ship – shape
sleek – slick – slake
steal – still – stale

[ɪ] – [e] – [ɛ]
bill – bail – bell
bit – bait – bet
dill – dale – dell
fill – fail – fell
hill – hail – hell
ill – ale – *l* (the letter)
kin – cane – ken
lid – laid – led
list – laced – lest

lit – late – let
mitt – mate – met
pin – pain – pen
pit – pate – pet
rick – rake – wreck
rid – raid – red
sill – sail – sell
sit – sate – set
till – tail – tell
will – wail – well

[e] – [ɛ] – [æ]
bait – bet – bat
caped – kept – capped
fade – fed – fad
flakes – flex – flax
gate – get – gat
lace – less – lass
laced – lest – last
laid – led – lad
later – letter – latter
mace – mess – mass
main – men – man
mate – met – mat
pain – pen – pan
paste – pest – past
pate – pet – pat
rain – wren – ran
rake – wreck – rack
sate – set – sat

[ɛ] – [æ] – [ʌ]
bed – bad – bud
beg – bag – bug
bet – bat – but
better – batter – butter
dead – dad – dud
dense – dance – dunce
fend – fanned – fund
flesh – flash – flush
guessed – gassed – gust
hem – ham – hum
leg – lag – lug
lest – last – lust
mess – mass – muss
messed – mast – must
met – mat – mutt
net – gnat – nut
peck – pack – puck
pedal – paddle – puddle

pen – pan – pun
pep – pap – pup
pet – pat – putt
send – sand – sunned
ten – tan – ton
trek – track – truck
wren – ran – run

[æ] – [ʌ] – [ɑ]
babble – bubble – bobble
backs – bucks – box
bag – bug – bog
bam – bum – bomb
cad – cud – cod
cap – cup – cop
cat – cut – cot
cracks – crux – crocks
gnat – nut – knot
hat – hut – hot
jag – jug – jog
lack – luck – lock
ma'am – mum – mom
pat – putt – pot
rat – rut – rot
sack – suck – sock
sadden – sudden – sodden
shack – shuck – shock
stack – stuck – stock
tack – tuck – tock
tags – tugs – togs

[ʌ] – [ɑ] – [ɔ]
cud – cod – cawed
cut – cot – caught
chuck – chock – chalk
done – don – dawn
fund – fond – fawned
huck – hock – hawk
nut – knot – naught
rut – rot – wrought
stuck – stock – stalk
tuck – tock – talk
tut – tot – taught

[ɑ] – [ɔ] – [o]
chock – chalk – choke
cod – cawed – code
cot – caught – coat
fond – fawned – phoned
knot – naught – note
nod – gnawed – node

rah – raw – row
rot – wrought – wrote
sod – sawed – sewed
stock – stalk – stoke
tot – taught – tote

$[ɔ] – [o] – [ʊ]$
ball – bowl – bull
calk – coke – cook
cawed – code – could
fall – foal – full
Paul – pole – pull

$[o] – [ʊ] – [u]$
code – could – cooed
foal – full – fool
pole – pull – pool
showed – should – shoed

$[ʊ] – [u] – [i]$
could – cooed – keyed
full – fool – feel
pull – pool – peel
wood – wooed – weed

PUNCTUATION   P.27

Punctuation serves two interrelated functions: it serves to make your writing clear or effective for your reader, and it serves to satisfy your reader's expectations. We could get along without periods, commas, etc.; English writers used to, and writers in some languages still do. You could get along without clothes, too. However, if you wore no clothes, people nowadays would think you were uncivilized or, more likely, insane. If you wear the wrong kinds of clothes—the socially unaccepted kind—people will think you are not intelligent.

It took you quite some time to learn how to tie a necktie or a shoelace, button a button, and zip a zipper. However, you can do those things automatically now without giving much conscious thought to them. So it is with learning how to use a period, comma, quotation mark, etc. It takes time, but a little effort will make it a habit soon. Your writing will look nice, too.

The uses of the various marks of punctuation are discussed in detail in the sections designated by the name of the mark of punctuation. See § Apostrophe, § Bracket, § Colon, § Comma, § Dash, § Exclamation Mark, § Hyphen, § Parenthesis, § Period, § Question Mark, § Quotation Mark, § Semicolon, and § Underlining.

QUESTION MARK
QUOTATION MARK

1. Use a question mark (or *interrogation point*) after a direct question.

What did you say?
Can you solve that problem?

2. Two questions may be put together as one sentence. Only one question mark is used.

Did you invent that story, or is it true?

3. A statement followed by a question may be put together as one sentence, but not a question followed by a statement. Also, see ¶ 4 below.

I know you are busy, but could you help me for a minute?
Could you help me for a minute? I know you are busy.

4. In sentences with direct quotations with questions, the general principle is that the smallest possible amount of punctuation is used. See § Direct vs. Indirect Speech.

a. Do not use a period after a sentence ending in a quoted question.

Robert asked, "Are you coming?"

b. If a question ends with a quoted statement, put the question mark outside the quotation marks, and use no period at the end of the statement.

Did Robert say, "I'm coming"?

c. If a question ends with a quoted question, use only one question mark, and place it inside the quotation marks.

Did Robert ask, "Are you coming?"

d. If a dialog guide comes after the quoted question, do not use a comma to set off the dialog guide. In the following example, *Robert asked* is the dialog guide.

"Are you coming?" Robert asked.

5. A question mark, generally within parentheses, is sometimes used to indicate doubt or uncertainty about a preceding word or figure.

One of the founders was Guillaume (?) Penn.
Chaucer's dates are 1340?–1400.

However, do not use a question mark after a statement that expresses doubt or uncertainty. The word *wonder* often occurs in such a statement.

I wonder if Alice is coming.

6. Either a period or a question mark may be used at the end of a sentence which has split word order but is intended as a request or command. A question mark is more frequent. See § Polite Expression.

> Would you tell me the time?
> Do you mind not talking so much.

7. Do not use a question mark after a question that is reported in *indirect speech* —that is, not given in the forms in which it was originally expressed.

> The man asked, "What do you want?" [The question "What do you want?" is reported in *direct speech:* it is given in the forms in which it was originally expressed.]
> The man asked what I wanted. [The original question is reported in indirect speech: notice all the differences in word order and forms.]

8. Do not use an inverted question mark at the beginning of a question.

9. Never use more than one question mark at a time, and never use an exclamation mark with a question mark.

QUOTATION MARK

1. The primary use of quotation marks is to indicate that you are repeating a person's words in the form in which he expressed them: you are using what is called *direct speech.*

> Abraham Lincoln said, "You can fool all the people some of the time, and some of the people all the time, but you can not fool all the people all the time."
> Longfellow wrote, "Life is real! Life is earnest!"

2. Quotation marks are used even though the person may not have said the words aloud.

> "Well," Henry said to himself, "if that's the way she wants it, that's the way it'll be."
> Wilhemina thought, "I really must show him that I don't like his attitude."

3. A second use of quotation marks is to indicate the definition of a word or phrase or to give the English equivalent of a foreign word or phrase. The foreign expression and the word or phrase to be defined are italicized in print and underlined in manuscript. See § Underlining.

> *Lie* meaning "recline" and *lie* meaning "tell a falsehood" have different forms for the past tense and the past participle.
> The term *Sturm und Drang* ("storm and stress") is applied to a period in German literature.

4. A third use of quotation marks is to indicate that a term is unusual or is being used in a special sense. Slang words are frequently set off by quotation marks. Use quotation marks for such a purpose only with the first occurrence of the term.

> In Marshall's plays the women are either "goffs" or "wipes." A goff happily marries the man she wants. A wipe also marries but later wishes she had not.

I must caution you against overusing quotation marks to indicate an emotional reaction—contempt, astonishment, and the like. Overuse is symptomatic of immature or careless writing.

> Sally's "hat" was a square inch of lace. [The sentence is better without quotation marks.]

5. A fourth use of quotation marks is to indicate the title of a piece of writing shorter than a book—such as an essay, a magazine article, a chapter of a book, a poem, a song, or a radio or television program—or the title of a work of art such as a statue, painting, or drawing. Capitalize the first and last word and all the other words except short prepositions, short conjunctions, and *a, an,* and *the.*

> Have you read "The Man Who Almost Made It" in the January *Harper's?*
> My favorite statue in the Louvre is "The Winged Victory."

Do not use quotation marks around nondescriptive headings such as Paragraph 6, Chapter 3, and Section 2.

6. In English, quotation marks always stand above the line.

7. Quotation marks come in pairs: one set before the quoted matter and one set after the quoted matter. Put the first set on the same line as the first word of the quotation, and put the second set on the same line as the last word of the quotation.

8. If the quotation consists of more than one sentence, put quotation marks before the first sentence and after the last sentence.

> Mrs. Walsh said plaintively, "Nobody tells me anything. I wish I were dead!"

9. If the quotation extends over more than one paragraph, put quotation marks at the beginning of the quotation and at the start of each paragraph but at the end of only the last paragraph.

> Mrs. Walsh said plaintively, "Nobody tells me anything. I wish I were dead!
> "When I was younger and more attractive, people used to tell me everything."

10. Commas and periods are placed to the left of the quotation marks. Notice all the examples. A comma may follow another punctuation mark before quotation marks as in the example below. However, such an occurrence is very rare.

> Glancing through the essay entitled "Why Not More?," Dr. Jefferson frowned thoughtfully.

Some writers would omit the comma in the above example.

11. A question mark or an exclamation mark is placed to the left of the quotation marks if the quoted matter itself is a question or an exclamation. Otherwise the question or exclamation mark is placed to the right of the quotation marks. Notice that a period or a second question or exclamation mark is not used.

Paul asked, "Have they gone?"
Did Paul say, "They have gone"?
Did Paul ask, "Have they gone?"
The frightened girl screamed, "Help!"
That wretch only said, "Sorry"!

12. Expressions like *he said* which indicate the speaker of the quotation are called *dialog guides.* A comma, not a colon, is the customary punctuation mark used to set off the dialog guide from the quoted matter. Dialog guides have three customary positions:

a. At the beginning of the quotation. Use a comma between the dialog guide and the quotation.

Mrs. Walsh said, "Nobody tells me anything."

b. Within the first quoted sentence. Such an interruption does not affect the capitalization of the quoted matter. Put commas and quotation marks before and after the dialog guide. Do not capitalize the dialog guide in this position.

"Nobody," said Mrs. Walsh, "tells me anything."
"Well," he replied, "it's all your own fault."

If the dialog guide interrupts a compound sentence before a semicolon, use a comma only before the dialog guide. The semicolon is placed to the left of the beginning of the second set of quotation marks.

"Nobody tells me anything," Mrs. Walsh said; "nevertheless, I'm not complaining."

c. At the end of the first quoted sentence. Use a comma, not a sentence period, at the end of that quoted sentence.

"Nobody tells me anything," said Mrs. Walsh.

If the quoted sentence ends with an abbreviation period, use a comma in addition.

"Nobody tells me anything in Washington, D.C.," said Mrs. Walsh.

d. Do not use a dialog-guide comma after a question mark or an exclamation mark.

"Why does nobody tell me anything?" that talkative woman asked.
"I wish I were dead!" she exclaimed.

13. In writing dialog, use a separate paragraph for every change of speaker. Be sure to use enough dialog guides so that your reader will know who the speaker is.

"Nobody tells me anything. I wish I were dead!" Mrs. Walsh said plaintively.
"Mother," Clarence replied calmly, "don't be childish." He had heard his mother complain so frequently that his response had become automatic.
Mr. Walsh's reaction to his son's utterance was also automatic. He said softly, "You should be ashamed of yourself, speaking to your mother like that, Clarence."

14. A long quoted passage is usually set off from the rest of the writing by indention both on the left and right side. A colon introduces the passage, and no quotation marks are used.

> Samuel Johnson wrote in the "Preface to the English Dictionary" in 1755:
>
>> It is the fate of those who toil at the lower employments of life, to be rather driven by the fear of evil, than attracted by the prospect of good; to be exposed to censure, without hope of praise; to be punished for neglect, where success would have been applause, and diligence without reward.
>> Among these unhappy mortals is the writer of dictionaries. . . .

Less frequently, a long quotation is incorporated within the piece of writing and is set off by quotation marks at the beginning and at the start of each new paragraph and at the end of the last paragraph.

> Samuel Johnson wrote in the "Preface to the English Dictionary" in 1755, "It is the fate of those who toil . . . without reward.
> "Among these unhappy mortals. . . ."

15. When you quote directly, be sure you quote exactly. Give the source of a direct quotation. If you use another person's words as your own without giving him credit, you are guilty of plagiarism.

16. There are two kinds of quotation marks: *double quotation marks* (" . . . "), which are the customary kind; and *single quotation marks* (' . . . '), which are used within a pair of double quotation marks. (The term *inverted commas* is sometimes used by British speakers.)

> The teacher asked, "Who said, 'Give me liberty or give me death'?"
> Did the teacher ask, "Who said, 'Give me liberty, or give me death'?"

On extremely rare occasions you might have a third quotation within a quotation. For that, you use double quotation marks within the pair of single quotation marks.

> Mae said, "The teacher asked, 'Who said, "Give me liberty, or give me death"?' "

17. Do not put quotation marks around an indirect quotation.

> Roxton said he was leaving.
> Mrs. Pearl asked who was staying.

18. Be careful about punctuating and capitalizing quoted sentences which have an intervening dialog guide. Test your punctuation and capitalization by mentally removing the dialog guide and its punctuation.

> "I must leave now," Lynn said . "Won't you come with me?"
> "I must leave now . Won't you come with me?"
> "Well," Mr. Jackson replied , "the boys try hard."
> "Well , the boys try hard."

19. The commas that are used for dialog guides are not used for quoted matter

331

that is not attached to a dialog guide. See the examples in ¶ 3 to 5. Here are some additional examples:

> The Constitution begins with the words "We, the people of the United States." "Hotel Service" is the title of an essay in that anthology.

Also, see § Direct vs. Indirect Speech.

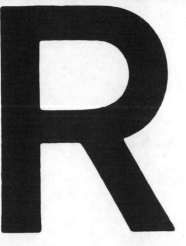

RATHER

1. The word *rather* is often used in conversation in the expression *would rather* with a verb to indicate preference.

> I don't want to go. I would rather stay home.

2. The *would* is often reduced.

> I'd rather stay home.

3. *Than* is used if the less desired thing is expressed.

> I'd rather stay home than go.
> Bob would rather meet us downtown than uptown.

4. *Not* is used after *rather.*

> I'd rather not go.
> Bob would rather not meet us uptown.

5. Notice the question forms.

> Would you rather stay home?   Wouldn't you rather stay home?
> Would you rather not go?   Wouldn't you rather stay home than go?

6. After *prefer,* the words *rather than* are also used before the less desired thing.

> I prefer to stay home.
> I prefer to stay home rather than go.
> William preferred to skate rather than swim.
> Bob would prefer to meet us downtown rather than uptown.

Also, see § Prefer, and § *Wish* vs. *Hope* vs. *Want* vs. *Would Like.*

RELATIVE PRONOUN

1. The words *who, whom, whose, which,* and *that* are sometimes called *relative pronouns* when they have an expressed antecedent—that is, a word or group of words which the relative pronoun refers to. The relative pronoun acts as a substitute for its antecedent.

> I saw the boy who did it. [*The boy* is the antecedent of *who.*]

2. Since the relative pronoun is a substitute, do not use another pronoun like *it* or *them* to refer to the antecedent. Some languages use a *double reference,* but English does not.

> I found a solution which my parents liked. [Since *which* is a substitute for *a solution,* do not use *it* after *liked* as a second substitute.]
> There are many terrors that we want to escape from. [Since *that* is a substitute for *many terrors,* do not use *them* after *from* as a second substitute.]

r

Also, see § Agreement—Pronoun, § Agreement—Verb, § Clause and its following sections, § Singular vs. Plural, § Subject and Simple Predicate, § *What* vs. *That* and *Which,* and § Word Order—Preposition.

REMEMBER VS. *REMIND*   R.3

1. The verb *remember* means "recall, recollect, or have in mind." The verb *remind* means "make or cause (somebody or something) to remember." The two words are not interchangeable.

> Can't you remember what I told you yesterday?
> That news item reminds me of a story I heard in Boston.
> My father's words made me remember my promise.
> My father's words reminded me of my promise.
> Mr. Lewis avoided people who remembered his dead wife because they would doubtless remind him of her.

2. *Remind* has two patterns. When it means "make remember from the past," its direct object is followed by the preposition *of.*

> This book reminds me of a play I saw two years ago.
> Edelweiss always reminds my sister of a trip she took to the Alps in 1950.

3. When *remind* means "make remember for the future," its direct object is followed either by a *to* infinitive or by a dependent clause.

> Mrs. Bell reminded her son to go to the store after school.
> Mrs. Bell reminded her son that he had to go to the store after school.

4. When *remember* means "recall from the past," it may be followed either by an *-ing* form or by a dependent clause.

> I remember seeing John yesterday.
> I remember that I saw John yesterday.

5. When *remember* means "have in mind now or in the future," it may be followed by a *to* infinitive, by a *wh* word with a *to* infinitive, or by a dependent clause.

> You must remember to bring your book tomorrow.
> You must remember what to do in case of fire.
> You must remember that Paul has to leave tomorrow.

RIGHT   R.4

1. The word *right* is used in the expressions *right away* and *right now,* both meaning "immediately."

> Don't hesitate; do it right away.
> Please give me some money right now.

2. *Right* is also used with *then* meaning "at that very moment, at the very same time."

> Amy did not delay about the letter; she wrote it right then.

-RY ENDING R.5

1. In words that end in the letters *ry*, the vowel letter before the *-ry* is silent in ordinary speech if the stress is on the syllable preceding that vowel letter. Some examples are *boundary, delivery, every, factory, history,* and *satisfactory.*

2. When some people speak slowly or emphatically, they pronounce an [ə] before the *-ry*—for example, *every* ['ɛvərɪ]. Ordinarily, *every* is pronounced ['ɛvrɪ].

3. The vowel letter *a* or *e* before a final *-ry* is pronounced [ɛ] and has a secondary stress if the syllable before that *a* or *e* is not stressed. Some examples are *cemetery, customary, dictionary, February, January, necessary, secretary,* and *vocabulary.*

SEARCH

1. We *search for* something we want.

People search for knowledge.
The police are searching for the criminal.

2. We *search* that which may have what we want.

People search libraries for knowledge.
The police are searching every house for the criminal.
The police searched the criminal for the stolen money.

SEMICOLON

1. Use a semicolon (;) between two independent clauses which could be but are not joined by the coordinating conjunctions *and, but, nor,* or *or.* A discussion of independent clauses is given under § Clause. Also, see § Clause—Independent and Adverbial, § Comma, and § Transition Expression for the punctuation with words like *nevertheless, however,* and *consequently.*

People make history; unusual people make history interesting.
Sarah works too hard; she does not get enough sleep, either.
Scott wanted to have a happy marriage; he hoped to be a great man in politics; he achieved neither goal.
Many problems seem insoluble; nevertheless, persistence frequently over- comes them.

2. Use a semicolon between sets in a series when there are commas within the sets.

Follow this procedure: first, get your application forms; next, fill them out; last, pay the charges.

SEQUENCE OF TENSE

1. The two sentences below mean the same thing, but notice the difference in the verb forms:

Today's paper *says* that it *will* rain tomorrow if it *does* not snow.
Today's paper *said* that it *would* rain tomorrow if it *did* not snow.

2. In general, the tense form of a dependent verb is determined by the tense of the principal verb: the dependent verb shows time *in relation to* the principal verb. The phenomenon is known as *sequence of tense.* It is found to varying extent in other languages, but it permeates English so thoroughly that it may be termed a distinctive characteristic of English. It appears not only in dependent clauses but also in infinitives and participles. See the following sections and § Tense and Time.

1. Notice the operation of sequence of tense in the following models:

Model 1

   a. She knows that John loves her. [The time of the dependent verb *loves* is the same as that of the principal verb *knows.*]

   b. She knows that John will love her. [The time of the dependent verb combination *will love* is later than (or subsequent to or future to) that of the principal verb *knows.*]

   c. She knows that John loved her. [The time of the dependent verb *loved* is earlier than (or anterior to) that of the principal verb *knows.*]

Model 2

   a. She knew that John loved her. [The time of the dependent verb *loved* is the same as that of the principal verb *knew.*]

   b. She knew that John would love her. [The time of the dependent verb combination *would love* is future to that of the principal verb *knew.*]

   c. She knew that John had loved her. [The time of the dependent verb combination *had loved* is earlier than that of the principal verb *knew.*]

2. Model 2 is so firmly entrenched in English that a general rule can be set up: if the principal verb is in the past, the verb in the dependent clause is also in the past.

3. You may see some violations of that general rule. Sometimes, if the dependent clause states a general truth, describes a habitual action, or expresses a permanent condition, the simple present tense is used in violation of the rule of sequence of tense. However, the sequential form is just as correct and is more usual, and I recommend that all speakers use it.

Columbus proved that the world was round.
The visitor discovered that the subway train always stopped at 96th Street.
The teacher asked me what my name was.

4. Use these past forms for these auxiliaries:

For *can,* use *could.*
For *may,* use *might.*
For *must,* use *had to.*
For *shall,* use *would.*
For *will,* use *would.*

For *should* and *ought,* see § *Ought* vs. *Should.* Also, see § *Can* vs. *Could* vs. *May* vs. *Might* and § *Must* vs. *Have to* vs. *Have Got to.*

5. The present perfect tense (*have* + a past participle) is a present tense. Do not use it in the dependent clause if the principal verb is in the past. Notice the difference in these two examples:

I know that you have studied your lesson.
I knew that you had studied your lesson.

6. Observe the operation of sequence of tense in the dependent verb of the following sentences:

The trip was planned carefully   so that I would see a lot.
The students did not remember   what I had taught them the day before.
I hoped   that Miss Brown would change the subject.
No one suspected   that a storm was approaching.
It reminded me of a chair   I had owned in my childhood.
The scientist was sure   that some day men would fly to the other planets.
I thought   that Americans' attitudes would be different.
Mr. Bowles said   that he did not intend to do what the women had asked.
The child cried   because he could not go to school.
The secretary announced yesterday   expenditures for next year would be greater.

7. If the time of the dependent clause is *unrelated* to the time of the principal verb, then sequence of tense is not involved. However, be careful.

Father bought the house in which we are living today.
Father bought the house so that we would have a place to live in.
In my opinion, Shakespeare wrote much better than his predecessors had been able to.
In my opinion, Shakespeare wrote much better than his contemporaries could.
In my opinion, Shakespeare wrote much better than modern dramatists can.
In my opinion, Shakespeare wrote much better than any playwright yet unborn will be able to.
Yesterday Congress passed a law that the President will veto tomorrow.
Yesterday Congress passed a law even though it was certain that the President would veto it two days later.

Also, see § Tense and Time and its following sections, § Conditional Sentence, and § Direct vs. Indirect Speech.

SEQUENCE OF TENSE—INFINITIVE AND PARTICIPLE   S.5

1. A *present infinitive* (the simple form of a verb, usually preceded by *to*) indicates time (*a*) contemporary with or (*b*) future to the time of the principal verb to which it is related.

a. Contemporary:

He needs to eat. [Present time in the principal verb *needs,* same time in the infinitive *eat.*]
He needed to eat. [Past time in the principal verb *needed,* same time in the infinitive *eat.*]
He will need to eat [Future time in the principal verb combination *will need,* same time in the infinitive *eat.*]

b. Future:

> He is planning right now to visit Europe next year. [Present time in the principal verb combination *is planning,* future time in the infinitive *visit.*]
> He was planning to go. [Past time in the principal verb combination *was planning,* future time in the infinitive *go.*]
> He will plan tomorrow to go next week. [Future time in the principal verb combination *will plan,* future time (actually, still farther in the future) in the infinitive *go.*]

2. A *perfect infinitive* (*to have* + a past participle) indicates time earlier than that of the principal verb.

> I am glad to have met you. [I am glad now that I met you in the past.]
> He was sorry to have missed the movie. [He regretted that he had not seen the movie.]
> You will be sorry to have missed the movie. [You will regret in the future that you did not see the movie.]

3. A *present participle* (the *-ing* form of a verb) indicates contemporary time in relation to the principal verb.

> The tornado departs, leaving destruction behind.
> The tornado will depart, leaving destruction behind.
> The tornado departed, leaving destruction behind.

4. A *perfect participle* (*having* + a past participle) indicates time earlier than that of the principal verb.

> The tornado departs, having caused severe damage.
> The tornado will depart, having caused severe damage.
> The tornado departed, having caused severe damage.

Also, see § Infinitive vs. Gerund.

SHALL   S.6

1. The word *shall* is sometimes used to indicate future time. In nearly all cases it is interchangeable with *will* or *be going to* although it is not used as frequently as those two forms. Most speakers do not consistently make a distinction between *shall* and *will* to express volition, determination, or simple futurity. Neither *shall* nor *will* is used very often in its full form in conversation: the reduced form *'ll* [l] is customary.

2. *Shall* has one use for which *will* and *be going to* can not be substituted: for questions with *I* or *we* as the subject, *shall* is used as a sort of polite expression similar in connotation to "Would you like me (or us) to. . . ." See § Polite Expression.

> Shall I leave now?
> Shall we dance?

For an extended discussion of *shall* and *will*, see C. C. Fries, *American English Grammar*, published by the Appleton-Century-Crofts Division of Meredith Publishing Company, pp. 150–167. Also, see § Auxiliary.

SILENT LETTER S.7

1. As you know, you can not always tell how to pronounce an English word from its spelling. Sometimes the same letter represents different sounds—for example, the letter *u* in *busy, bury, pull, sun,* and *rude*. Sometimes a letter represents no sound: it is "silent" or not pronounced. Many common words contain silent letters. Some of them are the following:

b	In *debt, doubt,* and *subtle*
d	In *Wednesday* (the first *d*)
gh	In *though, thorough,* and *through*
h	In *Thai, John, Thomas, Thames,* and in *hour, honor, heir* and their derivatives such as *hourly, honorable, honest, dishonest,* and *heiress*
i	In *business, bruise, fruit, juice,* and *suit*
l	In *could, should, would,* and *Lincoln* (the second *l*)
p	In *corps* and *receipt*
s	In *aisle, corps, island,* and *isle*
u	In *build, buy, guard, guess, guest, guide, guilt, guitar,* and *liquor*
w	In *answer, sword, two, who, whose, whom, whole,* and *wholly*

2. There are a few times when you can be sure that certain letters are not pronounced. Those times are the following:

b	After *m* at the end of a word: *bomb, climb, comb, crumb, dumb, lamb, limb, thumb*
g	Before *n* at the beginning of a word: *gnash, gnat, gnaw, gnome*
	Before *n* at the end of a word: *campaign, design, foreign, sign*
	Before *m* at the end of a word: *diaphragm, paradigm, phlegm*
gh	Before *t* at the end of a word: *light, night, bought, caught*
h	After *g* at the beginning of a word: *ghetto, ghost, ghoul*
	After *r* at the beginning of a word: *rhetoric, rhinoceros, rhubarb, rhyme, rhythm*
	After *ex* at the beginning of a word: *exhaust, exhibit, exhilarate, exhort*
	At the end of a word: *ah, catarrh, myrrh, Sarah, Utah*
k	Before *n* at the beginning of a word: *knee, knife, knock, know*
l	In the combination *alf* at the end of a word: *calf, half*
	In the combination *alk* at the end of a word: *chalk, stalk, talk, walk*
	In the combination *alm* at the end of a word: *calm, palm*
m	Before *n* at the beginning of a word: *mnemonic, Mnemosyne*
n	After *m* at the end of a word: *autumn, column, hymn, solemn*
p	Before *n* at the beginning of a word: *pneumatic, pneumonia*
	Before *s* at the beginning of a word: *psalm, pseudonym, psychic, psychology*
	Before *t* at the beginning of a word: *Ptolemy, ptomaine*

S

t	In the combination *sten* at the end of a word: *fasten, hasten, listen*
	In the combination *stle* at the end of a word: *apostle, castle, whistle*
w	Before *r* at the beginning of a word: *wrap, wreck, write, wrong*

Also, see § Phonetic Symbol, § *H-* Initial, § Syllabic Consonant, and § *-ry* Ending.

SIMPLE FORM OF VERB   S.8

1. The simple form of a verb is that form which occurs in the present infinitive (without *to*—e.g., *write*). For most verbs it is the same form that is used in the simple present tense, except for the third person singular (e.g., *writes*). (The verb *be* is a notable exception.) It is the form that is used in the affirmative imperative. It is also used in dependent clauses after certain verbs; see § Verb—Uninflected in Dependent Clause.

SINGULAR VS. PLURAL   S.9

1. Some words do not act as they may be expected to in the matter of *number* (singular and plural). Some words have a plural *form*—that is, an *s* on the end—but are singular in number. Other words which might be assumed to have a plural form do not have one. Still others can be either singular or plural in number without a change in their form.

2. A *singular* word is a word that is or can have as a substitute the words *I, me, he, him, she, her,* or *it.* A *plural* word is a word that is or can have as a substitute the words *we, us, they,* or *them.* The word *you* is singular if it applies to one person or thing, and *you* is plural if it applies to more than one person or thing. Singular and plural make up the concept of *grammatical number* in English.

> John came. He arrived. I saw him. [*He* and *him* substitute for *John;* therefore, *John* is singular.]
> Mary came. She arrived. I saw her. [*She* and *her* substitute for *Mary; Mary* is singular.]
> Food came. It arrived. I saw it. [*It* substitutes for *food; food* is singular.]
> Children came. They arrived. I saw them. [*They* and *them* substitute for *children; children* is plural.]
> Apples came. They arrived. I saw them. [*They* and *them* substitute for *apples; apples* is plural.]

3. A group of words also may be either singular or plural. Such a group of words is usually composed of a *head word* and a modifier or modifiers. A noun or pronoun is customarily the head word.

> The boy came. He arrived. [*The boy* is singular; *boy* is the head word.]
> One of the girls came. She arrived. [*One of the girls* is singular; *one* is the head word.]
> The food I ordered from the grocery store came. It arrived. [*The food I ordered from the grocery store* is singular; *food* is the head word.]

Some of the children from the neighborhood came. They arrived. [*Some of the children from the neighborhood* is plural; *some* is the head word.]
Those apples you spoke about came. They arrived. [*Those apples you spoke about* is plural; *apples* is the head word.]

4. The grammatical number of a word or group used as a subject influences the choice of form for the simple predicate when there is a choice, such as between *do* and *does;* see § Subject and Simple Predicate. Number also influences the choice of pronouns and adjectives; see § Agreement.

5. Many nouns and pronouns have different *forms* for the singular and for the plural. We say that such a word is "inflected for the plural." The majority of words which are inflected follow the rules given in ¶ 6, below: those words are called *regular.* A relatively few words which are inflected do not follow those rules: those words are called *irregular.* Still other words customarily occur in only one form: I will call them *one form.* Some of the one-form words may be singular in number, some of them may be plural in number, and some of them may be either singular or plural.

6. Here are the rules for the singular and plural forms of *regular words.*

a. The spelling rules for the inflection of regular words are the following:

1. We add *s* directly to the singular form of most regular words: *thing – things; house – houses; boy – boys; cup – cups; table – tables.*

2. We add *s* after *ch* pronounced [k]: *monarch – monarchs; epoch – epochs.*

3. We add *es* after *ch* pronounced [tʃ]: *inch – inches; match – matches.*

4. We add *es* when final *y* is changed to *i: baby – babies; story – stories.*

5. We add *es* if the singular form ends in *s, z, sh,* or *x: glass – glasses; buzz – buzzes; dish – dishes; box – boxes.*

b. In the majority of regular common words which end in the letter *s* in the singular, the *-s* (or *-ss*) is pronounced voiceless [s]—for example, *gas, kiss, circus,* and *mattress.* Their plural ending is *-es,* pronounced [ɪz]: *gasses, kisses, circuses,* and *mattresses.* Two words which end in the singular with *-s* pronounced voiced [z] are *lens* and *summons;* their plural form has *-es* pronounced [ɪz]: *lenses* and *summonses.* A number of singular proper names end in the letter *s;* some of those names end in [s] and some in [z]; see § Apostrophe for a list of them.

Further discussion of spelling is given in § Spelling—Word with Suffix; see that section for the doubling of final consonants such as *gas – gasses* and for the changing of *y* to *i* as in *baby – babies.*
The rules for the pronunciation of the regular plural words are given under § Suffix *-s.*

c. Most regular compound words like *grandfather* and *grown-up* form their plural by adding the *-s* or *-es* at the end of the compound. A few add the *-s* or *-es* elsewhere.

347

Compounds which end in *-in-chief* or *-in-law* add the *-s* to the part preceding those elements—for example, *brothers-in-law* and *editors-in-chief*. The plural for a few other similar compounds are the following: *aides-de-camp, hangers-on,* and *passers-by.*

7. The plural form of *irregular words* has to be memorized.

a. I will list the singular form and the plural form of the most important ones. A few words have alternate plural forms, either of which is acceptable but one of which is regular; those words will be excluded from the following list.

alumna – alumnae	hypothesis – hypotheses	psychosis – psychoses
alumnus – alumni	knife – knives	self – selves
analysis – analyses	leaf – leaves	sheaf – sheaves
axis – axes	life – lives	shelf – shelves
basis – bases	loaf – loaves	synopsis – synopses
calf – calves	louse – lice	synthesis – syntheses
child – children	man – men	that – those
crisis – crises	manservant – menservants	thesis – theses
diagnosis – diagnoses	mouse – mice	thief – thieves
echo – echoes	Mr. – Messrs.	this – these
elf – elves	Mrs. – Mmes.	tomato – tomatoes
ellipsis – ellipses	mulatto – mulattoes	tooth – teeth
embargo – embargoes	Negro – Negroes	torpedo – torpedoes
foot – feet	neurosis – neuroses	veto – vetoes
genus – genera	oasis – oases	wife – wives
goose – geese	ox – oxen	wolf – wolves
half – halves	parenthesis – parentheses	woman – women
hero – heroes	potato – potatoes	

b. Compounds with the word *man* or *woman* also have *men* or *women* in the plural form; for example, *fireman – firemen; gentleman – gentlemen; gentlewoman – gentlewomen.* Some words end in the letters *-man* but are not compounds of *man;* those words form their plurals regularly—e.g., *German – Germans; ottoman – ottomans; talisman – talismans.*

See § Abbreviation for the plural form of certain common abbreviations.

c. In scientific terminology there are a number of words taken from foreign languages, particularly Latin and Greek, which retain their foreign plural form.

One-form words are discussed in the remaining paragraphs of this section. In these paragraphs I will refer to one-form words as *singular form* if they do not end in an *-s* and as *plural form* if they end in an *-s.*

The two groups of one-form words listed in ¶ 8 and ¶ 9 may be used either as singular in number or as plural in number. The number is determined by the context: what the speaker or writer is talking about. Many of those words are frequently followed by phrases beginning with *of* which indicate the number.

The groups of one-form words in ¶ 10–13 have only one number: they are either singular or plural but not both.

8. Singular form, either number.

a. Indicators of quantity: *all, a lot, any, enough, half, the last, majority, minority, more, most, none, part, plenty, some, the remainder, the rest.*

Most of the pie has been eaten.   Most of the pies have been eaten.
A lot of sunshine is good for you.   A lot of women do not like him.
The last of the bread is gone.   The last of the rolls are gone.
Although the majority of Frank's examples were all right, the remainder were not quite exact.

b. Genitive pronoun: *mine.*

There is your mother.   Where is mine?
There are your parents.   Where are mine?

c. Relative and indefinite pronouns: *that, which, whichever, who, whoever, whom, whomever, whomsoever, whose, whosoever.* The number of these words is determined by their antecedent—that is, the word or group they refer to; see § Relative Pronoun. *That* is not used as an indefinite pronoun.

I like the boy who is standing by the door.
I like the boys who are standing by the door.

d. Nationalities ending in *-ese: Burmese, Chinese, Japanese, Javanese, Maltese, Portuguese, Siamese, Sudanese, Tyrolese,* etc. These words end in the sound [z].

There is only one Chinese in our class, but there are many Japanese.

e. The word *number* may be either singular or plural. It is used with countable things. If it is preceded by *the,* it is singular. If it is preceded by *a* in reference to quantity, it is plural. Also, see ¶ 12, *a,* and § Amount vs. Number.

A number of the members have resigned, but the exact number is not known.

f. Miscellaneous: *aircraft, craft* ("vessel" or "vessels"), *deer, fish* (and particular kinds such as *salmon, trout,* and *mackerel*), *offspring, sheep, swine.*

The Weather Bureau has put out storm warnings for all small craft.
Mr. Farley wanted to catch at least three fish, but he got only two trout.
The sheep are in the meadow, and the swine are in their pens.

9. Plural form, either number.

a. Genitive pronouns: *his, hers, its, ours, theirs, yours.*

There is my mother. Where is yours?
There are my parents. Where are yours?

b. Miscellaneous: *barracks, corps, crossroads, means, series, species, sweepstakes, Swiss.*

There is only one means by which real success can be achieved, but there are many means by which we can make money.

> A series of accidents has occurred at that crossroads.
> There are two series of readers: one for beginning students and one for advanced students.

10. Singular form, singular number. Except for those in *a* and *c* below, these words have *it* as their substitute.

a. Indicators of quantity with countable words: *another, each, either, neither.* These words have *he, him, she, her,* or *it* as their substitute, depending on the context; see § Agreement—Pronoun.

> I gave each of the boys what he had earned.
> Another of the girls was puzzled; she did not understand the question.
> That apple is green. Here is another; it is ripe.

b. Indicators of quantity with uncountable words: *amount, a good deal, a great deal, a great quantity, a large quantity, little, much.* These words have *it* as their substitute.

> The amount of money that Jackson has is unknown, but it is very large.
> Much of the food had spoiled; it had to be thrown away.

c. Indefinite pronouns: *anybody, anyone, anything, everybody, everyone, every-thing, nobody, no one, nothing, somebody, someone, something, what, whatever.* Most of these have *he, him, she,* or *her* as their substitutes. *What, whatever,* and those ending with *-thing* have *it* as their substitute. See § Agreement—Pronoun.

> Everything in their plans is sensible; there is nothing wrong.
> Since nobody has done his homework, everybody has to study harder.
> I do not know what is making that noise. It may be the wind.

d. Uncountable words. These words may cause trouble because they do not have a plural, unlike their equivalents in some other languages. These words differ from *collective* nouns such as *herd* and *crowd* in that they can not be modified by the words *a, one, two,* etc., or by *many* and *few.* However, they can be *quantified* by modifiers such as *much* or *little.* Several such indicators of quantity are possible, but they must be used with care: not every indicator may be used with each word. The following are the most frequent indicators: (1) *little,* (2) *a bit of,* (3) *much,* (4) *a great deal,* (5) *a lot of,* (6) *lots of,* (7) *kind of,* (8) *sort of,* (9) *piece of.* Those which can be used with the uncountable words listed below are designated by the numbers in the parentheses.

advice (1–9)	furniture (1–9)	nonsense (1–9)
attire (1–9)	grief (1–8)	optimism (1–8)
baggage (1–9)	homework (1–9)	pay (1–8)
cash (1–6)	information (1–9)	poetry (1–9)
clothing (1–9)	knowledge (1–9)	praise (1–9)
common sense (1–9)	luggage (1–9)	produce (1–9)
despair (1–8)	machinery (1–9)	progress (1–9)
entertainment (1–9)	mail (1–9)	propaganda (1–9)
equipment (1–9)	merchandise (1–9)	remorse (1–8)
fun (1–8)	music (1–9)	rice (1–9)

significance (1–8)   tuition (1–8)   wealth (1–9)
slang (1–9)   underwear (1–9)   weather (7–8)
traffic (1–8)

Dr. Gray's advice always reveals his common sense.
The teacher gave the students a great deal of advice.
That movie was just a lot of nonsense.
I discovered that I did not have a bit of cash.
I received several pieces of mail today.
David felt much remorse after he had shot the rabbit.
Don't you have some sort of homework to do?
We get various kinds of information from newspapers.
Although I like all of Mozart's music, I am particularly fond of his piano pieces.
Because slang is constantly changing, the significance of some words differs
     from time to time.
Women used to wear lots of underwear.

The words listed above are by no means all that can be used as uncountables; some others are given in § Article—*The* vs. No *The*. Still others are included in the next section.

e. Special words:

behavior, an uncountable, "conduct in general." Use *act* or *action* for specific deeds.

employment, an uncountable, "state of working." Countable equivalents are *job* and *position.*

lightning, an uncountable. Countable equivalents are *bolt* and *flash.*

the number. Use with reference to countable, plural words.

scenery, an uncountable. Countable equivalents are *scene, view,* and *sight.*

transportation, an uncountable. Use *means* for a device.

vacation, a countable that means "period of leisure which extends over several days or weeks."

vocabulary, a countable that means "stock of words of a language." Use *words* for items.

work, an uncountable when it means "toil" or "employment." Use *job* or *position* for a countable item. The sense of the word in *work of art* is "product"; you can use a plural in that sense: *an artist's works.*

Although the summer vacation lasts for four months, it is too short.
The vocabulary of English is tremendous, but you can increase your knowledge
     if it by studying and using new words as you encounter them.
The number of tickets that the box office sold was very large.
Transportation in New York is very good; the favorite means, because it is the
     fastest, is the subway.
Playwrights frequently draw attention to a character by having him perform an
     action which is not in keeping with his behavior.
Switzerland is famous for its beautiful scenery. The traveler gasps at one
     magnificent scene after another.
After days of looking for employment, Carl has finally got a good job.
Every job that Mildred gets seems to call for a lot of work.

S

11. Plural form, singular number. These words have *it* as their substitute.

a. Words ending in *-ics* denoting a science or a field of study or knowledge: *aeronautics, civics, economics, ethics, mathematics, mechanics, metaphysics, optics, phonetics, physics, politics, statistics, tactics, thermodynamics*, etc.

> Is statistics really a science?
> Economics is something Eva distrusts.
> Mathematics was Einstein's field.
> Physics was the only course I failed.

b. Diseases ending in *-s: arthritis, colitis, diabetes, measles, mumps, neuritis, phlebitis, rabies, rickets*, etc. The indicators that can be used are *case* and *attack*. The name of the disease comes after the indicator and *of*.

> Measles is really a dangerous disease.
> Rickets is caused by malnutrition.
> Oscar Johnson has just recovered from an attack of mumps.

c. A country, organization, or publication whose name is plural in form: *the United Nations, the United States, Honduras, Wales, General Motors, Standard Brands, the Boy Scouts, The New York Times*, etc.

> The United States is in the Western Hemisphere.
> The United Nations was established in 1945.
> General Motors produces many different types of cars.
> The Boy Scouts was founded by Baden-Powell.
> *The New York Times* is published daily.

d. Miscellaneous: *billiards* (the game), *checkers* (the game), *gallows, molasses, news* (indicator: *piece* or *item*), *shambles*.

> Almost all the news on the radio these days is distressing.
> I have just heard two alarming pieces of news.
> The room was a shambles after the children had finished playing.
> Billiards is Mr. Mixer's favorite recreation.

Also, see § Apostrophe for two lists of singular personal names that end in *-s*.

12. Singular form, plural number. These words have *they* or *them* as their substitutes.

a. Indicators of quantity: *both, few, many, a number, a good number, a great number, a large number, several, two, three*, etc.

> Several of the boys are going. Do you want to go with them?
> A few of the books are missing.
> A large number of Ralph's friends are coming to the party.
> A great number of people will be there. At least a hundred have accepted the invitation.

b. A large group of nouns formed from adjectives preceded by *the* or, less often, by a genitive or demonstrative adjective (*your, those,* etc.). These nouns always refer to people and usually mean "all those of that kind."

1. Nationalities. *British, Dutch, English, Finnish, Flemish, French, Irish, Polish, Scotch, Spanish, Swedish, Welsh,* etc. Notice that these words end with the sound [ʃ] or [tʃ].

The British drink a lot of gin.
The Dutch occupy Holland.
The French are noted for good food.
The Irish are supposed to be merry.

Those words have equivalents which can have both singular and plural forms— for example, *a Briton, some Britons; a Frenchman, two Frenchmen.*

2. Miscellaneous. This group is very large. Some frequent examples are the following: *dead, living, rich, poor, sick, hungry, lost, happy, lame, wounded.*

The rich get richer, and the poor get children. [Rich people become richer, and poor people have children.]
The sick have been cured; the lost have been found, and the dead have been revived.
"Give me your tired, your poor . . . ." [part of the inscription on the Statue of Liberty]

3. Less frequently, an adjective preceded by *the* means "that thing which is . . ." and is singular.

We can do the difficult immediately. The impossible takes a little longer.

c. Miscellaneous:

cattle (indicator: *head,* which has the same form for singular and plural)
clergy
intelligentsia
people (The times when this word means "nationality" or "race" and, there-fore, has both a singular and a plural form are relatively rare.)
police (The word *policeman* refers to one member of the police; *policemen,* to two or more members.)

People all over the world are pretty much the same.
Although his cattle were still lean, the rancher sold several head of them.
The intelligentsia are hailing Ronson as their spokesman.
The police are looking for the criminal.

13. Plural form, plural number. These words have *they* or *them* as their substitutes.

a. Indicator of quantity: *lots.*

Lots of the words were unusual.

In informal speech there are a number of expressions used similarly to *lots*—for example, *heaps, loads,* and *scads.*

b. Nouns representing a single item which is composed of two parts. The indicator *pair* can be used to show that one item is intended; *pairs*, to show that more than one item are intended.

(blue) jeans	trousers	(eye) glasses	scissors
breeches	coveralls	spectacles	shears
dungarees	overalls	bellows	tongs
knickers	pajamas	clippers	tweezers
pants	braces	forceps	
shorts	suspenders	pincers	
slacks	binoculars	pliers	

Your trousers are torn. You had better change them.
My new pair of pants is being altered.
The store sold forty pairs of shorts yesterday.
The ice company lost many pairs of tongs last year.
Those scissors are dull, but they are my only pair.
I have just broken my glasses. It is lucky I have an extra pair.

c. Miscellaneous:

aborigines	remains
archives	riches ("wealth")
auspices	savings
belongings	suds
clothes	surroundings
contents	thanks
customs ("tolls")	the blues ("melancholy")
dregs	the doldrums ("melancholy")
eaves	the Middle Ages
environs	the outdoors
goods (indicator: *piece*)	the outskirts
hysterics	the tropics
(living) quarters	tidings ("news")
manners ("behavior")	trappings
morals ("code of ethics")	victuals ("food")
nuptials	wages
proceeds	

Clothes certainly cost a lot, don't they?
These goods are fine, but they are too expensive.
Riches often go as quickly as they come.
The blues go away when the sun comes out.
Mr. Stevenson's morals are above criticism.
Did the customs officer inspect your baggage?

Also, see § Agreement, § *All* vs. *Whole*, § *Amount* vs. *Number*, § *Another* vs. *Other*, § *Any* vs. *Some*, §§ Article, § Comparison, § *Each* vs. *Every* vs. *All*, § *Few* vs. *A Few*, § *Hundred* vs. *Hundreds of*, § *Many* vs. *Much*, § *Many a*, § Noun—Not Repeated, § *Such* vs. *Such a*.

SO—SUBSTITUTE

1. With certain verbs the word *so* can be used as a substitute for the words "that is (or was) correct" in answers.

2. *So* may either precede or follow these verbs affirmatively: *appear, assume, believe, hope, presume, seem, suppose, tell, think.*

> Will we win? It seems so. Will we win? So it seems.
> Rob took the cake. I thought so. Rob took the cake. So I thought.
> Is John coming? I think so. Is John coming? So I think.

3. *So* follows the verbs listed above when they are used negatively. It also follows these verbs used either affirmatively or negatively: *be afraid, expect, imagine, say, trust.*

> Is John coming? I don't think so.
> Will we win? I would say so.
> Is it going to rain? I'm afraid so.
> Was he an honest man? I don't imagine so.

4. *So* precedes these verbs used affirmatively: *hear, notice, see.*

> Mr. Ross is an excellent teacher. So I have heard.

5. The word *not* is similarly used as a substitute for "that is (or was) not correct" after all the verbs listed above except *hear, notice,* and *see.*

> Will we win? It seems not.
> Rob took the cake. I thought not.
> Is it going to rain? I am afraid not.

Also, see § Verb—Not Repeated and § Word Order—Emphatic Adverb.

SPELLING

There is not much you can do about English spelling except to complain about it and learn it. Some rules that are helpful are given in § Spelling—Word with Suffix.

1. Another spelling rule is in the form of a popular rime that some people repeat to help themselves remember whether to spell a word with the letters *ei* or *ie.* It goes like this:

> *I* before *e*
> Except after *c*
> Or when sounded like *a*
> As in *neighbor* or *weigh.*

Some words which have *ie* are the following: *achieve, apiece, belief, believe, brief, besiege, chief, cashier, convenient, field, fierce, friend, grief, handkerchief, hygiene, mischief, niece, pier, piece, priest, relief, relieve, shield, shriek, siege, sieve, thief, view, wield,* and *yield.* As you can see, the *ie* words are quite numerous.

The words which have *cei* are relatively few: *ceiling, conceit, conceive, deceit, deceive, perceive, receipt,* and *receive,* but the exceptions (with *cie*) are even fewer: *ancient, conscience, conscientious, financier,* and *species.*

The words which have *ei* pronounced "*a* as in *neighbor*" are also few in number: *eight, freight, heir, neighbor, reign, rein, their, veil, vein, weigh,* and *weight.*

The remaining exceptions to the little rime are only these: *either, forfeit, height, foreign, leisure, neither, seize, sovereign,* and *weird.* However, most of the exceptions are used very frequently; therefore, you had better learn them.

2. Another group of words is also confusing: they are all pronounced with a final [sid]. However, they are only a handful, and they can be distinguished rather easily. Only one is spelled with *-sede: supersede.* Three are spelled with *-ceed: exceed, proceed,* and *succeed.* The others are spelled with *-cede: accede, cede, concede, intercede, precede, recede,* and *secede.*

3. There is something that you can probably do to help your reader: you can probably improve your handwriting. Remember that the purpose of writing is communication. If your reader can not read your handwriting, you are not writing: you are not communicating. Learning a new style of writing is difficult for certain groups of people—Slavic, Semitic, Japanese, etc. Such people have to be philosophical about the matter: they have learned how to speak and read a new language, and they must go ahead and learn how to write it. You should practice forming certain letters and figures in the English way rather than in the "European" way, particularly *z, f, p, r,* and *7*. A little tedious drill on your part will make the new style automatic for you, and you will undoubtedly discover that your spelling is making great improvement, too. Study and practice the formation of letters in § Handwriting.

4. In general, Americans and Englishmen spell certain groups of words differently. See § *-ize* vs. *-ise* for one such group. Another group is made up of those words ending in *-or* in American spelling and in *-our* in British spelling—for example, *honor* and *honour.* A third group involves the doubling of final *l* before a suffix—e.g., American *traveler* vs. British *traveller.* My advice to you on those groups is this: "In Rome do as the Romans do." If you are writing for an Englishman, use *-ise, -our,* and *ll;* if for an American, use *-ize, -or,* and *l.* That piece of advice is important: some Englishmen are not familiar with American spelling, and some Americans are not familiar with British spelling. If you use the unfamiliar form, your reader may think that you do not know how to spell. As you know, the ability to spell correctly is generally regarded as a trait of an educated person.

Words which a great number of persons have had trouble with are listed in the next section, § Spelling—Word Frequently Misspelled. Also, see § Abbreviation, § Adjective vs. Adverb, § Capitalization, § Cognate Word, § Homophone, § *-ize* vs. *-ise,* § Phonetic Symbol, § Silent Letter, § Singular vs. Plural, § Suffix *-ed,* § Suffix *-s,* § Verb—Regular vs. Irregular.

SPELLING—WORDS FREQUENTLY MISSPELLED   S.12

The spelling of certain words is particularly troublesome. For more than ten years some other teachers and I have collected the misspellings in thousands of compositions written by our students. The list under ¶ 3 contains the 430 words most commonly misspelled in those compositions. It is a very good list for you to study because it probably includes the words that you yourself misspell at times.

Don't be surprised that the words in the list are "ordinary" words; they are exactly the hardest ones to remember how to spell correctly. The irregular verbs are well represented in the list; see § Verb—Regular vs. Irregular.

1. The capitalizing of words is part of their spelling. The English rules for capitalization are, of course, quite different from those of other languages; see § Capitalization for a summary of the rules.

2. Closely allied to spelling is *grammatical number* (singular and plural). Some words have the same spelling for singular and plural; some words are used only in the singular or in the plural; etc. See § Singular vs. Plural.

3. After some of the words in the following list there are abbreviations and figures in brackets. The figures refer to the spelling rules (Rule 1, Rule 2, etc.) given in the next section, § Spelling—Word with Suffix. The other symbols in brackets are these:

2 pr	two pronunciations		pp	past participle
al	always		pres	present tense
pf	past form used for both past tense and		pt	past tense
	past participle		sg	singular
n	noun		v	verb
pl	plural			

accustom	always	automobile
achievement [1]	American	bad
acquainted [1]	among	baseball
acquire	an	beautiful [4]
across	analyze	because
address [2 pr]	and	bed
advertisement [1]	announce	before
advice [al sg]	another	began [pt]
advise [v]	answer	begin
afraid	any more	beginning [3]
afterward	anything [al sg]	behavior [al sg]
afterwards	apartment	being [1]
against	appearance [1]	believe
agreeable [1]	appreciate	besides
airplane	approach	between
all right	around	biggest [3]
almost	ashamed	born
already	atmosphere	break
although	attention	broken [pp]

brought [pf]	custom	family
build	daily	famous [2]
built [pf]	death	favorite [1]
business [4]	decide	feel
buy	decision	feeling [1]
came [pt]	department	fell [pt]
campaign	describe	felt [pf]
can't	destroy	finally [1]
career	develop	find
careful	didn't	foreign
Catholic	difference [1]	foreigner [1]
caught [pf]	different [1]	forgotten [pp]
center	difficult	forty
century	difficulty [1]	found [pf]
character	dining [2]	fourth [1]
characteristic [1]	disappear	French
cheap	disappoint	frequently [1]
children [pl]	discuss	friend
Chinese [sg & pl]	disease	funny [3]
choose [pres]	divide	German
chose [pt]	doesn't	government [1]
chosen [pp]	don't	grammar
Christian	easily [4]	great
Christmas	effect	Greek
cigaret	embarrass	group
cigarette	endeavor	happen
citizen	enemy	happened [1]
civilization [2]	engineer	happiness [4]
classical [1]	English	hear
climate	enjoy	heard [pf]
clothes [n, al pl]	enjoyed [1]	heart
coast	enough	high
college	entertainment [1]	holiday
color	equipped [3]	humor
comfortable [1]	especially [1]	hundred
coming [2]	etc.	imagine
committee [3]	European	immediately [1]
common	every	important
communism	everybody [al sg]	impossible
communist	everyone [al sg]	improve
comparison [2]	everything [al sg]	independence
completely [1]	exaggerate	Indian
concern	example	influence
consider	excellent	information [al sg]
continuous [2]	except	inhabitant
convenient	excite	in spite of
country	exercise	instead
course	existence	intellectual
create	experience	intelligent
criticize [1]	expression [1]	interest
crowded [pf]	extent	interested [1]

interesting [1]
Italian [4]
its [genitive]
it's [= it is, it has],
Japanese [sg & pl]
know
knowledge [al sg]
known [pp]
language
last
later [2]
Latin
learn
learned [1]
leave
led [pf]
left [pf]
life
like
literature
little
live [2 pr]
lives [2 pr]
lose
machine
made [pf]
magnificent
many
marriage [4]
maybe [perhaps]
means [sg & pl]
medicine
Mediterranean
men [pl]
middle
minute [2 pr]
money [al sg]
month
most
mountain
Mr.
museum
must
myself
necessary
neighbor
nervous [2]
New York
newspaper
nobody
noise

nowadays
occasion
occurred [3]
of course
off
old-fashioned
opinion
opportunity [2]
opposite [2]
organization [2]
origin
other
paid [pf]
particularly [1]
passed [pf]
passenger
people [pl]
philosophy
physical
plan
plane
planned [3]
pleasant [2]
pleasure [2]
possibility
possible
prefer
preferred [3]
prepare
pretty
privilege
probably
problem
profession [1]
professor [1]
program
promise
pronunciation
proof
psychology
quiet
quite
ran [pt]
read [pres & pf]
realize [1]
really [1]
reason
receive
recognize
recommend
referring [3]

remember
remind
responsibility
restaurant
rhythm
rich
right
running [3]
said [pf]
Saturday
scenery [al sg]
school
science
seat
seeing [1]
seem
seen [pp]
sense
sent [pf]
separate [2 pr]
should
similar
sit
skyscraper
small
so-called
soccer
somebody [al sg]
something [al sg]
sometimes
Spanish
speak
special
speech
spend
spent [pf]
standard
stayed [1]
stopped [3]
story
strange
strength
struck [pf]
student
studied [4]
studying [1]
succeed
success
successful
suddenly [1]
summer

Sunday	three	very
suppose	through	view
sure	today	wait
surprise	together	Washington, D.C.
surround	tomorrow	watch
swimming [3]	too	wear
taught [pf]	took [pt]	weather [al sg]
teacher [1]	traffic [al sg]	were [pt]
technique	traveling [1]	where
than	tried [4]	whether
theater	trouble	which
their	true	whole
themselves [al pl]	truth	with
then	two	without
there	type	woman
therefore	typical [2]	women [pl]
these [al pl]	understand	wonderful
they	unforgettable [3]	world
thing	unfortunately [1]	World War II
think	the United States	would
this [al sg]	until	writing [2]
thought [pf]	used to [pf]	written [pp]
thousand	usually [1]	young

SPELLING—WORD WITH SUFFIX   S.13

If you learn a few generalizations about the spelling of words with suffixes, you will greatly decrease the number of your headaches with English spelling. Also, you will get valuable aid for your struggles with the location of stress ("accent") in words: see Rule 3 below.

1. Three terms need to be defined for this discussion: *vowel letter, consonant letter,* and *suffix.*

a. The *vowel letters* of the English alphabet are *a, e, i, o, u,* and *y.* The following exceptions must be noted:

1. The *u* after *q* is a consonant letter. The combination *qu* is most often pronounced [kw], as in *equip, quart, quit,* and *quiz.* In a few words taken from French, the *qu* is pronounced [k], as in *croquet, bouquet,* and *liquor.*

2. The *w* after a vowel is usually a vowel letter. It and the preceding vowel letter may together represent one vowel sound (as in *law* [lɔ] or *show* [ʃo]), or they may represent a diphthong (as in *cow* [kaʊ]).

3. The *y* before a vowel is usually a consonant letter, pronounced [j], as in *yard, yellow,* and *young.*

b. All the other letters of the alphabet are classified as *consonant letters.*

c. A *suffix* is a letter or group of letters which is added to the end of a word to form a new word or meaning. Some of the most common suffixes are these:

-able	*-ation*	*-ence*	*-ful*	*-ish*	*-less*	*-ness*	*-s*
-age	*-ed*	*-er*	*-ing*	*-ist*	*-ly*	*-or*	*-y*
-ance	*-ee*	*-est*	*-ion*	*-ize*	*-ment*	*-ous*	

2. Now you are ready for the rules that govern the spelling of words with suffixes.

Rule 1: In the vast majority of cases, a suffix is added directly to the word.

comfort – comfortable	high – highest	heart – heartless
break – breakage	wonder – wonderful	sudden – suddenly
appear – appearance	go – going	govern – government
relax – relaxation	ski – skiing	good – goodness
happen – happened	impress – impression	profess – professor
absent – absentee	fool – foolish	zeal – zealous
exist – existence	special – specialist	begin – begins
murder – murderer	civil – civilize	luck – lucky

Note that Rule 1 operates with words like *finally, really,* and *stubbornness.*

Rule 2: Before a suffix beginning with a vowel, a final unpronounced *e* preceded by a consonant or *u* is dropped.

desire – desirable	divorce – divorcee	mule – mulish
value – valuable	confide – confidence	rogue – roguish
cleave – cleavage	office – officer	machine – machinist
persevere – perseverance	simple – simplest	mobile – mobilize
continue – continuance	true – truest	operate – operator
converse – conversation	come – coming	adventure – adventurous
hope – hoped	pursue – pursuing	continue – continuous
subdue – subdued	migrate – migration	assemble – assembly

a. Exception to Rule 2: Final *e* is retained after *c* or *g* when a suffix beginning with an *a* or *o* is added: *change – changeable; notice – noticeable; trace – traceable; courage – courageous; outrage – outrageous.*

b. The combination *-ee* is a spelling for the sound [i] at the end of a word, and, therefore, the second *e* is not "silent." Such words are governed by Rule 1—for example, *agree – agreeable* and *see – seeing.*

c. Note that Rule 1 operates for a final unpronounced *e* before a suffix beginning with a consonant. The *e* is not dropped: *immediate – immediately; complete – completely; vague – vaguely; excite – excitement.* The principal exceptions here are these words with suffixes: *argument, truly, truth,* and *wholly.*

Rule 3: If a word ends in a single consonant preceded by a single, stressed vowel, that final consonant is doubled when a suffix beginning with a vowel is added.

control – controlled	commit – committee	big – biggest
equip – equipped	occur – occurrence	begin – beginning
occur – occurred	swim – swimmer	get – getting
plan – planned	quiz – quizzes	refer – referring
prefer – preferred		

a. Rule 3 operates when the stress changes to the next to the last syllable in the new word with the suffix: *métal – metállic.*

b. Rule 1 operates with words which have more than one vowel letter in the final, stressed syllable: *obtain – obtainable; seem – seemed; fool – foolish; real – realize.*

c. Rule 1 operates with words which end in more than one consonant: *return – returning; interrupt – interrupted.*

d. Rule 1 applies to words which do not have the stress in the final syllable: *devélop – devéloped; ópen – ópened; lísten – lístening; trável – tráveler; márvel – márvelous.*

e. Similarly, if the location of the stress changes in the new word with the suffix, the doubling does not occur. The major examples are these: *confér – cónference; infér – ínference; prefér – préferable, préference; refér – réferee, réference.*

Rule 4: Final *y* preceded by a consonant usually changes to *i* before a suffix.

marry – marriage	supply – supplies	happy – happiness
try – tried	beauty – beautiful	mystery – mysterious
easy – easier	mercy – merciless	

a. Major exception to Rule 4: Final *y* does not change before a suffix beginning with *i: carry – carrying; study – studying; vary – varying; thirty – thirtyish.*

b. Personal names ending in *y* add only the suffix, without changing the *y* to *i: Mary – Marys; Allenby – Allenbys.* However, geographic names usually follow Rule 4: *Allegheny – Alleghenies; Germany – Germanies.*

c. Rule 1 operates when final *y* is preceded by a vowel: *enjoy – enjoyed; stay – staying; pay – payment; annoy – annoyance; play – plays.* The principal exceptions here are these: *day – daily; gay – gaily* (or *gayly*); *lay – laid; pay – paid; say – said.*

Rule 5: The letter *k* is added after *c* before the addition of a suffix beginning with *e, i,* or *y.*

shellac – shellacked	picnic – picnicker	panic – panicky
traffic – trafficking	mimic – mimicking	

These are the major exceptions: *criticize, publicize, publicity.* The final *c* in *critic* and *public* is pronounced [k], but in *criticize, publicize,* and *publicity* it is pronounced [s].

Rule 6: Add *-es* if a word ends in *ch* pronounced [tʃ]; add *-s* if a word ends in *ch* pronounced [k].

arch – arches	epoch – epochs
match – matches	monarch – monarchs

Also, see § Suffix *-ed* and § Suffix *-s* for some additional spelling rules.

STILL **VS.** *ANY MORE* **AND** *ANY LONGER*   S.14

1. The word *still* is used to indicate continuation without change. It customarily comes before the main verb or after the first auxiliary or *am, are, is, was,* or *were.* If the first auxiliary has *-n't, still* comes before the first auxiliary.

Professor Bronson still tells the same old jokes.
Mr. Swanson is still reading the paper; he has not finished yet.
Are you still working at Speyer's? Are you ever going to change jobs?
Edison was still quite young when he made his first invention.
When television was still a novelty, Harris foresaw its potentialities.
You're still not doing it right.
You still aren't doing it right.
You still haven't answered my question.

2. The words *any more* and *any longer* indicate the discontinuance of a habit or of a repeated action. They are used in negative sentences and come after the verb and its complements, if any.

I used to smoke a lot, but I don't any more.
Prof. Bronson does not tell those same old jokes any longer.
I am glad to hear that you are not working at Speyer's any more.
Nobody believes that theory any longer.

3. At times, particularly in writing, *no more* and *no longer* are used instead of *not ... any more* and *not ... any longer.* Their position in the sentence may vary.

I no longer believe you.
That day we read no more.
The glory of youth will be yours no longer.

Also, see § *Already* vs. *Yet,* § Opposition Expression, and § Word Order— Emphatic Adverb.

S

1. Certain kinds of words are usually stressed in phrases and sentences, and other kinds of words are usually not stressed.

a. In general, these kinds of words are stressed: nouns, main verbs, adjectives, adverbs, the demonstratives *this, that, these,* and *those,* and the *wh* words *who, whose, whom, which, what, when, where, why,* and *how* and their compounds such as *whoever.*

b. The kinds of words which are usually not stressed are these: the articles (*a, an,* and *the*), possessive adjectives, prepositions, conjunctions, personal pronouns, the verb *be,* and auxiliaries.

2. The articles *a, an,* and *the* are usually not stressed. Think of them as being an unstressed part of the next word. Say *a man* as if the two words were written together: *aman.* In the same way, say *the boy* like one word. Don't stop between the two words.

The article *an* should also be thought of as part of the next word. However, do not "carry over" the [n] to the vowel that follows it: stop your breath from coming out of your nose before you begin pronouncing the vowel.

3. The possessive adjectives *my, your, our, his, her, its,* and *their* are usually not stressed. Also, the words *his* and *her* are usually pronounced without the *h* unless they come at the beginning of a sentence.

4. Prepositions that precede their objects are usually not stressed, and neither are conjunctions. However, when the object is a personal pronoun (*me, him, it,* etc.), the preposition usually has some stress, but the pronoun does not. See § Part of Speech—Conjunction and Preposition for a listing of prepositions and conjunctions.

Be very careful about the pronunciation of the word *of:* it is almost always unstressed [əv].

The usual pronunciation of *toward* is [tɔrd].

When *with* is followed by the word *the,* the two words have only one *th* sound: [wɪðə]. In ordinary speech, *with the* and *with a* sound alike.

In ordinary conversation, *and* is often reduced to [n], and *or* is reduced to [ɚ]. See § Syllabic Consonant.

5. The personal pronouns *I, me, we, us, you, he, him, she, her, it, they,* and *them* are usually not stressed.

The *h* in the words *he, him,* and *her* is customarily not pronounced unless those words begin a sentence.

Unstressed *me* is pronounced [mɪ].

When *with* and *them* come together, there is only one *th* sound: [wɪðəm].

When a personal pronoun is the object of a preposition, the preposition usually has some stress, but the pronoun does not.

6. An auxiliary is usually not stressed when it precedes a verb. See § Auxiliary for a list of words used as auxiliaries. Also, see § *Must* vs. *Have to* vs. *Have Got to.*

Unstressed *am* is usually reduced to [m]; *are,* to [ɚ]; *will* and *shall* to [l]; *had* and *would* to [d].

Unstressed *have* is reduced to [v] after vowels and to [əv] after consonants.

Is and *has* are reduced to [s] after voiceless sounds and to [z] after voiced sounds. After a sibilant ([s, z, ʃ, ʒ, tʃ, dʒ]), unstressed *is* is pronounced [ɪz], and unstressed *has* is pronounced [əz].

All those reductions are customary in ordinary conversation even though in most writing the full form *am, is,* etc., are used.

If an auxiliary is the first or last word in a sentence, it receives stress. That auxiliary may have *-n't* with it. *Ought* is usually followed by unstressed *to.*

7. For certain reasons people stress words which are usually not stressed. The most important reason is to show contrast. That kind of stress is called *contrastive stress.*

> No, I did not tell *her;* I told *him.*
> The book is *on* the table, not *in* the table.

When a person stresses a word which is customarily not stressed, his listener expects it to be contrasted with another word or group. Therefore, if you unintentionally stress a customarily unstressed word, you may confuse your listener.

Also, see the following section, § Stress—Word, and § Pronunciation and § Phonetic Symbol.

STRESS—WORD S.16

1. Every English word of more than one syllable has at least one stressed syllable. A stressed syllable is pronounced in such a way that it is more prominent than an unstressed syllable. We stress a syllable by "saying it louder"; that is, we usually utter it with more volume of breath and with a higher pitch than we do the surrounding syllables.

Vowels in stressed syllables are usually "longer" than vowels in unstressed syllables. The lengthening is usually made by "gliding off" the vowel—that is, by adding a sound to the vowel. Add an unemphatic [ɪ] after the *front* vowels [i], [ɪ], [e], [ɛ], [æ]. Add an [ə] after the *back* vowels [u], [ʊ], [o], [ɔ], [ɑ]. See § Pronunciation—Vowel and § Phonetic Symbol.

Sometimes a word has a secondary stress. We pronounce the syllable that bears a secondary stress with a little less volume and lower pitch than the syllable with the primary stress, and we do not say it for as long as the syllable with the primary stress.

Syllables which are not stressed are pronounced with relatively little breath. Most important, the vowel in an unstressed syllable is usually [ə] or [ɪ]. There are no easy rules for determining whether [ə] or [ɪ] should be used in the unstressed. To be positive, you should consult a good dictionary. A reliable one is Kenyon and Knott's *A Pronouncing Dictionary of American English,* published by the G. & C. Merriam Company.

Since one of the characteristics of a poor speaker is stressing or forcefully pronouncing an unstressed syllable, my advice is this: don't worry about whether the unstressed vowel is [ə] or [ɪ]; use either and with relatively little clarity. One's concern should be about stressing the proper syllable and about *not* stressing the unstressed syllables.

A useful device for learning to distinguish stress is *tapping.* Take a pencil, and knock the end of it lightly on a chair or table for an unstressed syllable, and knock it more forcefully for a stressed syllable. For example, when you say the word *people,* strike once forcefully and once lightly. For the word *believe,* strike once lightly and once forcefully. For *returning,* strike once lightly, once forcefully, and once lightly. For *comfortable,* strike once forcefully and three times lightly. Give more time to the vowels in the stressed syllables than to those in the unstressed syllables.

2. Some speakers often misplace the stress on certain words. The following are some of those words; the vowel that should be stressed is underlined:

admirable	character	democracy	image	preface
afraid	comfortable	develop	italics	probably
apostrophe	comparable	development	machine	register
appetite	congress	distribute	mistake	responsible
Arabic	constantly	effort	obstacle	result
catastrophe	contribute	horizon	origin	theater
Catholic	degree	horizontal	politics	vegetable

3. The following pairs of words are spelled the same way, but the place of stress on them when they are used as verbs differs from the place when they are used as other than verbs.

NOT VERB—STRESS FIRST SYLLABLE	VERB—STRESS SECOND SYLLABLE
addict	addict
affix	affix
ally	ally
annex	annex
assay	assay
concert	concert
conduct	conduct
confine	confine
conflict	conflict
contest	contest
contract	contract
contrast	contrast
converse	converse
convert	convert
convict	convict
convoy	convoy
decrease	decrease
desert	desert
digest	digest
escort	escort

NOT VERB—STRESS FIRST SYLLABLE	VERB—STRESS SECOND SYLLABLE
exploit	exploit
extract	extract
frequent	frequent
import	import
incline	incline
increase	increase
insert	insert
insult	insult
object	object
perfect	perfect
permit	permit
present	present
produce	produce
progress	progress
project	project
protest	protest
rebel	rebel
record	record
refuse	refuse
subject	subject
survey	survey
suspect	suspect
transfer	transfer

Also, see the preceding section, § Stress—Group, § Cognate Word, § -ace, -ess, -ice, and -is, § -age, § -ate, § -ci-, -si-, and -ti-, § -ic, -ics, -ical, and -ically, § -ous Word, § -ry Ending, § Spelling—Word with Suffix, § -sure Ending, § Syllabic Consonant, § -ture Ending, and § X Word.

SUBJECT AND SIMPLE PREDICATE   S.17

1. *Subject* and *simple predicate* are technical terms used to refer to two specific components of one kind of syntactical relationship: they are the two parts of one of the numerous constructions of English.

2. In the following model sentence, the word *he* is the subject, and *lives* is the simple predicate:

Model 1	He	lives	here.

3. *Subject* is a grammatical term that is used to refer to the word *he* or to a word or group which can be substituted for *he* in that model sentence or in a similar sentence.

4. *Simple predicate* is a grammatical term that is used to refer to the word *lives* or to a word or group which can be substituted for *lives* in that model sentence or in a similar sentence.

5. Here are two more examples:

| Model 2 | They | live | here. |

The word *they* is the subject, and *live* is the simple predicate.

| Model 3 | They | work | here. |

The word *they* is the subject, and *work* is the simple predicate.

6. Let's take some more examples. Notice that a subject may be one word or a group of words.

SUBJECT	SIMPLE PREDICATE	
It	lives	here.
She	goes	there.
We	sleep	in a bed.
The boy	sits	in the garden every morning.
Some girls	left	early last night.
A few of the men	went	with them.

7. Here are some more sentences with the simple predicates in the middle. In the examples with more than one word in the simple predicate, we call the last of those words the *main verb* and each of the others is called an *auxiliary*. See § Auxiliary.

SUBJECT	SIMPLE PREDICATE	
It	eats	meat.
Dogs	like	bones.
Your teacher	will correct	your papers tomorrow.
Bob	has hurt	his finger.
You	may leave	in a short while.
The boys	have been	talking.
We	should have gone	with them.

8. Now you need some more technical terms. One of those is *grammatically complete sentence.* A grammatically complete sentence in English may be either of two kinds: an *imperative sentence* or a sentence containing a subject and simple predicate.

9. An imperative sentence is a sentence similar to the model below:

| Model 4 | Come | here. |

a. Such a sentence is directed as a request or order toward one or more listeners or readers who are customarily referred to by the word *you.* The typical imperative sentence contains the "simple form" or "uninflected form" of a verb, which we designate as the simple predicate; for example, *come* in the model above is the simple predicate. An imperative sentence may contain only that one verb form, as in the first example below, or it may contain that verb form and related words.

	SIMPLE PREDICATE	
	Stop!	
	Go	away.
	Be	quiet.
Please	stay	with me.
Before our next class,	study	the section on punctuation.

b. An imperative sentence is the only kind of grammatically complete sentence which may be composed of only one word, as in the first example above. It sometimes has as its subject the word *you* or an equivalent of *you* before the verb form to show emphasis or contrast.

	SUBJECT	SIMPLE PREDICATE	
	You	stop!	
	Everybody	pay	attention for a moment.
John may stay.	You	go	away.

c. The only auxiliary that is often used in an imperative sentence is *do.* In negative imperatives ("prohibitions") it is used with *-n't* or *not.* In affirmative imperatives it is used for emphasis.

	SIMPLE PREDICATE	
	Don't stop.	
	Do not stop.	
	Do be	quiet.
Please	do stay	with me.

10. The other kind of grammatically complete sentence contains a subject and a simple predicate. Now we can employ the terms *subject* and *simple predicate* in a number of generalizations or rules.

Rule 1: A grammatically complete sentence contains an expressed subject.

a. The only exception to that rule is an imperative sentence, as explained above.

b. This rule of English differs from the concept of a grammatically complete sentence in some other languages. For example, in expressions of weather, *it* is used in English as the subject.

SUBJECT	SIMPLE PREDICATE	
It	is	raining.
It	snowed	last night.
It	is	going to be a beautiful day.

At times, the word *it* is used as the grammatical subject but refers to a group of words which comes later in the sentence.

It	is	difficult	to explain that problem.

In the above example the *it* refers to "to explain that problem." Such a sentence can frequently be rewritten by making the group of words the subject in place of the *it.*

To explain that problem	is	difficult.

For a further discussion of that construction, see § Appositive, and § *It* vs. *There.* Here are some additional examples:

	SUBJECT	SIMPLE PREDICATE		
	It	will be	necessary	to repeat the course.
	It	seems	certain	that they will win.
I thought	it	would be	a good idea	to do that.

c. Some languages use a *summarizing* pronoun after a long subject. English does not. Do not add an *it* or *they* after the subject in sentences like the following:

SUBJECT	SIMPLE PREDICATE	
What Bob wanted to say	was	never made clear.
All the students in my class	work	very hard.

Rule 2: A grammatically complete sentence contains an expressed simple predicate.

This rule of English differs from the concept of a grammatically complete sentence in some other languages. For example, a form of the verb *be* is used as the simple predicate in English sentences whose equivalents in other languages do not have an expressed simple predicate.

SUBJECT	SIMPLE PREDICATE	
I	am	lazy.
That man	is	a doctor.

Rule 3: The subject and the simple predicate have fixed positions in relation to each other.

This rule involves the basic arrangement of words in English. For an extended discussion, see § Word Order and its following sections.

a. There are three arrangments or *patterns* of subjects and simple predicates. In the scheme below, *S* stands for "subject," and *P* stands for "simple predicate."

Pattern 1   Primary word order

S	+	*P*
A hero		lies	here.

Pattern 2   Split word order

P	+	*S*	+	*P*
Does		a hero		lie	here?

Pattern 3   Inverted word order

	P	+	*S*
Here	lies		a hero.

b. Pattern 1 is called *primary word order* because it is the most frequent of the three patterns. It is also sometimes called *statement word order* because the majority of statements in English have the subject before the simple predicate. However, some questions have primary word order; for example, in "Who is going?" *who* is the subject, and *is going* is the simple predicate.

370

c. Pattern 2 is called *split word order* because the subject comes between the two parts of the simple predicate. The pattern is sometimes called *question word order* because a large number of questions have an auxiliary before the subject. However, some statements have split word order; for example, in "Not once have you done that work correctly" the simple predicate *have done* is split by the subject *you.*

d. Pattern 3 is called *inverted word order* or *reverse word order* because the arrangement of subject and simple predicate is the opposite of Pattern 1. It is used frequently after the word *there* and other expressions of place. Here are some other examples:

	SIMPLE PREDICATE	SUBJECT
There	is	a man at the door.
There	have been	many wars in the past.
There	goes	your last chance.
Here	are	some examples.
At the base of our troubles	lies	a sense of insecurity.

e. Only certain kinds of words or groups come between a subject and its simple predicate or between the parts of a simple predicate. Adverbs, usually of frequency or degree or manner, most often separate the subject and the simple predicate or the parts of a simple predicate. The word *not* is probably the most common separator of a simple predicate.

That boy	*always*	works	hard.
I	*certainly*	like	that girl.
Mr. Baxter	*sadly*	shook	his head.
Mary	does *not* feel	well.	
You	must *first* take	the examination.	
That country	has *never* been	defeated in a war.	

Appositives—particularly *all, both,* and *each*—often intervene between a subject and a simple predicate, and so do vocatives and similar interjections.

We	*all*	waited patiently.
You must,	*my friend,*	be mistaken.
Mr. Thomas,	*indeed,*	is utterly wrong.

Rule 4: The subject and the simple predicate agree. This rule has to be remembered in relatively few instances since most simple predicates have the same form no matter what the subject is.

SUBJECT	SIMPLE PREDICATE	
He	stayed	home.
They	stayed	home.
She	can go	with him.
We	can go	with him.
It	had stopped.	
You	had stopped.	

a. The time when you have to be careful about observing Rule 4 is when there seems to be a choice between using and not using an *-s* form for the simple predicate. You choose the form with *-s* if the subject is *he, she,* or *it* or has one of those words as a possible substitute. You choose the form without *-s* if the subject is *I, we, you,* or *they* or has one of those words as a possible substitute. (Of course, when *I* is the subject, it customarily takes *am* instead of *be* and *was* instead of *were.*)

b. Let's take some examples of the simple predicate with the form with *-s*. The subject is followed by its possible substitute in brackets.

SUBJECT	SIMPLE PREDICATE	
The young man [He]	lives	here.
Every college girl [She]	wants	a degree.
My puppy [It]	does	not like milk.
The news [It]	is	alarming.
What they told you [It]	was	correct.

c. Here are some examples of the simple predicate with the form without *-s*. Notice that that form is used if the complete subject can have as its substitute two or more subject pronouns joined by *and.* Such a subject is called a *compound subject.*

SUBJECT	SIMPLE PREDICATE	
Girls [They]	want	degrees.
The young men [They]	live	there.
My puppies [They]	do	not like milk.
John [he] and Jim [he] [= They]	live	there.
John [he], Jim [he], and Paul [he] [= They]	live	there.
Ruth [she] and I [= We]	are	going.
You and your brother [he] [= You]	have	not been studious.
What you said [it] and what I said [it] [= They]	were	not the same.

Rather infrequently a compound subject has as its substitute *he, she,* or *it,* not *they.* In such an instance, the simple predicate has the *-s* form.

My best friend and severest critic [She]	is	my wife.

d. When you substitute a subject personal pronoun for the subject, be sure to include all the words of the subject. The pronoun substitutes for the *complete* subject.

SUBJECT	SIMPLE PREDICATE	
One of the boys [He]	is	leaving.
Two of the boys [They]	are	leaving.
The cause of the revolutions [It]	has	not been revealed.
The causes of the revolution [They]	have	not been revealed.

Rule 5: If the complete subject can be referred to by subject pronouns joined by *or, nor,* or *but,* make the simple predicate agree with the nearest pronoun. That kind of subject is also called a *compound subject.*

Let's take some of the preceding examples and see what happens to the form of the simple predicate. In such examples *nor* is preceded by the word *neither*, and *but* is preceded by *not*. The word *either* sometimes precedes *or*.

SUBJECT	SIMPLE PREDICATE	
John or Jim	lives	here.
Not John but Jim	lives	here.
Not only John but also Jim	lives	here.
Either Ruth or I	am	going.
Neither your brother nor you	have	been very studious.
Neither you nor your brother	has	been very studious.

a. Quite often a simple predicate has two or more auxiliaries or main verbs joined by *and, but,* or *or;* they are referred to as a *compound simple predicate.*

I	studied and read	last night.
Mr. Perkins	must and will get	a raise.
The boys	have left but will return	later.
Nobody	sang, smiled, or laughed	in that somber house.

b. Sometimes the *and* is omitted in a series of three or more.

The tiger	coughed, snarled, growled	in his cage.

Rule 6: The form of the simple predicate is determined by the subject, not by any other part of the sentence.

It	was	the boys who started the rumor. [*It* is the subject of the simple predicate *was; the boys* is a predicate nominative.]
What they want	is	wealth and fame. [*What they want* is the subject of the simple predicate *is; wealth and fame* is a predicate nominative.]

Rule 7: If the subject is the relative pronoun *that, which,* or *who,* the form of the simple predicate is determined by the antecedent of that pronoun. *Antecedent* means the "word or group of words which a pronoun like *he, it, that, who,* or *which* refers to."

He bought the bag. It was red. [*The bag* is the antecedent of the subject *it.*]
He bought the bag of apples that was red. [*The bag of apples* is the antecedent of the subject *that.*]
He bought the apples. They were red. [*The apples* is the antecedent of the subject *they.*]
He bought the bag of apples that were red. [*Apples* is the antecedent of the subject *that.*]
It is you who are wrong. [*You* is the antecedent of the subject *who.*]
It is Jim who is wrong. [*Jim* is the antecedent of the subject *who.*]
It is I who am wrong. [*I* is the antecedent of the subject *who.*]

Rule 8: Do not use a comma to separate the subject and the simple predicate. Since the subject and the simple predicate form a syntactic unit, a comma should not divide them. Go back over the examples in this discussion, and notice the lack of commas.

11. Nouns and verbs which are close to each other in a sentence are not necessarily subjects and simple predicates.

> John, did you tell Pauline?

In the above example, *John* is not the subject (it is a vocative). The word *you* is the subject, and the words *did tell* make up the simple predicate. The sentence has split word order.

> I heard John tell Pauline.

In the above example, *I* is the subject, and *heard* is the simple predicate. The word *tell* is not a simple predicate, and, therefore, *John* is not the subject of the sentence. The subject of a simple predicate may have as a substitute the words *I, you, he, she, it, we,* or *they*. If you substituted a pronoun for *John* in that sentence, it would be *him,* not *he:* "I heard him tell Pauline."

> I had John fired from his job.

In the above example, *I* and *had* go together to make up the subject and simple predicate. *John* is not the subject: if you substituted a pronoun, again it would be *him,* not *he:* "I had him fired from his job."

> I saw John running down the street.

In the above example, *I* and *saw* are the subject and the simple predicate. *John* is not the subject because the substitute would be *him,* not *he:* "I saw him running down the street."

> I wanted John to tell her.

In the above example, *I* and *wanted* are the subject and the simple predicate. *John* is not the subject because the substitute would be *him,* not *he:* "I wanted him to tell her."

12. The subject has one of two different meanings according to the kinds of words which make up the simple predicate:

a. The subject customarily means "performer" of the action expressed by the simple predicate.

SUBJECT	SIMPLE PREDICATE	
Lions	eat	meat.
The machine	ran	smoothly.
A minister	will marry	the couple.
Her father	should have given	Mary a spanking.

b. The subject means "describee"—i.e., "that which is described or identified"— if the simple predicate is or contains a form of *be, seem,* or a similar verb which is followed by a predicate nominative or predicate adjective.

SUBJECT	SIMPLE PREDICATE	
Lions	are	meat eaters.
The machine	seemed	efficient.
The couple	will appear	nervous.
Mary's father	should have been	a stricter disciplinarian.
Mary	ought to have been	more polite.

A subject of the describee category has the special meaning of "affectee"—either "that which undergoes the action" or "that to or for which the action is performed"—if the simple predicate is or contains a form of *be* or *get* and is followed by a past participle. The construction of "*be* or *get* + past participle" is called the *passive.* All other verbal constructions are called *active.*

SUBJECT	SIMPLE PREDICATE	
Meat	is	eaten by lions.
The machine	has been	repaired by the mechanic.
The couple	will get	married tomorrow.
Mary	should have been	given a spanking.
A spanking	ought to have been	given to Mary.

For a further discussion of subject and simple predicate, see § Clause and § Passive. Also, see § Infinitive vs. Gerund for a different kind of subject-and-verb relationship.

SUCH VS. SUCH A   S.18

1. *Such a* is used before singular nouns which are countable. *Such* is used before singular uncountable nouns. Both *such* and *such a* precede adjectives modifying the nouns.

It was such a hot day that we stayed indoors.
It was such good coffee that I drank two cups.
I told Mrs. Bryan she was lucky to have such a distinguished husband.
Have you ever heard of such nonsense?
You do not have the right to say such a thing.
You have no right to say such a thing.

2. If *no* is placed before *such,* the article *a* is not used.

You have the right to say no such thing.
There is no such animal in the world.

3. *Such* is used with all plural nouns.

Our teacher gives us such long assignments that we have time for nothing else.

4. Notice the equivalent constructions with *such . . . as* and with *like.*

Such men as he are dangerous.
Men like him are dangerous.

Also, see §§ Article, § *As* vs. *Like,* § Singular vs. Plural, and § Word Order—Adjective before Noun.

SUFFIX *-ED*   S.19

1. The suffix *-ed* is used to form the past tense and past participle of regular verbs. I will refer to that form as the *past form.*

2. The spelling of the past form follows a constant system.

a. The *-ed* is added directly to the simple form of most verbs. The simple form is the infinitive form without *to.*

approach – approached	develop – developed	interest – interested
consider – considered	enjoy – enjoyed	obtain – obtained
cough – coughed	enter – entered	pass – passed
destroy – destroyed	happen – happened	return – returned

b. If the simple form ends in *-e,* only *d* is added.

agree – agreed	decide – decided	like – liked
believe – believed	excite – excited	suppose – supposed
complete – completed	hoe – hoed	

c. If the simple form ends in *-y* preceded by a consonant, the *y* is changed to *i,* and *-ed* is added.

marry – married	reply – replied	study – studied	try – tried

d. If the simple form ends in a single consonant preceded by a single, stressed vowel letter, that final consonant is doubled, and *-ed* is added.

commit – committed	plan – planned	regret – regretted
impel – impelled	prefer – preferred	stop – stopped
occur – occurred	propel – propelled	

3. The pronunciation of the *-ed* follows a constant system. See § Phonetic Symbol for the explanation of the symbols in brackets.

a. If the simple form ends in [t] or [d], the final *-ed* of the past form is pronounced [ɪd].

commit – committed	decide – decided	interest – interested
connect – connected	divide – divided	surround – surrounded
create – created	excite – excited	

b. If the simple form ends in a voiceless sound except [t], the final *-ed* of the past form is pronounced [t]. Those voiceless sounds besides [t] with which the simple form may end are [p], [k], [f], [θ], [s], [ʃ], and [tʃ].

approach – approached	froth – frothed	pass – passed
cough – coughed	like – liked	stop – stopped
develop – developed	mash – mashed	

c. If the simple form ends in a voiced sound except [d], the final *-ed* of the past form is pronounced [d]. Those voiced sounds besides [d] in which the simple form may end are the vowels, diphthongs, and [b], [g], [m], [n], [ŋ], [v], [ð], [l], [r], [z], [ʒ], and [dʒ].

breathe – breathed	enjoy – enjoyed	sag – sagged
bang – banged	harm – harmed	star – starred
believe – believed	judge – judged	study – studied
call – called	plan – planned	suppose – supposed
consider – considered	rouge – rouged	try – tried
describe – described		

Also, see § -*ed* Adjective.

SUFFIX -*S*

1. The suffix -*s* has three different uses:

a. To indicate the third person singular, present tense, of regular verbs

b. To indicate the plural of regular nouns

c. To indicate the genitive of nouns

2. The spelling for the third person singular of verbs and for the plural of nouns is similar:

a. For most words we add -*s* directly.

ache – aches	cause – causes	laugh – laughs
actor – actors	freeze – freezes	like – likes
boy – boys	hate – hates	monkey – monkeys
breath – breaths	image – images	stop – stops
case – cases	judge – judges	thing – things

b. We add -*es* when a word ends in the letters *s, sh,* or *x.*

loss–losses	wish – wishes
campus – campuses	box – boxes

c. We add -*es* after *ch* pronounced [tʃ] but -*s* after *ch* pronounced [k].

church – churches
monarch – monarchs

d. We add -*es* when *y* is changed to *i.*

lady – ladies
carry – carries

For an elaboration of these rules, see § Spelling—Word with Suffix.

3. The rules for spelling the genitive can be simplified as follows:

a. Add -'*s* if the word does not end in the letter *s.*

b. Add only the apostrophe if the word ends in *s*.

actor – actor's	John – John's	actresses – actresses'
boy – boy's	lady – lady's	boys – boys'
man – man's	actors – actors'	James – James'
men – men's	actress – actress'	ladies – ladies'

For an elaboration of and some exceptions to those rules, see § Apostrophe.

4. The pronunciation of the suffix (*-s, -es,* or *-'s*) follows three rules. (See § Phonetic Symbol for the explanation of the symbols given in brackets below.)

a. If the preceding sound is [s], [z], [ʃ], [ʒ], [tʃ], or [dʒ], the suffix is pronounced [ɪz].

box – boxes	freeze – freezes	mirage – mirages
bus – busses	quiz – quizzes	image – images
case – cases	wish – wishes	church – churches'
cause – causes	brush – brushes	judge – judge's

b. If the preceding sound is [p], [t], [k], [f], or [θ], the suffix is pronounced [s].

hope – hopes	hat – hats	cake – cakes	chief – chiefs'
stop – stops	hate – hates	moth – moths	Jack – Jack's

c. If the preceding sound is not one of those listed in *a* or *b* above, the suffix is pronounced [z].

baby – babies	fur – furs	rule – rules
believe – believes	grow – grows	shade – shades
Bob – Bob's	knee – knees	shoe – shoes
breathe – breathes	Mary – Mary's	star – stars
calm – calms	ring – rings	way – ways
draw – draws	robe – robes	woman – woman's
fad – fads	rug – rugs	

5. The three rules above can be stated in another form. For this purpose, we can use the word *sibilants* for the sounds [s], [z], [ʃ], [ʒ], [tʃ], and [dʒ].

a. If the preceding sound is a sibilant, the suffix is pronounced [ɪz].

b. If the preceding sound is voiceless and not a sibilant, the suffix is pronounced [s].

c. If the preceding sound is voiced and not a sibilant, the suffix is pronounced [z].

6. The contraction *-'s* for the words *is* and *has* is pronounced like the suffix *-s*.

a. After a word ending with one of the sounds listed in ¶ 4, *b*, above, *-'s* is pronounced [s].

The shop's empty. It's been shut for a week.

b. After a word ending with one of the sounds listed in ¶ 4, *c*, above, -*'s* is pronounced [z].

> The man's in Chicago. He's been there since last Monday.

c. After a word ending with one of the sounds listed in ¶ 4, *a*, above, the contraction is not used. *Is* is pronounced [ɪz]. Stressed *has* is pronounced [hæz], and unstressed *has* is pronounced [əz].

> English is easy. My wish has come true, hasn't it?

-*SURE* ENDING   S.21

1. Unstressed -*sure* at the end of a word is pronounced [ʒɚ]. Some examples are *leisure, measure, pleasure,* and *treasure.*

2. The word *pressure* is pronounced [ˈprɛʃɚ].

3. The words *insure* and *assure,* as well as their derivatives such as *insurance* and *assurance,* are stressed on the second syllable: [ɪnˈʃʊr] and [əˈʃʊr].

SYLLABIC CONSONANT   S.22

1. A number of words have an unstressed syllable that is pronounced without a vowel. The syllable begins with [d] or [t] and ends in [n] or [l]. Such a syllable has a "syllabic *n*" or a "syllabic *l.*"

2. To make a syllabic *n*, put your tongue tip on your tooth ridge for the [d] or [t], and leave it there while you let your breath out through your nose. Don't move your tongue before you start the [n]; if you do, you will probably make a vowel sound. Don't stress the [n] syllable; stress the preceding syllable. Here are some words that are usually pronounced with syllabic *n:*

brighten	curtain	hidden
Britain	eaten	pardon
button	forgotten	satin
certain	garden	sudden

3. You can add other sounds after a syllabic *n.* Here are some examples:

certainly	important	suddenly
importance	pardoned	tightens

4. The contraction -*n't* is pronounced with a syllabic *n* in *didn't, wouldn't, couldn't,* and *shouldn't.* The word *and* is frequently pronounced only as a syllabic *n*, as in "bread and butter" and "right and left."

5. Syllabic *l* occurs under the same conditions as those for syllabic *n*—that is, in an unstressed syllable after [d] or [t]. Put your tongue tip on your tooth ridge for the [d] or [t], and leave it there while you pronounce the [l] by letting your breath come over the sides of your tongue. Here are some examples:

cattle	ladle	riddles
cradle	little	settles
fiddle	middle	bottled
huddle	noodle	paddled
idle	poodle	puddle
idol	battles	saddled

T

T INTERVOCALIC — T.1

1. Sometimes a *t* sounds like a *d.* That happens in ordinary speaking when the *t* comes between two voiced sounds. For example, *matter* may sound like *madder*, *atom* like *Adam*, *twenty* like *twendy*, *little* like *liddle*, *city* like *ciddy*, and *butter* like *budder.* When people speak slowly or emphatically, however, they usually pronounce that kind of *t* like [t] and not like [d]. Also, a *t* does not sound like [d] when it precedes a stressed vowel, as in *return*, or when it comes after a voiceless consonant, as in *after.*

TAKE—IN PHRASE — T.2

1. The verb *take* is used in the following phrases:

> *take [someone's] advice.* If you are wise, you will take Paul's advice and study hard.
> *take a course* (or *class*). I am going to take a course in economics next semester.
> *take a day* (or *some time*) *off.* I am going to take a day off and go to the beach.
> *take it easy,* "relax; don't worry." Don't get excited. Take it easy.
> *take [something] hard,* "be greatly affected emotionally by." Sam took Mary's death hard. Mr. Simmons' wife took it hard when he lost his job.
> *take place,* "happen." When did that meeting take place?
> *take a test* (or *examination, quiz*). You have to take a test before you register.
> *take time.* Learning takes time. There is no way of speeding it up.
> *take one's time.* Take your time; don't hurry.
> *take a train* (or *bus, car, plane, subway, taxi*). We are going to take the train soon. It is quickest to take the subway to Times Square. The strike made people take taxis instead of busses. I am going to take my car; you can ride with me.
> *take a trip.* Are you going to take a trip during the Christmas holidays?
> *take a vacation* (or *holiday*). Miss Cluny will take her vacation in October.
> *take a walk* (or *a stroll*). After lunch, Phillip takes a walk to aid his digestion.

Also, see § Preposition—Expression with.

TELL—IN PHRASE — T.3

1. The verb *tell* is used in the following phrases:

> *tell apart,* "recognize a difference between." Can you tell those twins apart?
> *tell [one] from [another],* "distinguish between." I can not tell Herbert from his brother: they look alike.
> *tell a story* (or *joke, lie, tale,* etc.). The children want you to tell them a story.
> *tell time.* Their six-year-old son is learning to tell time; now he wants a watch.
> *tell the time.* Can you tell me the time? I left my watch at home.
> *tell the truth.* You can't believe a thing Jack says. He just can't tell the truth. To tell the truth, I don't really like him.

t

2. If the person who is told something comes next to *tell,* the word *to* is not used.

> What did you tell the children? I told them a fairy story.   *but*   I told a fairy story to them.

For differences between *say* and *tell,* see § Direct vs. Indirect Speech. Also, see § Preposition—Expression with.

TENSE AND TIME   T.4

1. The English speaker, like speakers of many other languages, can conceive of many different kinds of time: "right now," "yesterday," "tomorrow," "the day before yesterday," "the day after tomorrow," etc. He can conceive of interrelationships between kinds of time: "yesterday and today and tomorrow," "yesterday and tomorrow even though not right now," etc. He has a wealth of words denoting time: "soon," "formerly," "Tuesday," "day after day," "last year," "a short time ago," etc.

As far as verb *forms* go, however, the English speaker has only two categories of time: *past* and *not past.*

2. It is extremely important for you to realize that every time an English speaker makes an utterance, he assigns one of those two kinds of verb time to every verb expression. He can put together some very complicated combinations of verb forms, but in each combination, usually at the very beginning, he asserts "past" or "not past." For example, in the following combinations, the first of each pair is stated to be "not past" and the second is stated to be "past" by the first word in the combinations:

can go	could go
is going to say	was going to say
has been raining	had been raining
will have been killed	would have been killed

3. I know that it is customary to talk about three kinds of time: *past time, present time,* and *future time.* As a matter of fact, I am going to follow that custom in the next sections. However, before doing so, I want to point out that the *future tenses* observe that division between "past" and "not past."

There are two kinds of *future time* in verb forms. The first is usually called *present future* although a better designation is *not-past future.* The second is called *past future.* In the two examples below I will express the same idea about John's winning something in the future:

> Today I *believe* that John *will* win.
> Yesterday I *believed* that John *would* win.

Notice that the verb form *will* is used in the first sentence, which expresses a not-past time, and that the verb form *would* is used in the second sentence, which expresses a past time. Such a distinction in forms is made automatically by the English speaker: it is a habit with him even though to speakers of some other languages that distinction seems quite unnecessary. See § Sequence of Tense.

Now I will get a bit philosophical, but I hope my philosophizing will help you learn the use of the English tense forms.

4. Suppose I want to express something that is *not* true. I have two tense forms to work with. I use the not-past form for something that *is* true. Therefore, why can't I use the past form for something that is not true? Isn't it more or less logical to do so? If I express a wish for something that I know can not happen, can't I use the past form of the verb *can* to indicate that I realize that impossibility?

> I wish I could go. [I know I can not go.]

See § *Wish* vs. *Hope* vs. *Want* vs. *Would Like.*

5. The same idea of "not true" is expressed by using the past verb forms in "unreal" not-past conditional sentences.

> If John had an excuse, he would be absent tomorrow. [John does *not* have an excuse; he will *not* be absent tomorrow.]

See § Conditional Sentence.

6. The important thing for you to remember is that *time* and *tense* are not synonyms. *Time* concerns matters like "right now" and "yesterday" and "tomorrow." *Tense* is a verb form or a combination of verb forms. *Tense* is used not only to express time; it also expresses grammatical relationship ("I believed he *would* win") and reality or unreality ("I wish I could go").

The following sections summarize the major tense forms and their uses. As I said before, I will use the ordinary terminology for the tenses even though some of the names are quite illogical with reference to time. You should remember that the operation of sequence of tense may require the converting of one tense form to another.

The order of discussion of the tenses will be this:

Simple present
Continuous present
Perfect present
Continuous perfect present

Simple past
Continuous past
Perfect past
Continuous perfect past
Habitual past

Simple future
Continuous future
Perfect future
Continuous perfect future
Future substitute

t

1. This tense is also called *timeless, factual, general, customary,* and *habitual.*

2. Forms:

[I, you, we, they] *work.*	[He, she, it] *works.*
[I, you, we, they] *do* not *work.*	[He, she, it] *does* not *work.*
Do [I, you, we, they] [not] *work?*	*Does* [he, she, it] [not] *work?*

3. Use:

a. To express a "general truth" or, similarly, a repeated or customary act or state. This form may be called *timeless* because it usually includes past, present, and future time. The word *whenever* and adverbs of frequency such as *always* and *usually* often accompany this tense.

> The earth rotates on its axis.
> Apples grow on trees.
> Mario speaks Italian; he does not speak English.
> Do you play the piano?
> I go to school four times a week.
> Does Mr. Caputo write very clearly?
> Katrinka gets up at seven o'clock every morning.
> Whenever Sylvester goes to Rome, he visits the Coliseum.
> I usually visit Burma in the summer.
> Conscientious students always study their lessons.
> Mrs. Simpson regularly goes to church on Sunday.
> It gets very hot in New York in the summer.

b. To express a state or condition with the following verbs. Most of the verbs indicate a mental or emotional state.

agree	distrust	love	resemble
appear	doubt	matter	result
be	equal	mean	see
believe	feel ("believe")	mind ("object to")	seem
belong	find	need	smell
care	foresee	notice	suffice
consist	forget	owe	suppose
contain	forgive	own	taste
depend	hate	please	think ("believe")
deserve	have ("possess")	possess	trust
desire	hear	prefer	understand
detest	hope	recall	want
differ	imagine	recognize	wish
disagree	know	recollect	
dislike	like	remember	

I agree with you completely.
My cat likes milk.

Oh, yes, I know his name.
This coffee tastes good.
Do you think so?
I want to go with you.
Stan prefers to stay home.
I remember Julia very well.

A few of the preceding verbs may also be used to indicate an act. When they do, they are often used in a continuous tense.

I am thinking about taking a trip.
The cook is tasting the milk to see if it is sour.

c. To quote an author or publication. The verb is usually *say* or *tell.*

Shakespeare *says,* "All the world's a stage."
The Bible *tells* us to honor our father and our mother.
The Bible *urges* us to love our neighbors.
Today's paper *says* that the weather will be fair tomorrow.
The poem *expresses* the poet's love of nature.

d. To express the "historical present." Some narratives are told almost entirely in the simple tense. However, since the technique is quite complicated, I recommend that you not use it.

e. To give stage directions.

The King (*walks* to throne and *sits* down): Where is the Queen?

Also, see § Tense—Future Substitute.

TENSE—CONTINUOUS PRESENT   T.6

1. This tense is also called *true, temporary, progressive,* and *definite.*

2. Forms:

[I] *am working*
[you, we, they] *are working*
[he, she, it] *is working*

3. Use: To express an action taking place in the present and having some duration, even if compared only with the instant or *now.* The time is essentially the present *in contrast to* the past or the future. This tense usually accompanies words like *right now, for the time being,* and *for the present.* A mnemonic aid is this: the verb form can frequently be divided by the phrase *in the act of;* for example, "I am [in the act of] reading this book right now."

Mary is writing a letter right now. She started a few minutes ago.
The room is getting dark. The sun is going down.
I am taking psychology this semester.

> Ralph is concentrating on English this semester.
> The idea of slavery is gradually being discarded.

Also, see § Tense—Future Substitute.

TENSE—PERFECT PRESENT   T.7

1. This tense is also called *present perfect* and *past indefinite.* The perfect present is a present tense because its use always implies a relationship with the present time. It may be said to preserve the idea of continuity between past time and present time (see ¶ 3, *c,* below), while the simple past and the other past tenses tend to make a sharp distinction between the past and the present.

2. Forms:

> [I, you, we, they] *have seen*
> [he, she, it] *has seen*

3. Use:

a. To express an action or state begun in the past which has continued *up to and into* the present. This tense usually accompanies the time words *since, so far, up to now,* and *up to the present.*

> Bill has lived in New York since 1940.
> I have studied English for a long time.
> For the past few years, my reading has been limited to newspapers.
> Americans have always wanted to be known as "rugged individualists."
> The essence of music has not changed since the beginning of time.

b. To express an action or state which was repeated in the past *and* which will possibly be repeated in the future

> We have eaten in that restaurant many times.
> I have used this razor blade only three times; it is still good.
> Since my arrival in the United States, I have lived in rather small rooms.
> Automobiles have constantly been improved by new inventions.

c. To express an action that occurred at an *unspecified* time in the past. Since words like *already, at last, ever, finally, just, lately, never, recently,* and *yet* do not necessarily indicate an exact time, they often accompany this tense.

   This use, I suppose, is the most illogical. Also, speakers seem to be inconsistent about using it or the simple past; they sometimes say, "Did you do it?" and sometimes "Have you done it?" My advice is this: choose the perfect present whenever your hearer or reader has no way of knowing the exact time when the action took place; it may have been a second before or years before.

> I have eaten there only once. [Compare: I ate there last night for the first time.]
> I have already seen that movie. [Compare: I saw that movie ten years ago.]

Jim has changed his attitude toward women. [Compare: Jim changed his attitude toward women when his fiancée jilted him.]

Although Barbara has traveled through most of Europe, she has not visited Rome. [Compare: Although Barbara used to travel through Europe, she never visited Rome.]

I have just remembered his name. [Compare: I remembered his name just a moment ago.]

Mrs. Rush's baby has finally begun to walk. [Compare: Mrs. Rush's baby began to walk yesterday.]

I have never met Mr. Watson. [Compare: I had never met Mr. Watson until you introduced us.]

TENSE—CONTINUOUS PERFECT PRESENT   T.8

1. Forms:

[I, you, we, they] *have been studying*
[he, she, it] *has been studying*

2. Use: To emphasize the duration of time more than the perfect-present use *a* does in expressing an action or state begun in the past which has continued into the present. Note that this tense is *not* used alternatively with the perfect-present uses *b* and *c.*

Ever since its premiere a year ago, we have been wanting to see that play.
The Johnsons' radio has been playing for two hours.
We have been having fine weather for the past few days.

TENSE—SIMPLE PAST   T.9

1. This tense is also called *past definite* and *preterit* or *preterite.*

2. Forms:

[I, you, we, he, she, it, they] *worked.*
[I, you, we, he, she, it, they] *did* not *work.*
Did [I, you, we, he, she, it, they] [not] *work?*

3. Use:

a. To express a completed action which occurred at a *specified* time in the past. This tense is almost always accompanied by a word, phrase, or dependent clause denoting the time in the past. The word *ago* is usually accompanied by this tense. Notice the time expressions in the examples.

I studied Italian before the war.
Robert arrived at ten o'clock last night.
My former teacher told me that.
Chaucer lived in the Middle Ages.

> Oh, yes, Bill and I met a couple of weeks ago.
> Mr. Billings came to New York a long time ago.
> I was in my room when the accident happened.

b. To express a series of past actions, all of which are viewed in relation to the present time, not to each other

> I got up this morning at seven o'clock, dressed, ate breakfast, and went to work.
> Charles got a job in a grocery store, but it did not suit him. Then, he worked for a time in a bank. Finally, he found a position in a finance company which he liked. He kept it for the rest of his life.

c. To convert a simple present in past direct speech into indirect speech. See § Direct vs. Indirect Speech.

> Marvin said, "I *live* on Fifth Avenue."
> Marvin said he *lived* on Fifth Avenue.

d. To express an unreal present condition. See § Conditional Sentence and § *Wish* vs. *Hope* vs. *Want* vs. *Would Like.*

> If you *governed* the world, what *would* you *do?*
> I *wish* I *had* a lot of money.

Also, see § Tense—Habitual Past.

TENSE—CONTINUOUS PAST   T.10

1. This tense is also called *imperfect* and *temporary past.*

2. Forms:

> [I, he, she, it] *was singing*
> [you, we, they] *were singing*

3. Use:

a. To express an action taking place when another action happened. The word *while* meaning "during the time that" is often used with this tense.

> Helen was driving when the accident occurred.
> While I was living in Africa, I went on a lion hunt.
> When the guest arrived, Mrs. Parker was sweeping the floor, and her husband was washing the dishes.
> I suddenly realized that the stranger was speaking to me.

b. To emphasize the duration of time more than the simple past does. It is frequently used to show the simultaneousness of two actions.

While I was hesitating, time was passing by.
Sarah did not care what people were saying about her.

c. To convert a continuous present in past direct speech into indirect speech

Millie replied, "I *am coming* at once."
Millie replied that she *was coming* at once.

TENSE—PERFECT PAST   T.11

1. This tense is also called *past perfect* and *pluperfect.*

2. Form:

[I, you, we, he, she, it, they] *had visited*

3. Use:

a. To express an action (1) which occurred or was completed before another action or time in the past or (2) which continued up to another time in the past. The earlier action is related to the later past time, not to the present time.

Karl thought he had met Miss Cochrane in Paris in 1940.
Until yesterday Martha had seen only one movie in her life.
By Easter, Mr. Gordon had planted his garden and had put a new roof on the tool shed.
The landlord believed that Miss Rostand had lived there for about eight years.
I supposed that my teacher had kept a record of my attendance.

The simple past is often employed instead of the perfect past with the words *before* and *after*—for example, "After he *finished* the book, he threw it away." The perfect past, however, is necessary to show your exact meaning with other words, as in the example below with *when:*

The guest of honor had left when we arrived. [Compare: "The guest of honor left when we arrived." Here the actions are simultaneous.]

b. To convert either a simple past or a perfect present in past direct speech into indirect speech

Mr. Lindley said, "I *was* there last night."
Mr. Lindley said that he *had been* there the night before.
Charlotte said, "I *have* never *seen* such a beautiful sight."
Charlotte said that she *had* never *seen* such a beautiful sight.

c. To express an unreal past condition. See § Conditional Sentence and § *Wish* vs. *Hope* vs. *Want* vs. *Would Like.*

If Paul had studied harder last semester, he would have got a better grade.
I wish I had gone to the movie last night.

t

TENSE—CONTINUOUS PERFECT PAST

T.12

1. Form:

[I, you, we, he, she, it, they] *had been waiting*

2. Use:

a. To emphasize the duration of time more than the perfect past does in expressing an action or state which continued up to a time in the past

> Mrs. Carlson had been working in the office for two years before she got a raise.
> The Joneses had been wanting to see the Metropolitan Museum a long time before they had a chance to see it.

b. To convert either a continuous past or a continuous perfect present in past direct speech into indirect speech

> Sue answered, "I *was listening* to the radio."
> Sue answered that she *had been listening* to the radio.
> Ruth exclaimed, "I *have been hoping* to hear him say that."
> Ruth exclaimed that she *had been hoping* to hear him say that.

TENSE—HABITUAL PAST

T.13

1. Forms:

[I, we, you, he, she, it, they] *used to smoke.*
[I, we, you, he, she, it, they] *used* not *to smoke.*
[I, we, you, he, she, it, they] *did* not *use to smoke.*
Did [I, we, you, he, she, it, they] [not] *use to smoke?*

2. Use: To express an action which was repeated or was habitual in the past but which occurs no longer. Contrast with the present time is always implied, if not expressed.

> I used to walk to my office, but now I take the bus.
> John used to say that he did not like girls.
> You didn't use to treat me like that.
> You used not to say unkind things to me.
> Did you use to see a lot of movies?
> Didn't you use to live on Fifth Avenue?

3. The *used to* can not be made to show present time by dropping the final *-d*. The simple present is the present-time equivalent of the habitual past.

> I take the bus to my office nowadays, but I used to walk.

4. *Be* (or *get* or *become*) **used to** means "be (get, become) accustomed to" and is followed by a noun, pronoun, or gerund, not an infinitive.

> Andrew is used to working ten hours a day.
> People prefer the kind of food they are used to eating.
> Have you got used to the noises of this city?
> Mrs. Patton finally became used to her husband's complaining.

5. The customary pronunciation of *used to* in all the above examples is ['justə].

6. Both the simple past (*smoked,* for example) and the past future (*would smoke*) are used to express a past habit, but they usually need a time word, phrase, or dependent clause to complete the connotation of habit.

> The boy's mother would punish him whenever he was naughty.
> In my childhood, ghost stories would always frighten me.
> I walked to my office every day before I bought a car.
> My father gave us exciting gifts every Christmas.

TENSE—FUTURE   T.14

As it is stated in § Tense and Time, there are two kinds of future tense: *present* (or "not past") and *past.* In the sections below, I will give the present-future form as the lead form and then give the past-future equivalent.

TENSE—SIMPLE FUTURE   T.15

1. Form:

> [I, you, we, he, she, it, they] *will learn*

For the form *shall learn,* see § *Shall.* In conversation or dialog, the contraction *'ll,* pronounced [l], is customary.

2. Use: To express intended or expected action in the future

> I will see you tomorrow.
> John will write the letter soon.

3. Past equivalent (*past simple future*): *would learn*

> I told you that I would see you tomorrow.
> His parents knew that John would write the letter soon.

4. The past simple future is also used to express the result of an unreal present condition. See § Conditional Sentence.

> If I had a lot of money, I would buy a car immediately.

t

1. Form:

[I, you, we, he, she, it, they] *will be writing*

2. Use: To express an action taking place *at* or *up to* a certain time in the future

I will be writing the letter when you arrive.
The cleaners will be working at twelve o'clock.
The doctor will be operating for another half hour.

3. Past equivalent (*past continuous future*): *would be writing*

I had no idea that I would be writing the letter when you arrived.
The nurse informed me a moment ago that the doctor would be operating for another half hour.

4. The past continuous future is also used to express the result of an unreal present condition. See § Conditional Sentence.

If I were you, I would be studying right now.

TENSE—PERFECT FUTURE   T.17

1. Form:

[I, you, we, he, she, it, they] *will have left*

2. Use: To express an action which will occur or will be completed before another action or a time in the future

We will have left before the mail arrives.
All the roses will have died before Christmas.

3. Past equivalent (*past perfect future*): *would have left*

I told the cook a few minutes ago that we would have left before eight o'clock tomorrow morning.
The youngster was not convinced that all the roses would have died before Christmas.

4. The past perfect future is also used to express the result of an unreal past condition. See § Conditional Sentence.

If I had known the train schedule, I would have met you at the station.

TENSE—CONTINUOUS PERFECT FUTURE   T.18

1. Form:

[I, you, we, he, she, it, they] *will have been writing*

2. Use: To emphasize that an action has been taking place up to the time of another action in the future

> By the time you arrive tonight, I will have been studying for two hours.

3. Past equivalent (*past continuous perfect future*): *would have been writing*

> I did not suspect that by the time you arrived last night, I would have been studying for two hours.

4. The past continuous perfect future is also used to express the result of an unreal past condition. See § Conditional Sentence.

> If I had been wise, I would have been studying at eight o'clock last night.

TENSE—FUTURE SUBSTITUTE   T.19

The following forms are sometimes called *future substitutes.*

1. *Be going to* + infinitive.

a. FORMS:

> [I] *am going to read*
> [you, we, they] *are going to read*
> [he, she, it] *is going to read*

b. USE: To express intended future action. This tense is considered to be less emphatic than the simple future and is probably used more frequently than the latter in conversation.

> Jack is going to buy a new hat some day.

c. PAST EQUIVALENT: *was* or *were going to read*

> Jack's wife stopped complaining when she found out that he was going to buy her a new hat.

2. Simple present tense

FORMS:

> [I, we, you, they] *leave*
> [he, she, it] *leaves*

USE:

a. To express future action, usually with a word, phrase, or clause indicating future time (e.g., *tomorrow, next week*). This tense is usually limited to verbs of motion such as *arrive, come, depart, go, head, leave, sail,* and *start.*

> Alice's brother leaves for Europe tomorrow.

PAST EQUIVALENT: usually not converted into the simple past; *would leave* and *was (were) leaving* are more common.

> Alice said that her brother was leaving for Europe the next day.

b. To express future action in an adverbial dependent clause beginning with *if, when, before, as long as, as soon as, until, unless,* etc., if the time of the principal verb is future. Also, see § Conditional Sentence.

> If I finish my homework soon, I will go with you.   *but*   I do not know when Mae will return. [In the second sentence the time of the principal verb is the present, and the dependent clause is not adverbial.]

This use of the simple present tense in dependent clauses expressing future time is one of the constructions which you should practice very much. Here is a helpful hint: the dependent clause expresses time just as the word *tomorrow* does in "I will pay him tomorrow."

I will pay him	tomorrow.
I will pay him	when I see him.
I will pay him	before he leaves.
I will pay him	as long as he works hard.
I will pay him	unless he objects.
I will pay him	as soon as I get some money.
I will pay him	until he gets a job.
I will pay him	if he works hard.

PAST EQUIVALENT (*simple past*): *left*

> Paul said that if he finished his homework soon, he would go with us.
> Mr. Smith said that when he returned, he would talk with you.

3. Continuous present tense

FORMS:

> [I] *am leaving*
> [you, we, they] *are leaving*
> [he, she, it] *is leaving*

USE: To express future action just as the simple present does in the use in ¶ 2, *a,* above.

> Mr. Johnson is leaving for Chicago tomorrow.

PAST EQUIVALENT: *was (were) leaving*

> The company announced that Mr. Johnson was leaving for Chicago the next day.

4. *Be to* + infinitive.

FORMS:

> [I] *am to take*
> [you, we, they] *are to take*
> [he, she, it] *is to take*

USE: To express future action, usually with the connotation of plan, appointment, obligation, or necessity.

> Miss Astor is to ride with us.
> We are to see the doctor tomorrow.

PAST EQUIVALENT: *was (were) to take*

> Miss Astor was happy when she learned that she was to ride with us.
> When Father heard about the epidemic, he said that we were to see the doctor at once.

5. *Be about to* + infinitive.

FORMS:

> [I] *am about to buy*
> [you, we, they] *are about to buy*
> [he, she, it] *is about to buy*

USE: To express a future action, usually with the connotation of "very soon"

> It is about to rain.

PAST EQUIVALENT: *was (were) about to buy*

> We stayed at home because it was about to rain.

THIS **AND** *THESE*   T.20

1. Be careful about the words *this* and *these* in writing. Use them to refer to things close at hand, either in place or time.

> I am glad I came to this city. Living in this community has broadened my out-look considerably.
> Next month I am going to Idaho. This month I have to stay home.

2. Very often the word *that, those,* or *the* is more appropriate than *this* or *these.*

> I have heard a lot about Burma and Thailand, but I have never been to those countries.
> I have been invited to my first college football game and prom next Saturday. The game is between Harvard and Princeton.

3. Do not use *this* to refer to something that you have not expressed. Remember that your reader can not read your mind, at least not easily. If he has to stop to figure out what you mean, you are giving him an unnecessary task.

4. Do not use *this, that, it,* or any similar word at the beginning of a composition to refer to the title. The title is not part of the body of the composition. If necessary, begin the body of the composition with the same words that the title has.

t

TRANSITION EXPRESSION

1. A transition word or phrase indicates an addition to a preceding statement. Such expressions are used like adverbs (some of them are sometimes called *conjunctive adverbs*). Most of them are movable: they usually come at the beginning of the addition, but some also occur in other positions. In the example below, the word *besides* is a transition expression.

> I do not want to go to that movie. Besides, I am too busy.

2. You help your reader by setting off transition expressions with punctuation. Commas are the usual marks.

3. Very frequently the addition is joined directly to the preceding statement without the coordinating conjunctions *and, but, or,* or *nor.* If the addition is an independent clause, a semicolon comes before it, and the transition expression is marked off with a comma or commas. In the following set of examples, *however* is a transition word.

> History is a record of mankind; however, different historians interpret it differently.
> History is a record of mankind; different historians, however, interpret it differently.
> History is a record of mankind; different historians interpret it differently, however.

4. The transition expressions can be divided into three groups according to the kind of addition they indicate: *including, contrasting,* and *summarizing.*

5. Including:

a. Set off the following transition expressions with commas wherever they occur:

besides	furthermore	incidentally
by the way	in addition	moreover

> Pat should not have told you that secret. Furthermore, you should not have repeated it.
> Water goggles and masks have become popular in underwater swimming. Masks are forbidden, by the way, at some beaches.

b. Set off the following *time-sequence* transition expressions with a comma only when they begin the addition.

first	afterwards	at last
first of all	later	last
second	next	finally
third	then	

> Registration is complicated. First, you select your courses. Next, you talk with an adviser. You then fill out your forms, and finally you pay your fees.

c. Set off *also, too,* and *similarly* with a comma when they begin the addition.

> You did your exercise incorrectly. Also, you did not turn it in on time. *or* You also did not turn it in on time.
>
> Icelanders complain about New York in the summer; similarly Ecuadorians suffer during the winter here.

d. Set off *either, too,* and *etc.* with a comma when they come at the end of the addition.

> Paul does not like Ruth, and I don't, either.
> Jonathan went to the movies, and his sister did, too.
> That store sells all kinds of pets: cats, dogs, monkeys, etc.

e. The words *especially, notably, particularly, in particular, chiefly, let alone, not to mention,* and *to say nothing of* often introduce an addition which is not an independent clause. Put a comma before them and, unless they end their clause, at the end of the addition.

> Juan's English improved rapidly after he came to this country, especially after he moved in with an American family.
>
> The speaker discussed the curriculum in high schools, particularly the senior high schools.
>
> Some students are not serious enough about their attendance, not to mention their assignments.
>
> A few children, chiefly girls, cried when they heard the news.

If the addition has internal punctuation and comes within a sentence, use dashes or parentheses instead of commas to set off the addition.

> All the students—especially Harry, Bob, and Charles—were disturbed by the new rule.

f. The words which frequently introduce appositives—*i.e., namely, specifically, that is, that is to say,* and *viz.*—are marked off by a following comma, and the whole appositive is marked off by dashes or parentheses.

> The outstanding Elizabethan dramatists—namely, Marlowe, Jonson, and Shakespeare—set off their era from all others.

g. The words which introduce an example—*e.g., for example, for instance, let us say,* and *say*—are followed by a comma. Use either dashes or parentheses to mark off the whole example.

> The outstanding Elizabethan dramatists—for example, Shakespeare—set off their era from all others.

If the example is an independent clause, it may be set off as a complete sentence, or it may be attached to the preceding statement with a semicolon.

> Hubert is a mechanical genius. For instance, he can take a watch apart and put it together again without having any screws left over.
>
> Hubert is a mechanical genius; for instance, he can take a watch apart and put it together again without having any screws left over.

t

h. Do not put a comma after *and* joining two words, two phrases, or two clauses. Of course, sometimes a comma appears after *and,* as in the last example below.

> Martha and Grant are coming.
> Martha and Grant are coming to the party and staying overnight.
> Martha is coming, and Grant is, too.
> Martha is coming, and, by the way, Grant is, too.

6. Contrasting:

a. Mark these transition expressions off with commas wherever they occur:

> | all the same | just the same | on the other hand | yet |
> |---|---|---|---|
> | however | nevertheless | otherwise | |
> | instead | on the contrary | still | |

> Bob was supposed to be here at nine; he appeared at noon, however.
> I know you had a reason; just the same, you should not have hit him.
> I study very hard. My grades, nevertheless, are poor.
> Henry has a bad reputation. Still, he is a likable fellow.
> Night classes are a good idea. Otherwise, working people could not go to school.

b. The word *not* often introduces a contrasting word or construction. Set off the whole group with commas if it follows what it is in contrast to.

> John, not Robert, was responsible.
> I stayed because I was tired, not because I wanted to.

However, if the *not* construction precedes a contrasting *but* construction, use no commas.

> Not Robert but John was responsible.
> I stayed not because I wanted to but because I was tired.

c. The word *though* is a transition expression when it does not begin its addition (at the beginning of its addition it is a conjunction). Mark it off with commas unless it begins its addition.

> I work very hard. I do not make much progress, though.
> Jake's fever did not go down, though, even after he had taken the medicine.

d. Do not put a comma after the conjunction *but* joining two clauses.

> Martha is coming, but Grant is not.

Also, see § Opposition Expression.

7. Summarizing. Mark these transition expressions off with commas wherever they occur:

accordingly	as a consequence	at least
after all	as a matter of fact	consequently
anyway	at any rate	hence

in brief	in short	therefore
in fact	in that case	thus
in other words	then ("therefore")	

Hemingway's latest novel is very popular; it is, therefore, hard to get.
Ask Mark. He is a specialist, after all.
Burton is very rich; at least, he gives everybody that impression.
"I don't have a driver's license." "In that case, you'd better not drive."
"That's very difficult to explain." "In other words, you don't know."

Also, see § Clause—Independent and Adverbial.

TRANSITIVE VS. INTRANSITIVE

T.22

1. A verb which has a direct object is called a *transitive* verb. A verb which does not have a direct object is called an *intransitive* verb.

> The boy ate the apple. [*The apple* is the direct object of the verb *ate;* therefore, *ate* is transitive.]
> The child slept. [The verb *slept* has no direct object; therefore, it is intransitive.]

2. Certain verbs are used only transitively; some are used only intransitively, and some are used at times transitively and at other times intransitively.

3. A few verbs occur in pairs: one verb is used transitively, and the other of the pair is used intransitively. The most common of those pairs are the following (the first verb of each pair is transitive, and the other is intransitive): *lay – lie; raise – rise; set – sit.*

> You should lay the baby on the bed. The baby is lying on the bed.
> The storm raised the level of the lake. The level of the lake rose.
> You can set the bag on the table. The bag is sitting on the table.

-TURE ENDING

T.23

1. Unstressed *-ture* at the end of a word is pronounced [tʃɚ] in most cases. Some examples are the following: *adventure, capture, creature, feature, fixture, furniture, future, lecture, mixture, nature,* and *picture.* The words *literature* and *temperature,* however, are pronounced either [tʃɚ] or [tjʊr].

2. The words *mature, immature,* and *premature* have stress on the *-ture,* which is pronounced [tjʊr] or [tʊr].

TWO-WORD VERB

T.24

1. A *two-word verb* is a combination of a verb and a particle which together have a meaning different from the customary meanings of the two words. A *particle* is a short word which is often used as a preposition or an adverb.

t

2. For example, in the sentence "The man will call up the stairs" the verb *call* has its customary meaning of "speak loudly," and *up* has its customary meaning of "from below to a higher point." However, in the sentence "The man will call up his friends" the words *call* and *up* have the meaning of the verb "telephone." Therefore, in the second sentence, the combination of *call* and *up* is classified as a two-word verb, but in the first sentence it is not.

3. Similarly, *run* and *across* in the sentence "Don't run across the street; walk slowly" have their usual meanings, but in "He likes to run across his friends" the two words mean "meet unexpectedly." In the second sentence *run* and *across* constitute a two-word verb; in the first sentence they do not.

4. Two-word verbs are extremely frequent in conversation and in all but the most formal writing.

5. One of the characteristics of two-word verbs is that almost all of the words which make them up are short and very common. The verbs are usually these:

back	catch	fall	hold	pick	take
be	come	figure	keep	put	talk
break	count	get	let	run	throw
bring	cut	give	look	see	try
call	do	go	make	set	turn
carry	draw	have	pass	stand	work

6. The particles are usually these:

about	around	back	for	of	out	to
across	at	by	in	off	over	up
along	away	down	into	on	through	with

7. With some combinations the particle may shift its position in the sentence, but with others the particle can not shift. For example, we may say either "The man will call up his friends" or "The man will call his friends up," and we have exactly the same *meaning*. That kind of two-word verb is called *separable* because a noun may separate the particle from the verb.

8. However, we can say only "He likes to run across his friends." We can not shift *across* from its position immediately after *run* and have the same meaning. That kind of two-word verb is called *inseparable* because a noun may not separate the particle from the verb.

9. In speech, the particle of a separable two-word verb usually receives more stress than the verb, but the particle of an inseparable two-word verb does not.

10. Another difference between the two kinds of two-word verbs arises when a short, one-syllable pronoun like *me, you, him,* and *them* is used as an object. The *pronoun object* is placed *before* a separable particle, and it is placed *after* an inseparable particle. For example, if we substitute *them* for *his friends* in the two examples above, we say, "The man will call them up," and we say, "He likes to run across them." The position of *them* can not be changed in either sentence. Pronouns of more than one syllable, like *anybody* and *everything,* act like nouns: they can go before or after the separable particle.

11. Is there any sure way of determining whether a two-word verb is separable or inseparable? The answer is, unfortunately, "No." For example, in the sentence "The committee will see through the plan which you have suggested," the words *see through* may mean either "understand the hidden bad purpose of" or "help to a successful conclusion." However, with the first meaning, *see through* is inseparable; with the second meaning, it is separable. If you replace the words "the plan which you have suggested" with the pronoun *it,* the sentence must be "The committee will see through it" for the first meaning and "The committee will see it through" for the second.

The only way to be sure of the word order of two-word verbs is observation: listening to speakers and reading newspapers, magazines, and books, particularly those with informal style. There are certain clues or helpful hints about the word order, but they must be used with caution.

12. One hint is this: if you are relatively positive that the combination is a two-word verb, put a noun object after the particle. It is true that a few combinations sound more natural if the particle follows the noun object, especially, if the object is not heavily modified. ("The committee will see your plan through" sounds better for the second meaning above.) On the other hand, an inseparable combination split up by an object sounds completely unnatural and is often unintelligible.

13. Here is a warning: if you are not sure whether the combination is separable or inseparable, do not use a pronoun object. A short pronoun can not go after a separable particle, nor can it go before an inseparable particle.

14. Another clue is this: the reflexive pronouns (*myself, himself,* etc.) are not used as extensively in English as they are in some other languages. There is a tendency to omit them unless they are needed for clarity. For instance, you can say, "I'm going to get my coat on," and your listener will understand that you are going to put the coat on *yourself* and not on somebody else. Similarly, you can say, "I have to get on the eleven-thirty train," and your listener will understand that you must put *yourself* on the train. (For clarity, you might use the reflexive in a sentence like "I must get my wife on the ten-o'clock train and *myself* on the eleven-thirty.")

15. Now, which *get on* above is separable, and which is inseparable? The answer is this: (*a*) If the "understood" reflexive pronoun comes before the particle, the two-word verb is inseparable. Substituting *it* for "the eleven-thirty train" in the example above, we have "I have to get on it." (*b*) If the "understood" reflexive pronoun comes after the particle, the two-word verb is separable. Substituting *it* for "my coat" in the other example, we have "I'm going to get it on."

16. Again, here is a caution: the test of understood reflexive pronouns can be applied to only some of the two-word verbs, not all. However, it seems especially applicable to those with *get, keep, put,* and *take.*

17. As you probably suspect, the two-word verbs had a natural development although some of their present meanings seem quite unrelated to the original. For instance, from the robber's command to his victim, "Hold your hands up!" it is easy to develop the statement "A robber held me up last night." The idea of stopping or delaying is then not so strange in the sentence "The accident held traffic up for two hours."

18. Some of the particles seem to add little meaning to the verb, like *up* in the sentences "Your child is growing up rapidly" and "I want to wash up before dinner." However, in other expressions, the word *up* is used as an intensifier and does convey a connotation of "very much" or "utterly," as in "The gangsters beat him up and threw him out of the car" and "She read the letter and then tore it up." In such uses, where the particle modifies the verb without changing its customary meaning, the particle is separable.

19. A number of two-word verbs, both separable and inseparable, are followed by a second particle, which is almost always a preposition that has an object. Sometimes that second particle is an integral part of the expression, as *with* is in *put up with* in the first example below, and sometimes it is used only if its object is stated, as *to* is with *catch on* in the second example below:

> Mrs. Blake is so bad-tempered that I do not see how her husband can put up with ("endure") her.
> Percy sometimes can not catch on to ("understand") a joke quickly. It has to be explained before he can catch on.

20. Quite a few two-word verbs have become nouns. Some of them are hyphenated, and some are written together as one word—for example, *take-off* and *holdup*.

> I got to the airport just before the take-off. I managed to get on the plane.
> There was a holdup near my apartment last night. The robber got away.

21. In summary, the word order of the two kinds of two-word verbs is the following:

INSEPARABLE:

VERB	PARTICLE	OBJECT (NOUN OR PRONOUN)
Get	on	the train.
Get	on	it.

SEPARABLE:

1.

VERB	PARTICLE	NOUN OBJECT
Get	on	your coat.

VERB	NOUN OBJECT	PARTICLE
Get	your coat	on.

2.

VERB	PRONOUN OBJECT	PARTICLE
Get	it	on.

A great number of two-word verbs are listed under § Preposition—Expression with. If a combination there is followed by "(S)," that combination is separable. If a combination is not followed by "(S)," you may assume that it is inseparable. However, in all instances, read the illustrative sentences with an eye to the position of the particle.

UNDERLINING

1. In handwritten or typed material, underline the kinds of words which are customarily italicized in print. (Some people use the term *underscore* instead of *underline*.)

2. Underline titles of books, magazines, newspapers, plays, motion pictures, and book-length poems. Capitalize the first and last word and all the other words except the articles *the, a,* and *an* and short conjunctions (e.g., *and, but,* and *or*) and short prepositions (e.g., *in, on, with,* and *for*).

> Samuel Butler wrote The Way of All Flesh.
> I read that article you recommended in The Saturday Review.
> You Can't Take It with You was a hit on Broadway.
> We had to read Dante's Inferno in our Italian class.

However, use quotation marks around the title of a piece of writing that is or could be printed as part of a book or magazine, such as an essay, a short story, or most poems.

> I read "The President's Dilemma" in The Saturday Evening Post.
> One of Tennyson's most famous poems is "Crossing the Bar."

For the capitalization of titles, also see § Capitalization.

3. Underline the names of ships, trains, and airplanes.

> There is a new book about the sinking of the Titanic.

4. Underline numbers, letters, words, or phrases which are used as *citation forms.* Citation forms frequently occur in writing which deals with words; notice the numerous instances in these pages. The *-'s* which indicates the plurality of citation forms is also underlined. Set off definitions with quotation marks.

> The grade A denotes superior work.
> John is the most common name for boys.
> The verb be is the most irregular verb in English.
> Tear meaning "rip" is pronounced differently from tear meaning "eye water."
> Join the top line of your 5's to the downstroke.

In manuscript, use quotation marks around long groups of words, but underline a series composed of single words or short phrases. Your paper will look neater.

> In that sentence the clause "which are referred to as such" is used like an adjective.
> The most frequently misspelled words are too, lose, and then.

Also, see § Quotation Mark and § Parenthesis.

5. Underline foreign words and phrases. Set off definitions with quotation marks, and if they are not part of the main structure of the sentence, enclose them in parentheses.

> Harry peppers his speech with expressions like <u>alors</u>, <u>mais non</u>, and <u>bien</u>. The land is serried with <u>klongs</u> ("canals").

a. Many foreign terms are included in the ordinary English vocabulary. When they are used without reference to their origin, they are not italicized or underlined. If you are in doubt about the status of such an expression, consult an up-to-date dictionary.

b. A number of terms and abbreviations used in literary, scientific, and legal writing are sometimes italicized. Some examples are the following: <u>infra</u> ("below"), <u>passim</u> ("here and there"), <u>sic</u> ("thus; as given"), <u>supra</u> ("above"), <u>vide</u> ("see").

c. See § Abbreviation for other similar terms and abbreviations, most of which are not italicized.

6. Underline words which would be heavily stressed if spoken.

> I wanted <u>three</u> copies, not four.

You should be careful about underlining for emphasis because overuse of underlining tends to become annoying to your reader. It is associated with the type of exaggeration that many schoolgirls are prone to use in their writing.

1. We ordinarily do not repeat a main verb or its complement in the same sentence or in a following sentence. We can say that we "suppress" the second instance.

> The girls go to the movies when they want to. [Suppressed: a second "go to the movies" after the final *to*]
> Johnny washes his hands only if his mother makes him. [Suppressed: a second "wash his hands"]
> "Won't you come along?" "Yes, I'd like to." [Suppressed: a second "come along"]

2. We ordinarily express the *to* of a suppressed infinitive, particularly after these words: *able, afford, care, expect, glad, going* (meaning "in the future"), *have* (meaning "be obliged"), *hope, intend, like, need, ought, plan, used* (meaning "had the habit of"), *want,* and *willing.*

> Dora studies only when she has to.
> The boys do not argue as much as they used to.
> I want to work hard, and with your help I think I will be able to.

3. We do not express a *to* after these verbs: *feel, have* (meaning "cause; order"), *hear, help, let, listen, make, notice, observe, overhear, see,* and *watch.*

> That boy is going to do a trick. He wants you to watch him.
> Sara wants to have dates, but her mother will not let her.

4. We ordinarily express the auxiliary that is associated with the suppressed second instance of the main verb. For this discussion, we can refer to such an auxiliary as the *second verb.* The full form of the auxiliary is used, not a contraction like *-'s, -'ll,* and *-'ve.*

> Peter works as hard as he can. [Suppressed: a second "work" after *can*]
> I have finished the assignment. Have you? [Suppressed: a second "finished"]

5. We use the auxiliary *do* or *does* if the tense of the suppressed verb is simple present.

> "Mary sings well." "Yes, she does."

6. We use *did* if the tense of the suppressed verb is simple past.

> You received a better grade in that class than I did.

7. The exception to the two preceding rules is the verb *be,* which uses *am, is,* or *are* for the simple present and *was* or *were* for the simple past in a second instance.

> "Mary is a good singer." "Yes, she is."
> You are a better student than your father was.

8. Adverbs of degree or frequency precede the second verb. Most other adverbs follow the second verb.

"Can you prove that?" "I certainly can."
Paul always says he will do better work next time, but he never does.
I do not like to be late, but I frequently am.
You used to study harder than you do now.
We know more about the world than people did a long time ago.
Come as early as you can tomorrow.

9. The expressed main verb may be affirmative, and its second verb may be negative, or vice versa. The negative is usually expressed by *-n't*, except with *am*.

John works hard, but Mary doesn't.
Mr. Walton is not here, but his wife is.
Your teacher will explain it to you; I can't.
If your friends won't tell you, who will?
Harry is going, but I'm not.

10. If the second verb shows *affirmative* agreement with the expressed main verb, two word-order patterns may be used. The word *too* is used in the first pattern, and *so* is used in the second pattern.

My wife liked the book very much. I did, too.
My wife liked the book very much. So did I.
John can go with you, and Mary can, too.
John can go with you, and so can Mary.

11. If the second verb shows *negative* agreement with the expressed main verb, two word-order patterns may be used. The word *either* is used in the first pattern, and *neither* is used in the second.

My wife did not like the book. I didn't, either.
My wife did not like the book. Neither did I.
John can not go with you, and Mary can't either.
John can not go with you, and neither can Mary.

12. A frequent method of asking a question, particularly in conversation, employs a second verb. The construction is called a *tag* or *attached* or *shortened* question. To a statement, we attach a second verb and the personal pronoun equivalent to the subject of the statement (notice the exception in the last example). If the expressed main verb is affirmative, its second verb is negative; if the expressed main verb is negative, its second verb is affirmative. If the second verb is negative, the contraction *-n't* is customary except after *am*. (This construction is not used if the question has a *wh* word—*who, why,* etc.)

You saw John yesterday, didn't you?
Philip never studies, does he?
That was an interesting story, wasn't it?
The boys could have tried harder, couldn't they?
There is nobody absent today, is there?

13. If the subject of the question is different from the subject of the statement, the shortened question is made a separate sentence.

> I saw Mr. Warner. Did you?
> I have done all my homework. Haven't you?
> Walter never studies. Does his sister?

14. The answer to a question without a *wh* word may be either "Yes" followed by the affirmative of the second verb or "No" followed by the negative of the second verb. This kind of answer is sometimes referred to as a *brief response* or *short answer* or *tag answer.* It is the customary answer in conversation.

> "Did you see Mary yesterday?"
>   Affirmative answer: "Yes, I did."
>   Negative answer: "No, I didn't."
> "You saw Mary yesterday, didn't you?"
>   Agreeing answer: "Yes, I did."
>   Disagreeing answer: "No, I didn't."
> "Doesn't John ever study?"
>   Agreeing answer: "No, he never does."
>   Disagreeing answer: "Yes, he does."
> "John never studies, does he?"
>   Agreeing answer: "No, he doesn't."
>   Disagreeing answer: "Yes, he does."

The disagreeing answer often starts with an interjection such as *oh* and *why* (pronounced [waɪ]).

> Oh, no, I didn't.
> Why, yes, he does.

15. In comparisons the second verb is often omitted, but it should not be if the meaning would be unclear without it. Notice the last two examples. Also, see § Comparison.

> William is as tall as his brother.
> Barbara can not sing as well as Alice.
> I have lost more weight than you.
> Mother scolds me worse than she does Father.
> Mother scolds me worse than Father does.

Also, see § Auxiliary, § *It* vs. *There*, § Negative, § *So*—Substitute, and § Word Order—Emphatic Adverb.

VERB—REGULAR AND IRREGULAR

V.2

1. A *regular* verb is a verb whose past-tense form and past participle are expressed by the addition of the sound [t], [d], or [ɪd] to the simple or present form and whose past-tense form and past participle are spelled with the addition of the letter *d* or *-ed* to the simple form. The past-tense form and the past participle of a regular verb have the same pronunciation and spelling. The rules are given under § Suffix *-ed.* The vast majority of English verbs are regular.

V

2. An *irregular* verb is a verb whose past-tense form and past participle are not expressed by the addition of the sound [t], [d], or [ɪd] and whose past-tense form and past participle are not spelled with the addition of the letter *d* or *-ed.* Very frequently the past-tense form and the past participle of an irregular verb are not the same. Although the number of irregular verbs is relatively small, they are very frequent in occurrence. The spelling and pronunciation of their forms have to be learned individually.

3. The following list of the major irregular verbs gives the *principal parts*—that is, the simple form, the past-tense form, and the past participle, separated by dashes. A few verbs have alternative past-tense forms or past participles. Some regular verbs which are often confused with similar irregular verbs are included.

Not included in the list are recognizable compounds which conform to the pattern of the root verb. Some such compounds are *foresee* (like *see*), *misunderstand* (like *understand*), *repay* (like *pay*), and *undertake* (like *take*).

Here are the principal parts of the major irregular verbs:

arise – arose – arisen
awake – awoke, awaked – awoke,
  awaked
be – was, were – been
bear – bore – borne
beat – beat – beat, beaten
become – became – become
begin – began – begun
bend – bent – bent
bet – bet – bet
bid ("offer") – bid – bid
bid ("order") – bade – bidden
bind – bound – bound
bite – bit – bitten
bleed – bled – bled
blow – blew – blown
break – broke – broken
breed – bred – bred
bring – brought – brought
broadcast – broadcast, broadcasted – broadcast, broadcasted
build – built – built
burst – burst – burst
buy – bought – bought
can – could (no past participle)
cast – cast – cast
catch – caught – caught
choose – chose – chosen
cling – clung – clung
come – came – come
cost – cost – cost
creep – crept – crept
cut – cut – cut

deal – dealt – dealt
dig – dug, digged – dug, digged
dive – dived, dove – dived
do – did – done
draw – drew – drawn
dream – dreamed, dreamt – dreamed,
  dreamt
drink – drank – drunk
drive – drove – driven
dwell – dwelled, dwelt – dwelled,
  dwelt
eat – ate – eaten
fall – fell – fallen
feed – fed – fed
feel – felt – felt
fight – fought – fought
find – found – found
fit – fitted, fit – fitted, fit
flee – fled – fled
fling – flung – flung
fly – flew – flown
forbid – forbade, forbad – forbidden
forget – forgot – forgotten, forgot
forgive – forgave – forgiven
forsake – forsook – forsaken
freeze – froze – frozen
get – got – got, gotten (see § *Get*)
give – gave – given
go – went – gone
grind – ground – ground
grow – grew – grown
hang ("execute") – hanged – hanged
hang ("suspend") – hung – hung

have – had – had
hear – heard – heard
hide – hid – hidden
hit – hit – hit
hold – held – held
hurt – hurt – hurt
keep – kept – kept
kneel – kneeled, knelt – kneeled,
  knelt
knit – knit, knitted – knit, knitted
know – knew – known
lay – laid – laid
lead – led – led
leave – left – left
lend – lent – lent
let – let – let
lie ("recline") – lay – lain
lie ("tell an untruth") – lied – lied
light – lighted, lit – lighted, lit
lose – lost – lost
make – made – made
may – might (no past participle)
mean – meant – meant
meet – met – met
must – (see § *Must*) (no past
  participle)
ought – (see § *Ought*) (no past
  participle)
pay – paid – paid
plead [plid] – pleaded, plead [plɛd],
  pled – pleaded, plead [plɛd], pled
prove – proved – proved, proven
put – put – put
quit – quit – quit
read [rid] – read [rɛd] – read [rɛd]
rend – rent – rent
rid – rid, ridded – rid, ridded
ride – rode – ridden
ring – rang – rung
rise – rose – risen
run – ran – run
say [se] – said [sɛd] – said [sɛd]
see – saw – seen
seek – sought – sought
sell – sold – sold
send – sent – sent
set – set – set
sew – sewed – sewed, sewn
shake – shook – shaken

shall – would (no past participle)
shed – shed – shed
shine ("give light") – shone – shone
shine ("polish") – shined – shined
shoe – shod – shod
shoot – shot – shot
should – (see § *Ought*) (no past
  participle)
show – showed – showed, shown
shred – shredded, shred – shredded,
  shred
shrink – shrank, shrunk – shrunk,
  shrunken
shut – shut – shut
sing – sang, sung – sung
sink – sank, sunk – sunk, sunken
sit – sat – sat
slay – slew – slain
sleep – slept – slept
slide – slid – slid, slidden
sling – slung – slung
slink – slunk – slunk
slit – slit – slit
smite – smote – smitten
sow – sowed – sown, sowed
speak – spoke – spoken
spend – spent – spent
spin – spun – spun
spit – spat, spit – spat, spit
split – split – split
spread – spread – spread
spring – sprang, sprung – sprung
stand – stood – stood
steal – stole – stolen
stick – stuck – stuck
sting – stung – stung
stink – stank, stunk – stunk
stride – strode – stridden
strike ("afflict") – struck – stricken
strike ("hit") – struck – struck
string – strung – strung
strive – strove – striven
swear – swore – sworn
sweep – swept – swept
swell – swelled – swelled, swollen
swim – swam – swum
swing – swung – swung
take – took – taken
teach – taught – taught

tear – tore – torn
tell – told – told
think – thought – thought
thrive – thrived, throve – thrived,
  thriven
throw – threw – thrown
thrust – thrust – thrust
tread – trod – trodden, trod
understand – understood – understood
wake – waked, woke – waked, woken

wear – wore – worn
weave – wove – woven
wed – wedded, wed – wedded, wed
weep – wept – wept
welcome – welcomed – welcomed
wet – wet, wetted – wet, wetted
will – would (no past participle)
win – won – won
wind ("coil") – wound – wound
wring – wrung – wrung
write – wrote – written

4. The present participle, gerund, or *-ing* form of a verb is always regular in pronunciation: the sound [ɪŋ] is added to the simple form. The spelling nearly always conforms to the rules given under § Spelling—Word with Suffix. Three verbs which end in *-ie* in the simple form have *ying* in the *-ing* form: *die – dying*, *lie – lying*, and *tie – tying*. A final, unpronounced *e* is retained in four words to indicate a difference between them and similar words: *dye – dyeing* (versus *die – dying*), *singe – singeing* (versus *sing – singing*), *swinge – swingeing* (versus *swing – swinging*), and *tinge – tingeing* (versus *ting – tinging*). These auxiliaries have no *-ing* form: *can, may, must, ought, shall,* and *will.*

5. The third-person singular, present-tense form of nearly all verbs is regular in pronunciation and spelling; the rules are given under § Suffix *-s.* The major exceptions are *is, has, does,* and *goes* (the pronunciation of the last is regular). These auxiliaries do not have an *-s: can, may, must, ought, shall,* and *will.*

VERB—UNINFLECTED IN DEPENDENT CLAUSE   V.3

1. After certain words expressing a request, order, or suggestion, the verb in the dependent clause is uninflected—that is, it is not changed to show number, person, or time. In other words, the form of the dependent verb is the same as the infinitive without *to.*

2. The dependent clause is customarily introduced by *that.*

3. Some of the "request" words are the following: *advice, advise, anxious, ask, command, demand, desire, desirous, direct, essential, imperative, indispensable, insist, necessary, order, prefer, proposal, propose, recommend, recommendation, request, require, requirement, suggest, suggestion,* and *urge.*

They required that he write a complete report.
The requirement that he write a report was dropped.
It is essential that everyone vote in the coming election.
Mrs. Burton proposed that we wait patiently.
My father's sole recommendation was that the car be bought.
I knew they had urged that she explain everything.

4. A mnemonic aid for the uninflected verb is this: the speaker is asking for something which does not exist or will not exist if his request is not fulfilled. Therefore, the unreality of the thing requested is shown by the use of the uninflected form of the verb. An inflected form customarily indicates time and, consequently, reality. See § Tense and Time.

5. Notice the difference in meaning in the following pairs of sentences:

The girl insisted that we be quiet. [At the time of her request, we were not quiet.]
The girl insisted that we were quiet. [Here she stated a fact.]

The supervisor asked that the work be done immediately. [A request]
The supervisor asked if the work had been done immediately. [A reported question]

The general demanded that his assistant do the same. [An order]
The general demanded whether his assistant had done the same. [A reported question]

6. The same idea of request can be expressed by different constructions.

The girl insisted on our being quiet.
The supervisor asked for the work to be done immediately.
The general demanded the same action from his assistants.

VOICED VS. VOICELESS   V.4

1. English sounds are divided into two kinds: *voiced* and *voiceless.* If there is noticeable vibration of the vocal cords, the sound is voiced. If there is not any noticeable vibration, the sound is voiceless. You can feel the difference in vibration by putting your fingers on your throat—on your "Adam's apple"—when you prolong the [s] in *see* [si] and the [z] in *zoo* [zu]. (For the explanation of the symbols in brackets, see § Phonetic Symbol.) You can detect the difference in vibration also by putting the palms of your hands over your ears as you alternate pronouncing [s] and [z]. Some people can feel the difference by putting their palms on the top of their heads.

2. All the vowel and diphthong sounds in English are voiced. Fifteen of the consonant sounds are voiced, and nine are voiceless. See § Phonetic Symbol for their distribution.

3. Unlike some languages, English does have voiceless sounds at the ends of words. Unlike some other languages, English does have voiced consonants at the end of words. The difference between a voiced and a voiceless final sound is important in the pronunciation of plural and past forms of words. See § Suffix *-ed* and § Suffix *-s.*

4. There are eight pairs of consonants in English that differ only by the presence or lack of vibration:

VOICED		VOICELESS		VOICED		VOICELESS	
[v]	vase	[f]	face	[dʒ]	gin	[tʃ]	chin
[ð]	either	[θ]	ether	[b]	buy	[p]	pie
[z]	zeal	[s]	seal	[d]	dime	[t]	time
[ʒ]	allusion	[ð]	Aleutian	[g]	gold	[k]	cold

5. The voiceless consonants are made with comparatively more volume of breath than the voiced consonants: the voiceless consonants are *aspirated*. You can think of the voiceless consonants as *strong* sounds and the voiced consonants as *soft* sounds. Also, stressed vowels are customarily longer before voiced consonants than before voiceless consonants.

6. There are several pairs of related words which differ in pronunciation by the voicing or voicelessness of the last sound. All of those words which have a voiced final sound are verbs. Most of those which have a voiceless final sound are nouns (*safe* may be either a noun or an adjective, and *close* is an adjective or an adverb). Sometimes the members of a pair differ in spelling; sometimes they do not. Make the vowel before the voiced final consonant longer than the vowel before the voiceless final consonant.

VOICED FINAL—VERB	VOICELESS FINAL—NOT VERB
abuse	abuse
advise	advice
believe	belief
close	close
descend	descent
devise	device
excuse	excuse
extend	extent
house	house
intend	intent
misuse	misuse
mouth	mouth
prove	proof
relieve	relief
save	safe
serve	serf
use	use

Five pairs differ not only in the last sound but also in the vowel sound:

VOICED FINAL—VERB	VOICELESS FINAL—NOT VERB
bathe	bath
breathe	breath
choose	choice
clothe	cloth
lose	loss

Also, see § Pronunciation and § Pronunciation—Consonant, particularly, the discussion of near-the-teeth sounds in ¶ 6 of the latter section.

WH WORD W.1

1. The "*wh* words" are *who, whom, whose, which, what, when, where, why,* and *how* and their compounds like *whoever.* They all begin with the letters *wh* (*how* is an exception, but it does have *h* and *w*). The *wh* words have special characteristics in English grammar, particularly in word order. See § Word Order—*Wh* Word.

WHAT VS. *THAT* AND *WHICH* W.2

1. As a pronoun, the word *what* has no antecedent—that is, a word to which it refers. Unlike its cognate or equivalent in some other languages, it is not used immediately after words like *all, anything, everything,* and *something.* The customary relative pronouns following *all,* etc., are *that* and *which.* However, *that* and *which* may be omitted if there is no possibility of ambiguity. In the following examples, if the *that* or *which* is in parentheses, it may be used or omitted. You can see from these examples that it is necessary to use *that* or *which* when they are subjects of verbs.

> I frequently try to guess what my friends are thinking about.
> Some students rely on what has been said in class.
> You have asked a question (that) nobody can answer.
> People often want things (which) nobody should.
> The nurse likes children and all that is connected with them.
> We have proved that anything which exists is real.
> Anything (that) you say to Hilton makes him angry.
> Everything which concerned life was important to Goethe.
> Bob got something that could be referred to as an education.
> The only thing (that) I am trying to do is to improve my English.
> It was only laziness on my part that kept me from going.
> Mr. Brewster is interested in what you said.

2. If the relative pronoun is the object of an immediately preceding preposition, *which,* not *that,* is used.

> Galileo made a tube in which he could insert lenses.
> Is this the book for which you paid fifty dollars?

Also, see § Word Order—*Wh* Word, § Clause and its following sections, § Direct vs. Indirect Speech, § Word Order—Preposition, and § Word Order—Adjective before Noun.

WHAT FOR W.3

1. *What for* is a colloquial equivalent of *why.* Notice that the *what* comes first in the sentence or clause and *for* comes last.

> What did you close that door for?   I do not know what he did it for.
> Why did you close that door?   I do not know why he did it.

1. The words *hope, want, wish,* and *would like* are all used in expressions of desire, but they are seldom interchangeable.

2. *Wish* is customarily used to express a desire that can not be fulfilled or is uncertain of fulfillment; the wish is "unreal." In this use *wish* is followed by a clause, and the word *that* may be used at the beginning of the clause. If *wish* is in a present, future, or present perfect tense, the tense form of the verb in the following clause is *shifted:*

a. The past-future form is used for the future.

> I wish that it would rain soon. [It is uncertain that it will rain soon.]

b. The past form is used for the present.

> I wish that it were raining now. [It is not raining now.]

See ¶ 3 and ¶ 4, below, for the use of *were* instead of *was.*

c. The past-perfect form is used for the past.

> I wish that it had rained last night. [It did not rain last night.]

3. I recommend that you use *were* instead of *was* for the first and third person singular in the dependent clause after *wish* even though some speakers use *was.*

4. If *wish* is in a past tense, the tense in the following clause is not shifted, but *were* is still used instead of *was.*

> Last night I wished that it would rain soon.
> Last night I wished that it were raining then.
> Last night I wished that it had rained the night before.

Here are some additional examples:

> I wish that I were tall. I am short.
> I wish I liked apples. I do not like apples.
> The girls wished John were going with them. He was not going.
> Mrs. Brown wishes her son would become a lawyer. He is not planning to be a lawyer.
> Have you often wished that you could be a different person?
> At the end of the semester you may wish you had been more studious.
> I wish I had more time to talk with you, but I must leave now.

5. *Wish, want,* and *would like* are used to express a desire with no reference to expectation. *Want* and *would like* are more frequent than *wish* in this use; *wish* in this use has a connotation of formality or command. All three verbs are followed by infinitives, not clauses. If the subject of the desired action is different from the subject of the *want,* etc., it comes before the infinitive, and if it is a personal pronoun, it has its object form. *Want* and *wish* occur in all tense forms, but *would like* is used almost exclusively as an equivalent of the present tense, and in conversational English it usually occurs in the contracted form *-'d like.*

I want to see him again.	I want him to visit me again.
I would like to see him again.	I'd like him to visit me again.
I wish to see him again.	I wish him to visit me again.
Carr wanted to be president.	Carr's wife wanted him to be president.
Carr wished to be president.	Carr's wife wished him to be president.

6. *Hope* is used to express the meanings of "anticipate with desire and with expectation of fulfillment."

a. If the subject of *hope* is the same as the subject of the desired action, *hope* may be followed by an infinitive or by a clause. The word *that* may be used at the beginning of that clause.

I hope to see him again.	John hopes to become a doctor.
I hope I will see him again.	John hopes that he will become a doctor.

b. If the subject of the desired action is different from the subject of *hope,* then *hope* is followed by a clause.

I hope that he will visit me again.
Mr. Brown hopes that his son will become a doctor.
Carr's wife hoped he would be president.

c. You will sometimes see the present tense used instead of the future tense for a future action after *hope*—for example, "I hope that he visits me again." However, that substitution can not be made in all cases, and, therefore, I recommend that you avoid using it.

Also, see § *Desire* and § *Like*—Verb.

WORD ORDER   W.5

1. *Word order* is the arrangement of words in a sentence, clause, or phrase to convey meaning. Some languages have relatively *free* word order: meaning is not changed by a change in the position of a word. Other languages have relatively *fixed* word order: meaning is changed or is not conveyed when the position of a word is changed.

2. English has relatively fixed word order. By placing eight words in varying positions, we get the following sentences, all of which convey different meanings:

The boy will hurt a really little dog.
The dog will hurt a really little boy.
The really little boy will hurt a dog.
The boy will really hurt a little dog.
The boy dog will really hurt a little.
The dog boy will really hurt a little.

> Will, a boy, hurt the dog really little.
> Boy! Will really hurt the dog a little!
> Will the boy really hurt a little dog?
> Will the dog really hurt a little boy?

Other meaningful arrangements are possible. The arrangement below might be encountered in poetry, which permits a slightly free word order. It is the customary word order of prose in another language, but it is not prose in English.

> The boy will a dog really little hurt.

The next arrangement conveys no meaning at all in English.

> The really dog hurt little will boy a.

3. In the first ten sentences above, a large number of the word-order patterns of English are illustrated: position of modifiers (adjectives and adverbs), of subjects, of objects, of verbs (auxiliary and main), of appositives, and of interjections.

Some of the English word-order patterns are surveyed in the following sections. Two of the most important are § Word Order—Primary and § Word Order—Split. In conjunction with these sections, you should refer to § Part of Speech and its following sections, § Clause and its following sections, § Phrase, and § Appositive.

WORD ORDER—ADJECTIVE AFTER NOUN AND PRONOUN   W.6

1. Single-word adjectives usually precede the nouns they modify. However, under certain conditions, adjectives follow the nouns they modify. Below, I will list some of the times when adjectives come after the nouns or pronouns they modify. Such adjectives are called *postposed.*

2. When a cardinal number (*one, two, three,* etc.) is used instead of an ordinal number (*first, second,* etc.), it follows its noun. See § Article—*The* vs. No *The.*

> Read Chapter Six for tomorrow. [= Read the sixth chapter for tomorrow.]

3. Adjectives follow the compounds of *any-, every-, no-,* and *some-,* such as *anyone, everything, nobody,* and *somewhere,* including those which are written as two words like *no one* and *any place.* Most of these compounds are usually classified as pronouns.

> A bride is supposed to wear something old, something new, something borrowed, and something blue.
> Anybody volunteering will be cited for merit.
> I am sure that Roger told nobody else.
> The searchers looked for the missing child everywhere possible.

4. The words *broad, deep, high, long, old, tall, wide,* and *young* follow nouns in expressions of measurement.

> I want a board twenty inches wide.
> The Browns' baby is eight months old.
> Mr. Boyle is at least six feet tall.
> The Empire State Building is 102 stories high.
> The boys worked all day long.
> I am going on a trip ten days long.

If the expression of measurement precedes the word it modifies, the noun in the expression is usually not inflected for number, and the words of the expression are hyphenated. The words *broad, deep,* etc., are usually omitted unless they are needed for clarity. See § Hyphen.

> I want a twenty-inch board. [To prevent misunderstanding: "I want a twenty-inch-wide board."]
> The Browns have an eight-month baby.   *or*   The Browns have an eight-month-old baby.
> Mrs. Boyle has a six-foot husband.
> Visitors marvel at the 102-story skyscraper.
> The boys worked at an all-day job.
> I am taking a ten-day trip to Bermuda.

5. A participle may follow the noun it modifies, particularly if the participle is used restrictively.

> The boy *selected* was my brother.
> Those girls *singing* practice every day.

6. Two coordinate descriptive adjectives joined by *and, but,* and *though* may follow the noun they modify. They are usually nonrestrictive.

> The young man, poor but proud, refused the offer.

7. The pattern of *verb + direct object + adjective* is very frequent. Such an adjective is a *predicate adjective;* see § Predicate Adjective. We can make this statement about the pattern: the adjective shows the condition of the direct object in relation to the verb. The adjective is frequently an *-ing* form or a past participle of a verb. The direct object can be either a noun or a pronoun. However, if it is the verb itself that is qualified, an adverb form is needed, not an adjective. Below, I have listed a number of examples with adjectives contrasted with adverbs.

To clarify what I said above about the adjective's showing the condition, I will group some types of sentences according to the pattern.

a. One type of sentence shows the verb's *result* on the direct object. The examples on the left illustrate that type.

ADJECTIVE	ADVERB
The boy made the girl angry.	The cook made the dinner quickly.
He pushed the door open.	He pushed the door violently.

b. Another type of sentence shows what the verb declares the direct object to be.

This construction is similar to that of the predicate objective discussed under § Predicate Objective. The examples on the left illustrate the type.

ADJECTIVE	ADVERB
The doctor pronounced me cured.	The student pronounced the word incorrectly.
The jury found the defendant guilty.	The police found the criminal easily.

c. A third type of sentence shows the state which the verb perceives the direct object to be in. The examples on the left illustrate the type.

ADJECTIVE	ADVERB
The maid watched the baby playing.	The maid watched the baby carefully.
He likes to see children happy.	He likes to see children occasionally.
She found her towels dirty.	She found her towels unexpectedly.

With those types as a beginning, you can probably see the similarity of all such constructions. Test yourself on the following examples:

I will have the package ready when the collector arrives.
The teacher had the papers corrected by the next day.
You have made your room very attractive.
The guests could smell the dinner burning.
Mothers try to keep their children healthy.
You must keep your wound bandaged.
Mrs. Dawson considered her friend's remark very foolish.
I want my coffee hot.
The accident left the girl helpless.
The new owner painted the house green.

In this connection, see § Part of Speech—Adjective and § Predicate Adjective.

8. An adjective with a following modifier or complement comes after its noun. There are three major kinds of such adjective phrases:

a. An adjective with a prepositional phrase

Paul's hands, *numb from the cold,* could not find the key.
The beggar, *shaking with laughter,* leaned against the wall.
The boy *dressed in white* is taller than the girl *dressed in green.*
Sammy demanded a book *different from his sister's.*
Mildred Engstrom, *angry at everybody,* left abruptly.

b. An *-ing* form with an object, an adverb, or a predicate adjective

The girl *wearing the red dress* is my sister.
Have you read the news item *describing the incident?*
The woman glared at the man *smoking the cigar.*
Mr. Johnson, *forgetting his dignity,* sang wholeheartedly.
Pete, *having lost the bet,* had to pay for the dinner.

> The tourist was unimpressed by the scenery *moving by.*
> The fisherman, *being poor,* could not buy another boat.

c. An adjective with a clause as a modifier or an object

> The puppy, *aware that he had done something wrong,* refused to eat.
> The students, *glad that school was finished,* ran out of the room.
> Mr. Ward, *knowing why I had not studied,* did not call on me.
> The janitor is still looking for the papers *lost when the wind blew this morning.*

9. The adjective phrases described in ¶ 8 above can shift their position under certain conditions. First, I must define some terms.

a. A phrase that is purely descriptive is called *nonrestrictive.* (Another term is *non-identifying.*) It adds information about the thing it modifies, but it does not necessarily distinguish that thing from all other things.

> **Model 1**   My father, *wearing a black suit,* came into the room.

b. A phrase that identifies a thing is called *restrictive.* (Another term is *identifying.*) It distinguishes that thing from all similar things.

> **Model 2**   The boy *wearing a black suit* is the one I was speaking of.

c. The phrase *wearing a black suit* is nonrestrictive in Model 1 above. The phrase does not identify *my father* in that sentence although it does add information about him. However, *wearing a black suit* is restrictive in Model 2 above. It does identify *The boy;* it does distinguish him from the other boys.

d. A nonrestrictive phrase is set off by commas from its preceding noun.

e. A restrictive phrase is not set off by commas from its preceding noun.

10. If a nonrestrictive adjective phrase modifies the subject, it can be moved to the beginning of the clause. A comma follows the phrase.

> *Numb from the cold,* Paul's hand could not find the key.
> *Shaking with laughter,* the beggar leaned against the wall.
> *Angry at everybody,* Mildred Engstrom left abruptly.
> *Forgetting his dignity,* Mr. Johnson sang wholeheartedly.
> *Having lost the bet,* Pete had to pay for the dinner.
> *Being poor,* the fisherman could not buy another boat.
> *Aware that he had done something wrong,* the puppy refused to eat.
> *Glad that school was finished,* the students ran out of the room.
> *Knowing why I had not studied,* Mr. Ward did not call on me.
> *Wearing a black suit,* my father came into the room.

11. Your reader expects to find a noun or pronoun near an adjective phrase like the ones which begin the preceding examples, and he expects the adjective phrase to modify that noun or pronoun. Suppose you changed the example "Wearing a black suit, my father came into the room" to read "Wearing a black suit, I saw my father come into the room." Your reader would assume that *I* was wearing a black suit even though you intended to say that your father was wearing a black suit. Such an adjective phrase is called a *misplaced modifier.* In order for your reader to understand what you mean to say, you would have to rearrange or reword the sentence so that that kind of adjective phrase is near the noun or pronoun it modifies.

12. Sometimes in haste you write down an adjective phrase and then forget to put the word it modifies into the sentence. Such an adjective phrase is called a *dangler* or a *dangling modifier:* it dangles because it is not "tied" to a noun or pronoun. Suppose you began a sentence with the phrase "Being unmarried." How should you continue—with the words "it is not necessary to go home at a regular time" or with the words "I do not have to go home at a regular time"? You should continue with the latter group of words so that the sentence reads "Being unmarried, I do not have to go home at a regular time." The adjective phrase "Being unmarried" is near the word *I,* which it modifies. Very often it is necessary to rewrite a sentence without using such an adjective phrase.

13. A nonrestrictive adjective phrase modifying the subject can also be shifted to the end of the sentence. However, adjectives are usually taken to modify the closest noun or pronoun. Therefore, if there is a noun or pronoun in the predicate, a reader or listener may think that the shifted phrase modifies that noun or pronoun. Such a phrase is also called a *misplaced modifier.* You should avoid using it because it may prevent your reader or listener from understanding your meaning easily. Also, notice that a comma is needed to prevent misreading in the following examples of acceptable shifted adjective phrases:

> Mildred Engstrom left abruptly, *angry at everybody.*
> Mr. Johnson sang wholeheartedly, *forgetting his dignity.*
> The puppy refused to eat, *aware that he had done something wrong.*

Also, see § *A-* Word, § Clause—Adjective, and § Phrase from Clause.

WORD ORDER—ADJECTIVE BEFORE NOUN W.7

1. Single-word adjectives usually precede the nouns they modify: they are *preposed.* For times when they do not, see the preceding section, § Word Order—Adjective after Noun and Pronoun.

2. When more than one modifier precedes a noun, the order of those modifiers is relatively fixed. The reason is that the modifiers do not modify the same thing: the modifier closest to the *head-word noun* modifies that noun; the immediately preceding modifier modifies not just the noun but the *nominal construction* composed of the noun and the closest modifier; that process may be repeated over and over. For illustration, I will take the sentence "Machines are expensive" and add modifiers before the noun *machines.*

> Laundry machines are expensive. [*Laundry* modifies the head-word noun
> *machines.*]

Electric laundry machines are expensive. [*Electric* modifies the nominal construction *laundry machines.*]

Automatic electric laundry machines are expensive. [*Automatic* modifies the nominal construction *electric laundry machines.*]

Enamel automatic electric laundry machines are expensive. [*Enamel* modifies the nominal construction *automatic electric laundry machines.*]

American enamel automatic electric laundry machines are expensive. [*American* modifies the nominal construction *enamel automatic electric laundry machines.*]

For practice you can analyze the string of modifiers in the following highly unusual but possible sentence, in which each word from *both* through *electric* modifies the nominal construction after it:

Both those next two attractive tall new square pink American enamel automatic electric laundry machines are expensive.

3. Now, after having given you that fantastic example, I will give you a warning: do not write that kind of sentence. A string of modifiers preceding a noun often retards a reader's comprehension of a sentence or diverts his attention. Be frugal with modifiers at all times, and particularly shun clusters of them.

4. The customary order of modifiers before nouns is given in the following list. (The examples under ¶ 5 below will show you how this is applied in sentences.) The words listed in Groups *a* to *h* can be called *indicating*, and those in the remaining groups can be called *descriptive*.

a. *all, any, both, double, each, every, half, no, triple, twice, which,* and *what.*

b. The following three kinds of words:
  1. Articles (*a, an,* and *the*).
  2. Demonstratives (*this, that, these,* and *those*).
  3. Genitives (*my, John's,* etc.).

c. *own* (this follows only genitives).

d. *whole.*

e. Sequence words: ordinal numbers (*first, second,* etc.), *next, last, preceding, following, present,* and *past.*

f. Quantifiers: cardinal numbers (*one, two,* etc.) and other *count* or *quantity* words like *certain, few, little, many* (this precedes *a* and *an*), *most, much, numerous, several,* and *some.*

g. *additional, more,* and *other* (this usually precedes a cardinal number).

h. *such* (this precedes *a* and *an*).

i. Descriptive modifiers (*beautiful, interesting,* etc.) other than the words in Groups *j* to *r.*

j. Common adjectives of size, height, or length (*big, tall,* etc.).

k. Common adjectives of age or temperature (*old, hot,* etc.).. ,

l. Common adjectives of shape (*round, square,* etc.).

m. Common adjectives of color (*green, gray,* etc.).

n. Modifiers denoting nationality, origin, or location (*American, city,* etc.).

o. Modifiers denoting material or composition (*silver, wood,* etc.). These can frequently be converted into a phrase beginning with *of* and placed after the modified noun (*of silver, of wood*).

p. Modifiers denoting operation (*automatic, mechanical,* etc.).
q. Modifiers denoting power (*gas, vacuum,* etc.).
r. Modifiers denoting purpose or destination. These, like many of those of Group *o*, frequently have the same form for noun uses. They can often be converted into a phrase beginning with *for* and placed after the modified noun (*a party dress - a dress for a party*).

5. Study the arrangement of the modifiers in the examples below. The letters in parentheses refer to the groups above. Note that no punctuation is used if a modifier of one group is followed by a modifier of another group in the customary sequence.

> Pete ate (*a*) all (*b*) the pie.
> Pete ate (*b*) the (*d*) whole pie.
> Laura paid (*a*) double (*b*) his (*i*) regular fee.
> The tourists saw (*a*) each (*i*) towering (*o*) steel skyscraper.
> Bea has (*b*) her (*c*) own (*k*) new (*q*) gas (*r*) ice freezer.
> Read (*b*) the (*e*) next (*f*) few pages for tomorrow.
> The company is (*b*) a (*i*) typical (*j*) large (*r*) industrial organization.
> Have you met (*b*) that (*i*) brilliant (*k*) young (*n*) Spanish philosopher?
> The bus went up (*b*) the (*i*) winding (*n*) mountain highway.
> The teacher recited (*f*) several (*h*) such examples.
> Have you ever seen (*h*) such (*b*) a (*i*) fine (*n*) spring day?
> The Smiths bought (*b*) those (*f*) three (*i*) handsome (*k*) old (*n*) colonial (*o*) mahogany (*r*) writing desks.

6. Two modifiers of the same group can be joined by the conjunctions *and, although, as well as, but, nor, or,* and *though.* Such modifiers are called *coordinate* modifiers.

> The psychiatrist spoke in a (*i*) gentle but (*i*) persuasive voice.
> Sarah had a (*m*) black and (*m*) blue spot on her arm.

7. If the conjunction is not used, a comma is used.

> The orchestra played a (*i*) swaying, (*i*) enchanting waltz.
> Millie has a (*i*) smooth, (*i*) creamy complexion.
> The United States used to be a (*i*) raw, (*i*) sparsely settled, (*i*) tradition-less country.

8. A modifier of Group *j, k, l,* or *m* is sometimes placed before descriptive modifiers which customarily precede it. The reason for doing so seems to be to emphasize that modifier. A comma is customarily placed after it.

> The woman gave a low, shuddering sigh.
> Bob's former employer sent him a short, unkind reply.

9. An adverb is usually placed directly before the modifier it modifies. Do not use a hyphen between an adverb with the suffix *-ly* and the word it modifies or between the adverb *very, quite, rather, more, most, less,* or *least* and its following adjective or adverb. Also, see Word Order—Adverb Modifying Adjective and Adverb.

430

The student gave an entirely wrong answer.
Jane is a very sweet little girl.
George's question put me into a highly embarrassing position.
Lisa was stunned by the quite unexpected news.
She was the most disappointed child in the group.

10. If the adverbs *as, how, however, so,* and *too* precede an adjective, that adjective is placed before all others except those in Group *a.*

It was too terrible an experience to talk about.
The speculator offered me twice as much money as I had paid.
The girl is so much a part of him that he can not live without her.

11. Use a comma to prevent an adjective from being interpreted as an adverb. Two words that can be either adjectives or adverbs are *pretty* and *mighty.*

Sue is a pretty, young girl. [Sue is a nice-looking young girl.]
Sue is a pretty young girl. [Sue is a rather young girl.]

12. Quite often, for emphasis, a modifier is repeated. Use a comma after the first instance.

That happened a long, long time ago.
The old man was very, very tired.

13. If a whole number and a fraction modify a noun, either of two arrangements may be used.

Philip has lived there for two and a half years.
Philip has lived there for two years and a half.

For the arrangement of two modifiers of Group *b* (articles, demonstratives, and possessives), see § Apostrophe. For the use of hyphens in preposed modifiers, see § Hyphen. For the three positions of adjectives in sentences, see § Part of Speech—Adjective. Also, see § *All* vs. *Whole,* § Noun—Not Repeated, and § Phrase from Clause.

WORD ORDER—ADVERB MODIFYING ADJECTIVE AND ADVERB W.8

1. An adverb that modifies an adjective or another adverb usually directly precedes that adjective or adverb. Some of the most frequent of such adverbs are the following: *almost, as, even, how, however, just, less, more, most, only, quite, rather, so, still, too,* and *very.*

Johnson has been late only twice. [*Only* modifies the adverb *twice.*]
The other road is less dangerous. [*Less* modifies the adjective *dangerous.*]
The storm arose quite unexpectedly. [*Quite* modifies the adverb *unexpectedly.*]

Many adverbs ending in *-ly,* usually derived from adjectives, also modify adjectives and other adverbs—for example, *really, surely,* and *certainly.* A number of those adverbs are listed as adverbs of degree under § Word Order—Adverb Modifying Verb.

> A really nice boy came by to see you. [*Really* modifies *nice.*]
> There was a fairly large crowd there. [*Fairly* modifies *large.*]
> The frightened man was barely able to speak. [*Barely* modifies *able.*]

2. The adverb *enough* is an outstanding exception to the rule of position: it occurs only after the adjective or adverb it modifies. See § *Enough.*

> That seems fair enough.
> Haven't we walked far enough?

3. In conversation and informal writing, *awful, awfully, real, sure,* and a number of other words are used as modifiers; see § Intensifier.

> The test was awfully easy.
> I'm sure tired.

4. *Any, much,* and *no* are used before adjectives and adverbs in the comparative degree.

> Is the patient any better today?
> This lesson is much more difficult than the preceding one.
> I must be home no later than eight o'clock.

5. When *how* or *however* modifies an adjective or adverb, that group always goes to the beginning of the sentence or clause. See § Word Order—*Wh* Word and § Opposition Expression.

> How far did you walk?
> How pretty Mary looks in her new dress!
> No matter how hard I try, I can not learn that poem.
> However hard I try, I can not learn that poem.

Also, see § Word Order—Adjective before Noun for the relative position of adjectives modified by *as, how, however, so,* and *too.*

6. Most of the adverbs listed in this section can also modify verbs; see the next section, § Word Order—Adverb Modifying Verb. *Very, pretty,* and *real* modify only participial verb forms which are used as adjectives or adverbs.

> I am very surprised about that.
> That movie was pretty disappointing.

Any and *no* are not used to modify verbs.

WORD ORDER—ADVERB MODIFYING VERB   W.9

1. Adverbs or adverbial phrases modifying a verb usually follow the verb and its objects. The customary word order is the following (but also see ¶ 11 to ¶ 14, below):

SUBJECT	VERB	OBJECT(S)	ADVERB OF PLACE	ADVERB OF MANNER	ADVERB OF TIME
Bus drivers	take	people	to New Jersey	cheerfully	every night.
Everything	produced	fear and terror	in my mind.		
The scheme	failed	its goal		entirely.	
Juan	spent	a few weeks	in Boston		last winter.
I	had	a good time	at the party		yesterday.
His speech	made	an impression	on me.		
His wife	bought	him some ties	at Macy's		a week ago.
The teacher	will be		here		soon.
All papers	had sent	reporters	to the event.		
Mary	went		to the movie	with John	last night.
The police	chased	the burglar	up the street.		
We	got		home		before dawn.
George	changes	his theme	in class	a little bit	afterwards.

2. Make this a general rule: never put an adverb between a verb and its object unless you have an excellent reason.

3. If two adverbs of the same kind are used in the same sentence, they may usually be interchanged in position.

> I have an appointment *at ten o'clock tomorrow.*
> I have an appointment *tomorrow at ten o'clock.*

4. When the word *not* modifies a verb, it comes after the first auxiliary or after the subject if the first auxiliary precedes the subject.

> They must not stay.
> Should the boys not go?

a. If the tense of the verb is simple present, we use *do* or *does* before *not*. See § *Do*—Auxiliary.

> Paul smokes a great deal.
> His brother does not smoke at all.

b. If the tense of the verb is simple past, we use *did* before *not.*

> Sam went there last night.
> Charles did not go there last night.

c. Not is used after *am, is, are, was,* and *were* without *do, does,* or *did.*

> Oscar is not here.
> Were they not happy to see you?

5. If the contraction *-n't* is used, it is attached to the first auxiliary or *is, are, was,* and *were* but not *am.* That contraction is customary in conversation.

> The boys mustn't stay.
> Tim doesn't smoke a great deal.

> I didn't go to the show yesterday.
> Shouldn't the girls go?
> George isn't here.
> Weren't they happy to see you?

6. Adverbs of degree generally precede the main verb. (For an exception, see § *Be—Verb.*) Certain adverbs of degree are often called *adverbs of frequency*. Those are the following:

always	frequently	occasionally	regularly	still
continually	generally	often	repeatedly	usually
customarily	never	ordinarily	seldom	
ever	not	rarely	sometimes	

> Diamonds often play the role of insurance.
> Mr. Parker occasionally had good ideas.
> We rarely see Mr. and Mrs. Johnson.

Other adverbs with a similar meaning of frequency act like adverbs of time: they usually go at the end of the sentence. Some of those are *once, twice,* etc., *three times a week,* and *every now and then.*

> I go to school every day.
> Louise has been in the office twice.

7. Some other adverbs of degree are the following. Most of them are stressed in conversion to convey emphasis.

absolutely	definitely	merely	really
actually	distinctly	nearly	scarcely
almost	even	obviously	simply
already	evidently	only	surely
barely	fairly	positively	truly
certainly	hardly	possibly	
clearly	just	probably	

> Diamonds certainly play the role of insurance.
> Mr. Bayberry almost missed the train.
> Your supervisor possibly had good ideas.
> Miss Brewster distinctly told you to leave.
> Charles clearly smokes a great deal.

8. If there are auxiliaries, the adverb of degree usually follows the first auxiliary or the subject if the first auxiliary precedes the subject.

> I have frequently explained that to you.
> Mr. Linden has never been asked his opinion on that matter.
> Do you sometimes visit the Joneses?
> Have those boys ever done their homework on time?
> Mr. Robertson has surely told his supervisor about that matter.
> Do you really believe that rumor?

9. When the first auxiliary is stressed, the adverb of degree precedes it. The auxiliary is stressed in contradictions and in its uses as a *second verb* in shortened clauses. See § Verb—Not Repeated.

> "You did not tell John." "I certainly did tell him."
> "Are New Yorkers always in a hurry?" "They usually are."
> I will go to the party if I possibly can.

10. When *not* or *-n't* occurs with an adverb of degree, the arrangement is usually this: the word that is more prominent in the user's mind comes second and is stressed. If the adverb of degree is the first word, it generally precedes the *not* or the first auxiliary and *-n't*.

> Mr. Lewis does not always answer his letters promptly.
> Those young children certainly don't understand that novel.
> Don't you sometimes visit the Joneses?
> I simply can't make up my mind about that boy.
> Haven't those boys ever done their homework on time?
> Harrison's wife clearly did not approve of his choice.
> We don't generally go to school on Friday.
> Your supervisor obviously will not give his permission to your request.
> You just don't try as hard as you should.
> After six months my next-door neighbor still doesn't know my name.

11. The position of adverbs modifying verbs can be changed for specific reasons. The most important reason is clarity.

> A month ago Betty thought she would leave town.
> Betty thought she would leave town a month ago.

The two examples above indicate two different meanings. In the first, the "thinking" was a month ago; in the second, the "leaving" was a month ago. In each sentence the *a month ago* has been placed closest to the verb it modifies.

12. Another reason for changing the position of adverbs is emphasis or contrast.

> *Now* you have spoiled all my plans!

The adverb *sometimes* frequently begins a sentence or clause to indicate contrast.

> I usually stay home in the evening. Sometimes I go to a movie.

However, the adverb *always* does not take an initial position.

13. A third reason for changing the position of adverbs is style or effective expression. For instance, the first example in ¶ 1—"Bus drivers..."—is syntactically correct but stylistically poor: there is an excess of modifiers at the end of the sentence. The arrangement is improved by placing the adverb of manner *cheerfully* in the same position as an adverb of degree.

> Bus drivers cheerfully take people to New Jersey every night.

14. Single-word adverbs of manner may be placed in the positions of adverbs of degree, and adverbs or adverbial phrases of time can be shifted to the beginning of the sentence or clause. Single-word adverbs of sequence (*first, next, then,* etc.) can begin or end the sentence or take the positions of an adverb of degree. The adverbs of frequency, with the exception of *always* and *ever,* can begin or end the sentence or clause.

> The detective carefully observed everything in the room.
> A week ago my wife bought two dresses in that store.
> Last night Mary went to the movies with John.
> Before catching him, the police chased the burglar down the street for ten blocks.
> First, you take your examination. Then, you register.
> You first take your examination. You then register.
> You take your examination first. You can register then.
> Mr. Paulson's assistant made good suggestions very often.

Also, see § Word Order—Emphatic Adverb, § *Already* vs. *Yet,* § *Enough,* § *Only,* § Opposition Expression, § *Still* vs. *Any More* and *Any Longer,* and § Two-word Verb.

WORD ORDER—EMPHATIC ADVERB   W.10

1. Certain adverbs which are negative or have a negative implication are often placed at the beginning of a statement in order to indicate emphasis. Then, they are followed by *split word order* (auxiliary verb + subject + main verb) or *inverted word order* (verb + subject). Those adverbs are the following:

> never   rarely   hardly
> nowhere   seldom
>
> Never have I heard of such a thing.
> Nowhere would he look for a job.
> Rarely has Jean failed to do what I have asked.
> Seldom does such a person show much improvement.
> Hardly had I left the room before she called me back.

2. In initial position those adverbs and the words *not* and *only* can be followed by other adverbial expressions. The following subject and verb will keep their split or inverted word order.

> Never in my life   have I heard of such a thing.
> Nowhere else in the world   can you hear so many languages spoken.
> Hardly ever   will you see Mr. Robertson without a smile on his face.
> Not always   can people do what they want to.
> Not once   have you copied your sentences correctly.
> Not only   did I forget to close the window, but I also forgot to sweep.
> Only seldom   does Miss Rivers take part in a conversation.
> Only with this kind of education   will they have adequate preparation.
> Only when a child grows up   does he understand his parents' intentions.
> I realized that only with supervision   would Joe perform his tasks.

3. The word *no* in an introductory adverbial phrase is followed by split or inverted word order.

> In no case   do I want to argue with you.
> On no account   can the driver be held responsible.
> By no means   should you buy that kind of car.
> Under no circumstances   will your money be refunded.
> No sooner   do I get one problem settled before another appears.
> No longer   will I believe a word you say.

4. The word *nor* introducing a clause has the same effect on word order.

> I do not believe it, nor   can you make me believe it.

5. Split or inverted word order is also used after so + an adjective or adverb at the beginning of a sentence or clause.

> So simple   does the trick seem that we are likely to overlook the magician's dexterity.
> So earnestly   did the boys beg that their father gave his permission.

6. The word *so* expressing affirmative agreement and the word *neither* expressing negative agreement are followed by split or inverted word order. If the main verb is the same, it is usually not repeated; see § Verb—Not Repeated.

> John likes Mildred very much. So   do I.
> Sue can not go, and neither   can I.
> Just as the poet seeks to express similarities, so   does the actor endeavor to be accepted as the character he is portraying.

7. Similarly, in shortened comparison clauses introduced by *as* and *than,* split or inverted word order is often used.

> Many idioms had their origin in metaphor, as   did many two-word verbs.
> Students with strong motivation are more likely to succeed than   are those with poor motivation.

Also, see § Negative.

WORD ORDER—INVERTED W.11

1. *Inverted word order* or *reverse word order* is the arrangement of words which has the complete verb before the subject.

2. The verb agrees in number and person with the following subject. Notice the examples below.

3. Inverted word order occurs most frequently after the word *there.*

	VERB	SUBJECT
There	is	your friend.
There	are	your friends.
There	have been	many wars in the past.
There	may have been	some cause for his behavior.

4. Inverted word order is used rather often in what is called *formal style.* You should be familiar with it because you will encounter it in literature and scientific and legal writing. You, however, may seldom have occasion to use it except in sentences with *there.* Notice that all the following examples begin with expressions of *place.*

	VERB	SUBJECT
Here	is	an example.
Here	are	some examples.
There	goes	your last chance.
In every man	are	potentialities that can be developed.
Rooted deep in our traditions	is	free elementary school education.

5. Inverted word order is frequently used in dialog guides, particularly with the word *say.* However, primary word order is just as good.

"That,"	said John, "is another story."
"That,"	John said, "is another story."

If the person spoken to is mentioned, use primary word order.

"That,"	John said to me, "is another story."
"Don't you think that's right?"	John asked me.

Also, see § *It* vs. *There.*

WORD ORDER—OBJECT OF VERB   W.12

1. The order of a verb and its direct and indirect objects customarily follows either of two patterns:

Pattern 1	Verb + indirect object + direct object
Pattern 2	Verb + direct object + *to* or *for* + indirect object.

Grammatically, the *indirect object* in Pattern 2 is the object of the preposition *to* or *for;* the preposition and its object compose an *equivalent of an indirect object.*

His mother gave	John	a ball.
His mother gave	a ball	to John.
Mr. Lewis bought	his niece	some toys.
Mr. Lewis bought	some toys	for his niece.

2. If the direct object is a pronoun, the order is usually Pattern 2.

His mother gave	*it*	to John.

His mother gave	*it*	to him.
Mr. Lewis bought	*them*	for his niece.
Mr. Lewis bought	*them*	for her.

3. If the indirect object is a pronoun and the direct object is a noun, the order is usually Pattern 1.

| His mother gave | him | a ball. |
| Mr. Lewis bought | her | some toys. |

4. If the indirect object is long or greatly modified, the order is usually Pattern 2.

| His mother gave | a ball | to the little boy who was crying. |
| Mr. Lewis bought | some toys | for his niece, the daughter of his sister. |

5. The following verbs generally require *to* or *for* before the indirect object, and, consequently, the order is usually Pattern 2 if there is a direct object.

admit. The clerk admitted his mistake to me.
answer. A secretary frequently has to answer letters for her boss.
arrange. I will arrange an appointment for you.
begin. If I begin the story for you, do you think you can finish it?
clarify. I wish you would clarify that statement for me.
confess. The robber confessed his guilt to the jury.
declare. He declared his innocence to the judge.
dedicate. The author dedicated the book to his wife.
describe. The child described the party to us.
drive. Let John drive the car for you.
explain. Did the teacher explain the lesson to you?
finish. Since you must leave, I will finish your work for you.
indicate. Talbert indicated his willingness to me.
introduce. Later on, Mrs. Palfrey introduced her husband to me.
mention. Mr. Gilbert did not mention the incident to his wife.
outline. The professor outlined the course to his students.
pronounce. Please pronounce those last two words for me.
propose. Marcia proposed another system to her superintendent.
prove. The scientist proved his theory to his audience.
quote. The student quoted their poems to me.
recall. Mrs. Francis recalled his excuse to him.
recite. Must you recite all your troubles to me?
recommend. The librarian recommended a number of books to me.
report. The sergeant reported the incident to the lieutenant.
return. Betty returned the books to the librarian at ten o'clock.
reveal. Who revealed my secret to my sister?
say. Now, I want you to say the poem to me again.
speak. The actor spoke his lines to his wife in order to memorize them.
start. The garageman will start the car for you.
suggest. A teacher gets tired of suggesting composition topics to his students.
translate. Can you translate this French word for me?

6. However, if the direct object after one of those verbs above is long or greatly modified, the indirect object with *to* or *for* may precede. Sometimes the indirect object must precede for the sake of clarity.

> Our teacher declared   to us   that the English language could be learned.
> The frightened woman described   to the policeman   the appearance of the man who had attempted to rob her.
> Can't you suggest   to him   that he ought to be more careful?
> Sue proved   to me   that there were nice things in the city.
> Please explain   to me   what happened.

7. If either the direct object or the indirect object is or contains a *wh* word, it goes before the subject and the verb. It is followed by split word order (auxiliary + subject + verb) or inverted word order (not a subject) in questions and by primary word order (subject + verb) in statements.

> What   did his mother give   to John?
> Which ball   did his mother give   to John?
> How many toys   did Mr. Lewis buy   for his niece?
> What nice toys   Mr. Lewis bought   for his niece!

In sentences like the above, the *to* or *for* is sometimes omitted before the indirect object, but for the sake of clarity I urge you to use the *to* or *for.*

a. If the indirect object is a *wh* word, three arrangements are possible: (1) the *to* or *for* is placed before the *wh* word; (2) the *to* or *for* is placed at the end; (3) the *to* or *for* is omitted.

> To whom did his mother give a ball? (Arrangement 1)
> Whom did his mother give a ball to? (Arrangement 2)
> Whom did his mother give a ball? (Arrangement 3)
> For whom did Mr. Lewis buy some toys? (Arrangement 1)
> Whom did Mr. Lewis buy some toys for? (Arrangement 2)
> Whom did Mr. Lewis buy some toys? (Arrangement 3)

Arrangement 1 is customary in formal writing. Arrangement 2 is probably most frequent in speech, and *who* is often used instead of *whom* although there are grammarians who consider the use of *who* incorrect.

> Who did his mother give a ball to?
> Who did Mr. Lewis buy some toys for?

Arrangement 3 is sometimes used, but I recommend that you not use it because at times it seems awkward.

b. A *wh* word in a dependent clause is customarily followed by primary word order. It does not matter whether the whole sentence is a statement or a question.

> I know   what his mother gave to John.
> Did you find out   how many toys Mr. Lewis bought for his niece?

Also, see § Word Order—Adverb Modifying Verb and § Word Order—*Wh* Word.

440

WORD ORDER—POLITE   W.13

1. For the sake of politeness, words referring to one's own self (*I, me, mine,* and *myself*) are placed after those referring to another or others (*you, they,* etc.).

> Both you and I should study harder.
> Sue invited Sam and me to dinner.
> Some friends and I went to a show last night.
> Is this yours or mine?
> The teacher asked neither Mary nor me about our assignments.

See § Apostrophe for sentences like "A friend of mine and I went."

WORD ORDER—PREPOSITION   W.14

1. Prepositions usually precede a word or group, which is called their *object.* See § Part of Speech—Noun and § Part of Speech—Conjunction and Preposition.

> They were talking *about* the accident.
> He painted a chair *for* her.
> She is interested *in* the plan.
> Those students have changed *to* the morning class.

2. In direct questions, if the object is or contains a *wh* word (*who, what, which,* etc.), it is customarily placed first in the sentence. In formal writing, the preposition is usually placed before the *wh* word.

> *About* what were they talking?
> *For* whom did he paint the chair?
> *In* how many things is she interested?
> *To* which class have those students changed?

3. In conversation, the preposition is probably more often placed at the end of the question. In that position, it is sometimes called a *delayed* or *deferred* preposition.

> What were they talking *about?*
> Whom did he paint the chair *for?*
> How many things is she interested *in?*
> Which class have those students changed *to?*

4. In dependent clauses, the positions of the preposition and its *wh* object may be the same as their positions in direct questions. Notice, however, that the subject and the verb in the dependent clause have *primary word order* (subject before the verb). The second pattern is probably the more frequent in conversation.

		DEPENDENT CLAUSE
	I asked	about what they were talking.
	I asked	what they were talking about.
	Do you know	for whom he painted the chair?

	DEPENDENT CLAUSE
Do you know	whom he painted the chair for?
She will tell you	in whose plans she is interested.
She will tell you	whose plans she is interested in.
Those students can not remember	to which class they have changed.
Those students can not remember	which class they have changed to.

5. If the pronoun *whom* or *which* is the object of the preposition in the dependent clause and has an immediately preceding antecedent, *whom* or *which* can be omitted and the preposition placed last. All three of the following patterns may be heard in speech, but the last is probably the most frequent. The first pattern is customary in formal writing. The antecedent is italicized in the left-hand column in the following examples.

	DEPENDENT CLAUSE
Thomas was *the boy*	about whom they were talking.
Thomas was *the boy*	whom they were talking about.
Thomas was *the boy*	they were talking about.
Was Elizabeth *the one*	for whom he painted the chair?
Was Elizabeth *the one*	whom he painted the chair for?
Was Elizabeth *the one*	he painted the chair for?
She discovered *the plans*	in which she was interested.
She discovered *the plans*	which she was interested in.
She discovered *the plans*	she was interested in.
Do you remember *the class*	to which those students have changed?
Do you remember *the class*	which those students have changed to?
Do you remember *the class*	those students have changed to?

All the above three patterns may be used only for *restrictive* dependent clauses. The third pattern is not used for *nonrestrictive* clauses. See § Clause—Adjective.

6. If the whole dependent clause is the object of a preposition, only the second pattern of ¶ 5 above is used.

	DEPENDENT CLAUSE
It depended on	what they were talking about.
Do you have any idea about	whom he painted the chair for?
I will look into	whose plans she is interested in.
Please remind those students of	which class they have changed to.

7. In conversation, *whom* is rarely used unless it comes immediately after the preposition. *Who* is used instead although there are grammarians who consider this incorrect.

For whom did he paint the chair?
Who did he paint the chair for?

Also, see § Clause, § Word Order—Object of Verb, and § Word Order—*Wh* Word.

WORD ORDER—PRIMARY

1. Primary word order is the arrangement of words which has the subject before the verb. It is used predominantly in statements of fact *(declarative sentences)*.

	SUBJECT	VERB
	He	understands.
	They	are reading.
	Everybody	can hear.
	The animal	ate.
	A baby	was crying.
	The boy and the girl	have arrived.
	My book	has been found.

Some questions have primary word order; see § Word Order—*Wh* Word. Some statements do not have primary word order; see § Word Order—Emphatic Adverb. Also, see § Word Order—Split and § Word Order—Inverted.

WORD ORDER—SPLIT

1. *Split word order* is the arrangement of words which has an auxiliary verb preceding the subject and the main verb of a sentence or clause. It is used predominantly in direct questions which do not begin with one of the *wh* words (*who, what,* etc.) as the subject or part of the subject. For that reason, the arrangement is sometimes called *question word order.*

	AUXILIARY	SUBJECT	MAIN VERB
	Does	he	understand?
Why	did	you	leave?
	Can	everybody	hear?
What	did	the animal	eat?
	Have	the children	arrived?

2. If there is more than one auxiliary verb, only the first is placed before the subject.

	AUXILIARY	SUBJECT	MAIN VERB
	Could	he	have misunderstood?
When	should	that baby	have been fed?

3. If the negative contraction *-n't* is used, it is attached to the first auxiliary.

	AUXILIARY	SUBJECT	MAIN VERB
	Doesn't	he	understand?
Why	haven't	the children	arrived?

4. Adverbs of degree follow the subject.

	AUXILIARY	SUBJECT	ADVERB	MAIN VERB
	Does	he	not	understand?
Which book	have	they	already	read?
When	does	he	usually	eat?

Not all questions have split word order; see § Word Order—*Wh* Word. Some statements have split word order; see § Word Order—Emphatic Adverb. Also, see § *Do* —Auxiliary, § *Be*—Verb, and § Word Order—Adverb Modifying Verb.

WORD ORDER—TRANSPOSED   W.17

1. *Transposed word order* is the arrangement of words which has a predicate complement before the subject and the verb. The predicate complement may be a direct object, an indirect object, a predicate nominative, a predicate adjective, a predicate objective, the object of a preposition, or an adverb modifying the verb.

> What did she say? [*What* is the direct object; it precedes the subject *she* and the verb *say.*]
> Whom did you tell? [*Whom* is the indirect object; it precedes the subject *you* and the verb *tell.*]
> Which boy is your brother? [*Which boy* is the predicate nominative; it precedes the subject *your brother* and the verb *is.*]
> How pretty she looks! [*How pretty* is the predicate adjective; it precedes the subject *she* and the verb *looks.*]
> What are you thinking about? [*What* is the object of the preposition *about;* it precedes the subject *you* and the verb *thinking.*]
> When will they leave? [*When* is an adverb modifying *leave;* it precedes the subject *they* and the verb *leave.*]

2. Transposed word order occurs most frequently when a *wh* word is the predicate complement or part of the predicate complement. The *wh* words are *who, whom, whose, which, what, when, where, why,* and *how* and their compounds like *whoever* and *however.* Notice their occurrence in the examples above and below.

3. Transposed word order occurs in direct questions when the predicate complement is or contains a *wh* word. The subject and the verb have split word order (auxiliary + subject + main verb) or inverted word order (main verb + subject— see § Word Order—*Wh* Word, ¶ 2, *b* for the rule governing the last example below).

	AUXILIARY	SUBJECT	MAIN VERB
What	did	she	say?
Which suit	could	he	have worn?
When	can	we	leave?
On which day	will	they	arrive?

4. Transposed word order occurs in a dependent clause when the predicate complement of the dependent clause is or contains a *wh* word. However, that predicate complement is customarily followed by primary word order (subject + verb). It does not matter whether the whole sentence is a statement or a question.

	DEPENDENT CLAUSE		
He knows	what	she	said.
Does he know	what	she	said?
John wants to find out	whom	you	told.
Does John want to find out	whom	you	told?

5. Transposed word order occurs in statements when the *wh* words *what* and *how* are used for emphasis. The following subject and verb have primary word order.

	SUBJECT	VERB
What a nice boy	Jimmy	is!
How hard	that girl	works!

For a fuller discussion of the word order with *wh* words, see § Word Order—*Wh* Word and § Word Order—Preposition.

6. Particularly in writing, transposed word order is used for emphasis or contrast even when the predicate complement is not or does not contain a *wh* word. You should become aware of that use since you will encounter it rather often in your reading.

This I believe. [= I believe this.]
Money he did not have. [= He did not have money.]
Free you are, and free you must remain. [= You are free, and you must remain free.]
Away the boy ran. [= The boy ran away.]
Good cause they have for their complaints. [= They have good cause for their complaints.]
Certain it is that he was wrong. [= It is certain that he was wrong.]
His promise you can rely on. [= You can rely on his promise.]
His life had been entangled with women. Some he had loved; others he had liked. [= He had loved some; he had liked others.]
Mrs. Boyle I could not avoid, but her son I could get away from. [= I could not avoid Mrs. Boyle, but I could get away from her son.]

Such transposed word order often occurs in poetry. Here are some examples from the poetry of Henry Wadsworth Longfellow.

And the song, from beginning to end,
I found again in the heart of a friend. [= I found the song....]

Your silent tents of green
We deck with fragrant flowers. [= We deck your silent tents....]

A blind man is a poor man,
And blind the poor man is, [= And the poor man is blind]
For the former seeth no man,
And the latter no man sees. [= And no man sees the latter]

7. Transposed word order is sometimes used humorously.

> Garlic I do not like on other people. [= I do not like garlic on other people.]

8. Since transposed word order sometimes has a humorous or even ridiculous effect, you should be careful about using it with other than *wh* words. Your reader may smile when you do not want him to.

Also, see § Word Order—Emphatic Adverb and § Word Order—Inverted.

WORD ORDER—*WH* WORD   W.18

1. The "*wh* words" are *who, whom, whose, which, what, when, where, why,* and *how* and their compounds like *whoever.* They are used in statements and in questions. In a statement they are customarily part of a dependent clause. In a question they may be part of a main clause or part of a dependent clause.

2. In main clauses in questions, the *wh* word is placed before the verb. (A *simple sentence* is composed of one main clause; see § Clause.)

a. If the *wh* word is the subject or part of the subject, it is followed by the verb.

SUBJECT	VERB	
Who	took	my pencil?
Whose book	was	lost?
What sort of person	would do	a thing like that?
Which boy	said	that?
Who	found	the house?
What	happened	after that?

b. If the *wh* word is not the subject or part of the subject, it is followed by split word order (auxiliary + subject + main verb). If the main verb is *am, are, is, was,* or *were*, the *wh* word is followed by inverted word order (main verb + subject); e.g., the main verb, *am, are, is, was,* or *were* precedes the subject.

	AUXILIARY OR *be* VERB	SUBJECT	MAIN VERB	
What	did	he	take?	
Whom	did	you	see	last night?
Whose book	can	I	borrow?	
What kinds of flowers	did	the girls	find	in the woods?
Why	did	the boy	say	that?
When	are	they	leaving?	
Where	will	I	meet	you?
How many times	have	you	seen	that movie?
Who	is	that man?		

3. In dependent clauses of both statements and questions, a *wh* word is placed at the beginning. That dependent clause has primary word order (subject before verb). If the *wh* word is not the subject or part of the subject, it goes before the subject.

		DEPENDENT CLAUSE		
		SUBJECT	VERB	
I want to know		who	took	my pencil.
Tell me		what	happened	after that.
I can not find out		whose book	was	lost
Paul was surprised	when	Mary	began	to cry.
Make a record of	what	the boy	took.	
Were you at home	when	the phone	rang?	
Is that the boy	whom	you	saw	last night?
Let me know	whose book	I	can borrow.	
I can guess	which boy	you	like	the best.
Can you imagine	why	the boy	said	that?
Does she know	when	they	are leaving?	
She knows	when	they	are leaving.	
He did not remember		who	brought	the package.
Didn't he remember		who	brought	the package?
It depends on	what	the schedule	is.	
Why does it depend on	what	the schedule	is?	
They found the house	where	their friend	was living.	
Who found the house	where	their friend	was living?	
I wonder	who	that man	is.	
Do you know	who	that man	is?	

4. The dependent clause keeps primary word order when it is placed at the beginning of the sentence.

DEPENDENT CLAUSE				
	SUBJECT			
When	she	began	to cry,	Robert was surprised.
When	the man	struck	you,	what did you do?
What	baseball	is	to America,	soccer is to Europe.
How	music	affects	people	is interesting to psychologists.
Why	those girls	like	that boy	I can not understand.

5. The *wh* words *how* and *what* are sometimes used for emphasis. They and the words they modify go at the beginning of the clause, and they are followed by primary word order.

How pretty	you look today!
What strange things	people believed in the Middle Ages!
How beautifully	Melissa sings!

6. The *wh* words are frequently used in titles of books, articles, etc. Such titles are like shortened statements, as if the words "The Following Composition Describes..." had been omitted. They are followed by primary word order.

> What I Expect to Learn in College
> How People Can Improve Their Pronunciation
> Why Boys Want to Be Policemen
> When Knighthood Was in Flower

a. Many titles begin with the words *How to.*

> How to Repair a Radio
> How to Play the Piano in Ten Lessons

b. Some titles are intended as questions. They have question marks at the end.

> Is There No Hope for Mankind?
> What Would You Have Done?
> Why Can't We Have Peace?
> Who Was the Culprit?

7. We frequently use the following *opinion-asking* formulas in questions beginning with *wh* words:

> do you guess   do you suppose
> do you imagine   do you think
> would you say

a. We insert those formulas after the *wh* words or at the ends of the questions. If the *wh* words are modifiers, the formulas come after the modified words.

b. If the formulas come at the end of the sentence, they do not affect the word order.

c. If the formulas come within the sentence, the rest of the question has primary word order, and the question auxiliaries *do, does,* or *did* are not used.

d. Notice the punctuation in the examples.

> Who is coming?
> Who is coming,   do you suppose?
> Who   do you suppose   is coming?
>
> Who is he?
> Who is he,   do you think?
> Who   do you think   he is?
>
> Where was that man born?
> Where was that man born,   would you say?
> Where   would you say   that man was born?

What excuse did he give?
What excuse did he give,   do you guess?
What excuse   do you guess   he gave?

8. Study the word order in the following sentences with *wh* words.

Practically nobody knows what the origin of the celebration is.
The boy repeated the words without knowing what their meaning was.
The scientist wanted to know what effect the new medicine had had.
I do not know what the definition of that word is.
Don't you remember what their names are?
Did you try to find out what his explanation was?
A hunter has to go where animals live.
I would like to know why I can not remember everything I study.
The minister thought of how hard it would be to live without hope.

Also, see § Word Order—Preposition.

X WORD

The letter *x* represents different sounds in different words. However, you can usually tell how an *x* in a particular word is pronounced.

1. *X* is usually pronounced [ks].

exchange	exercise	explain	extra	next
excuse	expect	expression	mix	taxi

2. In words spelled with *exce-* or *exci-*, there is only one [s] sound.

except	exceed	excess
excite	excellent	

3. *X* at the beginning of a word is pronounced [z]. There are not many English words that begin with an *x.* Two examples are *Xavier* and *xylophone.*

4. *X* before a stressed vowel is pronounced [gz].

exact	examination	exist
exaggerate	example	

5. The *h* in the words *exhaust, exhibit, exhilarate,* and *exhort* and their derivatives is not pronounced. The vowel after the *h* in those words is stressed; therefore, the *x* is pronounced [gz].

6. In a few words, *x* represents special pronunciations:

anxiety [æŋˈzaɪətɪ]	luxurious [ləgˈʒʊrɪəs]	X ray [ˈɛksˈre]
anxious [ˈæŋʃəs]	luxury [ˈlʌkʃərɪ]	

7. The *x* in *exile* and *exit* may be pronounced either as [ks] or as [gz]. The abbreviation *Xmas* is pronounced like the full form, *Christmas.*

appendix

Barbara F. Matthies
Iowa State University

In the following finding list, the numbers refer to the page or pages where you will find each item. Items that are not italicized are subjects or concepts. Items that are italicized show the correct use of that word.
For example:
    number   14, 16-17, 20, 26, 41-54, 346-354
If you look on these pages, you will find information about the subject or concept of "number."
    number   24, 349
If you look on those pages, you will find information about the *word* "number."